the baker's bible

the baker's bible

Over 350 recipes for breads, tarts, cakes, cookies, and pastries

Edited by Deborah Gray

CHARTWELL
BOOKS, INC.

A QUINTET BOOK

Published by Chartwell Books
A division of Book Sales, Inc.
114 Northfield Avenue
Edison, New Jersey 08837

ISBN 0-7858-0920-1

Reprinted 1999, 2000

This book was designed and produced by
Quintet Publishing Limited
6 Blundell Street
London N7 9BH

Creative Director: *Richard Dewing*
Art Director: *Clare Reynolds*
Designer: *James Lawrence*
Senior Editor: *Sally Green*
Editor: *Deborah Gray*

Typeset in Great Britain by
Central Southern Typesetters, Eastbourne
Manufactured in Hong Kong by Regent Publishing Services Ltd,
Printed in China by Leefung-Asco Printers Ltd.

THE MATERIAL IN THIS PUBLICATION PREVIOUSLY APPEARED IN:
The American Harvest Cookbook, *Rosemary Moon*;
The Bread Book, *Audrey Ellison*; The Bread Machine Book, *Marjie Lambert*;
Breakfast Bakes, *Elizabeth Wolf-Cohen*;
The Chocolate Book, *Valerie Barret*; The Coffee Book, *Rosemary Moon*;
The Complete Book of Gingerbread, *Valerie Baxter*;
The Encyclopedia of Desserts, *Elizabeth Wolf-Cohen*;
High-Fibre Cooking, *Rosemary Moon*; Irish Cooking, *Ethel Minogue*;
Leith's Cookery School, *Prue Leith and Caroline Waldegrave*;
Low-Fat Vegetarian Cooking, *Jenny Stacey*;
New Jewish Cooking, *Elizabeth Wolf-Cohen*;
Recipes from a Polish Kitchen, *Bridget Jones*;
Scandinavian Cooking, *Sonia Maxwell*;
Traditional Cakes and Pastries, *Barbara Maher*;
The Ultimate Bagel Cookbook, *Sarah Maxwell*;

CONTENTS

INTRODUCTION

Enjoy your baking.

There can be nothing so welcoming as the smell of home baking and nothing more appetizing than hot muffins at breakfast time or a scrumptious snack of fresh cookies with milk on returning from school or work. Anyone who bakes knows the satisfaction of presenting the family with a delicious cake, or setting an indulgent pie down at the dinner table. Many of us are tired of the synthetic tastes that purchased foods offer us and value the good wholesome tastes of fresh, natural ingredients. Nothing can equal home cooking for flavor.

There is no great mystery to the art of baking. It is simply a matter of careful measuring and following the instructions. Nor need baking take a great deal of time. There are many recipes in this book that take only a few minutes to prepare, particularly with the help of electric mixers and food processors.

Let this book indeed become your Baker's Bible. In it you will find all you will ever need to know about baking techniques. There are comprehensive sections on baking basics covering all the various types of pastries, cakes, cookies, and breads, large and small, baked with and without yeast. Whether you want to make a fancy, rich pie crust, learn how to bake bread, or make the perfect birthday cake, all the knowledge is here. In addition, there are hundreds of recipes from home and abroad, traditional and contemporary to inspire your baking. The information and recipes are written in a clear no-nonsense style so that whether you are an experienced cook or a keen novice you will find the instructions easy to follow.

Baking Tips

- Always measure ingredients precisely and use the exact ingredients suggested. It can make a difference if you substitute different types of flour or sugar for example.
- Use medium-sized eggs unless otherwise specified.
- Preheat the oven to the given temperature. Some ovens run hot, particularly fan ovens, in which case, follow the manufacturer's recommendations for heat reduction.
- As a general rule, yeast mixtures and pastries should be placed near to the top of the oven, cakes and cookies in the center.
- Avoid opening the oven door while baking. This is particularly important in the first 15 minutes of baking (5 minutes for cookies) when a sudden blast of cold air can ruin a cake by making it sag in the middle.
- Prepare can pans or sheets prior to making up the batter. This is particularly important for cakes as the rising agent begins work immediately on contact with liquid.
- Always lightly dust the worksurface before rolling out pastry and cookies, too much flour and it will become incorporated into the dough. If it proves

very difficult to roll out, return to the refrigerator for 30 minutes. If it is too hard after refrigeration, leave to stand at room temperature for 5 minutes.

- Test cakes using a wooden pick for sponge-type cakes and a metal skewer for fruit cakes. Insert into the center of the cake, if it comes out clean with no batter clinging to it, then the cake is done. Repeat at 5 minute intervals.
- If the cake or pastry is over-browning, cover with foil or waxed paper.
- Leave cakes to sit in their pans for 5 minutes before turning out, that way they will come away from the sides more easily.
- Baked foods are more easily removed from their pans when cooked on waxed paper.
- Double up ingredients and make double the quantity; most cakes (unfrosted), breads and pastries can be frozen for 3 months. Most will keep in an airtight container in a cool, dark place for no more than 2 weeks.

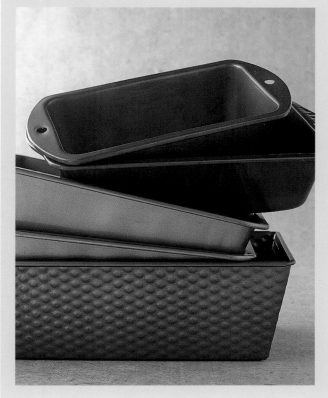

Pastry

Almost anything can be encased in pastry to form a pie or tart. Featured in this section are a wide range of pastry types to suit every filling of your choice from fruits and chocolate to vegetables and meat. There are wonderful recipes too, ranging from classical pastries from France and Austria to modern tarts and desserts, using ingredients once thought of as delicacies but now available in every market.

INTRODUCTION

Tarts and pastries, play a part in many culinary traditions, but have played a very important part in British, American, and French cuisines. Most are easy to prepare and, with a little forethought, can be put together quickly. Remember pastry can be bought from markets and home-made pastry freezes well, so make it in batches and freeze ahead. Fillings can be assembled in no time, so use your imagination and enjoy the treat of a simple tart or pie made with delicious tender pastry, warm from the oven.

Every cook I know aspires to make light, tender flaky pastry. There are a few basic commandments that must always be obeyed, regardless of what kind of pastry you choose:

- **Chill all the ingredients.**
- **Work as quickly as possible and, unless you are one of those natural born pastry makers, use a pastry blender or a food processor.**
- **Chill the pastry after every stage of making and assembling: chill after patting into a disc and after rolling out and lining the tart or pie pan. Do not be tempted to cheat—your pastry will shrink unevenly.**
- **Pastry likes a hot oven; butter-rich pastries and puff paste especially require a hot blast of heat to seal the pastry and release the steam. If longer cooking is required for a filling, the temperature can be reduced so the pastry does not burn.**

A succulent slice of the ever-popular lemon tart.

The Ingredients

Most kinds of pastry are made with a combination of flour, fat and a liquid to bind. The texture, flavor and color of the resulting pastry will vary tremendously depending on the proportions and types of ingredients used.

Flour

All-purpose flour is used throughout this section. Even the same brand of flour can vary from season to season, depending on humidity or how long it has been stored, so the amount of liquid necessary to bind the pastry will always vary; 1/8 teaspoon baking powder can be added to 1 1/2 cups flour to achieve a lighter result. Whole-wheat or rye flour can replace some of the white flour but produces a heavier result. Use equal amounts or more white flour proportionally to whole-wheat or other flours for easier handling. Please note that it is always essential to be consistent when using either metric or imperial, and not to mix the two.

Fat

Lard was probably the first fat used in pastry making, but has fallen out of favor for health reasons. It does make a very short and tender pastry, but has a distinctive taste. Pure butter gives pastry a rich flavor and color and a crisp texture, but it can be difficult to handle. Most bakers use a combination of butter or hard margarine (not the soft tub variety) and shortening to achieve a balance of good buttery color and flavor with the short flaky texture provided by white fat. Unsalted butter is preferable because it has a lower water content and the amount of salt can be more easily controlled. Experiment until you find your own preference.

The normal proportion of fat to flour is usually half fat to flour (i.e. one part fat to two parts flour), although some rich European-style pastries, such as *pâte sucrée* have a higher percentage of fat. The more fat the dough has, the more difficult it will be to handle, so be sure the dough is chilled at all stages of handling.

Liquid

Most pastry is bound with water, although milk or other liquids can be used. Normal tart pastry uses about 1 teaspoon of water per 1/4 cup flour; this varies if eggs or an egg yolk is added. The water should be water so it does not melt or soften the fat(s). Too much water will make a sticky pastry, which is difficult to handle and produces tough pastry. Be careful when using a food processor, since the mixture can form into a pastry before the correct quantity of liquid has been added. This can produce a dough that is too short and is difficult to handle and results in a brittle, too crumbly pastry. Many recipes call for an egg yolk mixed with water to a certain measure. This adds a golden color and helps to bind the pastry. Sometimes a little juice is added for flavor, but be careful as certain juices, such as lemon, contain a high proportion of acid, which can shorten the pastry too much for easy handling. A little grated orange or lemon rind should add just the right kind of flavor. Flavorings such as vanilla, almond, or lemon can be used to enhance the chosen fillings, as can spices such as cinnamon, nutmeg, ginger, or cardamom.

Eggs

Eggs are added to pastry for richness in texture and flavor, and because they help bind all the ingredients. Normally only the yolk is used and, for a very rich biscuit-like pastry used in some European style-tarts, yolks are used without any other liquid.

Sugar

Sugar is used both to sweeten the final pastry and create a crisper texture. A teaspoon or two is often added even to savory doughs, because the sugar helps the pastry to color and gives a more golden look. Superfine sugar or confectioner's sugar is usually used because these types dissolve more quickly than granulated. Granulated sugar can be used but can result in a crunchy texture, which is not always desired.

Commercial Pastry

Excellent quality pie crust, puff paste, and phyllo paste can be purchased in markets, and all give good reliable results. Puff paste is available chilled or frozen and gives excellent results. Look for the all-but variety since the flavor is superior. Phyllo paste is also available chilled or frozen and is a great freezer stand-by. These paper-thin sheets of paste need to be defrosted before being carefully un-wrapped. Because the thin layers dry so quickly, it is advisable that they be covered with a damp cloth when working.

Although many good-quality, ready-made pastries are available, there is nothing quite as satisfying as making your own. The method for making Basic Pie Crust is easy to follow and, once mastered, can be adapted for both sweet and non-sweet tarts simply by adding a few extra ingredients.

8 OZ QUANTITY

2 cups all-purpose flour

½ tsp salt

1½ tsp superfine sugar, optional

1 stick cold unsalted butter, cut into small pieces

2 Tbsp cold margarine or shortening fat, cut into small pieces

2–4 Tbsp iced water

Basic Pie Crust (*Pâte Brisée*)

Brisée in French means broken. In this pastry the flour and fats are "broken together," or cut in. After adding the liquid, the pastry is blended until the mixture begins to bind together. If the pastry becomes sticky at any stage, refrigerate until it is easy to handle. This recipe should produce a firm, yet flaky crust which can support a filling but at the same time is still tender. Sifting flour is not absolutely necessary, but it can help lighten the pastry if you are using the hand method.

Hand Method

1 Into a large bowl, sift the flour, salt, and sugar if using. Sprinkle the pieces of butter and margarine or shortening over the flour mixture. Using a pastry blender or two knives scissor-fashion, cut in the fat until the mixture forms coarse crumbs. Do not over-work, as this causes a tough crust.

2 Sprinkle about 2 tablespoons of the water over the flour-crumb mixture and toss lightly with a fork. Gather the parts of pastry that have bound together to one side of the bowl. Add a little more water to any dry crumbs and toss again.

3 Gather the pastry into a rough ball and turn on to a sheet of plastic wrap. Lightly press the pastry into a disc shape and flatten slightly. Wrap the pastry tightly and refrigerate for at least 1 hour or overnight.

Food Processor Method

If you have warm hands, are working in hot weather, tend to have a heavy touch or just have not got the knack, the food processor should be the answer to your prayers. Used carefully, it produces perfect pastry every time; just take care not to over-process. Although shortcrust pastry is easily made by hand, the sweeter pastries do benefit from the food processor method. The more sugar and fat added to the pastry, the more difficult it is to handle.

1 **Put the flour, salt, and sugar in the bowl of a food processor fitted with the metal blade. Process for 5–7 seconds just to blend. Sprinkle the pieces of butter and margarine or shortening over the surface and process for 10–15 seconds until the mixture resembles coarse crumbs.**

2 **Sprinkle about 2 tablespoons of the water over the flour-crumb mixture and, using the pulse button, process the mixture until the pastry just begins to hold together, 10–15 seconds. DO NOT OVERPROCESS.**

Test the pastry by pinching a piece between your fingers: if it is still too crumbly, add more water, little by little, and pulse again until the pastry begins to stick together in clumps.

Do not allow the pastry to form into a ball or add too much water because the baked pastry will be tough. Turn the pastry on to a sheet of plastic wrap and continue with step 3 on page 12.

Rich Pie Crust (*Pâte Brisée Riche*)

Richer than basic pie crust, this is excellent for fruit tarts and special occasion pies.

8 OZ QUANTITY

2 cups all-purpose flour	**½ tsp salt**
1 stick cold unsalted butter, cut into small pieces	**1 egg yolk beaten with 2 Tbsp iced water**

Proceed as for Basic Pie Crust Pastry (*Pâte Brisée*), using the beaten egg yolk and water to bind.

Rich Herb Pie Crust

This tender green-flecked pastry is ideal for vegetable pies and tarts. Vary the herbs to suit the filling and your taste.

8 OZ QUANTITY

2 cups all-purpose flour	**2 Tbsp chopped chives**
½ tsp salt	**1 Tbsp fresh parsley, chopped**
1 stick cold unsalted butter	**4–6 fresh basil leaves, torn into small pieces**
½ tsp fresh thyme leaves or ¼ tsp dried thyme	**1 egg yolk beaten with 2 Tbsp iced water**
½ tsp fresh oregano or marjoram chopped or ¼ tsp dried oregano or marjoram	

Prepare as for Rich Pie Crust, adding the herbs when the flour and butter have been combined to form coarse crumbs, and before adding the water.

Light Whole-wheat Crust

This wholewheat crust remains light and flaky by substituting less than half the white flour for whole-wheat. Substitute 1 tablespoon of shortening for that amount of butter if you would like to produce a very flaky pastry.

8 OZ QUANTITY

1¼ cups all-purpose flour	**¼ stick shortening or hard margarine**
¾ cup whole-wheat flour	**1 egg yolk beaten with 2 Tbsp iced water**
½ tsp salt	
½ stick cold unsalted butter, cut into small pieces	

Proceed as for Basic Pie Crust, combining the two flours and salt before cutting in the fats.

Basic Sweet Crust (*Pâte Sucrée*)

Pâte sucrée, "sweetened pastry," is made in the same way as *pâte brisée*, but contains more sugar and is generally bound with egg yolks or a combination of egg yolks and water. Use powdered sugar as it dissolves instantly, although superfine sugar can also be used. These additions make the pastry sweeter and a little crisper than ordinary pie crust pastry, which is ideal for dessert and fruit tarts. After the pastry is formed, it is lightly kneaded by a process the French call *fresage* where the heel of the hand blends the pastry until it is soft and pliable. The addition of sugar and egg yolk makes the pastry softer and more difficult to handle, so be sure to chill all the ingredients and work quickly. However, because this is a soft pastry, it is easy to patch; just press any tears together—they will not show. This pastry can be made by hand by following the instructions for Basic Pie Crust, but it is easier to use the food processor.

6 OZ QUANTITY

1½ cups all-purpose flour	1 stick cold unsalted butter, cut into small pieces
½ tsp salt	
3–4 Tbsp confectioners' sugar	2 egg yolks beaten with 2 Tbsp iced water and ½ tsp vanilla extract (optional)

- Put the flour, salt, and sugar in the bowl of a food processor, fitted with the metal blade. Process for 5–7 seconds. Sprinkle the butter over the flour mixture and process for 10–15 seconds until the mixture resembles coarse crumbs. Pulse 2–3 times more if the crumbs are not evenly distributed.
- With the machine running, pour the yolk-water mixture through the feed tube and process just until the pastry begins to hold together. **DO NOT OVERPROCESS.**

   Test the pastry by pinching a piece between your fingers; if it is still crumbly add a little more water and pulse once or twice. Do not allow the pastry to form into a ball at this stage because the baked crust will become tough. Turn out the pastry on to a sheet of plastic wrap.
- Using the plastic wrap as a guide, hold each side with one hand and push the pastry away from you, turning the pastry and holding the opposite sides of the plastic wrap to contain it, until it is smooth and just blended. Flatten into a disc and wrap with the plastic wrap. Refrigerate for 1 hour or overnight.

Extra Sweet Crust (*Pâte Sucrée Riche*)

With a little more sugar and egg yolk, pastry becomes a melting, rich biscuit, or shortbread pastry, that is ideal for encasing fruit tarts and tartlets. This pastry is very tricky to handle; although chilling is important, do not chill for too long or it will be too firm to roll out. If you cannot roll it out, simply press it in the tart tin using flour-dipped fingers.

6 OZ QUANTITY

1½ cups all-purpose flour	3 egg yolks beaten with 1 Tbsp iced water and ½ tsp vanilla extract (optional)
½ tsp salt	
4–5 Tbsp confectioners' sugar	
1 stick cold unsalted butter, cut into small pieces	

Proceed as for Basic Sweet Pastry.

Easy Nut Crust

This is a delicious flavorful crust, which makes an ideal base for custards and cooked fillings. It does not need rolling out and can be pressed straight into a pie dish with lightly floured hands, chilled and then baked without weighting with beans.

8 OZ QUANTITY

2 sticks unsalted butter at room temperature	2 cups all-purpose flour
1 egg, lightly beaten	½ tsp sugar
1 tsp vanilla or almond extract (optional)	1 cup walnuts, peanuts, almonds, hazelnuts or macadamia nuts, finely chopped

- Lightly spray or brush the pie dish with a vegetable cooking spray or a little melted butter or oil.
- Using an electric mixer, cream the butter in a large bowl. Add the egg and vanilla extract and beat until blended. Sprinkle over the flour, sugar, and nuts and beat on low speed until well blended.
- Scrape the mixture into the prepared dish and press evenly on to the bottom and up the side of the tart pan or pie plate. Using a fork, prick the bottom of the pastry. Place in a refrigerator and chill for at least 30 minutes.
- Preheat the oven to 350°F. Bake the crust 6–8 minutes until set. Remove to a wire rack to cool. It must be completely cool before filling.

Cream Cheese Crust

Cream cheese pastry is a moist, flaky pastry often used with sugary or nutty fillings. It is ideal for rich tartlets and tiny petit fours.

FOR A 9-IN TART PAN OR
TWELVE 2–3 IN TARTLET PANS

1½ cups all-purpose flour	1 stick unsalted butter, at room temperature
½ tsp salt	
1 tsp sugar	½ package (4 oz) full-fat soft cheese, at room temperature

● In a large bowl, sift together the flour and salt. Add the butter, sugar, and soft cheese and, with an electric mixer, beat the ingredients together until well blended and a soft pastry forms. Shape into a ball, flatten to a disc and wrap tightly. Refrigerate about 1 hour before rolling and shaping.

Crumb Crust

This easy crumb crust, popular for cheesecakes, is ideal for chilled tarts since it remains crisp and crunchy, and is particularly good for ice cream tarts and chilled chiffon mixtures. For alternative flavorings to suit different fillings, use vanilla, ginger, chocolate, or Amaretti cookies (about 24) instead of graham crackers, or replace ½ cup of the crumbs with ½ cup chopped nuts for a Nut Crumb Crust.

FOR A 9-IN TART PAN

1½ cups graham cracker crumbs (about 20 squares) or other cookie crumbs	¾ stick butter or margarine, melted
	1–2 Tbsp sugar, or to taste

● If making your own crumbs, put the graham crackers or alternatives in the bowl of a food processor fitted with the metal blade and process for 20–30 seconds until fine crumbs form. Alternatively, put them in a heavy-duty freezer bag and press into fine crumbs with a rolling pin. Pour them into a bowl and stir in the melted butter or margarine and sugar, if using. Pour into a tart pan and press crumbs on to the bottom and up the side of tart pan or pie plate. Chill, uncovered, for at least 20 minutes in the refrigerator.

● Preheat the oven to 375°F. Bake the crust 6–8 minutes until set. Remove to a wire rack to cool. It must be completely cool before filling.

Rich Cheese Crust

This pastry is based on a Rich Pie Crust. Use a grated hard cheese, such as Cheddar.

8 OZ QUANTITY

2 cups all-purpose flour	3 Tbsp cold shortening, cut into small pieces
¼ tsp salt	
⅛–¼ tsp cayenne pepper	¾ cup grated mature Cheddar cheese
½ tsp dry mustard	
1 stick cold unsalted butter, cut into small pieces	1 egg yolk beaten with 3 Tbsp iced water

Proceed as for Rich Pie Crust, adding the cheese after the butter and white vegetable fat are cut in, and mix well to combine.

Chocolate Crust

This makes a stunning background for fruit tarts and tartlets, as well as chocolate fillings.

8 OZ QUANTITY

1¼ sticks unsalted butter, softened	3 tsp vanilla extract
½ cup superfine sugar	½ cup cocoa powder (preferably Dutch processed)
½ tsp salt	
	2 cups all-purpose flour

● Put the butter, sugar, salt, and vanilla into the bowl of a food processor fitted with the metal blade and process for 25–30 seconds until creamy. Add the cocoa and process about 1 minute, until well blended. Add the flour all at once and, using the pulse button, process for 10–15 seconds until the flour is well blended. Scrape the pastry out on to a sheet of plastic wrap and shape into a flat circle. Wrap and refrigerate.

● Soften the pastry for 10–15 minutes at room temperature. Unwrap and sandwich between two large pieces of plastic wrap. Roll out to about ¼ inch thick. Peel off the top sheet and invert into a greased tart pan. Ease on to the bottom and sides of the pan, then remove the bottom layer of plastic wrap. Press the pastry around the pan, then roll the rolling pin over the top of the pan to cut off any excess pastry. Prick the base of the pastry with a fork and refrigerate 1 hour.

● Preheat the oven to 400°F. Blind bake for 10 minutes. Remove the paper or foil and beans and continue baking for 5 more minutes until just set. Transfer to a wire rack to cool.

Rolling and Shaping the Pastry

If the pastry has been refrigerated for more than an hour, allow it to soften slightly at room temperature for about 10 minutes.

To Form a Pastry Circle

TIP

To freeze rolled-out pastry, carefully slide on to a flat baking sheet and freeze, uncovered, until very firm. Remove from freezer and slide on to freezer paper, wrap well and re-freeze, with paper in between each layer. Wrap tightly and store in the freezer. Defrost in the refrigerator overnight or at room temperature several hours before using.

1 Unwrap the pastry and place on a lightly floured surface. Using a lightly floured rolling pin, press parallel grooves into the pastry. Turn the pastry 45°, flouring the surface underneath and press more parallel grooves. Continue rotating and pressing the pastry, being careful the pastry does not stick, until it is about ½ inch thick. This method avoids overworking the pastry before actually rolling it.

To Form a Square or Rectangle

Proceed as for rolling out a circle but rotate the pastry 90° rather than 45° when making the grooves. This will cause the pastry to elongate to fill a square or rectangular tin.

2 Beginning from the center, lightly roll out the pastry to the far edge, but do not actually roll over the edge. Return to the center and roll to the near edge, but do not roll over the edge. Turn the pastry 45° and continue rolling until it is about ⅛ inch thick and forms a 12–14- inch round. Do not allow the pastry to stick to the work surface; lightly flour the surface and rolling pin as necessary, using a small pastry brush to remove any excess flour from the pastry.

3 If the pastry is tender or tears, patch it with a small piece of moistened pastry. As the pastry circle enlarges, fold it in half or into quarters to rotate and dust with flour to avoid stretching it.

Lining a Pie Pan

The traditional pie pan is shallow with no rim. It usually has a fluted side and removable base that gives the characteristic edge and allows the side of the pan to be removed for presentation without disturbing the base of the tart. Tart rings are generally smooth-sided rings which are set on a heavy cookie sheet to form its base; these are generally used by professionals. The best pans are dull metal or non-stick since shiny metal reflects the heat and prevents the crust from browning properly. Butter-rich pastry does not generally stick, but lightly spray the pie pan with a vegetable cooking spray. Alternatively, brush the bottom and side of the pie pan with a little oil.

Lining Tartlet Pans

For very small tartlet pans (less than 2 inches), arrange the pans on the work surface close together and unroll the rolled-out pastry over them, loosely draping the pastry into them. Roll the rolling pin over them to cut off the excess pastry, then, using a floured thumb, press the pastry on to the bottom and up the side of the pans. Prick the bottoms with a fork. For larger tartlets, follow the steps for lining a round pie pan, since this gives adequate pastry and a firm high edge to support any filling.

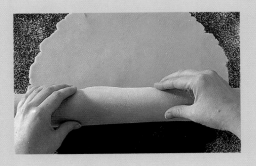

1 To transfer rolled-out pastry to a pie pan, set the rolling pin on the near edge of the pastry round, square, or rectangle. Fold the edge of the pastry over the rolling pin, then continue to roll pastry loosely around the pin.

2 Hold the far edge of pastry and rolling pin over far edge of the pie pan and gently unroll the pastry, allow it to settle into the tin without stretching or pulling.

3 Using floured fingertips, lift the outside edge of the pastry and ease into the bottom and side of pan, allowing excess pastry to overhang the edge. Smooth the pastry on to the bottom of the pan and press the overhang down slightly toward the center of the pan, making the top edge thicker.

4 Roll the rolling pin over the edge, cutting off any excess pastry and flattening the top edge. Press the thickened top edge against the side of the pan to form a stand-up edge. This makes the edge slightly thicker and higher, reinforcing the side of the crust. Prick the bottom of the pastry with a fork and, if you like, crimp or decorate the edge. Refrigerate 1 hour or freeze for 20 minutes.

Tips for Filling Tarts

- For easier handling, and to avoid any overflows, always set tart pan on a heavy baking sheet.
- Beat the eggs and milk or cream mixture in a large measuring cup or pitcher, rather than a bowl, since it will be easier to pour.
- To fill the tart case with a liquid filling, set the tart on a baking sheet. Pull out the middle oven rack halfway and set the tart on its baking sheet on the rack. Pour in as much filling as possible and gently slide the rack back in place. Bake 5 minutes as this allows a thin crust to form over the top. If any mixture remains, pull the oven rack out and carefully pour the remaining mixture into the center of the tart. Slide the rack back in place.
- To remove the side of the tart pan, set the bottom on a sturdy can and allow the side to drop down gently on to the surface, leaving the tart on the bottom of the pan. Slide on to a serving plate.
- For a vegetable or meat tart, sprinkle cheese over the partially baked tart case to keep the pastry from getting soggy. When the cheese melts it forms a barrier between the pastry and the filling.
- Rubbing an unbaked tart case with 1 tablespoon of softened butter and chilling before filling helps prevent a soggy crust.
- Brushing a warm, baked blind tart case with a little beaten egg or egg white and returning it to the oven for 2 minutes, creates a seal between pastry and filling, preventing a soggy crust. Brushing a baked tart case with melted preserves helps prevent a fruit tart becoming soggy.
- There are many tart pans on the market. Use a dull metal or non-stick pan as they produce the most well-cooked, crisp pastry. Shiny metal reflects heat, and glass and china absorb it, preventing the pastry from browning well. To present or transport a tart, bake the tart in a metal, removable-bottomed pan. Remove the side of the pan from the baked tart, leaving it on the metal bottom, then slide into a quiche dish of the same size.
- To test if the filling is set, insert a sharp knife into the center. It should come out clean and should feel hot to the touch.
- If the pastry edge begins to brown before the filling is set, cover with foil.

Blind Baking

Blind baking is a method of prebaking a pastry case, either partially or completely, to prevent the pastry from becoming soggy and to ensure the base cooks evenly.

1 Cut out a circle of waxed paper or foil about 3 inches larger than the pie pan. Fold the paper or foil in half and lay it across the center of the pastry-lined pie pan. Unfold it and press on to the bottom, into the edge and up the side of the pastry.

2 Fill the paper- or foil-lined crust with dried beans, rice, or pastry weights, spreading them evenly over the bottom and up the side. The dried beans, rice or pastry weights can be cooled and saved to use again.

3 To partially blind bake pastry: bake in a 400°F oven for 15–20 minutes until the pastry is set and the rim looks dry and golden. Remove to a heatproof surface and remove the paper or foil and beans. The pie crust can now be filled and the baking completed.

4 To completely blind bake pastry: bake in a 400°F oven for 10 minutes. Remove to a heatproof surface and carefully remove the paper or foil and beans. Prick the pastry bottom again with a fork and bake for 5–10 minutes until golden. The bottom should look dry and set. Cool on a wire rack before filling.

Hot Water Crust

This is made by heating water and fat together and mixing them into the flour. Because of the high proportion of water, this pastry is inclined to be hard. Its strength and firmness allows it to encase heavy mixtures, such as English pork pie, without collapsing. Also, as the fat used is generally lard, the pastry can lack flavor, so add a good spoon of salt. Many old recipes recommend throwing the pastry away uneaten once it has done its duty as container. The recipe for Veal and ham pie is a better-tasting modification of hot water crust, containing butter and egg.

Do not allow the water to boil before the fat has melted. If the water reduces by boiling, the proportion of water to flour will not be correct.

Quickly mix the water and melted fat into the flour in a warm bowl, then keep it covered with a hot damp cloth. This prevents the fat from becoming set and the pastry flaking and drying out.

MAKES I LB OF HOT WATER CRUST

4 cups all-purpose flour	³⁄₄-cup plus 2 Tbsp water
I tsp salt	⁵⁄₈ stick butter
2 beaten eggs	⁵⁄₈ stick lard

- Sift the flour and salt into a bowl. Make a dip in the middle of it, break the eggs into it and toss a liberal covering of flour over the egg.
- Put the water, butter, and lard into a saucepan and bring to a boil. Once the liquid is boiling, pour it on to the flour, mixing with a knife as you do. Knead until the pastry is smooth. Wrap in a piece of plastic wrap and refrigerate for 15 minutes.

Choux Pastry

This pastry contains water and eggs and depends on the rising of the steam within it to produce a puffy hollow pastry case. It is easy to make if the recipe is followed closely. The following points are particularly important:

- Measure ingredients exactly. Proportions are important with choux.
- Do not allow the water to boil until the butter has melted, but when it has, bring it immediately to a full rolling boil. Boiling the water too soon will cause too much evaporation.
- Have the sifted flour ready in a bowl so that the minute the rolling boil is achieved, you can tip in the flour, all in one go.
- Beat fast and vigorously to get rid of lumps before they cook hard.
- Do not over-beat. Stop once the mixture is leaving the sides of the pan.
- Cool slightly before adding egg—otherwise you'll scramble them.
- Do not beat in more egg than is necessary to achieve a dropping consistency. If the mixture is too stiff, the pastry will be stodgy. If it is too thin, it will rise unevenly into shapeless lumps.
- Bake until it is a good even brown, otherwise the inside of the pastry will be uncooked.
- If the pastry is to be served cold, split the buns/rings, or poke a hole in each of them with a skewer to allow the steam inside to escape. If steam remains trapped inside, the pastry will be soggy and a little heavy.

Opened-up pastry or small buns with holes in them can be returned to the oven, hole uppermost, to dry out further.
- Serve the pastry on the day it is made (or store frozen), as it stales rapidly.

Choux Paste

MAKES I QUANTITY CHOUX USING I CUP FLOUR

6 Tbsp unsalted butter	¹⁄₈ tsp salt
I cup water	4 eggs, lightly beaten
I cup all-purpose flour	

- Put the water and the butter, cut into 3–4 pieces, into a heavy saucepan and place over a gentle heat.
- Bring to the boil slowly so that by the time the liquid boils all the butter has melted.
- As soon as the liquid is boiling fast, tip in all the flour and remove the pan from the heat.
- Beat vigorously until a smooth paste is formed. The trick is to beat out the lumps before they are cooked solid by the heat. Once the paste curls away from the sides of the pan, stop.
- Allow the paste to cool slightly then beat in the liquid egg, a little at a time. It may not be necessary to add all the egg.
- Continue adding egg until you have a soft dropping consistency. The mixture will be shiny and smooth and will fall reluctantly from a spoon if it is given a sharp jerk.

Suet Crust

This is made like pie crust except that the fat (suet) is generally chopped or shredded before use. Because self-rising flour (or all-purpose flour and baking powder) is used in order to produce a less heavy, doughy pastry, it is important to cook the pastry soon after making while the raising agent is at its most active. During cooking the raising agent causes the dough to puff up and rise slightly and as the paste hardens during cooking, air will be trapped. This makes the suet crust lighter and more bread-like.

Butter for greasing

3 cups self-raising flour

Salt

6 oz shredded beef or vegetable suet

Water to mix

- Grease a pudding basin.
- Sift the flour with a good pinch of salt into a bowl. Blend in the shredded suet and add enough water to mix, first with a knife, and then with one hand, to a soft dough.
- Roll out the paste and line the oven-proof bowl or pudding mold.
- Fill the paste bag with the desired mixture.

Lining a Bowl

- Cut a third from the prepared suet paste and reserve it. Roll the rest out on a lightly floured board to a round about ½ inch thick. Flour the round well on top then fold it lightly in half, bringing the far edge toward you when you fold.
- Gently roll it to a round again, pushing the flat folded edge into a curved shape. Use floured hands to separate the two layers of pastry to give a bag-shape. Carefully lift the "bag" and ease gently into the greased bowl or mold.
- Trim off the excess paste leaving 1 inch above the edge. Fill. Roll out the remaining third of the paste to make a round lid. Put in place, wet the edges and press them together securely.

Flaky and Puff Paste

These are made rather like the first stage for preparing pie crust pastry, though the consistency of these pastries is initially softer and less "short," containing a high proportion of water. Then more fat is incorporated into the paste, which is rolled, folded, and re-rolled several times. This process creates layers of pastry which, in the heat of the oven, will rise into light thin leaves. For instance, puff paste, which is folded in three and rolled out six times, will have 729 layers.

As the whole aim is to create the layers without allowing the incorporated fat to melt, start with everything cool, including the bowl, the ingredients and even the worktop if possible. Short, quick strokes (rather than long steady ones) allow the bubbles of air so carefully incorporated in the pastry to move about while the fat is gradually and evenly distributed in the paste. Work lightly and do not stretch the paste—or the layers you have built up will tear and allow the air and fat to escape. Chill the pastry between rollings or at any point if there is a danger of the fat breaking through the pastry, or if the pastry becomes sticky and warm. Although it sounds complicated, it is easy to do.

Pastry rises evenly to a crisp crust in a steamy atmosphere. For this reason flaky and puff pastries (which are expected to rise in the oven) are generally baked with a roasting pan full of water at the bottom of the oven, or on a wet baking sheet. The oven temperature is set high (about 425˚F) to cause rapid expansion of the trapped layers of air and quick cooking of the dough before the fat has time to melt and run out.

Flaky Paste

2 cups all-purpose flour

Pinch of salt

¾ stick unsalted butter

½ cup plus 2 Tbsp cold water

¾ cup shortening or lard

- Sieve the flour with a pinch of salt. Blend in half the butter. Add enough cold water to mix with a knife to a doughy consistency. Turn out on to a floured board and knead until smooth.
- Roll into an oblong about 5 x 10 in. Cut half the shortening or lard into tiny pieces and dot them evenly all over the top two thirds of the pastry, leaving a good margin.
- Fold the pastry in three. Fold the unfatted third up, then the top fatted third down. Press well to seal the edges.

- Repeat the rolling and folding process (without adding any fat) once more so that the folded, closed edge is on your left.
- Roll out again, dot with butter as before, fold and seal as before to prevent the fat escaping during rolling.
- Roll out again, dot with the rest of the lard, fold, seal, and roll once more.
- Fold, wrap the pastry and "relax" (or chill) for 10–15 minutes.
- Roll and fold once again (without adding any fat) and then use as required.

Puff Paste

4 cups all-purpose flour	1¼ cups iced water
2 tsp salt	1 tsp lemon juice
4 sticks unsalted butter	

- Sieve the flour and salt into a bowl and blend in 1 stick of butter with the fingertips or pastry cutter. Add sufficient water and lemon juice to bind into a pliable dough. Turn on to a lightly floured surface and lightly knead until smooth.
- Shape the pastry into a round and cut a cross in the top to about half its depth. Open out the resulting four flaps and roll them out until the center is about four times as thick as the flaps. Shape the remaining butter to fit the center of the dough and fold over the flaps envelope-style. Seal the edges with the fingertips.
- On a floured surface, roll out the dough into a rectangle 8 x 16 in using quick, short strokes. Fold the dough in three. Wrap the pastry in plastic wrap and leave for 20 minutes in the refrigerator.
- Fold the pastry in three and roll into a rectangle as before. Fold into three again. Repeat the rolling and folding for a total of six times. Leave the dough to chill for at least 30 minutes before using it. Puff paste should rise to about six times its height and should be cooked at 450°F.

NOTE

If the pastry becomes too warm or sticky and difficult to handle, wrap it up and chill it for 15 minutes before proceeding.

Strudel Paste

This differs from most other pastries in that it actually benefits from heavy handling. It is beaten and stretched, thumped and kneaded. This treatment allows the gluten to expand and promotes elasticity in the dough. The paste is rolled and stretched on a cloth (the bigger the better) until it is so thin that you should be able to read fine print through it. Keep the paste covered and moist when not in use. When the pastry is pulled out, brush it with butter or oil to prevent it cracking and drying, or keep it covered with a damp cloth. Strudel paste can be bought in ready rolled leaves from specialist food shops, especially Greek-owned ones. Called "phyllo" or "filo" pastry, it is used to make the Middle Eastern baklava.

TIP

Bought phyllo pastry is obtainable from markets and from specialty food shops. It comes ready rolled and in convenient leaves. It can be frozen.

2½ cups all-purpose flour	¼ cup plus 2 Tbsp water
Pinch of salt	1 tsp oil
1 egg	

- Sieve the flour and salt into a bowl.
- Beat the egg and add the water and oil. First with a knife and then with one hand mix the water and egg into the flour, adding more water if necessary to make a soft dough.
- Beat the paste until smooth and elastic, as follows: lift the dough up in one hand and with a flick of the wrist throw it on to a lightly floured marble slab or board without letting go of it. Gather it up again and repeat the flinging down. Keep doing this for a few minutes. The paste will gradually become more elastic and less sticky.
- Keep folding and flicking until the paste is smooth, shiny and elastic. Cover and leave in a warm place for 15 minutes.
- Put the pastry into a clean floured bowl. Cover and leave in a warm place for 15 minutes.
- The pastry is now ready for rolling and pulling, as described.

Vegetarian Tarts

Sun-dried Tomato and
Mozzarella Tart

Spinach and Walnut
Whole-wheat Quiche

Rich Ratatouille and Goat's
Cheese Quiche

Sweet Garlic, Thyme and
Olive Tart

Spinach, Camembert, and Pine Nut
Square

Yellow Squash and Provolone Tart

Broiled Eggplant and Pepper Pie

Fancy Asparagus Tranche

Cheese Soufflé Tart

Sun-dried Tomato and Mozzarella Tart

T ransform the idea of the classic tomato and cheese pizza by updating the ingredients and arranging them on a pastry base.

MAKES 6–8 SLICES

1 recipe Rich Pie Crust (*Pâte Brisée Riche*, see page 13)

¾ cup home-made thick tomato sauce or ready-made pizza topping

1½ cups shredded mozzarella cheese

4–5 large Italian-style plum tomatoes, sliced

6 sun-dried tomatoes, packed in oil, drained and sliced

8 oz smoked mozzarella cheese, sliced

6–8 fresh basil leaves, torn into small pieces plus extra for garnish

Virgin olive oil for drizzling

Freshly ground black pepper

Preheat the oven to 400°F. Roll out the pastry into a 11-in round and use to line a 10-in lightly greased pizza plate or shallow tart pan. Prick the bottom and blind bake for 10 minutes.

Remove from the oven and prick the bottom again. Immediately spread the bottom evenly with the tomato sauce or pizza topping and sprinkle with the grated cheese. Return to the oven until the cheese just begins to melt, 3–5 minutes. Remove from the oven and cool slightly.

Arrange the sliced tomatoes, sun-dried tomatoes and smoked mozzarella overlapping on the surface of the tart case in a decorative pattern. Sprinkle with the torn basil. Drizzle with about 1 tablespoon of olive oil and season with the pepper.

Return to the oven until the pastry is golden and the cheese melted, and just beginning to color, about 8 minutes. Serve, hot, drizzled with additional olive oil and garnish with fresh basil leaves.

Spinach and Walnut Whole-wheat Quiche

The fillings in vegetable quiches can easily become one dull mass of indistinguishable textures. In this quiche, walnuts are mixed with the spinach, giving a good crunch to the filling.

SERVES 4–6

PASTRY	FILLING
1 stick butter	1 lb frozen chopped leaf spinach
1¼ cups fine whole-wheat flour	Salt and freshly ground black pepper
Pinch of salt	Freshly grated nutmeg
	⅔ cup walnut pieces, roughly chopped
	½ cup blue cheese, crumbled (Stilton or Danish)
	1¼ cups milk
	2 large eggs

Preheat the oven to 400°F. Blend the butter with the flour and salt in a bowl until the mixture resembles fine crumbs. Mix to a manageable dough with warm water, then roll out and use the pastry to line a 9-inch loose-bottomed pie pan. Line with paper towels then fill with baking beans. Bake in the oven for 20 minutes.

Cook the spinach gently in a covered pan until piping hot; shake from time to time to prevent it from burning. Squeeze the spinach dry then season to taste with salt, pepper, and nutmeg.

Remove the paper and beans from the shell and fill with a layer of the spinach, then a layer of walnuts. Crumble the blue cheese over the top of the filling.

Beat the milk and eggs and season with salt and pepper. Pour the custard over the spinach filling then grate a little nutmeg over the top. Reduce the oven temperature to 375°F and bake the quiche for 25–30 minutes, until the custard has set. Serve warm or cold.

Rich Ratatouille and Goat's Cheese Quiche

Fillings for quiches are almost infinitely variable and this one is great for using up leftover ratatouille. Alternatively you can use a can of vegetables for ease and speed, and add chopped nuts to the vegetables—about ¼ cup—to give a little extra texture interest.

SERVES 4

PASTRY	FILLING
¾ stick butter	1 Tbsp basil leaves, roughly torn
¾ cup whole-wheat flour	⅔ cup soft goat's cheese
Pinch of salt	Salt and freshly ground black pepper
15-oz canned or fresh ratatouille	1¼ cups milk or milk and light cream, mixed
	2 large eggs, beaten

Preheat oven to 400°F. Prepare the pastry by blending the butter into the flour and salt until the mixture resembles fine bread crumbs. Mix to a firm, manageable dough with warm water, then knead lightly on a floured surface and roll out to line a deep 7-inch pie pan. Chill the pastry lightly for 10–15 minutes, then line the pastry case with paper towels and fill with baking beans. Bake for 15 minutes in the oven.

Remove the paper and the beans and spread the ratatouille over the partly-cooked pastry. Sprinkle the basil leaves and goat's cheese over and season with pepper. Beat together the milk, the eggs, and some seasoning, then pour the mixture into the pastry case over the vegetables and cheese. Return the quiche to the oven, reduce the heat to 375°F and cook for a further 35 minutes or until set. This quiche is best served warm.

Rich Ratatouille and Goat's Cheese Quiche ▶

Sweet Garlic, Thyme, and Olive Tart

This strong-flavored tart is served with goat's cheese and basil on top—it makes a great talking point. Substitute arugula or watercress for basil if you like.

SERVES 6

8–9-in tart pan lined with **Rich Pie Crust** (*Pâte Brisée Riche*, see page 13) partially baked blind	I cup whipping cream
	2 eggs
¼ stick butter	I cup mixed good quality black and green olives, rinsed, stoned, and halved
4–6 large young garlic cloves, unpeeled	½ cup diced feta cheese
2 tsp fresh thyme leaves, chopped, or I tsp dried thyme	⅛ tsp dried chili flakes
2 Tbsp extra-virgin olive oil	Handful fresh basil leaves or watercress or arugula
I large sweet onion, thinly sliced	

In a small saucepan over a low heat, melt the butter. Add the garlic and thyme and cook, covered, for 15–20 minutes, stirring occasionally, until the garlic is soft. Remove from the heat to cool slightly. Squeeze the garlic from its skin and discard skins. Mash the pulp to combine with the butter and thyme.

Preheat the oven to 375°F. In a medium skillet, heat 1 tablespoon of the olive oil. Add the onion and cook, stirring frequently, until soft and translucent, about 10 minutes. Spread evenly over the bottom of the tart case.

Beat the cream and eggs and stir in the garlic purée. Pour into the onion-filled tart case and sprinkle the olives over the top. Bake until just set and lightly colored, about 30 minutes. Remove to a wire rack to cool slightly.

In a small bowl, toss the diced feta cheese in the remaining olive oil with the chili flakes. Arrange on the warm tart with the basil leaves or watercress or arugula. Serve immediately.

Spinach, Camembert, and Pine Nut Square

The Camembert and sour cream combine to create a rich creamy filling in this tart.

SERVES 4

10-in square tart pan lined with Rich Pie Crust (*Pâte Brisée Riche*, see page 13) baked blind	6 oz Camembert, brie or other semi-soft cheese, rind removed and cut into small pieces
2 Tbsp butter	¼ cup sour cream
2 shallots, finely chopped	2 eggs
8 oz baby spinach, washed and dried	salt
	Freshly grated nutmeg
	2 Tbsp pine nuts

Preheat the oven to 350°F. Place the shell on a cookie sheet for easier handling. In a medium skillet over a medium heat, melt 1 tablespoon of the butter. Add the shallots and cook, stirring often, until just softened, 3–5 minutes. Spread evenly over the bottom of the shell.

Melt the remaining butter in the same pan and add the spinach, stirring gently, until it wilts, about 1 minute. Spread over the bottom of the shell and sprinkle the cut-up cheese over the spinach.

Beat the sour cream and eggs until well-blended. Season with salt and nutmeg and pour into the shell. Sprinkle over the pine nuts. Bake until set and golden, 20–25 minutes. Transfer to a wire rack to cool slightly; serve immediately.

Yellow Squash and Provolone Tart

If yellow squash is hard to find or out of season, simply use young zucchini.

SERVES 4

9-in tart pan lined with Rich Pie Crust (*Pâte Brisée Riche*, see page 13), baked blind	I small red bell pepper, diced
	½ tsp salt
I Tbsp olive oil	Freshly ground black pepper
I Tbsp butter	2 Tbsp bottled pesto sauce
10 oz yellow squash or zucchini, diced	I cup heavy cream
	2 eggs
	½ cup grated Provolone cheese, preferably aged

Preheat the oven to 375°F. Set the shell on a cookie sheet for easier handling.

In a large skillet over a medium-high heat, heat the oil and butter. Add the yellow squash or zucchini and red bell pepper and cook, stirring frequently, until just beginning to soften, about 5 minutes. Season with salt and pepper and spread on to the bottom of the shell. Drizzle the surface with the pesto sauce.

Beat the cream and eggs until blended., Stir in the grated cheese and pour over the filled shell. Bake until set and golden, about 35 minutes. Transfer to a wire rack to cool slightly. Serve hot or warm.

Broiled Eggplant and Pepper Pie

Broiling the vegetables before baking them in the tart really intensifies the flavors and brings out their sweetness.

SERVES 6

9-in tart pan lined with Rich Pie Crust (*Pâte Brisée Riche*, see page 13), partially baked blind	I large red onion, thickly sliced
	4 oz soft goat's cheese, crumbled
I medium eggplant, thinly sliced crossways	½ cup whipping cream
2 zucchini, sliced diagonally crosswise	I egg
	I egg yolk
¼ cup olive oil	I oz Parmesan cheese, freshly grated
I red bell pepper, quartered and seeded	½ tsp dried oregano
I yellow bell pepper, quartered and seeded	I Tbsp tomato paste
	¼ tsp dried chili flakes

Preheat the broiler. Line the broiler pan with foil and arrange the eggplant and zucchini slices in a single layer on the foil. Brush the surfaces generously with some of the olive oil. Broil the vegetables until just beginning to char, about 5 minutes. Turn and broil 5 more minutes. Arrange on the bottom of the shell. Set on a cookie sheet for easier handling.

Arrange the red and yellow bell pepper quarters, skin-side up, together with the onion rings, on the foil and brush with the remaining oil. Broil until just beginning to char, about 6–7 minutes. Remove any loosened skin and arrange them over the other vegetables in the shell, distributing them evenly. Sprinkle the crumbled goat's cheese over the vegetables.

Preheat the oven to 400°F. Beat the cream with the egg and egg yolk. Stir in the Parmesan cheese, oregano, tomato paste and chili flakes until well blended. Pour over the vegetables in the tart case. Bake until the filling is set and top is well colored, about 25 minutes. Transfer to a wire rack to cool slightly. Serve warm.

◄ *Broiled Eggplant and Pepper Pie*

Fancy Asparagus Tranche

Atranche is a "slice" in French. This rectangular tart makes an elegant presentation, as well as being easy to slice.

SERVES 4

14 x 4-in tart pie pan lined with Rich Pie Crust, see page 13, partially baked blind	2 eggs
	I egg yolk
	½ tsp salt
I Tbsp butter	¼ tsp cayenne pepper
I lb thin asparagus tips, well washed	3 Tbsp freshly chopped dill or chives
½ cup heavy cream	2 tsp Dijon mustard

Preheat the oven to 350°F. Set the shell on a cookie sheet for easier handling. In a large skillet over a medium-high heat, melt the butter. Add the asparagus tips and cook, tossing gently until tender-crisp and brightly colored, 1–2 minutes. Remove from the heat and cool slightly. Arrange the asparagus spears crosswise and top to tail in the shell.

Beat the cream, eggs, and egg yolk until well blended. Season with salt and cayenne pepper, then stir in the dill or chives and mustard. Pour into the shell. Bake until set and golden, about 25 minutes. Transfer to a wire rack to cool slightly. Serve hot or warm.

Cheese Soufflé Tart

This cheese soufflé in a pastry shell makes a great supper. For a special presentation, make individual tartlets but bake 10 minutes less.

SERVES 6

9-in pie pan lined with Rich Pie Crust (*Pâte Brisée Riche*, see page 13), partially baked blind	1¼ cups milk
	2 eggs, separated
	I Tbsp Dijon mustard
I oz Parmesan cheese, freshly grated	1¼ cups grated Cheddar cheese
¼ stick butter	Salt
I small onion, finely chopped	Cayenne pepper
¼ cup plain flour	I egg white

Preheat the oven to 425°F. Sprinkle the shell with Parmesan cheese. Set on a cookie sheet for easier handling.

In a medium saucepan over a medium heat, melt the butter. Stir in the onion and cook for 1–2 minutes. Stir in the flour all at once and cook, stirring constantly, for 2 minutes. Gradually whisk in the milk, stirring until thick and smooth. Bring to a boil and cook for 1 minute. Remove from the heat. Beat in the egg yolks, one at a time, then beat in the mustard and cheese. Season with a little salt and cayenne pepper. Set aside.

In a medium bowl, with an electric mixer, beat all the egg whites with a pinch of salt until soft peaks form. Stir a spoonful of the whites into the cheese sauce to lighten it, then gently fold in the remaining whites and spoon the mixture into the shell.

Bake until the soufflé is puffed and golden, about 25 minutes. Serve immediately in the same way as you would a traditional soufflé.

Meat and Fish Pies, Quiches, and Tarts

Cheese, Ham, and Broccoli Pie

Spanish Tortilla Tart

Quiche Lorraine

Smoked Salmon, Creamy Leek, and Orange Tart

Crab and Red Pepper Tartlets

Beef Wellington

Steak and Kidney Pudding with Smoked Oysters

Scandinavian Meat Loaf en Croûte

Game Pie

Veal and Ham Raised Pie

Chicken and Mushroom Pie

Cheese, Ham, and Broccoli Pie

The classic flavors of ham and cheese marry well with broccoli.

SERVES 8

- 8 x 12-in rectangular pie pan lined with 8 oz Cheese Pastry, partially baked blind
- 2 cups broccoli flowerets, blanched
- 1 cup diced cooked ham
- ½ cup whipping cream
- ½ cup milk
- 3 eggs
- 2 egg yolks
- Salt
- Freshly ground black pepper
- 1¼ cups grated Gruyère or Swiss cheese

Preheat the oven to 375°F. Arrange the blanched broccoli evenly over the bottom of the pie case, then sprinkle over the ham pieces or slices.

Mix the cream, milk, eggs, and egg yolks until well blended. Season with salt and pepper and stir in the cheese. Pour over the filling. Bake until set and golden, 30–35 minutes. Transfer to a wire rack to cool slightly. Serve hot or warm.

Spanish Tortilla Tart

The pie crust creates a tender, flaky container for an omelet-like filling with typical Spanish-style flavors.

SERVES 6

9-in pie pan lined with 6 oz Rich Pie Crust (*Pâte Brisée Riche*), partially baked blind

1 Tbsp olive oil

1 small onion, thinly sliced

1 red or green bell pepper, seeded and thinly sliced

2 garlic cloves, chopped

2–3 sun-dried tomatoes packed in oil, chopped

8–10 pitted black olives, chopped

1 large potato (about 8 oz), cooked and sliced

¼ cup chorizo, cut into thin strips

2 tsp chopped canned jalapeño chiles

4 eggs

⅔ cups milk

¼ cup whipping cream

½ tsp salt

Freshly ground black pepper

½ tsp paprika

⅓ cup grated Cheddar cheese

Preheat the oven to 375°F. In a medium skillet over a medium heat, heat the oil. Add the onion, pepper, and garlic and cook, stirring occasionally, until softened, about 8 minutes. Reserve one quarter of the mixture and spread the remainder evenly on the bottom of the pie crust. Set on a cookie sheet for easier handling.

Sprinkle the onion mixture with three-quarters of the sun-dried tomatoes and olives, and arrange the potato slices over the top. Sprinkle over the remaining onion-pepper mixture, sun-dried tomatoes, and olives.

Beat the eggs, milk, and cream. Season with salt, pepper, and the paprika, then stir in the cheese. Pour over the vegetable layers. Bake until set and golden, about 30 minutes. Transfer to a rack to cool slightly. Serve hot, warm, or at room temperature.

Quiche Lorraine

The authentic "quiche," which originates in the Lorraine region of France, is a custard-based tart containing bacon, cream, and eggs, and is served as an hors d'oeuvre. Purists say that only this tart can truly be called a quiche. If you like, add 1 cup grated Gruyère or Swiss cheese to the custard mixture.

SERVES 6

9-in pie pan lined with 6 oz Rich Pie Crust (*Pâte Brisée Riche*), partially baked blind

8 oz bacon, cut into ½-in slices

1½ cups whipping cream

3 eggs

1 egg yolk

½ tsp salt

Freshly ground black pepper

Freshly grated nutmeg

Preheat the oven to 375°F. Set the pie crust on a cookie sheet for easier handling.

Put the sliced bacon in a skillet over a low heat. When the fat begins to melt, increase the heat to medium and fry, stirring occasionally, until crisp. Drain on absorbent paper, then sprinkle over the bottom of the pie crust.

Beat the cream and eggs until well blended. Season with salt and pepper and a little grated nutmeg. (Stir in the cheese, if using.) Pour into the pie crust. Bake until the filling is set and golden, about 35 minutes. Transfer to a rack to cool slightly. Serve at room temperature.

Smoked Salmon,
Creamy Leek, and Orange Tart

A hint of orange zest brings out the flavor of the leeks and smoked salmon.

SERVES 6

9-in pie pan lined with 6 oz Rich Pie Crust Pastry (*Pâte Brisée Riche*), partially baked blind	2 Tbsp chopped fresh chives or dill
	Freshly ground black pepper
3 leeks, trimmed, washed and cut into ¼-in slices	8 oz smoked salmon, cut into thin strips
1 cup whipping cream	3 Tbsp sour cream
Grated zest of ½ orange	1 egg
	1 egg yolk

Preheat the oven to 375°F. Put the leeks, whipping cream, and orange rind into a medium saucepan. Set over a medium-high heat and bring to a boil. Simmer until the leeks are tender and cream reduced to a thick purée consistency. Remove from the heat and stir in the chives or dill and season with pepper. Spread evenly on the bottom of the pie crust.

Arrange the smoked salmon strips evenly over the leek mixture. Set on a baking sheet for easier handling.

Beat the sour cream, egg, and egg yolk and pour over the leeks and smoked salmon strips. Bake until the filling is set and golden, about 25 minutes. Transfer to a wire rack to cool slightly. Serve warm or at room temperature.

Crab and Red Pepper Tartlets

Buy good quality fresh white crabmeat for these delicate tartlets. Use a mini-muffin pan to make hors d'oeuvre-size tartlets.

MAKES 8

4 sheets phyllo pastry, defrosted if frozen

½–⅔ stick butter, melted

3 red bell peppers, seeded and cut lengthwise into thin strips

I Tbsp chopped dill

¼ cup Parmesan cheese, freshly grated

8 oz fresh white crabmeat

2 Tbsp mayonnaise

I Tbsp lemon or lime juice

In a large skillet over a medium heat, melt 2 tablespoons of the butter. Add the red pepper strips and cook until softened. Remove from the heat and stir in the dill.

Preheat the oven to 350°F. Lightly grease eight 2½ × 1¼ inch muffin cups. Stack the phyllo pastry sheets on a work surface and cut into 4–5 inch squares.

Place one square on the work surface and brush lightly with a little butter; do not brush right up to the edge. Sprinkle with a little Parmesan cheese. Place a second square on top of the first at a right angle, to create a star shape. Brush lightly with butter and sprinkle with a little Parmesan. Top with a third square, at an angle to the first two, but do not brush with butter. Ease into one of the muffin pan cups, keeping the edges pointing up to form a flat-bottomed tulip shape. (Keep the phyllo pastry sheets you aren't working with covered with a damp tea-towel to prevent them from drying out.) Line the remaining cups.

Bake until crisp and golden, about 10 minutes. Transfer to a rack to cool slightly. Carefully remove each phyllo case and set on a rack to cool. Divide the pepper mixture evenly among the tartlet cases and top each with a little crabmeat. Mix the mayonnaise with the lemon or lime juice and drizzle a little sauce over the crabmeat. Garnish with dill sprigs.

Beef Wellington

This pastry-wrapped beef makes an impressive pastry dish hot or cold.

SERVES 6

1 lb flaky or puff paste	2½ cups mushrooms
2-lb beef tenderloin, in one piece	1 medium onion
	2 garlic cloves
Salt and pepper	Mixed fresh herbs
1½ sticks butter	1 egg, beaten, to glaze

Preheat the oven to 425°F. Make the pastry dough and chill in the refrigerator.

Trim the beef and season with salt and pepper. Rub with butter and roast in a hot oven for about 10 minutes.

Finely chop the mushrooms, onion, garlic, and herbs and cook in the rest of the butter. Drain well and put in a layer on the top of the beef.

Roll out the dough large enough to fit around the beef and meet at the top. Brush beaten egg on the edges of the dough and squeeze together with your fingers. If you are worried about the dough opening during cooking, put the seam under the beef and decorate the top with dough leaves made from the trimmings. Brush all over with beaten egg and roast for about 20 minutes or until the pastry is golden. Serve hot or cold.

Steak and Kidney Pudding with Smoked Oysters

This is a classic English steak pudding. The smoked oysters (and indeed the kidney) can be left out of the pie. Mushrooms could be substituted for oysters in the Steak pudding.

SERVES 4

12 oz flour-quantity suet crust	1 small can smoked oysters, drained
1½ lb chuck steak	Salt and pepper
8 oz lambs' kidney	2 tsp chopped onions
Flour	2 tsp chopped fresh parsley

NOTE

Traditionally, steak and kidney puddings served from the bowl are presented wrapped in a white linen napkin. Alternatively, they can be unmolded on to a large deeply-lipped dish and cut like a cake.

As the filling of the pudding may, with long cooking, dry out somewhat, it is worth having a gravy boat of hot beef gravy or bouillon handy to moisten the meat when serving.

Cut the steak into ¾-in cubes. Chop the kidneys, discarding any sinew. Place both the steak and the kidneys in a large sieve. Pour over flour and shake until the meat is lightly coated.

Line the pudding bowl with the prepared suet pastry. Fill the lined bowl with the meat and add the smoked oysters. Sprinkle plenty of seasoning, chopped onion, and parsley in between the layers. Add water to come three quarters of the way up the filling.

Roll the remaining third of suet pastry ¼ in thick and cover the pudding filling.

Cover the pudding with a piece of waxed paper, pleated down the center (this is to allow room for the pastry to expand), and a similarly pleated piece of foil. Tie down with string.

Place in a saucepan of boiling water with a tightly closed lid, or in a steamer, for 5 hours, taking care to top up with boiling water occasionally. (If using the saucepan method, the water should come two thirds up the side of the pudding bowl. If too full the water bubbles over the top. If too empty it risks boiling dry.)

Remove the paper and foil and serve the pudding.

▲ *Beef Wellington*

Scandinavian Meat Loaf en Croûte

The chicken liver filling adds a gourmet touch to the meat loaf. An attractive dish which tastes as good as it looks.

SERVES 4–6

PASTRY

1 lb basic pie crust

MEAT LOAF

⅓ cup dried bread crumbs

½ cup cream

½ cup water

½ onion, chopped

Butter for frying

¼ lb frozen chicken livers, thawed

14 oz ground beef, veal, or pork, as available

1½ tsp white pepper

½ tsp salt

Prepare the pastry and leave to rest in the refrigerator for 1 hour.

Mix the bread crumbs with the cream and water. Fry the onion in a little butter. Slice the chicken livers, fry, and season. Mix the minced meat with salt, pepper, bread crumb mixture, and fried onion. Pat the mixture into a meat loaf shape on moistened greaseproof paper. Cut a line along the to and fill with the livers, season, then smooth over to cover.

Preheat the oven to 425°F. Roll out the pastry between sheets of plastic wrap. Remove the wrap now and then to sprinkle with flour. Roll out one rectangle large enough to wrap around the meat loaf. Trim away uneven edges and save for decoration.

Ease the meat loaf on to the pastry. First fold up the short ends, trimming away the pastry at the corners so that it is not too thick. Fold up the long sides but not too tightly. Seal the join. Ease the parcel on to a greased baking sheet. Decorate with pastry trimmings. Bake for 30–35 minutes.

If liked, serve with chopped iceberg lettuce and bell peppers dressed in a mixture of 3 tablespoons mayonnaise, 2 tablespoons tomato paste, 3 tablespoons water, salt, and pepper.

Game Pie

Serves 8–10. It is not really worth making a game pie for less than eight people.

SERVES 8–10

1–1½ lb Basic Pie Crust	½ lb veal, ham or pork
2–2½ lb venison for stewing, or a mixture of rabbit and venison	¼ lb chicken livers
	2 Tbsp chopped fresh thyme
8–12 oz pheasant, partridge, or pigeon	Chopped fresh savory, tarragon, and parsley
1 onion	Grated zest of 1 orange
2 leeks	Salt and freshly ground black pepper
2 carrots	
1 turnip	Pinch of ground cloves
Fresh parsley, thyme and bay leaf tied together	Pinch of grated nutmeg
	2 cups fresh bread crumbs
1 stick butter	1 egg, beaten
10 Tbsp chopped shallots	1 glass Madeira or port
3 cups chopped mushrooms	5 hard-cooked eggs, chopped
½ lb bacon slices	1 egg, beaten, to glaze

Put any bones you have, together with the venison trimmings, in a pot. Add the onion, leeks, carrots, and turnip with enough water to cover. Submerge the herbs and simmer while you prepare the rest of the pie.

In ¼ cup of the butter, fry the jointed birds until cooked "pink." Remove. In a little more butter fry the shallots and mushrooms.

Preheat the oven to 375°F. Line a 10–12 in deep baking dish with half the bacon slices. Grind the rest of the bacon with the veal, ham, or pork. Add the chicken livers and the reserved livers from the birds used in the pie. Put the ground meat into a bowl and mix with the fried shallots and mushrooms, herbs, orange zest, salt, pepper and spices. Add the bread crumbs, the whole egg and the Madeira. Mix well.

Put a layer of game joints over the bacon slices. Season and sprinkle with parsley. Add a layer of hard-cooked eggs, then the cooked liver mixture rolled into balls. Continue until full, cover with foil and bake for up to 1 hour.

Take out of the oven and cool. Put a pie funnel in the middle, cover with the pastry dough and let some of the funnel protrude. Glaze with egg and cook in a hot oven until the pastry is golden. Serve with a fruit jelly.

Veal and Ham Raised Pie

This traditional pie makes an impressive center-piece for a buffet party and is excellent served with beet or potato salad.

SERVES 4

1 lb quantity Hot Water Crust (see page 19)	1 onion, finely chopped
1½ lb boned shoulder of veal	2 Tbsp chopped parsley
4 oz ham	1 hard cooked egg
Salt and pepper	1 egg, beaten
	1 pt meat aspic

Preheat oven to 325°F. Cut the veal and ham into very small cubes. Season with a little salt, plenty of pepper, onion, and parsley. Leave on one side.

Wrap a large piece of waxed paper around the outside of a tall, wide jar. Smooth it down as well as possible and try to cover the jar tightly. Leave upside down while you make the pastry.

Reserve about a quarter of the paste for the lid, keeping it covered. Roll out the remaining paste to a round and shape to cover the upturned jar. Leave to chill until really firm, about 20 minutes. When hard turn the jar over and remove it carefully, leaving the greaseproof paper inside the pastry case. Trim and carefully remove the greaseproof paper from the pastry. Stand the pastry case on a baking sheet.

Fill the pie, pushing the filling well into the corners, with half the seasoned meat. Press in the hard-cooked egg and cover with the remaining meat. Shape the filling so that there is a central dome.

Cover the pie with the pastry reserved for the lid. Using a little water secure the lid to the sides of the pie. Press firmly together. Cut off any excess pastry and "crimp" the top edge. Secure a double piece of waxed paper around the whole pie with paper clips at top and bottom to prevent the sides from bulging.

Make a few pastry leaves from any pastry trimmings. Brush the top of the pie with egg white. Make a neat hole (for the steam to escape) in the middle of the lid and decorate the top with the pastry leaves.

Bake for 2 hours. After 1½ hours remove the paper and brush the sides evenly with the egg glaze. Remove from the oven and allow to get completely cold on a wire rack, but do not refrigerate yet.

Warm the meat aspic until just runny. Using a funnel, fill the pie with aspic. The aspic will take some time to filter through the meat so keep repeating the topping up process until you are sure that it is absolutely full. Leave to cool and set before serving.

TIP

For curly pastry leaves cut diamonds from a wide pastry strip. Use a knife blade held at a non-cutting angle to mark the leaf "veins," while pulling the leaf into a curved shape.

Thicker, more robust leaves can be curved in situ. The leaves can be glazed with egg to stick them in place and to give them a shine when baked.

Chicken and Mushroom Pie

A home-cooked favorite with a light rich pastry, quite unlike the purchased counterpart.

SERVES 6–8

1 lb flaky paste	1 lb button mushrooms, or wild mushrooms, if available
1 good-sized chicken	
1 Spanish onion	Knob of butter, softened and worked with 1 Tbsp flour
Fresh parsley, thyme, and bay leaf tied together	1 Tbsp chopped fresh herbs, including tarragon
Carrots, celery, and leeks	
Dry white white (optional)	1 egg, beaten, to glaze

Place the chicken in a pot with the onion, bouquet garni, and vegetables. Cover with water and some dry white wine, if you have any.

When the chicken is cooked, remove it from the pot and reserve the broth. Take off all the skin and remove the bones and any tough sinews. Cut the chicken into bite-sized pieces.

Sauté the mushrooms in a little butter. Remove from the butter and place in a deep baking dish together with the prepared chicken.

Into the pan juices from the mushrooms, gradually add 2½ cups or more of the reserved chicken broth. Cook for a few minutes over a high heat. Thicken with a knob of butter worked together with 1 tablespoon of flour. Add the fresh herbs and seasoning and pour over the chicken and mushrooms. Cool.

Roll out the flaky paste dough. Cover the contents to the edges of the baking dish, and brush an egg glaze on the pie. Cook in the oven, preheated to 425°F, until golden brown.

Fruit and Nut Tarts and Pies

Summer Berry Tart on Hazelnut Crust

The nuttiness of the pastry goes beautifully with the sweetness of summer berries. If you like, substitute other favorite fruits cut into bite-sized pieces.

SERVES 6

9-in tart pan lined with Easy Nut Crust made with hazelnuts (see page 14), baked blind

1½ lb mixed summer berries, such as strawberries, raspberries, loganberries, red or black currants

⅓ cup red currant or raspberry preserve

2 Tbsp raspberry-flavor liqueur

Mint leaves for garnish (optional)

Cut any large strawberries in half or quarters and put in a large bowl. Add the remaining fruit and then toss lightly just to combine.

In a small saucepan over a medium heat, heat the preserve with the liqueur until melted and smooth, stirring frequently. Drizzle over the fruit and shake the bowl to help lightly coat the fruit.

Pour the fruit mixture into the shell, gently distributing the fruit evenly over the surface and into the edge. If you like, garnish with fresh mint leaves.

Blueberry Pie

Asimple classic. If fresh blueberries are
unavailable, frozen blueberries work
equally well.

SERVES 4

CRUST

1½ sticks butter

⅓ cup sugar (optional)

1 egg

⅓ cup whipping cream

2¼ cups flour

FILLING

2 pints blueberries

Sugar to taste (optional)

1 tsp bread crumbs or
   potato flour

Soften the butter and add the sugar, if using. Mix in the
egg thoroughly, then add the cream and flour. Mix well, but
do not beat the dough. Leave the dough to stand in a cool
place for 15 minutes.

Preheat the oven to 400°F. Roll out the dough into a
thin sheet and transfer to a greased baking sheet, shaping a
raised edge all the way around. Mix the blueberries with
the sugar, if using, and the bread crumbs or potato flour.
Spread the filling on the dough. Bake until the crust is
golden brown.

Curd's Cheese Strudel

Curd's cheese is the traditional name for what is now called soft cheese.

SERVES 6–8

FILLING

½ cup golden raisins

1 Tbsp rum

1 stick butter, softened

¾ cup superfine sugar

4 egg yolks

11 oz soft cheese, sieved

¼ cup sour cream

1 tsp lemon zest

1 portion strudel dough or 12 sheets of phyllo pastry

Confectioners' sugar to dust

Soak the golden raisins in the rum for 30 minutes to plump. Beat the butter and sugar until light and fluffy. Beat in the egg yolks one at a time. Mix in the cheese, sour cream and zest.

Spread the filling over two-thirds of the pastry and sprinkle with golden raisins and rum. Using the cloth to help, roll the pastry loosely over the filling; tuck in the ends carefully, so that the filling cannot leak out, and transfer to a large, greased cookie sheet, seam side down. Brush with more melted butter and bake in the oven preheated to 400°F for about 30 minutes until crisp and well-browned. Serve warm or cold dusted with confectioners' sugar.

If using phyllo pastry, use six sheets at a time. Brush one sheet with melted sweet butter and cover with a second sheet of pastry; brush with more melted butter and continue layering and brushing with butter with the remaining layers. Place half the cheese filling in the middle and roll up in the same way as for strudel. Finish with the rest of the phyllo sheets in the same way.

Summer Berry Strudel

This is a delicious summer recipe—the almond cream adds a distinctive richness and flavor.

SERVES 6–8

ALMOND CREAM

⅔ cup blanched almonds

¼ cup sugar

2 Tbsp all-purpose flour

6 Tbsp unsalted butter, softened and cut into pieces

1 egg

1 egg yolk

½ tsp almond extract

FOR THE STRUDEL

1½ sticks butter, melted

2 cups fresh bread crumbs

2 lb mixed summer berries, such as raspberries, blueberries, strawberries (hulled and chopped), plus extra for serving

½ cup sugar plus extra for sprinkling

Grated zest of 1 lemon

8 large sheets phyllo pastry

Confectioners' sugar for dusting, sifted

Whipped cream or crème fraîche for serving

For the cream: Grind almonds, sugar, and flour in a food processor. Blend butter a little at a time until creamy, then add egg, egg yolk, and almond extract. Blend well.

For the strudel: Heat 5 tablespoons of the melted butter in a large skillet, then add the bread crumbs and stir-fry for 5 minutes.

Preheat oven to 375°F. Grease a large baking sheet. Toss the berries in a large bowl with ½ cup sugar and lemon zest.

Place a phyllo pastry sheet on to the work surface. Brush with a little melted butter and sprinkle with about ¼ cup of the bread crumbs. Lay a second sheet of pastry over the top, and repeat. Continue layering the remaining phyllo sheets with butter and crumbs.

Spread the almond cream over the stack of pastry. Spoon the berry mixture over the center and roll up jelly-roll fashion. Slide the strudel, seam-side down; on to the cookie sheet. Brush with any remaining butter and sprinkle with a little sugar.

Bake about 45 minutes until crisp; cover with foil if it browns too quickly. Cool on a wire rack. Dust with confectioners' sugar and serve with whipped cream or crème fraîche and extra berries.

Lemon and Almond Strudel

A rich but light tangy filling that goes well with good Italian coffee.

SERVES 6–8

FILLING

½ stick butter

2 egg yolks

1 whole egg

1½ cups superfine sugar

Grated zest of 2 lemons

1½ Tbsp lemon juice, strained

2 egg whites

½ cup superfine sugar

1 portion strudel dough or 12 sheets of phyllo pastry

¾ cup ground almonds

Confectioners' sugar, to dust

Beat the butter until pale and creamy. Whisk in the egg yolks one at a time and the whole egg. Beat in 1 cup sugar and mix in the lemon zest. Set aside. Beat together the lemon juice and remaining sugar. Whisk the egg whites until they stand in stiff peaks and beat the lemon juice and sugar mixture into them until they are thick and glossy.

Brush the strudel dough with melted butter and cover two-thirds with the butter and egg yolk filling. Scatter the ground almonds all over and cover with the lemon and egg white mixture. Roll up the strudel lightly. Brush with melted butter.

Preheat oven to 400°F. Bake the strudel for 30 minutes until crisp and well browned. Serve dusted with confectioners' sugar.

Fruit Flans

These classic tarts are easy to make and always look impressive filled with fresh fruits. However, soft fruits must not be cooked so make a quick and easy dessert. Simply, bake an 8–10 inch blind pie case from Rich Pie Crust as described on page 13, and fill shortly before serving to prevent the pastry from going soggy.

For the simplest fruit flan, fill the pie case with the prepared fruits arranging them attractively in concentric rings or in colorful segments as desired. The fruit can then be glazed with 3 tablespoons grape jelly warmed with 2 tablespoons kirsch or lemon juice.

Many fruit flans include a custard filling known as crème pâtissière. Fill the case with the custard filling before topping with the fruit.

Crème Pâtissière

4 eggs	4¼ cups milk
⅔ cup sugar	¼ cup butter
1 cup plus 2 Tbsp flour	Few drops vanilla extract

Beat together the eggs and sugar until the mixture becomes pale in color. Add the sifted flour. Bring the milk to a boil and pour over the custard, beating continuously.

Transfer the custard to the pan and cook over a low heat, stirring with a wooden spoon until the mixture thickens as it begins to boil. Remove from the heat.

Cut the butter into small cubes and stir into the custard along with the vanilla extract.

Place a sheet of dampened baking parchment or sprinkle superfine sugar over the custard until it is cold to prevent a skin from forming.

Tarte Tatin

This classic French tart was made famous by two sisters in a small town in France called Sologne; now it is served all over the world. It is equally delicious made with pears.

SERVES 6–8

12 oz ready-made puff paste or 1 recipe Basic Sweet Paste (*Pâte Sucrée*, see page 14)	¾ stick unsalted butter
	1¼ cups sugar
10 large Golden Delicious apples	¼ tsp ground cinnamon
	Sour cream for serving
Juice of 1 lemon	

On a lightly floured surface, roll out the pastry into an 11-inch round, about ¼-inch thick. Slide on to a lightly floured cookie sheet and refrigerate until needed.

Using a swivel-bladed vegetable peeler, peel the apples, then halve and core them. Sprinkle the apples with a little lemon juice as you work, to prevent them from darkening.

In a 10-inch heavy-based, ovenproof deep skillet over a medium-high heat, melt the butter. Add the sugar and cinnamon, stirring occasionally, until the sugar dissolves. Cook, stirring occasionally, until the sugar is a rich golden caramel color. Remove from the heat.

Carefully arrange the apple halves, rounded side down, around the outside edge of the pan, pressing them together tightly. Press the remaining apple halves into the center, squeezing them into a circle (remember the apples shrink as they cook). Be very careful not to touch the caramel as it is dangerously hot.

Return the apple-filled pan to the heat and bring to a boil. Simmer until the apples begin to soften and the caramel darkens, about 20 minutes. Remove from the heat to cool slightly.

Preheat the oven to 425°F. Remove the pastry round from the refrigerator and allow to soften slightly, about 5 minutes. Carefully slide the rolled-out pastry round over the apple-filled pan, centering the pastry over the apples. Using a knife, carefully tuck the overhanging dough inside the edge of the pan. Pierce the pastry in 2 or 3 places. Bake until golden, 25–30 minutes. Transfer to a wire rack to cool, about 5 minutes.

Run a knife round the edge of the pan to release any pastry that might be stuck. Place a heatproof serving plate over the pan and, using oven mitts, carefully invert them together (unmold this tart over the sink in case the caramel runs out). Gently remove the pan, loosening any apple that may have stuck. Serve warm or at room temperature. Serve with sour cream or crème fraîche.

Lavender-scented Apple Tart

The heady scent of lavender in this tart evokes the hills of Provence in France. Use fresh lavender if you can find it, or substitute rosemary or thyme for an equally intriguing flavor. For a pretty effect, do not peel the apples, but core and thinly slice them. The peel on the edge gives the cooked tart a colorful finish.

SERVES 6

10-in tart pan lined with
  Basic Pie Crust (*Pâte
  Sucrée*, see page 14)

4 large Gala or Golden
  Delicious apples

½ cup Pineaux de Charente
  or other sweet dessert
  wine

3 Tbsp granulated sugar

GLAZE

¼ cup honey

1 tsp dried lavender or to
  taste

Preheat the oven to 400°F. Using a swivel-bladed vegetable peeler, peel the apples, if desired, then halve and core them. Place cut-side down on a work surface and cut crossways into thin slices. Toss with 3–4 tablespoons of the wine and 2 tablespoons of the sugar.

Starting at the outside edge, arrange the apple slices in overlapping concentric circles in the shell. Sprinkle with the remaining sugar. Bake until the apples are tender and the pastry crisp and golden, about 40 minutes. Transfer to a wire rack to cool slightly.

In a small saucepan over a medium-high heat, simmer the remaining wine, honey, and lavender until reduced by half, about 5 minutes. Carefully brush the hot glaze over the tart. Serve warm.

Plum Crumble Tarts

Almost any firm fruit can be substituted for the plums. The sharpness of the fruit contrasts perfectly with the sweet crumble topping.

MAKES 6

six 3½-in tartlet pans, lined with Basic Pie Crust (*Pâte Sucrée*, see page 14), partially baked blind

CRUMBLE TOPPING

1 cup all-purpose flour

¾ stick cold butter, cut into small pieces

¼ cup sugar

3 Tbsp light or dark brown sugar

½ cup walnuts or pecans, chopped

½ tsp ground cinnamon

FILLING

1½ lb plums

1 Tbsp butter

2 Tbsp sugar

½ tsp ground cinnamon

Lemon juice

Prepare the crumble topping. Put the flour in a large bowl and sprinkle the pieces of butter over the top. Using a pastry blender, cut in the butter until the mixture resembles coarse crumbs. Do not over-blend or the topping will be too dense. Stir in the sugars, nuts, and cinnamon until well blended. Refrigerate until ready to use.

Preheat the oven to 400°F. Halve the plums and, using a small spoon, remove the stones; chop coarsely. In a large skillet over a medium-high heat, melt the butter. Add the plums and toss to coat. Sprinkle with the sugar and cinnamon, and cook for about 1 minute. Cool slightly.

Divide the plum mixture equally among the tartlet crusts and set them on a cookie sheet for easier handling. Spoon the crumble mixture over the plums, mounding it generously. Bake for 15–20 minutes until the topping is crisp and golden. Transfer tartlets to a wire rack to cool. Serve warm with sour cream, if liked.

Apple and Golden Raisin Crumble

Adjust the quantity of cinnamon, or use apple pie spice to taste.

SERVES 4–6

CRUMBLE TOPPING

1½ cups all-purpose flour

Pinch of salt

1 stick butter

½ cup sugar

FILLING

2 lb apples

Butter

2 Tbsp golden raisins

3 Tbsp brown sugar

Squeeze of lemon juice

Pinch of cinnamon

Prepare the crumble by sifting the flour into a bowl with the salt. Rub in the butter using a pastry blender until the mixture resembles coarse crumbs. Stir in the sugar.

Peel, quarter, core, and slice the apples thinly into a deep buttered pie plate. Mix in the golden raisins, sugar, lemon juice, and cinnamon. Press down firmly to flatten.

Sprinkle the crumble mixture evenly over the apple so that it is well sealed. Bake in an oven preheated to 400°F for 30 minutes until golden brown.

> **TIP**
>
> *For the crumble, use a deep dish that takes apple and topping easily. The apple swells slightly as it cooks and can push bits of crumble off the top if the dish is overfilled, or the juices may overflow.*

Plum Crumble Tarts ▶

Strawberry Heart Tart

Aheart-shaped cake pan can be used to make this tart, carefully unmolding the pastry before filling. Alternatively, a free-form heart shape can be made on a baking sheet.

SERVES 6

10 oz ready-made puff paste	½ cup red currant jelly
1½ lb strawberries	2 Tbsp Kirsch, cherry-flavor liqueur, or water (optional)

Preheat the oven to 425°F. Lightly spray a 9-inch heart-shaped cake pan with vegetable oil. On a lightly floured surface, roll out the pastry to a circle about ⅛ inch thick. Line the cake pan with the pastry, pressing into the base. Trim and crimp the edges.

Line the heart-shaped dough with foil and fill with beans. Bake blind for 10–15 minutes. Reduce the oven temperature to 400°F, remove foil and beans and continue baking until crisp and golden brown, about 15 more minutes. Transfer to a wire rack to cool completely. Carefully remove the pastry heart from the pan.

Cut off the stem end of the strawberries and slice each lengthwise. If they have a rounded not pointed tip, cut them through the narrowest part to make them appear more pointed. Arrange them, tightly together, pointed ends up, in the tart case.

In a small saucepan over a medium heat, heat the jelly with the liqueur or water until melted and bubbling. Cool slightly, then brush the berries with a thick layer of glaze, allowing it to dribble between the berries. Serve at room temperature.

Rustic Strawberry Rhubarb Pie

The classic strawberry-rhubarb combination is an ideal filling for an easy-to-make pie. It is also excellent made with apples and blackberries.

SERVES 6–8

1 recipe Basic Pie Crust (*Pâte Sucrée*) or Extra Sweet Pie Crust (*Pâte Sucrée Riche*, see page 14)

1 Tbsp butter

1 lb rhubarb, cut into 1-in pieces

Sugar

2 Tbsp all-purpose flour

1 lb strawberries, hulled and halved if large

2 Tbsp fresh bread crumbs, toasted, or 4 Tbsp home-made dried bread crumbs

Lightly spray or oil a large cookie sheet. On a lightly floured surface, roll out the pastry to a 13–14-inch round; it doesn't matter if the shape is not perfect or if the edges tear, as this is a rustic pie. Slide on to the cookie sheet and refrigerate 30 minutes.

In a large skillet over a high heat, melt the butter. Add the rhubarb and stir-fry until the juices begin to run and it just begins to lose its color. Sprinkle in 3–4 tablespoons sugar and the flour and toss to coat. Remove from the heat and add the strawberries, tossing lightly to combine. Cool for about 5 minutes.

Preheat the oven to 400°F. Remove the pastry round from the refrigerator to soften for about 5 minutes. Sprinkle the surface of the pastry with the toasted or dried bread crumbs and spoon the fruit on to the pastry to within 3–4 inches of the border.

Using your fingertips, fold and crimp the wide border of the pastry over the fruit toward the center. Sprinkle with a little sugar. It doesn't matter if the pastry cracks or is uneven, just pinch it together. Bake until the pastry is crisp and golden and fruit is bubbling, 35–40 minutes. Transfer the pie on its cookie sheet to a wire rack to cool slightly. Serve hot or warm.

Summer Fruit Pizza Tart

This freeform tart resembles a pizza—cover it with any soft fruit you like. It's delicious with ice cream!

SERVES 10–12

1 recipe Basic Pie Crust (*Pâte Sucrée*, see page 14) or Walnut- or Almond-Enriched Basic Pie Crust (see page 12)	halved or quartered strawberries
	½ cup raspberries
	½ cup blackberries
2 Tbsp honey	½ cup blueberries
1 small peach, thinly sliced	1 Tbsp butter, melted
1 small nectarine, sliced 1 cup	2–3 Tbsp sugar

Lightly spray or brush a large cookie sheet with vegetable oil. On a lightly floured surface, roll out the pastry to 11–12-inch round, about ⅛-inch thick. Transfer to the baking sheet. Crimp the edge and prick the bottom all over. Refrigerate for 30 minutes.

Preheat the oven to 400°F. Line the pastry round with foil and weight with the bottom of a pie pan or ovenproof dinner plate. Bake 10 minutes until the pastry edge begins to color. Remove the weight and foil.

Gently brush the surface with the honey and arrange the fruits in triangles or circles over the surface of the pastry. Brush the fruit with the melted butter and sprinkle with the sugar.

Bake until the fruit is tender and pastry is golden, 5–7 minutes. If you like, turn on the broiler and broil the tart until the fruit begins to caramelize, 1–2 minutes. Cover the edge of the pastry with foil if it browns too quickly. Cool slightly and serve warm.

Southern Pecan Tart

This all-American classic pie is delicious served warm with whipped cream, sour cream, or vanilla ice cream.

SERVES 8–10

1 9-in tart shell, lined with Basic Sweet Pie Crust	¼ cup light corn syrup
2½ cups pecan halves	Grated zest and juice of ½ lemon
3 eggs	4 Tbsp butter, melted
1 cup dark brown sugar, packed	½ tsp vanilla extract

Preheat oven to 350°F. Pick out about 1 cup of perfect pecan halves and set aside. Coarsely chop the remaining nuts.

Beat the eggs and sugar together in a large bowl. Then beat in the corn syrup, grated lemon zest and juice, melted butter, vanilla extract, and finally the chopped pecans. Then pour this mixture into the tart shell and carefully set on to a cookie sheet.

Arrange the perfect pecans in concentric circles on top of the egg-sugar mixture and bake until the filling is set and slightly puffed and pecans are well colored, about 40 minutes. Transfer to a wire rack to cool. Serve warm or at room temperature.

◀ *Summer Fruit Pizza Tart*

California Prune Linzer Tart

This cookie-like tart is popular in Eastern Europe. Dried apricots or fresh cherries can be substituted for the prunes.

SERVES 6–8

---

12 oz ready-to-eat pitted prunes

Grated zest and juice of 1 orange

¾ cup water

2 Tbsp sugar

½ tsp ground cinnamon

½ tsp almond extract

CHOCOLATE-ALMOND PASTRY

½ cup blanched almonds

⅔ cup superfine sugar

1½ cups all-purpose flour, sifted

2 Tbsp unsweetened cocoa powder, sifted

1 tsp ground cinnamon

½ tsp salt

Grated zest of 1 orange

2 sticks unsalted butter, cut into pieces

2–3 Tbsp iced water

Confectioners' sugar for dusting, sifted

Bring the prunes to a boil with the orange zest and juice and water. Simmer until the liquid is absorbed and the prunes soft and plump, 15 minutes. Stir in the sugar and the cinnamon and almond extract. Process in a food processor, 20–30 seconds. Cover and chill.

Spray or butter an 11-inch tart pan. Process the almonds and half the sugar to fine crumbs. Add the remaining sugar, flour, cocoa, cinnamon, salt, and orange zest and process to blend. Add the butter and process until coarse crumbs form, about 20 seconds. Add the water a tablespoon at a time and process until the dough just begins to form.

Turn the dough on to a large piece of plastic wrap and knead lightly. Press half the dough on to the bottom and sides of the pan. Prick the bottom and refrigerate 30 minutes. Roll out the remaining dough and cut into ½-inch strips.

Preheat oven to 375°F. Spread the prune filling on to the pastry-lined tart pan. Arrange the dough strips on the top in a lattice pattern. Bake about 35 minutes. Cool then dust with confectioners' sugar.

Coffee and Apple Parcels

These unusual little parcels make a decorative dessert.

SERVES 4

3½ cups all-purpose flour	Zest of 1 orange
Pinch of salt	4 apples
⅓ cup sugar	**SAUCE**
1½ sticks butter	2 Tbsp butter
2 eggs, beaten	¼ cup all-purpose flour
FILLING	⅔ cup milk
1 banana, mashed	¼ cup cooled extra strong coffee
2 rings pineapple, chopped finely	⅔ cup light cream

Sift the flour, salt, and ¼ cup of sugar into a bowl. Blend in the butter until the mixture resembles fine crumbs. Mix to a stiff paste with the eggs.

Mix together the banana, pineapple, remaining sugar and orange zest. Peel and core the apples.

Put all the sauce ingredients into a pan, except the light cream, and heat, whisking all the time. When thick, remove from the heat and use a little of the sauce to moisten the fruit filling.

Roll out the pastry to a square. Cut out four circles. Place an apple in the center of each square and fill with the banana and pineapple mixture.

Brush the edges with water and completely enclose the apple, pressing joins neatly together.

Place the apple parcels, join side down, on a cookie sheet and make a small hole in the centers. Decorate with pastry trimmings.

Preheat the oven to 425°F and bake for 30 to 35 minutes on the center shelf until golden.

Gently heat the coffee sauce and add the cream. Do not boil. Serve with the apples.

Traditional Fruit Pies

These classic fruit pies are guaranteed to please family and friends. Follow the instructions for the apple, pear, and plum pies. For the peach pie the fruit needs no precooking and the fruit can be placed directly on the crust base.

Mom's Apple Pie

10 oz-flour quantity Basic Pie Crust (see page 12)

2 lb pared tart apples (McIntosh, Rome Beauty, Jonathan)

½ cup golden raisins

1 tsp cinnamon

½ cup superfine sugar

2 tsp cornstarch

1 egg

1 Tbsp milk

1 Tbsp granulated sugar

Prepare the pastry and place it in the refrigerator, pastry behaves better when cold.

Wash, peel (if necessary) and slice the fruit and put into a saucepan with the golden raisins, cinnamon, and superfine sugar. Bring to a boil, simmer for 5 minutes, then remove from the heat and cool.

In the meantime, remove half the pastry from the refrigerator and roll out on a well floured surface with a floured rolling pin to a circle just larger than the pie plate. Place the pastry on the greased pie plate and cut around the edges with a sharp knife. Sprinkle the cornstarch on to the base of the pie to absorb any excess juices.

Preheat the oven to 400°F. Beat the egg into a small bowl with a little milk. Remove the other half of the pastry from the refrigerator and roll out in the same way. Brush a little of the egg around the edge of the pastry base and place cover with the pastry top pushing down on to the edges. Cut around the pie and crimp the edges together using either your fingers or a fork. Brush the top of the pie with the egg mixture. Decorate the pie with fruits and leaves made from pastry scraps. Make two slits in the center of the pie with a sharp knife and sprinkle the granulated sugar over the top.

Bake in your preheated oven for 25–30 minutes or until the pie is golden brown. Remove from the oven and leave to cool a little before serving with whipped cream or vanilla ice cream.

VARIATIONS

Pear and Ginger Pie

10 oz-flour quantity Basic Pie Crust

2 lb pears

½ cup chopped candied ginger

½ cup superfine sugar

2 tsp cornstarch

1 egg

1 Tbsp milk

1 Tbsp granulated sugar

Peach Pie

10 oz-flour quantity Basic Pie Crust

2 lb peaches, skinned and sliced

1 tsp lemon juice

½ cup superfine sugar

¼ tsp cinnamon

2 tsp cornstarch

1 egg

1 Tbsp milk

1 Tbsp granulated sugar

Plum and Mint Pie

10 oz-flour quantity Basic Pie Crust

1 lb plums

½ cup chopped mint

¾ cup superfine sugar

2 tsp cornstarch

1 egg

1 Tbsp milk

1 Tbsp granulated sugar

Custard and Cream Tarts

Orange Cardamom Tart

Pear and Chocolate Cream Tart

Cherry Almond Tart

Lemon Tart

Florida Key Lime Tart

Strawberry Shortcake

Chocolate Banoffee Tart

Paris–Brest

Coffee Pear Tart

Raspberry Tart

Prune and Walnut Tart

Pumpkin Pie with
Pecan Praline Topping

Gingered Créme Brûlée Tartlets

Chocolate Ganache and Berry Tart

Butterscotch Pie

Coconut Custard Pie

Millefeuilles with
Raspberries or Strawberries

Orange Cardamom Tart

This delicious orange tart is flavored with cardamom seeds, which give it a slightly exotic touch. Topped with orange slices, it looks stunning.

SERVES 6–8

- 9-in pie pan lined with Extra Sweet Pie Crust (*Pâte Sucrée Riche*, see page 14), partially baked blind
- 5 Tbsp fine-cut orange marmalade
- 2½ cups sugar
- 1¼ cups freshly squeezed orange juice, strained
- 2 large navel oranges, thinly sliced
- 1 stick unsalted butter, softened
- 2 eggs
- 2 egg yolks
- ⅔ cup whipping cream
- Seeds from 4–5 cardamom pods, lightly crushed
- Grated rind of 3 oranges
- ¼ cup golden raisins,

In a small saucepan over a low heat, heat 3 tablespoons of the marmalade until melted. Use to brush the bottom of the tart case with an even layer. Set on a cookie sheet for easier handling.

In a medium saucepan, combine 1¼ cups sugar and 1 cup of the orange juice. Bring to a boil and cook until thick and syrupy, which should take about 10 minutes. Add the orange slices to the syrup and simmer gently until they are completely glazed, about 10 minutes. Carefully transfer to a rack set over a baking sheet so that you can catch any drips. Reserve the syrup.

Preheat the oven to 375°F. With an electric mixer, beat the butter, eggs, egg yolks, and 1¼ cups sugar until lightened, about 2 minutes. Gradually beat in the cream, cardamom seeds, and then the remaining marmalade. Finally stir in the orange rind, remaining juice, and the golden raisins. (The mixture may look curdled at this stage, but don't worry it will be fine.)

Pour the mixture into the crust. Bake until the filling is just set, about 35 minutes. Transfer to a wire rack to cool slightly. Arrange the orange slices in overlapping concentric circles on top of the tart. Bring the reserved syrup to a boil and brush over the orange slices to glaze. Serve at room temperature.

Pear and Chocolate Cream Tart

Sweet ripe pears baked into a rich, chocolate, creamy custard are a heavenly combination.

SERVES 6

9-in pie pan lined with Extra Sweet Pie Crust (*Pâte Sucrée Riche*) or Chocolate Paste

4 oz dark chocolate, melted

1 cup whipping cream

½ cup superfine sugar

1 egg

1 egg yolk

1 tsp vanilla or almond extract

3 medium ripe pears

In a medium saucepan over a low heat, melt the chocolate, cream, and 2 tablespoons of the sugar, stirring frequently, until smooth. Remove from the heat and cool slightly. Beat in the egg, egg yolk, and vanilla extract and spread evenly in the tart case.

Preheat the oven to 375°F. Using a swivel-bladed vegetable peeler, carefully peel the pears, then halve and core them. Put them on a work surface cut-side down and cut crossways into thin slices.

Arrange the pears spoke fashion in the crust and gently with the heel of your hand to fan out the pear slices toward the center. Tap the tart gently on the work surface to eliminate air bubbles.

Bake for 10 minutes. Reduce the oven temperature to 350°F. Sprinkle the surface of the tart with the remaining sugar and bake until the custard is set and pears are tender and glazed, about 20 more minutes. Transfer to a wire rack to cool slightly. Serve warm.

Cherry Almond Tart

In this tart, dried tart cherries are combined with fresh cherries for maximum flavor.

SERVES 6–8

9-in pie pan lined with Basic Sweet Pastry (*Pâte Sucrée*)

1 cup dried tart cherries

½ cup water

⅔ cup blanched almonds

2 Tbsp all-purpose flour

¾ stick sweet butter, softened

Sugar (see recipe)

½ tsp almond extract

1 egg

1 egg yolk

10 oz pitted fresh sweet cherries

Confectioners' sugar for dusting

In a small saucepan, combine the dried cherries and water. Bring to a boil over a medium-high heat. Reduce the heat and simmer over a low heat until the water is absorbed and cherries are soft and plump, about 15 minutes. Cool completely.

Preheat the oven to 400°F. Put the almonds in a food processor fitted with a metal blade. Process until fine crumbs form. Add the flour and pulse to blend. Add the butter, 1 cup sugar, the almond essence, the egg, and egg yolk and process for 10–15 seconds until smooth and creamy, scraping down the sides of the bowl once. Spread the mixture evenly in the pie crust.

In a bowl, combine the fresh cherries and plumped dried cherries and sprinkle with 2–3 tablespoons of sugar (or to taste). Toss well and spoon over the almond mixture, distributing the cherries evenly.

Bake for 15 minutes. Reduce the oven temperature to 350°F, sprinkle the surface with another teaspoon of sugar and continue baking until the filling is puffed and golden, about 25 more minutes. Transfer to a wire rack to cool slightly. Serve warm or at room temperature.

Pear and Chocolate Cream Tart ▶

Lemon Tart

This is one is always popular, a creamy sweet-sharp lemon filling encased in crisp tender pastry—simple but delicious.

SERVES 6–8

9-in pie pan lined with Extra Sweet Pie Crust (*Pâte Brisée Riche*, see page 14), partially baked blind	⅔ cup sugar
	½ cup whipping cream
	3 eggs
Grated zest of 2–3 lemons	3 egg yolks
⅔ cup freshly squeezed lemon juice	Confectioners' sugar for dusting

Preheat the oven to 375°F. With an electric mixer on low speed, beat together the lemon zest, juice, and sugar. Slowly beat in the cream until blended, then beat in the eggs and yolks, one at a time.

Set the tart case on a cookie sheet for easier handling and carefully pour in the filling. (If you prefer a completely smooth filling, strain into the crust, removing the zest.)

Bake until the filling is just set, but not colored, about 20 minutes. If the tart begins to color, cover with foil. Transfer to a wire rack to cool completely. Dust with confectioners' sugar before serving.

Florida Key Lime Tart

Originally made with the small, yellowish limes that come from the Florida Keys, this tart can be made with any limes. Florida key lime juice is available in bottles from larger markets and some specialty stores.

SERVES 6–8

9-in pie pan or pie plate lined with Ginger Crumb Crust (see page 15)	½ cup Key lime or freshly squeezed lime juice (about 3 limes)
3 egg yolks	1 Tbsp grated lime zest
15 fl oz can sweetened condensed milk	1 cup whipping cream

With an electric mixer, beat the egg yolks until thick and creamy, about 3 minutes. Gradually beat in the condensed milk, lime juice, and zest. Pour into the crust and refrigerate until completely set, for at least 4 hours or overnight.

Beat the cream until stiff peaks form. Spoon the cream into a decorating bag fitted with a medium star nozzle and pipe a decorative border between the outer edge and center. Alternatively, serve cold with whipped cream passed separately.

WARNING

People with weak immune systems, or pregnant women may wish to avoid this dish because it contains uncooked eggs.

◀ *Lemon Tart*

Strawberry Shortcake

This mouth-watering dessert should be eaten while it is still warm. The shortcake dough may be prepared 1 to 2 hours ahead of time and kept in a cool place. Have the butter, fruits, and the cream ready too, so that the warm cake can be assembled in just a few minutes.

SERVES 8

CRUST

2¼ cups all-purpose flour

2 tsp baking powder

½ tsp salt

Pinch of nutmeg

½ cup superfine sugar

5 Tbsp unsalted butter, chilled and cubed

1 egg

⅔ cup heavy cream or half and half

1 stick unsalted butter, softened for spreading on cooked layers

FILLING AND TOPPING

2 cups strawberries, red currants or raspberries

3 Tbsp sugar

2 Tbsp kirsch or Grand Marnier

1 cup heavy or whipping cream

Reserve a few fruits for decoration. Slice one third of the strawberries but leave other fruits whole. Crush the rest of the fruit and stir in 2 tablespoons of sugar and 1 tablespoon of the liqueur. Fold in the sliced fruit and set aside.

Sift together the flour, baking powder, salt, nutmeg, and sugar into a bowl. Drop in the butter pieces and quickly rub to a crumb texture. Lightly whisk the egg into the cream and pour on to the dry mixture. Combine quickly into a smooth dough. Butter and flour an 8-inch spring-form pan and press in the dough. Preheat the oven to 425°F and bake for about 20 minutes on a wire rack.

Split the shortcake in two and spread half the butter on the bottom layer and the rest on the underside of the top layer. Spread the fruit filling over the bottom cake and sandwich with the top layer. It does not matter if the fruit oozes out.

Whisk the cream until softly peaked and beat in the rest of the sugar and liqueur. Spoon the cream on to the shortcake and decorate with reserved fruits.

Chocolate Banoffee Tart

B anoffee pie is an all-time favorite. Covering it with white chocolate whipped cream sends it right over the top. The toffee layer can be made ahead, but don't add the bananas and cream more than a few hours before serving.

SERVES 8

9-in deep pie pan lined with Chocolate Pie Crust or Chocolate or Ginger Crumb Crust (see page 15), baked blind

2 15-oz cans sweetened condensed milk

6 oz good-quality dark chocolate, chopped

⅔ cup heavy cream

1 Tbsp corn syrup

2 Tbsp unsalted butter

3 ripe bananas

WHITE CHOCOLATE WHIPPED CREAM

1¾ cups whipping cream

6 oz good-quality white chocolate, grated

½ tsp vanilla extract

Cocoa powder, for dusting

Puncture each of the cans of milk (this prevents any possible explosion while cooking). Put them in a medium saucepan and add enough water to cover. Bring to a boil then reduce the heat and simmer, covered, for about 2 hours. Be sure to top up with water. (Some milk may leak but this does not matter.) Carefully remove tins from water and cool.

In a medium saucepan over a medium-low heat, combine the chocolate, heavy cream, syrup, and butter. Cook until smooth and melted, stirring constantly. Pour into the prepared crust and refrigerate until set, which should take about 1 hour.

Prepare the white chocolate whipped cream. In a small saucepan over a medium heat, bring ½ cup of the cream to a boil. Remove from the heat and stir in the grated white chocolate all at once, stirring until completely smooth. Stir in the vanilla essence. Strain into a medium bowl and cool to room temperature.

Scrape the condensed milk into a bowl. Whisk the thickened "toffee" until smooth. Immediately spread evenly over the chocolate layer in the pie shell.

Slice the bananas thinly and arrange them in overlapping concentric circles over the toffee layer in the tart case. In a medium bowl, whisk the remaining cream until stiff peaks form. Fold a spoonful into the white chocolate cream to lighten it, then fold in the remaining cream. Spoon over the banana layer and spread to the edge. Dust the top with cocoa if you like. Refrigerate until ready to serve.

Paris–Brest

This dessert was created to celebrate a famous bicycle race from Paris to Brest and back again. A delicious variation of a classic recipe!

SERVES 6–8

CHOUX PASTE	FILLING
⅔ cup water	1 lb cherries, stoned and marinated overnight in kirsch
4 Tbsp unsalted butter	
⅔ cup all-purpose flour	1¼ cups heavy cream
Pinch of salt	3 Tbsp confectioners' sugar
2 eggs, beaten	2 Tbsp instant coffee dissolved in 1 Tbsp hot water
⅓ cup flaked almonds	

Heat the water and butter in a saucepan until the butter melts and the water boils. Remove from the heat and quickly beat in the flour and salt. Continue beating over a low heat until the paste is smooth and leaves the sides of the pan clean.

Remove from the heat and add the eggs a little at a time, beating well between each addition until the mixture is smooth and shiny.

Preheat oven to 400°F. Spoon the mixture into a pastry bag fitted with a plain 1-inch nozzle. Pipe a circle about 1½ inches wide and 8 inches in diameter on a greased cookie sheet. Sprinkle the almonds evenly over the dough and bake for 30 minutes. remove from the oven and slice through the middle with a sharp knife. Cool both halves separately.

Place the pastry base on to a serving plate, then spoon the drained cherries into the bottom half of the ring. Whip together the cream, sugar, and coffee, and spoon this mixture on to the cherries.

Cover with the top of the pastry and dust with confectioners' sugar.

Coffee Pear Tart

T̲he flavor of coffee and pears works surprisingly well in this tart.

SERVES 10

CRUST

1½ sticks butter

3½ cups all-purpose flour

1 Tbsp sugar

2 Tbsp powdered instant coffee dissolved in 1 Tbsp warm water

1 egg

FILLING

2 lb firm ripe pears

2 eggs beaten

⅓ cup heavy cream

2 Tbsp powdered instant coffee dissolved in 1 Tbsp warm water

1 liqueur glass of coffee liqueur

Preheat oven to 400°F. Blend the butter into the flour and stir in the sugar. Mix together the coffee and egg and use to bind the mixture together. If more liquid is required use water. Roll out the pastry and line a 12 inch loose-bottom pie plate. Bake for 15 minutes.

Peel, halve, and core the pears and arrange in a circle in the pie shell.

Mix together the eggs, cream, coffee, and liqueur. Pour over the pears and bake for 30 minutes. Serve warm.

Raspberry Tart

Adelicious fresh tart consisting of a thin, rich pie shell filled with a fine lemon cream and raspberries, topped with lemon jello. Suitable both as coffee cake and a dessert.

SERVES 6

CRUST

2 cups flour

Pinch of salt

1 stick soft butter

2 Tbsp sugar

1 egg yolk

LEMON CREAM

2 egg yolks

2 Tbsp sugar

¾ Tbsp cornstarch

Generous 1 cup light cream

2 Tbsp softened butter

Grated zest of ¼–½ lemon

JELLO

Gelatin

1 cup water

2 Tbsp sugar

juice of ½ lemon

About 2 cups fresh raspberries, or ½ lb packet of frozen raspberries

Preheat the oven to 200°F. Place the flour and salt in a bowl, then blend in the butter until the mixture resembles crumbs. Stir in the sugar. Add the egg yolk, and stir until it forms a dough. Add water as necessary. Knead lightly. Use to line a shallow, straight sided pie dish, 9-inches in diameter. Bake blind for about 10 minutes, until golden. Cool slightly, then release carefully from the pan.

For the lemon cream, whisk together the egg yolks, cream, cornstarch, and sugar in a saucepan. Simmer the mixture, whisking, until the cream is thick and fluffy. Remove from the heat, add the butter, and whisk occasionally while it cools. Flavor the cold cream with the lemon zest.

Dissolve the gelatin in the water for the jello. Add the sugar and lemon juice.

Fill the crust with the lemon cream, and cover with raspberries. Pour the jello over the top when it starts to set. Leave the tart in a cold place until serving.

Prune and Walnut Tart

Baked in a crisp pastry and made with cream for a special occasion. One mouthful of this tart conjures up images of prune country in southwest France or California, soaking up the sunshine and planning the next trip to the local vineyard…

SERVES 6

PASTRY

6 Tbsp butter

1¼ cups fine whole-wheat flour

1 Tbsp light brown sugar

1 large egg, beaten

FILLING

2 Tbsp plum preserve or apple jelly

⅓ cup pitted prunes, chopped roughly

⅓ cup walnut pieces, chopped roughly

1¼ cups milk or light cream

2 large eggs, beaten

1 tsp superfine sugar (optional)

Freshly grated nutmeg

Prepare the pastry by blending the butter into the flour and sugar. Bind together with the beaten egg then knead gently on a lightly floured surface. Cover the pastry with plastic wrap and chill in a refrigerator for 30 minutes.

Preheat an oven to 400°F. Roll out the pastry to line a deep, 8-inch flan or cake pan, preferably with a loose base. Fill the pastry case with baking parchment and baking beans, then bake for 15 minutes. Remove the baking beans and parchment and continue cooking for a further 5 minutes, until the base is dry.

Reduce the oven heat to 350°F. Spread the preserve over the base of the flan case then top with the prunes and walnuts. Beat the milk or cream with the eggs and sugar, if used, then pour the custard into the flan case and grate some nutmeg over the top. Bake for 40 minutes, or until the custard is lightly set. Allow to cool, then serve warm or cold.

Pumpkin Pie with Pecan Praline Topping

This is the traditional Thanksgiving pumpkin pie with a face lift. The pecan topping is easy to make and adds a crunchy contrast to the creamy filling.

SERVES 6–8

9-in tart pan lined with Basic Pie Crust (*Pâte Sucrée*, see page 14), partially baked blind

10½ oz canned solid-packed pumpkin

1 cup sugar

½ cup packed light brown sugar

¾ cup whipping cream

5 Tbsp milk

2 eggs

1–2 Tbsp bourbon or whisky (optional)

¾ tsp ground cinnamon

½ tsp ground allspice

½ tsp ground ginger

¼ tsp ground cloves

¼ tsp grated nutmeg

TOPPING

½ cup pecans, chopped

1 cup packed light brown sugar

2 Tbsp unsalted butter, melted

Whipped cream or vanilla ice cream for serving

Preheat the oven to 350°F. With an electric mixer, beat the pumpkin with the remaining ingredients (except the topping and whipped cream) until smooth and well blended. Set the tart on a cookie sheet for easier handling and carefully pour the mixture into the crust.

Bake until the filling is just set (tart will continue to bake once removed) and pastry is golden, about 45 minutes. Cover the pastry edge with foil if it browns too quickly. Remove to a wire rack to cool completely, then refrigerate.

Preheat the broiler. Combine the pecans, sugar, and butter, and sprinkle evenly over the tart. Cover the edge of the pastry with a strip of foil if necessary. Broil about 4 inches from the heat until the topping bubbles and caramelizes, watching carefully, about 1 minute. Allow to cool, then serve the tart at room temperature or chilled with whipped cream or ice cream if desired.

Gingered Crème Brûlée Tartlets

The deliciously thick custard in these tartlets can be flavored still further by infusing the cream with a split vanilla pod if you prefer, but it is the ginger that adds a subtle hint of exotic Eastern flavor.

MAKES 4

Four 4-in tartlet tins lined with Basic Pie Crust (*Pâte Sucrée*, see page 14), or Ginger Crumb Crust (See page 15), baked blind	1 Tbsp sugar
	1 Tbsp ginger syrup (from the bottle)
1¼ cups whipping cream	1 piece bottled stem ginger, finely chopped
1 egg	4–6 Tbsp light brown granulated sugar
2 egg yolks	

Preheat the oven to 325°F. You will find that if you set the tartlet crusts on a baking sheet it will make for easier handling later on.

In a small saucepan over a medium heat, bring the cream to a boil. Whisk the egg and egg yolks with the sugar and ginger syrup until lightened, about 1 minute. Slowly whisk in the hot cream. Strain into a measuring jug and stir in the chopped ginger.

Divide the mixture evenly among the tartlet crusts. Bake until the custard is lightly set, about 15 minutes. Transfer to a wire rack to cool, then refrigerate for at least 4 hours or overnight.

Just before serving, preheat the broiler. Sprinkle a thin layer of sugar evenly over the custard right to the pastry edge. If the pastry is already very brown, protect with a thin strip of foil while broiling. Broil close to the heat until the sugar melts and begins to bubble, about 1 minute; do not over-broil or the custard will begin to curdle. Refrigerate immediately to allow the caramel to harden, about 5 minutes, then serve.

Chocolate Ganache and Berry Tart

Summer berries make a perfect match for a rich chocolate crust filled with a dark chocolate and raspberry truffle mixture.

SERVES 6–8

9-in pie pan lined with Chocolate Pastry, baked blind	chocolate, chopped
2¾ cups whipping cream	4 Tbsp framboise or other raspberry-flavored liqueur
1 cup seedless raspberry preserve	1½ lb mixed fresh summer berries, such as raspberries, blackberries, strawberries (quartered if large), or blueberries
8 oz good quality dark	1–2 Tbsp superfine sugar

In a medium saucepan over a medium heat, bring 1¾ cups of the cream and three-quarters of the raspberry preserve to a boil, whisking to dissolve the preserves. Remove from the heat and add the chocolate all at once, stirring until melted and smooth. Strain the mixture directly into the shell, lifting and turning the tart to distribute the filling evenly. Cool completely or refrigerate until set, at least 1 hour.

In a small saucepan over a medium heat, heat the remaining raspberry preserve and 2 tablespoons of the framboise or other raspberry-flavored liqueur until melted and bubbling. Drizzle over the berries and toss to coat well. Arrange the berries over the top of the tart. Refrigerate until ready to serve.

Bring the tart to room temperature at least 30 minutes before serving. Whip the remaining cream with the sugar and remaining framboise- or raspberry-flavored liqueur until soft peaks form. Spoon into a serving bowl and serve with the tart.

Butterscotch Pie

A wickedly rich dessert for those with a decidedly sweet tooth! The cream adds the final luxurious touch.

SERVES 6–8

9-in pie-pan lined with Basic Pie Crust, baked blind	3 Tbsp unsalted butter
2¼ cups scalded milk	¼ tsp salt
1 vanilla bean, split	4 egg yolks
1 cup brown sugar	¾ cup chopped pecans
¼ cup all-purpose flour	½ cup whipping cream
	Pecan halves to decorate

Bring the milk and vanilla pod to a boil Draw off the heat and leave to infuse for 15 minutes. Remove the pod. Place a double boiler over hot water and combine sugar, flour, butter, and salt. Stir and cook until blended. Slowly add the infused milk. Beat the egg yolks until light, add a little of the milk mixture to lighten, then stir into the mixture in the double boiler. Stir and cook until the mixture thickens. Remove from the heat and stir in the chopped pecans.

Pour the cooled butterscotch into the pie shell. Beat the cream until soft peaks form and spoon into a decorating bag fitted with a medium star nozzle. Pipe a border of cream around the edge and decorate with pecan halves.

Chocolate Ganache and Berry Tart ▶

Coconut Custard Pie

This is a classic pie—a sweet creamy coconut filling in a tender flaky pastry crust.

SERVES 4

1 9-in pie plate lined with Basic Sweet Pie Crust (see page 14) baked blind

⅔ cup sugar

4 Tbsp cornstarch

⅛ tsp salt

2 cups milk

¾ cup heavy cream

3 egg yolks

2 Tbsp sweet butter, diced

2 tsp vanilla extract

2½ cups flaked sweetened coconut

1 cup heavy cream

In a medium saucepan, combine the sugar, cornstarch, and salt. Slowly whisk in the milk and half the cream and bring to a boil over medium heat.

Beat the egg yolks with the remaining cream and slowly pour into the thickened milk mixture, whisking constantly and rapidly to avoid lumps. Boil for 1 minute, whisking constantly. Remove from the heat and beat in the butter, vanilla extract, and 1½ cups of the coconut. Pour into the tart shell and smooth the top evenly. Cool, then refrigerate.

Preheat the oven to 425°F. Spread the remaining coconut on a baking sheet and toast until golden, stirring occasionally, about 5 minutes. Cool the coconut completely.

Beat the cream until soft peaks form. Spoon into a decorating bag filled with a medium star nozzle and pipe a border of cream around the edge. Alternatively spoon cream on to the tart and swirl with the back of a spoon. Sprinkle with the toasted coconut and serve cold.

Millefeuilles with Raspberries or Strawberries

One thousand leaves is the literal translation, and it is almost true! For by the time the puff paste has been rolled, folded, and turned half a dozen times, there are more than 700 layers of trapped air and butter dough. This feather-like assemblage needs only the simplest embellishment, and it makes a sumptuous after-dinner dessert.

SERVES 4

- 1 lb puff paste chilled (see page 21), or use a ready-made fresh or frozen pastry
- 2 cups whipping cream
- 4 Tbsp vanilla sugar
- 2 Tbsp kirsch or Grand Marnier
- 1 lb raspberries or strawberries, cleaned but not washed
- Confectioners' sugar to dust

Roll out the paste on a chilled, floured surface to ⅛ inch thick, and use a sharp knife to cut it into three equal rectangles, 7 × 12 inches. Leave to chill for at least 1 hour, or overnight if possible.

Preheat the oven to 425°F. Chill a cookie sheet under running cold water and then shake off the excess moisture. Transfer one of the pastries to the wet tray, prick all over with a fork to prevent it from puffing too much and bake it in the hot oven until it is well puffed and golden. Cool on a wire rack. Prepare and bake the other pastries in exactly the same way.

Whisk the cream into soft peaks; lightly beat in the sugar and liqueur.

Smooth half the whipped cream on to a puff pastry rectangle. Cover with a second layer of pastry and spread over the rest of the cream. Reserve one perfect fruit for decoration, and embed the rest in the cream. Lay the last pastry rectangle on top. Dredge the top heavily with sifted confectioner's sugar. Heat a long metal skewer and quickly burn a trellis pattern into the sugar, reheating the skewer as necessary. Place the reserved fruit in the center as decoration and serve on an elegant platter. Use the remaining whipped cream to pipe rosettes on the top of the dessert.

Small Pastries

Profiteroles

Chocolate-dipped Palmiers

Walnut-raisin Rugelach

Poppy Seed Parcels

Apple Pastries

Mango Galettes

Irish Cream Barquettes

Raspberry Chocolate Eclairs

Cheddar Pennies

Parma Ham, Fig,
and Fontina Barquettes

Cheese Straws

Profiteroles

These delicious pastries are a guaranteed dinner party hit.

SERVES 6

4 Tbsp unsalted butter

⅔ cup water

⅔ cup all-purpose flour

2 eggs, beaten

FILLING

1¼ cups heavy cream

¼ cup confectioners' sugar, sieved

a little Grand Marnier

2 tsp finely-grated orange zest

CHOCOLATE SAUCE

⅔ cup semisweet chocolate chips

2 Tbsp orange juice

½ cup confectioners' sugar

2 Tbsp butter

Melt the butter in a pan with the water. Bring to a boil and immediately tip in the flour. Beat well until the mixture forms a ball that comes cleanly away from the pan. Leave to cool. Beat or whisk in the eggs, a little at a time. Continue beating until the mixture is smooth and glossy.

Put mixture into a decorating bag fitted with a ½-inch plain nozzle. Pipe about 24 small balls on to a greased and floured cookie sheet.

Preheat oven to 400°F. Bake in the oven for 15–20 minutes until well risen and golden brown. A few minutes before removing from the oven, pierce them with a sharp knife to release the steam. Cool on a wire rack.

To make the filling, whisk the cream until stiff. Stir in the confectioner's sugar, Grand Marnier and orange zest. Put the cream in a decorating bag fitted with a small nozzle and pipe the cream into the choux buns through the slits.

To make the sauce, put all the ingredients into a bowl over a pan of hot water and heat until melted. Stir well.

Pile the profiteroles on a serving dish and just before serving, pour over the warm sauce.

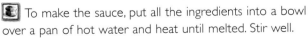

Chocolate-dipped Palmiers

These classic French pastries are deceptively quick and easy to make as they can be made from purchased puff pastry.

MAKES ABOUT 40

½ cup finely chopped hazelnuts

2 Tbsp sugar

½ tsp ground cinnamon

8 oz fresh or frozen puff pastry (see page 21),

defrosted if frozen

Sugar for rolling

1 egg, lightly beaten

8 oz semisweet chocolate

Lightly grease 2 large baking sheets. In a small bowl, combine hazelnuts, sugar, and cinnamon. Set aside.

Cut pastry into quarters. Generously sprinkle work surface with sugar and roll out one quarter of pastry to a thin rectangle. Lightly brush pastry with beaten egg, and sprinkle evenly with the nut mixture.

Fold long edges of pastry inward to meet, edge to edge, in center. Brush surface with a little more beaten egg, and sprinkle with more nut mixture. Then fold outside edges inward to meet, edge to edge, in center to make 4 even layers.

Preheat oven to 425°F. Using a sharp knife, cut pastry crosswise into 1-inch strips, and place ½ inch apart on cookie sheets. Open from center fold to form a "V" shape. Refrigerate 15 minutes.

Bake until golden, about 10 minutes, turning palmiers over half-way through cooking time. Remove baking sheets to wire racks to cool slightly. Then remove palmiers to wire racks to cool completely.

In a small heat-proof bowl set over a saucepan of just simmering water, melt the chocolate until smooth, stirring frequently. Line baking sheets with waxed paper or foil. Dip each palmier halfway into chocolate and place on lined baking sheets. Allow to set.

Walnut-raisin Rugelach

Rugelach are one of the most popular Jewish pastries in the United States. Often made with a simple cream cheese paste, these little filled crescents melt in the mouth. The fillings can vary from poppy seed to cinnamon and walnuts, to cheese or chocolate or commonly raspberry or apricot preserves.

MAKES ABOUT 60 PIECES

CREAM CHEESE PASTE

2 sticks unsalted butter, softened

½ lb cream cheese, softened

1 Tbsp sugar

2 to 3 Tbsp sour cream

2 cups all-purpose flour

¼ teaspoon salt

FILLING

¾ cup golden raisins

1 cup finely chopped walnuts

2 teaspoons ground cinnamon

⅓ cup sugar

Milk for glazing

2 Tbsp sugar mixed with ½ tsp cinnamon for sprinkling

In a large bowl with electric mixer (or by hand), cream butter and cream cheese together until well blended. Add sugar and beat until smooth, then beat in sour cream and mix in flour and salt until a soft dough is formed. Shape into a ball and flatten to disc. Wrap dough well and refrigerate until dough is firm, at least 2 hours.

Preheat oven to 350°F. Lightly grease 2 large cookie sheets. In a small bowl, toss raisins and walnuts with the cinnamon and sugar to mix. Set aside.

Place dough on lightly floured surface and cut into quarters; work with one-quarter at a time, keeping remaining dough refrigerated. Roll out one-quarter of the dough ⅛ inch thick. Using a 10-inch plate cut dough into a 10-inch circle. Sprinkle dough with about one-fifth of the filling to within 1 inch of the edge.

With a long-bladed, sharp knife, cut dough circle into 10- to 12-equal wedges. Starting at the curved edge, roll up each wedge jelly-roll fashion. Place each on cookie sheet, point side down (to keep filling from escaping) about 1 inch apart, curving ends down to form a crescent.

Brush each crescent with a little milk and sprinkle with a little sugar-cinnamon mixture.

Bake until golden brown, 20–25 minutes. Remove pastries to a wire rack to cool. Repeat with remaining dough and reroll trimmings to make extra cookings. Store in an airtight container.

VARIATION

Poppy Seed Rugelach

Use 1¼ cups canned poppy seed filling, spreading about one-fifth on each dough circle before cutting. Shape and bake.

Poppy Seed Parcels

These unusual pastries come from Poland. The poppy seeds are mixed with butter, raisins, honey, and nutmeg and are terrific with a steaming mug of coffee.

MAKES 16

2 cups all-purpose flour	2 Tbsp butter
6 Tbsp unsalted butter	4 Tbsp raisins, chopped
2 Tbsp superfine sugar	2 Tbsp liquid honey
1 egg, separated	½ tsp grated nutmeg
3 Tbsp sour cream	Superfine sugar to sprinkle
½ cup poppy seeds, ground	

Sift the flour into a bowl. Rub in the butter, then stir in the sugar. Mix in the egg yolk with the sour cream to make a fairly stiff dough. Knead the dough, then wrap in plastic wrap. Chill for 30 minutes.

Meanwhile, make sure the poppy seeds are ground. Mix them with the butter in a small pan. Cook for a few minutes, stirring all the time. Add the raisins, honey, and nutmeg and set aside to cool. Set the oven at 375°F.

On a lightly floured surface, roll out the dough into a 14 inch square. Cut this into sixteen 3½ inch squares. Divide the poppy seed mixture between the squares, piling it in the middle of each with a teaspoon. Lightly whisk the egg white and brush it on the edges of the pastry. Fold the corners of each pastry square up to meet over the middle of the poppy filling. Pinch all the pastry edges together to seal them thoroughly. Use the blunt edge of a knife to knock the pastry edges down, holding them with two fingers, to ensure they are sealed and neat.

Place the parcels on greased cookie sheets and brush them with a little egg white. Bake for 20 to 25 minutes, until golden. Sprinkle with superfine sugar as soon as they are cooked. Cool on a wire rack.

Apple Pastries

These are slightly fiddly to make but they are worth the effort.

MAKES ABOUT 30

1½ cups all-purpose flour

6 Tbsp unsalted butter

3 Tbsp superfine sugar

½ cup cottage cheese

2 Tbsp sour cream

3 full-flavored eating apples, peeled, cored, and quartered

1 egg, beaten

Confectioners' sugar to dust

Sift the flour into a bowl. Rub in the butter and stir in the sugar. Drain any liquid from the cheese, then press it through a sieve. Mix the cheese and sour cream into the flour mixture to form a soft dough. Knead gently into a ball and cut in half.

Preheat the oven at 400°F. Roll out one piece of dough quite thinly and cut out 2½ inch rounds, using a pastry cutter. Cut each apple quarter into two or three pieces. Place a piece of apple on a round of pastry. Brush the edge of the pastry with egg, then fold it in half to enclose the apple in a miniature case Pinch the edges together to seal them well. Place on a greased cookie sheet. Fill and seal all the pastry rounds, re-rolling the trimmings. Repeat with the second piece of pastry. Brush the pastries with beaten egg.

Bake for about 20 minutes, until golden and cooked. Cool on a wire rack and dust with confectioners' sugar while warm. Serve warm or cold.

Mango Galettes

This idea can be used with any tender fruit which cooks quickly, such as nectarines, peaches or even papayas. Puff paste also makes an easy-to-make base.

MAKES 6

1 recipe Extra Sweet Pie Crust (*Pâte Sucrée Riche*, see page 14)	1 Tbsp unsalted butter
	2 Tbsp superfine sugar
2 medium ripe mangoes	2 Tbsp apricot preserves or honey

On a lightly floured surface, roll out the pastry ¼ inch thick. Using a large fluted cutter or saucer as a guide, cut out six 4-inch rounds, re-rolling pastry scraps if necessary. Transfer to a large cookie sheet, scallop the edges if you like and prick the bases to within ¾ inch of the edge. Refrigerate 30 minutes.

Preheat the oven to 400°F. Peel the mangoes. Cut off each half and lay cut sides down. Slice thinly crosswise.

Arrange the mango slices over the pastry circles to within ¾ inch of the edge. Brush with a little melted butter and sprinkle each with a quarter of the sugar. Bake until the mango begins to caramelize and the pastry is set and golden, which should be about 15 minutes. Transfer to a wire rack to cool slightly.

In a small saucepan over a medium heat, melt the apricot preserves or honey. Brush over the galettes and serve warm.

Irish Cream Barquettes

These little tartlets make an ideal accompaniment to an after-dinner coffee. Use other shapes to form the tartlets, such as hearts, squares, or circles.

MAKES 12

12 mini-barquettes or other mini-tartlet pans lined with Extra Sweet Pie Crust (*Pâte Sucrée Riche*, see page 14), baked blind

⅔ cup semisweet chocolate, melted

½ cup milk

3 egg yolks

2 Tbsp sugar

3 Tbsp all-purpose flour

4 Tbsp Irish cream liqueur

4 Tbsp whipping cream, whipped

Chocolate shavings or cocoa powder for dusting

Brush the bottom of each tartlet with a little melted chocolate. Set the tartlets on a cookie sheet to make for easier handling.

In a heavy-based saucepan over a medium heat, bring the milk just to a boil. Beat the egg yolks and sugar until light, about 1 minute, then stir in the flour. Add the hot milk, whisking constantly.

Return the custard to the heat and cook, until it thickens, about 2 minutes, whisking constantly. Remove from the heat and whisk in the Irish cream liqueur. Allow to cool. Gently fold in the cream and refrigerate until thickened, about 30 minutes.

Spoon the custard-cream into a decorating bag fitted with a medium star nozzle. Pipe into the tartlet crusts and refrigerate. Garnish with chocolate shavings or dust with cocoa just before serving.

Raspberry Chocolate Eclairs

Eclairs are irresistible and the addition of raspberries adds a juicy, sharp contrast to the sweetness of the chocolate.

MAKES ABOUT 10

½ **stick butter, cut in pieces**	**FILLING**
⅔ **cup water**	⅔ **cup heavy cream**
⅔ **cup all-purpose flour**	1½ **cups raspberries**
2 eggs, beaten	**A little sugar**
	TOPPING
	6 oz semisweet chocolate
	2 Tbsp butter

Put the butter or margarine and water into a pan and bring to a boil. Remove from the heat and tip all the flour into the pan at once. Beat with a wooden spoon until the paste forms a ball. Cool. Whisk the eggs into the paste, a little at a time. Continue beating until mixture is glossy.

Preheat oven to 400°F. Put the pastry into a decorating bag fitted with a large plain nozzle. Pipe 3 inch lengths on to greased cookie sheets.

Bake for about 25 minutes, until golden brown. Remove from the oven and make a couple of slits in the sides of each one to allow steam to escape. Return to the oven for a few minutes to dry. Cool on a wire rack.

To make the filling, whisk the cream until stiff. Fold in the raspberries and sugar to taste. Make a slit down the side of each éclair and fill with the cream mixture. Melt together the chocolate and butter. Dip the tops of the éclairs into the chocolate and then leave to set.

Cheddar Pennies

Although not a sweet cookie, these spicy cheese rounds are really popular. They are usually served with a drink and make a change from peanuts and chips.

MAKES ABOUT 4 DOZEN

1 stick unsalted butter, softened

1 cup grated medium or sharp Cheddar cheese

1 cup all-purpose flour

3 Tbsp fresh chopped chives

⅛ tsp salt

¼ to ½ tsp cayenne pepper or chili powder

TIP

This is a good way to use up small pieces of hard cheese, such as Cheddar or Monterey Jack, but the cheese should be well flavored and not bland or the pennies won't have a good flavor.

In a bowl with electric mixer, beat butter until creamy, 30 seconds. Stir in grated cheese, flour, chives, salt, cayenne pepper or chili powder to form a soft dough.

Scrape on to a piece of plastic wrap or waxed paper and using wrap or paper as a guide, form into a long log about 1½ inches in diameter (for smaller pennies, form dough into a 1 inch log). Wrap tightly, and refrigerate several hours or overnight until firm. (Dough can be made up to five days ahead or frozen.)

Preheat oven to 350°F. Lightly grease 2 large cookie sheets. Using a sharp knife, cut dough log (or logs) into ⅜ inch slices and place on prepared cookie sheets. Bake until slightly puffed and golden, 10 to 12 minutes. Using a metal pancake turner or palette knife, remove cookies to a wire rack to cool. Store in airtight containers.

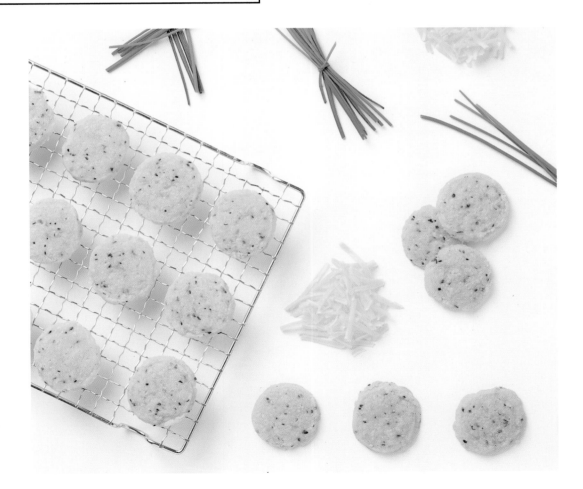

Parma Ham, Fig, and Fontina Barquettes

The saltiness of the Parma ham and sweetness of the figs are balanced by the fontina cheese to create a delicious pastry hors d'oeuvre.

MAKES 12

12 barquette molds lined with Rich Pie Crust (*Pâte Brisée Riche*), baked blind

12 slices Parma ham, trimmed, and cut in half lengthwise

4 figs, halved and thinly sliced

1¼ cups diced fontina cheese

Freshly ground black pepper

Parsley or basil leaves for garnish

Preheat the oven to 375°F. Roll the Parma ham and fill the barquettes with fig slices and diced cheese and Parma ham rolls. Grind a little black pepper over each barquette. Set on a cookie sheet for easier handling.

Bake until the cheese is just melted and pastry heated through, 3–5 minutes. Serve hot or warm.

Cheese Straws

This paste uses self-rising flour. The raising agent lightens pastry that might otherwise be slightly heavy, on account of the cheese.

MAKES 30

1½ cups self-rising flour

Pinch of salt

¾ stick butter

½ cup grated Parmesan and Swiss cheese

1 egg yolk

Salt and pepper

Pinch of cayenne pepper

Pinch of dry mustard

Beaten egg

Preheat the oven to 375°F.

Sift the flour into a basin with a pinch of salt. Blend the butter into the flour until the mixture looks like coarse crumbs. Add the grated cheese, egg yolk, salt, pepper, cayenne, and mustard. Mix to a stiff dough with the beaten egg. Chill for 15 minutes.

Line a cookie sheet with waxed paper. Roll the paste into a large rectangle and cut into strips about ½ inch wide. Twist each strip two or three times like a candy cane and press the ends down on the paper firmly to prevent unraveling.

Bake for 10–15 minutes. They should be golden brown. Leave to cool on a wire rack.

TIP

Bake any mixture with a high cheese content—and therefore likely to burn—on waxed paper. If twisting the cheese straws, press the ends down firmly to prevent unraveling.

Cakes

There is no mystery to making cakes, but this section gives plenty of background information on baking techniques as well as a wide selection of recipes. There are impressive big cakes suitable for the most special occasions right down to simple little cakes suitable for community bake sales. A selection of frostings is included too and instructions on how to decorate and make the most of the finished cake.

INTRODUCTION
AND BASIC RECIPES

A deliciously tempting slice of carrot cake, the great favorite.

Successful cake making is a most satisfying activity for the cook. It is almost most demanding on account of the accuracy needed in measuring the ingredients and the skill necessary in preparing certain cakes. Confidence is best built by beginning with the easier types, such as gingerbread or fruit cakes. The first attempt at making more difficult cakes such as a genoise sponge are often disappointing. Happily, practice—with good ingredients, proper utensils, careful weighing and measuring, precise oven temperatures and exact timing (in short careful attention to detail)—makes perfect.

Most cakes are made by mixing fat, sugar, flour, eggs, and liquid. Air or another gas is incorporated to make the mixture rise while baking. As it bakes, strands of gluten in the flour are stretched by the gas until the heat finally hardens the cake. It is even rising that gives a cake a light sponge-like texture.

Ingredients

Fats

Butter makes the best flavored cakes. Margarine, particularly the soft or "tub" variety, has its place in baking both for speed and (if the margarine is high in polyunsaturated fats) for health reasons, though it has less flavor than butter. Shortenings are flavorless but give light cakes. Lard cakes are often delicious but heavy and for this reason lard is little used in cake making. Oils are not used much as they do not easily hold air when they are creamed or beaten, and the resulting cakes can be heavy.

Sugars

The finer creaming possible with superfine sugar makes it most suitable for cake making. Very coarse granulated sugar can give a speckled appearance to a finished cake unless the sugar is ground down first in a blender or food processor. Soft brown sugars give color and flavor to dark cakes like gingerbread, but they give sponge cakes a drab look and a too-caramel flavor.

Corn syrup, honey, treacle, or molasses are used in cakes made by the melting method. Such cakes are cooked relatively slowly as these thick liquid sugars tend to caramelize and burn at higher temperatures.

Eggs

Unless specified, most recipes assume a medium sized egg weighing about 2 oz. The eggs should be used at room temperature—cold eggs tend to curdle the mixture and this results in the cake having a tough, coarse, too open texture. When using whisked egg whites in a cake, be sure that not even a speck of yolk gets into the whites. Any yolk, or fat on the whisk, will prevent proper whisking (and therefore the air-holding ability) of the whites and thus reduce the lightness of the finished cake.

Flours

All-purpose white flour is used in cake making unless otherwise specified. Self-rising flour has a rising agent (baking powder) added to it and should only be used if specified in the recipe. All flours, even if labeled "ready-sifted" should be sifted before use to eliminate any lumps and to incorporate air.

Rising Agents

Air

Air is incorporated into cake mixtures by agitating the ingredients. Methods include sifting the flour, beating the butter and beating or creaming it again with the sugar to a fluffy, mousse-like consistency, and whisking the eggs. The heat of the oven causes the air trapped in the mixture to rise and lighten the cake, either by itself or in conjunction with other rising agents.

Steam

Steam rises some mixtures even when air has not been beaten into them. Flour mixtures with a high proportion of liquid in them will rise in a hot oven since, as the water vaporizes and the steam rises, the uncooked flour mixture rises with it. While in this puffed-up state, the mixture hardens in the oven heat with the steam trapped inside. The pockets of air created by steam are uneven and very open as in choux pastry so steam is not used on its own for making cakes. But steam is a contributing factor in rising wet cake mixtures such as gingerbread.

Baking Soda

Baking soda is a powder which, when mixed into cake mixtures, quickly gives off half its substance as carbon dioxide gas. In a cake the trapped gas causes the mixture to puff up. Heat sets the mixture once it has risen. By the time the cake cools, the gas will have escaped and will have been replaced by air.

Unfortunately, the unused portion of baking soda remaining can give a cake a slightly unpleasant smell and taste, and a yellowish color. For this reason, baking soda is most often used in strongly tasting cakes such as those flavored with chocolate or molasses. The carbon dioxide reaction is speeded up by acidic substances, so baking soda is usually used in cake mixtures with ingredients such as sour milk, vinegar, buttermilk, sour cream, cream of tartar, and yogurt. This makes is especially suitable for quickly mixed items like fruit cakes. It also gives them a soft texture and spongy crust with a deep color. Unfortunately the process destroys some of the vitamins present in the flour.

Baking Powder

Baking powder in commercial forms consists of bicarbonate of soda and an acid powder which varies according to the brand, plus a starch filler, usually cornstarch, arrowroot, or ground rice. The starch keeps the mixture dry by absorbing any dampness in the air which might cause the soda and acid in the powder to react. The presence of the filler explains why more commercial baking powder than mixed baking soda and cream of tartar would be needed to raise the same cake. A "double action" baking powder is sold which needs heat as well as moisture to produce carbon dioxide gas. The advantage of it is that it can be added to mixtures in advance of baking—it only works once in the oven.

Preparing a Cake Pan

All pans should be greased before use to prevent the cake mixture from sticking or burning at the edges or bottom. Melted shortening or oil are the most suitable fats. Always turn the pan upside down after greasing to allow any excess fat to drain away. Use a pastry brush to get a thin layer.

Bread pans and non-stick springform pans need no preparation other than greasing. Pans for cakes made by the melting or creaming methods should be greased, then the base lined with waxed paper or baking parchment, cut exactly to size and the paper brushed out with more melted shortening or oil. (To cut the paper

1 Cut a length of non-stick paper long enough to encircle the cake pan and overlap slightly.

2 Fold the paper along one side to give a 1 inch margin. Make small cuts along its length up to the margin line, as shown. Cut 2 circles of non-stick paper to fit bottom of tin.

4 Fit the strip of paper around the edge of the pan, allowing the cut flanges to lie flat on the bottom.

5 Fit the second paper circle in the bottom to keep the cut flanges flat. Brush the side and base of the lined pan with butter or oil.

accurately draw round the pan, then cut just inside the line.) For cakes made by the whisking method, a dusting of superfine sugar and flour should be given after lining and greasing.

For fruit cakes, grease the tin, then line the sides and base with waxed paper following the steps as shown below:

3 Brush the pan with melted butter or oil and fit one of the paper circles in the bottom. Brush with butter or oil.

6 Finally, dust the inside of the pan lightly with flour, shaking out any excess.

A Blended-in Method Cake

The blended-in method gives a fairly substantial cake with a crumbly moist texture. The rising agent is always baking soda. In this example the agent is in the self-rising flour. The cake is delicious served sliced and spread with butter.

Marmalade Loaf

2 cups self-rising flour	2 eggs, lightly beaten
$\frac{1}{2}$ tsp salt	3 Tbsp orange marmalade
1 stick butter	3 Tbsp milk
$\frac{1}{4}$ cup superfine sugar	

● Heat the oven to 350°F. Grease a medium size (1½ lb) loaf pan or 6 inch cake pan or charlotte mold.

● Sift the flour and salt into a bowl and blend in the butter: to do this first cut the butter with a knife into tiny dice, and stir them into the flour with a knife, so that each piece is floured and separate. Then using the tips only of well floured fingers, or a pastry cutter, gently rub a few dice at a time to break them up, dropping them back into the flour as soon as they are squashed or crumbled. Keep dipping your fingers into the flour and dropping the butter pieces from a height into the bowl— this both cools them and aerates the mixture.

● When the mixture resembles coarse crumbs stir in the sugar, eggs, marmalade, and milk. Mix well.

● Turn into the prepared pan and bake for about 55 minutes, or until a skewer inserted into the middle of the cake will emerge clean.

● Allow to cool in the pan for 10 minutes, then turn out and cool, right side up, on a wire rack. Serve sliced and spread with butter.

Creaming Method Cakes

All-in-one Creaming Method

The all-in-one method is any easy version of the creaming method, because all the ingredients are beaten together at the same time, but a strong electric mixer is necessary to make these cakes really successful, and soft "tub" margarine gives a lighter result than butter.

Chocolate All-in-one Cake

This cake is made with an electric mixer.

I stick soft butter or margarine

½ cup superfine sugar

2 eggs

¼ cup unsweetened cocoa powder, sifted

¾ cup self-rising flour

Milk, if necessary

FILLING

4 oz semi-sweet chocolate

½ stick unsalted butter

Approx. cup confectioners' sugar, sifted

I egg yolk

NOTE

If the chocolate is hot when added it will melt the butter, which will then lose the beaten-in air that makes the frosting fluffy. This also happens if the butter or frosting is beaten for too long (and so over-heated) in the processor. In this case leave till cool and solid, then beat again.

● **Preheat the oven to 375°F. Lightly oil two 7 inch cake pans and line the bottom with waxed paper. Brush out with oil.**

● **Put all the ingredients except the milk into the bowl of a strong electric mixer or processor and beat until smooth. Start beating slowly—otherwise the flour will shoot out of the bowl. Gradually build up speed. The mixture should be of dropping consistency. That is, it should drop reluctantly off a spoon. If it sticks obstinately it is too thick. Add enough milk to achieve the correct consistency.**

● **Divide the mixture between the pans and bake for 20 minutes or until the cakes are well risen and feel spongy to the fingertips. Allow to cool for a few minutes in the pans,**

then turn out on to a wire rack, remove the baking papers and allow to cool completely.

● **For the frosting, break the chocolate into small, equal sized pieces. Place on a plate and set over a saucepan of simmering water until completely melted. Beat the butter. When soft add sugar. Beat until light and fluffy. Beat in the egg yolk followed by the melted and cooled chocolate.**

● **Sandwich the cakes with the frosting. Dust the top with a little confectioners' sugar.**

Creaming Method Fruit Cake

Fruit cakes use another version of the creaming method. Softened butter and sugar are creamed in a mixing bowl to incorporate air. The eggs and any other liquid are gradually beaten into the creamed mixture, with the flour added with the last few additions of egg to reduce the risk of curdling. After the mixture is well combined, the dry fruit is folded in well to distribute it throughout the cake. The mixture should have a soft dropping consistency (it should fall reluctantly off a spoon given a slight shake—neither sticking obstinately nor running off) and be spread out evenly in the prepared pan, with a slight dip in the center of the mixture to counter-act the cake "peaking." Because these cakes are generally large and dense and contain a high proportion of fruit (which burns easily), they are cooked extremely slowly. To prevent burning they can be placed on a folded newspaper in the oven and can be covered in several layers of brown paper—but not foil, which traps the steam and produces too doughy a result.

Rich Fruit Cake

2 sticks butter	2 cups golden raisins
1 cup soft brown sugar	2 cups currants
2½ cups self-rising flour	1 tsp mixed spice
1 tsp salt	1¼ cups dark beer or
4 large eggs, lightly beaten	Guinness (for an even richer
¾ cup ground almonds	flavor replace half the beer
2 Tbsp chopped mixed	with rum or brandy)
candied peel	
2 Tbsp chopped candied	
cherries	

- Preheat the oven to 350°F. Line a cake pan as described on page 106.
- Beat the butter and sugar together until light, fluffy and pale in color. This is easily achieved in a machine. If doing it by hand start with the butter, soft but not melted, and beat hard for a few minutes, then add the sugar and continue for a good 10 minutes more.
- Sift the flour with the salt and stir it into the butter mixture with the eggs, adding first a spoon of flour, then a spoon of egg, and so on. Add all the rest of the ingredients, alternating spoons of fruit or dry ingredients with the beer. Once all is in, beat the mixture briefly to ensure even mixing.
- Turn into the prepared cake pan and bake for 1 hour. Turn the oven down to 300°F. Cover the cake with a sheet or two of brown paper and bake for a further 3 hours or until a skewer will emerge clean when pushed into the cake. Allow the cake to cool in the pan. Once cold store in an airtight container.

Classic Creaming Method

The creaming method, ie the creaming of fat and sugar to a mousse-like consistency (and thereby incorporating air) is the secret of lightness in this type of cake, although a little chemical rising agent is usually added. First the butter or margarine is beaten until it is smooth and very light in color, but the fat is never allowed to melt (if it did the carefully incorporated air beaten into it would escape). The sugar is then beaten in by degrees until the mixture is pale and fluffy.

The eggs are lightly beaten and added, also by degrees, to the creamed mixture. The mix is beaten after each addition to thoroughly incorporate them. At this point the batter can curdle— usually caused by too-cold eggs—but beating in a tablespoon of sifted flour taken from the recipe after each addition of eggs should prevent this. Cakes made from curdled mixtures are acceptable, but they have a less delicate, more open and coarse texture than those made from uncurdled mixture.

All-purpose or cake flour, if used, should be sifted with the baking powder and salt. Self-rising flour should be sifted with salt. The flour mixture is then folded carefully into the creamed mixture with a metal spoon and with as little mixing as possible to ensure a minimum loss of air in the batter.

Victoria Sandwich

1 stick butter	Milk, if necessary
½ cup superfine sugar	FILLING
2 eggs, at room temperature	Raspberry preserves
1 cup self-rising flour	Confectioners' sugar

- Preheat the oven to 375°F. Lightly oil two 7 inch cake pans and line the bottom with waxed paper. Brush again with oil.
- Beat the butter until soft. Add the sugar and beat again until light and creamy. It should look fluffy and pale. Beat the eggs in a separate bowl until smooth. Gradually add the beaten egg to the butter mixture, beating well at the time. If the mixture begins to curdle add a little of the flour.
- Sift the remaining flour and fold it into the cake mixture using a large metal spoon. The mixture should be of dropping consistency. That is, it should drop reluctantly off a spoon. If it sticks obstinately it is too thick. Add enough milk to achieve the correct consistency.
- Divide the mixture between the pans and bake for 20 minutes or until the cakes are well risen, golden and feel spongy to the fingertips. Allow the cakes to cool for a few minutes in the pans, then turn out on to a wire rack. Remove the baking papers and allow to cool.
- Sandwich the cakes with the preserve. Sift a little confectioners' sugar over the top.

A Melting Method Cake

The melting method is used for very moist cakes like gingerbread. The fat, sugar, syrup, and any other liquid ingredients are heated together to melt, then they are cooled slightly. The flour and other dry ingredients are sifted together and the warm sugar mixture is stirred, not beaten, into the dry mixture along with the eggs. The rising agent is always baking soda. These cakes are the perfect cake for the beginner—easy, reliable, and delicious.

Gingerbread

¾ cup crystallized ginger	½ tsp salt
¾ stick butter	⅔ cup milk
¾ cup dark corn syrup	I egg, beaten
½ cup brown sugar	½ tsp baking soda
2 cups all-purpose flour	½ tsp cream of tartar
I tsp ground ginger	

- **Prepare a shallow rectangular cake pan; grease the bottom and sides and then line the bottom with waxed paper and grease again. Set the oven to 325°F.**
- **Chop the preserved ginger finely. Melt the butter, syrup, and sugar together without boiling. When the sugar has dissolved add the ginger and allow to cool.**
- **Sift the flour into a bowl with the ground ginger and salt. Make a well in the center. Warm the milk and pour it into the egg. Add it to the syrup mixture. Slowly beat the syrup mixture into the flour, pouring a little at a time into the well, and drawing the flour in from the sides as you mix. When all the flour is incorporated in the mixture, stir in the baking soda and cream of tartar.**
- **Turn the mixture into the prepared pan and bake for about I hour. The gingerbread should feel moist and slightly tacky but firm. Let it cool before turning it out. It will keep for about 2 weeks in an airtight container, and freezes perfectly.**

A batter is whisked "to the ribbon" when a lifted whisk will leave a thick ribbon-like trail on the surface of the batter.

Whisked Method Cakes

In the whisking method, the only rising agent is air that has been trapped in the cake batter during mixing. As the air expands in the heat of the oven, the cake rises.

The simplest whisked sponge contains no fat. Sugar and eggs are whisked together until they are thick and light, then flour is folded in gently to keep in as much air as possible. In a lighter but more complicated whisked sponge, the eggs are separated and the yolks are whisked with the sugar and the flour added. The whites are whisked in another bowl, then folded into the batter. Sometimes half the sugar is whisked with the yolks, and half with the whites to give a meringue.

To make these sponges, the sugar and eggs (or egg yolks only) are whisked in a bowl set over a pan of barely simmering water. Make sure that the bowl does not touch the water or the heat will scramble the eggs.

The gentle heat from the steam speeds up the dissolving of the sugar and slightly cooks and thickens the eggs, so encouraging the mixture to hold the maximum number of air bubbles. The mixture should change from yellow to almost white in color and increase to four times its original volume. The mixture is ready when a lifted whisk will leave a ribbon-like trail. Whisking is traditionally done with a balloon whisk but a hand-held electric one works excellently. If a powerful food mixer is used, the heat can be dispensed with, though this process is speeded up if the mixture is put into a warmed bowl.

When the flour is folded in, great care should be taken to fold rather than stir or beat, as the aim is to incorporate the flour without losing any of the beaten-in air which alone will rise the cake. The correct movement is more of lifting the mixture and cutting into it, rather than stirring it.

Although they are light and springy, a drawback to these cakes is that they stale quickly. Always plan to make a fatless sponge on the day of serving, or freeze the cake once it is cool.

Whisked Fat-less Sponge

3 eggs	FILLING
6 Tbsp superfine sugar	Strawberry preserve
¾ cup all-purpose flour	Double cream, lightly whipped
Pinch of salt	Confectioners' sugar

- Preheat the oven to 350°F. Prepare a deep 8 in cake pan or jelly roll pan. Grease the pan with oil, then line the base with waxed paper, cut exactly to size. Brush again with oil. Dust with superfine sugar and then flour. Shake out any excess sugar or flour.
- Place the eggs and sugar in a bowl and fit it over (not in) a saucepan of simmering water. With a balloon whisk (or hand-held electric one) whisk the mixture until it has doubled in bulk and will leave a thick "ribbon" trail on the surface when the whisk is lifted. Start whisking slowly and gradually build up speed. It is essential that the eggs and sugar are not allowed to get too hot—do not let the water get above simmering point and take care that it does not touch the bowl. Remove the bowl from the heat and whisk occasionally until it becomes cool.
- Sift the flour and salt. With a large metal spoon sprinkle it evenly over the surface of the mixture, then fold it in gently but thoroughly.
- Turn into the prepared pan and bake in the middle of the oven for about 25 to 30 minutes. When the cake is cooked it will be risen and brown with the edges slightly shrunk from the edge of the pan and crinkled. When pressed gently with a finger, it will spring back, and will feel spongy. Another point to note is that the cake will sound "creaky," if held close to the ear.
- Leave to cool for a few minutes in the pan and then turn out on to a wire rack. Remove the waxed paper and leave to cool.
- Split in half with a large sharp bread knife. Spread the bottom half with preserve and spoon on the cream. Sandwich together again. Dust the top of the cake with a little confectioners' sugar.

Chocolate Feather Cake with Chestnuts

This cake is a non-classic whisked one and can be made by hand, but is time- and labor-intensive. With the help of an electric mixer and food processor or blender, it is simplicity itself. It can be served plainly dusted with confectioners' sugar for tea, or as a dessert with a chestnut cream filling and hot chocolate sauce. It is interesting because a variety of rising methods are used: a meringue is made with the egg whites (the acid cream of tartar being added to improve volume); a mousse-like emulsion is made with the oil and yolks; the powder ingredients are sifted to aerate them; and a tiny quantity of baking powder is added to guarantee lightness.

3 eggs, separated	FILLING
Pinch of cream of tartar	1¼ cups heavy cream
Scant cup superfine sugar	8 candied chestnuts or chestnuts in syrup
¼ cup vegetable oil	1 Tbsp confectioners' sugar
1 tsp vanilla extract	HOT CHOCOLATE SAUCE
6 Tbsp water	3 Tbsp unsweetened cocoa powder
1 cup all-purpose flour	½ pt water
¼ cup unsweetened cocoa powder	2 tsp cornstarch
¼ tsp baking powder	3 Tbsp dark corn syrup
½ tsp salt	

- Preheat the oven to 375°F. Separate the eggs. Put the egg whites and pinch of cream of tartar into a bowl and whisk until they will hold their shape, then add about half the sugar and whisk until stiff and glossy. (This is only possible with an electric whisk. In the absence of one, whisk the whites to stiff peak and fold in the sugar carefully without further beating.)
- Put the egg yolks with the oil, vanilla, and water into the processor or blender and beat until creamy, pale, and smooth. If doing this by hand, use a balloon whisk. Beat well.
- Sift the flour, cocoa, baking powder, and salt together and stir in the rest of the sugar. Add to the liquid mixture and whisk until smooth. Fold into the meringue mixture.
- Turn carefully into an ungreased 8 inch angel cake or tube pan, or into a 9 inch springform cake pan, prepared as for whisked cakes (page 110). Bake for 50 minutes or until the cake has slightly shrunk from the sides of the

pan and feels springy to the touch. Allow to cool and shrink in the pan, then turn out and transfer to a wire rack. Do not attempt to turn it out before it is cool—it will stick and then break.

- Whip the cream stiffly. Chop three of the chestnuts roughly. Mix into the cream. Split the cake horizontally with a bread knife and carefully remove the top layer. Use half the whipped cream to sandwich the two layers together, and fill the central hole with the rest. (If the cake has been made in an ordinary, rather than ring shaped, pan use all the cream to sandwich it.)
- Sift the confectioners' sugar over the top of the cake, and decorate with the remaining five whole candied chestnuts.
- Serve the sauce separately if the cake is to be eaten as a pudding. Mix the cocoa powder with 2 tablespoons water in a saucepan until smooth. In a cup mix the cornstarch with 1 tablespoon water until smooth. Add the syrup and water and slaked cornstarch to the pan and stir until boiling.

TIP

The cake may be split and filled as Whisked Sponge, filled and frosted with either of the following butter frosting or eaten plain.

The Genoise

This is a whisked sponge that has just-runny butter folded into it with the flour. Butter gives it flavor and richness and makes it keep a day or two longer than fatless sponges. A richer genoise cake (genoise fine) has a greater proportion of butter to flour, and the egg whites are whisked separately and folded in after the butter. The butter for both types of genoise sponges should be poured in a stream around the edge of the bowl and then folded in. If the butter is poured heavily on top of the whisked mixture, it forces out some of the air, and needs excessive mixing, with the danger of loss of more air.

Whisked cakes are cooked when the surface will spring back when pressed with a finger. The cakes should be cooled a few minutes in the pan and then turned out on to a cake rack. The baking paper should be carefully peeled off to allow the escape of steam.

Rich Genoise Cake

4 eggs	Pinch of salt
½ cup plus 1 Tbsp superfine sugar	½ stick very soft but not melted butter
1 cup plus 1 Tbsp all-purpose flour	

- Preheat the oven to 375°F. Prepare a deep 8 in cake pan as above.
- Place the eggs and sugar in a bowl and fit it over (not in) a saucepan of simmering water. With a balloon whisk (or hand-held electric one) whisk until the mixture has doubled in bulk, and will leave a thick "ribbon" trail. Start whisking slowly, and gradually build up speed. Remove the bowl from the heat and whisk occasionally until cool.
- Sift the flour with the salt and dust it evenly and lightly over the egg mixture. Fold it in gently with a large metal spoon.
- Beat the butter until it is soft enough to be just liquid without being clear or melted. It should still be opaque and have the consistency of half-whipped cream. Pour it as thinly as possible round the edge of the bowl. (Dumping it in a lump on the surface requires too much mixing and consequent loss of air.) Fold in gently.

1 Cut a circle of non-stick paper to fit the base of the pan. Brush the pan with oil.

2 Put the non-stick paper in the pan and brush with oil.

3 Dust evenly all over with superfine sugar. Shake off the excess. Then dust with plain flour and again shake out the excess.

4 Place eggs and sugar in a bowl over simmering water. Whisk the eggs and sugar together, slowly at first, then gradually build up speed.

5 Whisk until doubled in bulk, leaving a thick ribbon behind when the whisk is lifted. Remove from the heat and whisk occasionally until cool.

6 Dust the flour and salt over, keeping the sieve as close to the egg and sugar mixture as possible.

7 Blend in the flour with a large metal spoon. Turn the bowl with your left hand and use a three-dimensional figure-of-eight movement to ensure an even fold.

8 Pour in the softened butter around the edge of the bowl. Blend in gently. Pour into the prepared pan and bake for 30 to 35 minutes.

9 Leave to cool on a wire rack. Remove the non-stick paper and cut the cake in half with a bread knife.

● Pour the mixture into the prepared pan. Bake for 30 to 35 minutes. The cake is cooked when risen and golden brown, with the edges slightly shrunk from the pan edge and crinkled. The surface will feel spongy and will spring back when pressed with a finger and the cake will sound "creaky" if held close to the ear.

● Cool for a few minutes in the pan and then turn out on to a wire rack. Remove the waxed paper and leave to cool.

Frosting

Not all cakes need frosting, but adding one is a sure way to jazz up a simple cake. Frostings and garnishes should be chosen to add contrast in texture and color. The flavor should either blend with that of the cake, such as a chocolate fudge frosting on a chocolate cake, or add a contrasting taste, such as the hint of lemon in the cream cheese frosting used with a carrot cake.

Frostings are nearly always used when the cake is for a gift or a special occasion. Then you have the opportunity to add various garnishes and decorations to suit the occasion. Although using a decorating bag takes a little practice to perfect, it is not necessary to be highly skilled to make simple star and leaf shapes which make excellent borders and decorations. Royal Glaze and Butter Frosting both pipe well.

Garnish the cake with orange and lemon candy slices, frosted grapes, nuts, coconut, or chocolate flakes, and curls. There are wonderful purchased flowers that are made specially for cake decoration that add a professional touch to the cake. Some of them, such as candied mimosa and violets, are made from real flowers, others are made from sugar and come in a range of varieties and colors. For children, use candies such as jelly beans, licorice, and confetti candy, which always go down well.

7-Minute Frosting

2 egg whites

1½ cups sugar

5 Tbsp cold water

¼ tsp lemon juice or cream of tartar

1 tsp vanilla extract

● **Place all the ingredients, except the vanilla in a heat-proof bowl and place in a double boiler over a pan of rapidly boiling water. Beat continuously with a wire beater or electric mixer for seven minutes by which time the frosting should be thick and fluffy. Stir in the vanilla and use immediately.**

7-Minute frosting should be used immediately.

Variations

Lemon or Orange Frosting

Use only 3 tablespoons water and omit the vanilla. Add 2 tablespoons lemon or orange juice and half a teaspoon grated lemon or orange zest to the finished frosting.

Marshmallow Frosting

Add 1 cup mini marshmallows to the egg white mixture. The heat and beating action will melt the marshmallow and make the frosting smooth.

Chocolate Frosting

Add 2 squares semi-sweet chocolate to the ingredients in the bowl. For chocolate marshmallow frosting, add both marshmallows and chocolate.

Cream Cheese Frosting

3 oz cream cheese, at room temperature

1½ Tbsp milk

1 cup confectioners' sugar, sifted

1 tsp lemon zest

1 tsp lemon juice

1 tsp vanilla extract

● Beat the cream cheese, milk, and confectioners' sugar until smooth. Stir in the lemon zest, juice, and vanilla.

Fudge Frosting

¾ stick butter

1 cup brown sugar

1 Tbsp milk

½ tsp vanilla extract

2 cups confectioners' sugar, sifted

● Place the butter, brown sugar, and milk in a pan and heat gently until the sugar has dissolved. Remove from the heat and add the vanilla and confectioners' sugar. Beat until the frosting is smooth and of spreading consistency.

● Fudge Frosting can be flavored with one of the following:

Chocolate: add 2 squares of semi-sweet chocolate to the pan.

Coconut: stir ½ cup shredded coconut into the finished frosting.

Coffee: omit vanilla and add 1 Tbsp instant coffee to the pan.

Nut: stir ½ cup chopped pecans, hazelnuts, or mixed nuts into the finished frosting.

Liqueur: Add 2 Tbsp rum, Irish Cream or other suitable liqueur into the finished frosting. As this makes the frosting slightly runnier, add 2 to 4 Tbsp additional confectioners' sugar.

Butterscotch Frosting

½ stick butter

½ cup brown sugar

Pinch salt

⅓ cup evaporated milk

About 2 cups confectioners' sugar

½ tsp vanilla extract

● Place the butter, brown sugar, salt, and evaporated milk in a double boiler and place over a pan of rapidly boiling water. Beat until the sugar has melted and the frosting is smooth. Beat in sufficient confectioners' sugar to make the frosting of spreading consistency, then stir in the vanilla.

Butter Frosting

¾ stick unsalted butter   1–2 tsp warm water or milk

1½ cups confectioners' sugar

● Beat the butter until light and fluffy, then gradually beat in the confectioners' sugar adding a little water if necessary to make the frosting of spreading consistency. Flavor with one of the following:

Vanilla:	¼ to ½ tsp vanilla extract
Orange/ Lemon	stir in the grated zest of 1 small orange or ½ lemon, use orange or lemon juice in place of water.
Chocolate:	add 1 square melted semi-sweet chocolate to the softened butter.
Mocha:	as for chocolate but dissolve 1 tsp instant coffee in the water or milk.
Pineapple:	omit milk or water and add ⅓ cup drained crushed pineapple to the finished frosting.
Maple:	omit milk or water and add ¼ cup maple syrup or maple flavored syrup, add chocolate pecans if desired.

Fondant Frosting

This is not as complicated to prepare as at first seems, and it does keep fresh for several months. If you make a large quantity it will always be on hand when you need it. Half the quantity is enough to cover an 8½ to 9½ inch cake.

● Pour the water into a heavy-based pan, or unlined copper sugar boiler; add the sugar and lemon juice. Heat gently until the sugar has all dissolved, then bring to a boil and cook briskly until the syrup reaches the soft ball stage (240°F); 2 to 3 minutes of boiling. Pour the syrup straight on to a cold wet marble slab or wet work surface and leave to cool for 1 minute.

● Using a wooden spatula or metal scraper, work all round the syrup, lifting it from the edges and slapping and folding it over into the middle. It will change from a clear transparent syrup to a dense creamy mass.

● The syrup will now be cool enough to handle. Continue working—it will set hard otherwise—kneading and punching by hand, and folding in the same way as one handles dough. After about 10 minutes it should look matt white and feel smooth and firm.

● Wrap in plastic wrap and leave to rest for 1 hour; or store in the refrigerator. Divide the mixture in two. Store one half for later use.

● The fondant must be softened before use. Place in a heat-proof bowl and set it over a pan half-filled with simmering water; in this instance the water may come up the sides of the bowl. Warm very gently and add just a little tepid water (about 2 tablespoonfuls is enough for ½ pound of fondant), for an unperfumed flavor. When the fondant mixture has the texture of thick cream it is ready for instant use.

● To color the fondant, add a drop of orange vegetable coloring. For a spiritous flavor, use Grand Marnier instead of the water.

● Spread the fondant over the cake as you would glacé frosting. Decorate with candied orange zest while still soft. Leave to set for several hours or overnight.

How Much Frosting?

Top and sides of two layer 8 inch round cake	1¼ cups
Top and sides of two layer 9 inch round cake	1½ cups
Top and sides of three layer cake	2¼ cups
Top and sides of 8 x 8 inch square cake	1½ cups
Top and sides of 9 x 5 x 3 inch loaf cake	1¼ cups
Filling 10 x 15 inch jelly roll	2 cups
24 cup cakes	1¼ cups

Marzipan

1 cup confectioners' sugar	1 tsp lemon juice
1 cup superfine sugar	3 drops almond extract
2½ cups ground almonds	1 egg, beaten

- Sift the confectioners' sugar into a bowl, then stir in the superfine sugar and the almonds. Add the lemon juice and almond extract, then using a wooden spoon, stir in sufficient egg to form a stiff paste. Knead lightly on a board dusted with confectioners' sugar.

Basic Transparent Glaze

1 cup confectioners' sugar	Few drops vanilla extract or
Water	lemon juice
	Food coloring, optional

- Sift the confectioners' sugar into a bowl and stir in sufficient water to achieve spreading consistency. Stir in the vanilla extract or lemon juice. Stir in a few drops of food coloring to tint the glaze, if desired. Use immediately as the glaze sets quickly.

Royal Glaze

2 large egg whites	½ tsp lemon juice
3½ cups confectioners' sugar, sifted	1 tsp glycerine

- In a bowl, break up the egg whites with a fork. Stir in the confectioners' sugar a little a time, beating well with a wooden spoon. When about half of the sugar has been added, stir in the lemon juice. Continue adding the sugar until the icing forms soft peaks, stir in the glycerine to prevent the frosting from setting rock hard. At this stage it can be used for frosting. For piping, add a little more sugar until the icing holds its shape when formed into peaks. Do not add more sugar if the frosting appears soft after adding all the sugar, continue to beat until it thickens or it will set too hard. To allow air bubbles to settle, cover with a damp cloth and leave for 5 minutes before using.

A glaze adds the finishing touch to a fruit and nut topping

Plain Cakes

Eivor's Orange Cake

Acacia Honey Cake

Boiled Orange and Almond Cake
with Cottage Cheese Frosting

Light Pound Cake

Passionfruit-glazed Pound Cake

Sunshine Cake

Sandcake

Seed Cake

Finnish Lemon Cake

Sour Cream Cake

Angel Cake

Lekach

Eivor's Orange Cake

This Scandinavian orange cake is light and airy, with a fresh flavor. Try it served with coffee or tea, or as a dessert accompanied by fruit salad.

MAKES ONE 9 INCH CAKE

⅔ cup butter

½ cup sugar

3 eggs

Grated zest of 2 lemons

¼ cup fresh orange juice

2 cups flour, sifted with 2 tsp baking powder

Butter for greasing

Bread crumbs for coating pan

GLAZE

½ cup confectioners' sugar

2 Tbsp fresh orange juice

A few drops of oil and yellow food coloring

Candied orange peel

Whisk the butter and sugar until smooth and pale. Add the eggs, one at a time, stirring vigorously. Mix in the lemon zest and orange juice, together with the flour. Grease a 9 inch round cake pan with the butter, and sprinkle in the bread crumbs. Pour the batter into the pan. Place in a cold oven. Heat the oven to 325°–350°F and bake for 1 hour. Turn out and leave to cool under the upturned pan.

Mix the confectioners' sugar and orange juice to a smooth glaze. Add a couple of drops of oil, and color the glaze light yellow with food coloring. Spread over the cake and scatter the orange peel on top.

Acacia Honey Cake

Honey cakes are among the oldest cakes in history and were usually served for festive occasions. Best made a week in advance.

MAKES 12 TO 16 SLICES

¾ cup acacia honey	2 Tbsp dark rum
3 whole eggs, lightly beaten	½ tsp baking soda
2¼ cups rye flour, unsifted	1 Tbsp milk
1 tsp ground cinnamon	Almond halves to decorate
Large pinch ground cloves	
½ cup coarse, ground almonds or hazelnuts	

Preheat oven to 350°F. Grease and flour a deep rectangular pan 12 x 8 inches.

Warm the honey in the jar set in a pan of hot water, then pour it into a large mixing bowl and whisk until it is frothy, thick and white. Beat in the eggs and add the flour a spoonful at a time. Mix together the spices and nuts and stir in the rum, and combine with the honey and egg mixture. Dissolve the baking soda with the milk and beat it into the batter. Leave to mature in a covered bowl overnight as this helps to lighten the batter.

Press into the prepared pan. Stud with almond halves and bake for 30 to 35 minutes. Avoid letting it brown too much as this gives a bitter taste. When the cake has cooled in the pan, cut it into rectangular pieces and store for at least a week in an airtight container before serving.

Boiled Orange and Almond Cake with Cottage Cheese Frosting

A simple cake with a moisture texture and a bright tangy flavor.

MAKES ONE 9 INCH CAKE

2 oranges

6 eggs

½ cup sugar

2 cups blanched almonds, ground

1 tsp baking powder

Flour to dredge the pan

FROSTING

1 cup cottage cheese

½ cup confectioners' sugar

2 Tbsp heavy cream

1 Tbsp Grand Marnier, or Cointreau

Preheat the oven to 375°F. Boil the oranges in their skins in water on top of the stove until they are very soft—this takes about 1 hour. Drain thoroughly.

Beat the eggs and add the sugar, almonds, and baking powder. Purée the chopped oranges in a food processor and add to the mixture. Oil and flour a 9 inch cake pan and pour in the mixture. Bake for about 1 hour. This is a very moist cake and may be served as a dessert, plain with cream, or with the cottage cheese frosting.

To make the frosting, put all the ingredients into a mixer or food processor. Blend. When they are well creamed, spread on top of the cake.

Light Pound Cake

Pound cake is an equal-weight cake, in which each of the main dry ingredients weighs the same as the eggs. It originated centuries ago and was highly spiced, flavored and perfumed, and filled with seeds or dried fruits. Using potato flour gives the cake a finer flavor and the whipped egg white makes it much lighter.

MAKES ONE LOAF CAKE OR EQUIVALENT

2¼ sticks butter

1 cup plus 2 Tbsp superfine sugar

2 in vanilla bean, split

1 tsp lemon zest

4 large eggs

1 cup all-purpose flour, unsifted

1 cup potato flour

1 tsp baking powder

1 tsp orange-flower water

1 Tbsp dark rum

Confectioners' sugar, for dusting

Beat the butter and half the sugar until light and fluffy. Beat in the seeds of vanilla bean and the lemon zest. Beat in, one at a time, one whole egg and the three yolks.

Sift together two or three times the flours and baking powder; then lightly beat 3 tablespoons at a time into the butter and sugar mixture, together with the orange-flower water and the rum, taking care not to over-beat. Whisk the egg whites in a separate bowl until they are firm, and beat in the rest of the sugar until the mixture looks silky and smooth. Lighten the main mixture by beating in 2 to 3 spoonfuls of the egg whites, then tip in the rest and gently fold in using a large metal spoon.

Preheat oven to 350°F. Use a deep 8 inch cake pan or a 9 x 5 inch loaf pan or 9 to 10 inch tube pan. Butter well and dust with flour. Pour in the cake batter and smooth level. Make a slight hollow in the middle. Bake in the warmed oven until well risen and golden brown about 1¼ hours. Leave to cool in the tin for 10 minutes before turning out on to a wire rack. Dredge with confectioners' sugar before serving. Pound cake keeps fresh for at least one week.

VARIATIONS

This basic pound cake is quite simple, but it may be enriched in a variety of exciting ways.

Dried Fruit

Try a mixture of dried fruits—apricots (soaked in water for 2 to 3 hours, then dried and chopped), 1 cup each of golden raisins and raisins; you need two loaf pans for this.

Citrus Peel

Mixed candied citrus peel also tastes good.

Chocolate and Ginger

Chocolate and ginger make the cake rich and spicy. Pour half the cake mixture into a 7 inch tube pan and to the remaining mixture add 2 tablespoonfuls cocoa powder, 1 teaspoon powdered ginger, and ⅓ cup candied ginger, chopped small. Blend the mixture well and spoon it on to the first quantity in the tin; gently drag a fork through it to give a marbled effect.

Fresh Fruit

Fresh fruit can also be added to the basic batter. Choose any seasonal firm fruit, but avoid soft or citrus ones: plums, grapes, apples, cherries, rhubarb, apricots, and pears are all good. You will need about 1½ lb stone fruits, 1 lb others.

Wash, dry, peel, and core or remove the stones. Pour half of the cake mixture into the pan and cover with a layer of fruit; spoon over the rest of the cake batter and cover with the remaining fruit. The baking time will be a little longer, and the cake will not keep for more than about 5 days.

Streusel

Combine ½ cup brown sugar, ½ cup toasted slivered almonds, ½ tablespoonful ground cinnamon and ¼ stick melted butter. Spoon half the batter into a tube pan and cover with the streusel mixture. Cover with the rest of the batter.

Passionfruit-glazed Pound Cake

The flavor of this cake comes from the intensity of the passionfruit glaze. Be sure to use the blackest, most wrinkled fruits, as they are usually the ripest.

MAKES 8 TO 10 SLICES

1½ cups all-purpose flour

¼ tsp baking powder

1½ sticks unsalted butter, softened

1 cup sugar

Grated zest of 1 small orange

1 tsp vanilla extract

3 eggs, lightly beaten

PASSIONFRUIT GLAZE

8 to 10 ripe passionfruits

About ¼ cup sugar

4 seedless oranges, peeled and segmented

Confectioners' sugar for dusting (optional)

Preheat the oven to 350°F. Grease a 9 × 5 inch loaf pan. Line the bottom with nonstick baking parchment. Grease the paper and dust the pan lightly with flour. Sift the flour and baking powder into a bowl.

Beat the butter until light and creamy, for 1 to 2 minutes in a large bowl with an electric mixer. Gradually beat in the sugar until light and fluffy, then beat in the grated orange zest and vanilla extract. Beat in the eggs on low speed until well blended. Fold the flour mixture into the egg mixture, until just blended. Scrape into the pan, smoothing the top evenly.

Bake until risen and golden, and a cake tester inserted into the center comes out clean, about 1 hour. (Cover the top with foil if the cake browns too quickly.) Remove to a wire rack to cool, about 20 minutes.

To prepare the glaze, cut six of the passionfruits crosswise in half, and scoop the pulp into a nylon sieve or strainer placed over a medium bowl and press through with a wooden spoon. Stir in about ⅓ cup sugar; the amount required will depend on the sweetness of the passionfruits. Stir until the sugar is dissolved.

Using a long wooden or metal skewer or cake tester, pierce holes from the top to bottom all over the cake (about 30 holes). Slowly spoon over the glaze and allow to stand for about 20 minutes. Carefully unmold on to the rack, top-side up. If you like, dust with confectioners' sugar before serving.

Meanwhile, cut the remaining passionfruits crosswise in half, and then scoop the pulp into a bowl; sweeten to taste with 2 to 3 tablespoons of sugar. Serve slices of the cake with a few orange segments drizzled with the passionfruit glaze.

Sunshine Cake

S unshine cake belongs to childhood, and the ditty, "...we ought to bake a sunshine cake, it isn't really so hard to make ..."

MAKES ONE 9 INCH ANGEL CAKE

Scant 1½ cups all-purpose flour, sifted	2 in vanilla bean
Pinch salt	1 tsp cream of tartar
6 eggs, separated	1 tsp lemon juice, strained
1 cup plus 2 Tbsp superfine sugar	Confectioners' sugar, to dust

Carefully wash and dry a 9 inch angel cake pan and dust with flour. Preheat oven to 350°F.

Sift the flour and salt several times to aerate well. Whisk the egg yolks and half the sugar until thick and frothy, then mix in the seeds of the vanilla bean. Set aside. Lightly whip the egg whites in a clean bowl until they are foamy, add the cream of tartar and continue whisking until they have expanded into firm white peaks. Pour the remaining sugar in until glossy and smooth.

Carefully fold in the beaten egg yolks and lemon juice on a low speed, or by hand. Sift over one-third of the flour and gently fold it in; repeat in two more stages.

Pour the sponge batter into the floured pan. Drag a knife through it to break any pockets of air. Bake for 50 minutes or until well risen and springy to the touch, turn over on a wire rack to cool, leaving the cake pan in place.

Dust with confectioners' sugar to serve.

Sandcake

S andcake is related to pound cake, but the method of preparation is quite different. The mixture has to be beaten for a considerable time so that when it has been baked the texture is fine and sand-like. Potato flour gives added refinement with a powdery dense texture and a sweet, nutty flavor.

MAKES ONE LOAF CAKE

1½ sticks butter	Scant 1½ cups potato flour, sifted
¾ cup superfine sugar	¼ tsp baking powder
1 large egg	2 large egg whites
3 large egg yolks	Confectioners' sugar, to dust
1 Tbsp rum	
½ tsp lemon zest	

Gently melt the butter in a small pan, taking care not to let it brown. As it starts to bubble, draw the pan off the heat and carefully pour the clear liquid into a small mixing bowl, leaving the thick sediment in the bottom of the pan. Allow to cool. As it starts to solidify, set the bowl on a bed of ice-cubes and beat the clarified butter for 10 minutes with a food mixer (20 minutes by hand) until it is very thick and almost white.

Preheat oven to 325°F. Grease and flour a 9 x 5 inch loaf pan.

Transfer the butter to a large bowl. Add the sugar, egg, and egg yolks a little at a time, making sure that the mixture never becomes runny, and beat for a further 15 minutes.

Slowly add the rum, beating all the time, then the zest. Sift the flour and baking powder and fold in half but do not over-blend. Whisk the egg whites until they are stiff and fold them into the main mixture in three stages, alternating with siftings of flour. Pour into the prepared pan and smooth out. Bake for 1 hour. Turn out of the pan to cool on a wire rack. Dredge with confectioners' sugar to serve. Keeps fresh for up to a week.

Seed Cake

Seed cake, or "seedy cake" as it was known in Dublin, Ireland, was very popular with the ladies. It is traditionally washed down with a glass of port.

MAKES ONE 8 INCH CAKE

2 sticks butter	1 heaped Tbsp caraway seeds
Heaped 1 cup sugar	2 Tbsp milk
4 eggs	2 Tbsp Kirsch
1½ cups self-rising flour	Confectioners' sugar

Cream the butter and sugar. Beat in the eggs, 1 at a time, adding a little flour each time to prevent the mixture curdling.

Fold in the rest of the flour and the caraway seeds. Stir in the milk and Kirsch.

Bake in a round 8 inch pan, lined and greased, for about 1½ hours. Leave in the pan for a few minutes, then cool on a wire rack. Dredge the top of the cake with confectioners' sugar, if wished. This cake keeps for a long time in an airtight container.

Finnish Lemon Cake

The sharp lemon flavor and smooth, creamy texture of this cake makes a perfect contrast to the accompanying preserves or fruit.

MAKES ONE 9 INCH CAKE

4 eggs, separated

3 Tbsp sugar

5 Tbsp all-purpose flour

Grated zest of 1 lemon

1¼ cups heavy cream or sour cream, or 1 cup plain yogurt

Butter for greasing

Bread crumbs for coating pan

Preheat the oven to 350°F.

Whisk the egg yolks with the sugar and flour. Add the lemon zest. Whip the cream, and stir it into the egg mixture. If using yogurt, just mix it in. Whisk the egg whites into peaks, and fold into the mixture. Mix well, but do not stir or the batter might sink.

Pour the mixture into a greased and breadcrumbed 9 inch cake pan. Bake for 35 to 40 minutes. Do not open oven door during the first 25 minutes. Serve the cake freshly baked as dessert with any kind of preserves, or berries and soft fruit.

Sour Cream Cake

A feather-light sponge, is made with sour cream and delicately spiced with cinnamon, cardamom, or ginger.

MAKES ONE 9 INCH CAKE

⅔ cup softened butter	I tsp ground cardamom or ginger
I cup sugar	I cup sour cream
3 eggs	I tsp vanilla sugar
4 cups all-purpose flour	Butter for greasing
I tsp baking soda	Bread crumbs for coating pan
I tsp ground cinnamon	

Preheat the oven to 325°F.

Mix the butter and sugar until light and creamy. Add one egg at a time, stirring constantly. Mix all the dry ingredients together, except the vanilla sugar (sugar that has been left with a vanilla pod to absorb the flavor) and bread crumbs. Beat half of the flour mixture into the creamed mixture. Whisk in the sour cream, the rest of the flour mixture, and the vanilla sugar.

Grease a 9 inch round cake pan with the butter, and sprinkle with the bread crumbs. Spoon in the mixture. Bake for 50 minutes. When ready, turn out on to a wire rack and leave to cool.

Angel Cake

Although it sounds complicated, this low-fat recipe is very easy to make. Be sure to treat the mixture gently so as not to beat out all of the air.

MAKES ABOUT 12 SLICES

3 eggs	**FILLING**
6 Tbsp superfine sugar	Scant cup low-fat soft cheese, such as curd or cream cheese
¾ cup self-rising flour	
Few drops of pink food coloring	2 Tbsp confectioners' sugar
Few drops of yellow food coloring	

Preheat the oven to 400°F. Line three 9 x 5 inch loaf pans with baking parchment paper. Whisk the eggs and sugar in a large bowl until thick and pale and the whisk leaves a trail in the mixture when lifted. Sift the flour into the mixture and fold in gently.

Divide the mixture into three equal quantities and place in separate bowls. Add a few drops of pink coloring to one bowl and stir in gently. Add a few drops of yellow food coloring to another bowl and stir in gently.

Spoon the pink mixture into one prepared pan, the yellow into another and the plain mixture into the third. Bake for 10 minutes until the mixture springs back when gently pressed. Turn out and leave to cool completely on a wire rack.

Trim the sides from each cake. Mix together the filling ingredients. Place the yellow cake on a chopping board and spread half of the filling on top. Place the pink cake on top and spread with the remaining filling. Top with the white cake.

Dust with confectioners' sugar and slice to serve.

Lekach

This honey cake is the traditional Jewish New Year's cake. Heavily flavored with ginger and other spices, it resembles German-style gingerbread.

MAKES 12 SLICES

2½ cups all-purpose flour

I cup whole-wheat flour

½ cup dark brown sugar

I Tbsp baking powder

I tsp baking soda

2 tsp ground ginger

I tsp ground cinnamon

½ tsp ground allspice

½ cup chopped walnuts or almonds, toasted (optional)

½ cup golden raisins (optional)

1¾ cups good-quality natural honey

I cup strong black coffee

3 Tbsp bourbon whiskey, brandy, or water

4 eggs

¼ cup vegetable oil

½ cup ginger preserve or chopped stem ginger in syrup

Confectioners' sugar for dusting or honey for glazing

Preheat oven to 350°F. Grease a 9 x 13 inch cake pan; line with waxed paper, then grease and flour paper.

In a large bowl, combine flours, brown sugar, baking powder, baking soda, ginger, cinnamon, and allspice. Stir in chopped walnuts or almonds and raisins if using. Set aside.

In a small saucepan, over medium-low heat, heat honey with coffee until warm and remove from heat. Stir in bourbon whiskey, brandy, or water.

In a large bowl, beat eggs with vegetable oil until well blended. Beat in ginger preserve or stem ginger. Alternately, in 3 or 4 batches, stir in the warm honey mixture and the flour mixture into the beaten egg mixture until well blended.

Pour batter into the prepared pan. Bake until the skewer inserted in the center comes out with just a few crumbs attached and the top springs back when gently pressed with a finger, I hour. Remove pan to the wire rack and cool completely.

Turn out the cake on to a rack and then back on to a serving plate, so the cake is right side up. Dust with confectioners' sugar or, if you do not mind a sticky cake, brush with slightly heated honey, and cut into squares to serve.

Family Cakes

Zucchini Passion Cake

Cranberry and Coffee Cake

Coffee Almond Slice

Pear Upside-down Cake

Cranberry-orange Upside-down Cake

Apple Bran Cake

Walnut Torte

Coffee Sponge

Coffee Jelly Roll

Carrot Cake

Polish Honey Cake

Lime Coconut Layer Cake

Zucchini Passion Cake

This passion cake is usually made with carrots and grated zucchini—for extra color use some green and some yellow if at all possible.

MAKES ONE 9 INCH CAKE

2 cups cake flour	**FROSTING**
2 tsp baking powder	⅔ cup cream cheese
I tsp baking soda	I stick butter, softened
I tsp salt	½ tsp vanilla extract
I cup superfine sugar	2 cups sieved confectioners' sugar
⅓ cup pine nuts	
⅓ cup golden raisins	Finely shredded mixed carrot and zucchini for decoration (optional)
¾ cup ripe bananas, mashed (about 2 fruits)	
3 large eggs, beaten	
2 cups shredded mixed carrots and zucchini	
⅔ cup sunflower oil	

Preheat the oven to 350°F, and line a 9 inch deep cake pan with baking parchment—a loose-bottomed, spring-form pan is best.

Sift the flour, baking powder, baking soda, and salt into a large mixing bowl, then add the sugar, pine nuts, and golden raisins. Mix well, then add the mashed bananas and beaten eggs. Stir in the grated vegetables and finally the oil, then beat the cake thoroughly for a minute, to a thick, slightly lumpy batter.

Scrape the batter into the prepared pan then bake in the preheated oven for I hour, until a skewer inserted into the center of the cake comes out clean. Leave for a few minutes, then carefully remove the cake from the pan and leave it to cool completely on a wire rack.

To make the frosting, beat the cream cheese and butter together with the vanilla until smooth, then gradually beat in the sugar. Leave the frosting to stand in a cool place for about 30 minutes, to harden it slightly, then spread over the cake. A little finely shredded mixed carrot and zucchini makes a perfect decoration, either in tiny mounds around the edge of the cake, or in the center.

Cranberry and Coffee Cake

This is a very light sponge cake made with oil, flavored with coffee, with dried cranberries folded into the mixture. It may be served as a plain sponge cake or decorated with whipped cream and fresh fruits, such as apricots, blueberries, or cherries, or whatever fruits are in season.

MAKES ONE 9 INCH CAKE

3 large eggs	I tsp coffee essence
½ cup light brown sugar	⅓ cup dried cranberries, chopped roughly
⅔ cup fine whole wheat flour	
I Tbsp sunflower oil	Whipped cream and fresh fruit (optional)

Preheat an oven to 375°F then lightly grease an 8 to 9 inch cake pan and line the base with baking parchment.

Whisk the eggs and sugar together until pale and fluffy—this is best done in an electric mixer and may take up to 10 minutes. Fold in the flour a few spoonfuls at a time, then add the oil and essence, drizzling them down the side of the bowl. Finally, add the cranberries, folding in lightly. Transfer the mixture immediately to the prepared cake pan and bake in the preheated oven for 20 to 25 minutes, until the mixture springs back when pressed lightly and shrinks away from the sides of the pan.

Turn the cake out on to a wire rack to cool completely. Decorate with fruit and whipped cream, if wished, then serve sliced.

Coffee Almond Slice

This sophisticated-looking cake is surprisingly easy to make and well worth the effort. A rich tea-time treat.

MAKES 10 SLICES

I stick butter	FILLING AND TOPPING
½ cup sugar	I oz semi-sweet chocolate
2 eggs	1¼ cups heavy cream
I cup plus 2 Tbsp self-rising flour	4 tsp instant powdered coffee dissolved in I Tbsp hot water
I Tbsp baking powder	
⅓ cup ground almonds	3 Tbsp confectioners' sugar
2 drops almond extract	½ cup chocolate vermicelli
I Tbsp water	

Preheat an oven to 350°F. Grease and line a 7 x 11 inch pan with baking parchment.

Put all the cake ingredients in a bowl. Mix together and beat until smooth. Pour the batter into the prepared pan. Bake for 25 to 30 minutes until firm to the touch. Turn out, remove paper and cool.

Melt the chocolate until runny and keep warm. Whisk the cream with the dissolved coffee and confectioners' sugar until it forms soft peaks.

Trim the edges of the cake and cut into three even-sized pieces. Spread a layer of cream on one piece, top with a second layer and spread with more cream. Top with the final layer of cake.

Spread the sides with cream and coat with the chocolate vermicelli. Spread the remaining cream on the top. Spoon the chocolate into a decorating bag with a fine tip. Pipe straight lines along the length of the cake and with the point of a knife draw lines backward and forward across the chocolate lines creating a chevron effect. Chill for at least I hour and serve.

Cranberry and Coffee Cake ▶

Pear Upside-down Cake

In the low-fat version of this recipe, sliced pears are set on a caramel base and topped with a spicy sponge mixture. Once cooked, turn out and serve immediately with plain yogurt.

MAKES ONE 8 INCH CAKE

2 Tbsp honey	¼ cup superfine sugar
2 Tbsp granulated brown sugar	3 egg whites
2 large pears, peeled, cored and sliced	1 cup self-rising flour
4 Tbsp polyunsaturated margarine	2 tsp ground allspice
	Walnuts, to decorate (optional)

Preheat the oven to 350°F. Heat the honey and sugar in a pan until melted. Pour into an 8 inch round cake pan lined with baking parchment. Arrange the pears around the base of the pan.

Beat together the margarine and sugar until light and fluffy. Whisk the egg whites until peaking and fold into the mixture with the flour and allspice. Spoon on top of the pears.

Bake for 50 minutes or until risen and golden. Let sit for 5 minutes, then turn out on to a serving plate. Remove the lining paper. Decorate with walnuts if desired, but remember that nuts are high in fat and are best saved for special occasions.

Cranberry-orange Upside-down Cake

"Upside-down" cakes became very popular in the 1940s, the most famous being made with canned pineapple rings.

MAKES ONE 9 INCH CAKE

CRANBERRY TOPPING	CAKE
4 Tbsp unsalted butter, melted	⅔ cup all-purpose flour
2 cups fresh cranberries	1 tsp baking powder
⅔ cup sugar	¼ tsp salt
Grated zest of 1 orange	3 eggs
¼ tsp ground cinnamon	½ cup sugar
	½ tsp vanilla extract
	Grated zest of 1 orange
	3 Tbsp unsalted butter, melted

Preheat the oven to 350°F. Pour the melted butter into a 9 inch cake pan. Mix the cranberries, sugar, orange zest, and cinnamon in a bowl. Spread the mixture over the bottom of the pan, pressing gently into the butter.

Sift the flour, baking powder, and salt twice. Put the eggs in a heat-proof bowl and set over a pan of simmering water. With an electric mixer, beat until frothy. Gradually beat in the sugar until thick and pale. Beat in the vanilla extract and orange zest.

Remove from heat and fold in the flour mixture in three batches; drizzle in the melted butter and fold into the batter. Spoon batter over the cranberry layer. Bake 35 minutes. Remove to a wire rack to cool, about 7 minutes.

Run a knife around the edge of the pan to loosen the cake. Place a plate over the pan, bottom side up, and quickly unmold the cake.

Pear Upside-down Cake ▶

Apple Bran Cake

Chunks of apple add moisture to this filling low-fat cake. Decorate with apple slices just before serving or brush with a little lemon juice if wishing to store the cake.

MAKES ONE 8 INCH CAKE

½ cup plus 2 Tbsp apple sauce

½ cup plus 2 Tbsp brown sugar

3 Tbsp skim milk

1½ cups all-purpose flour

¼ cup all bran breakfast cereal

2 tsp ground baking powder

1 tsp ground cinnamon

2 Tbsp honey

1½ cups peeled and chopped apples

2 egg whites

Apple slices and 1 Tbsp honey to decorate

Preheat oven to 300°F. Grease a deep 8 inch round cake pan and line with baking parchment.

Place the apple sauce in a mixing bowl with the sugar and milk. Sift the flour into the bowl and add the bran, baking powder, cinnamon, honey, and apples. Whisk the egg whites until peaking and fold into the mixture. Spoon the mixture into the prepared pan and level the surface.

Bake for 1¼ to 1½ hours or until cooked through. Cool in the pan for 10 minutes, then turn on to a wire rack and cool completely. Arrange the apple slices on top and drizzle with honey.

Walnut Torte

A classic cake made with ground nuts in place of flour. Keeps well for up to two weeks.

MAKES ONE 9 INCH CAKE

2 cups ground walnuts	I Tbsp toasted bread crumbs
½ cup superfine sugar	I Tbsp cocoa powder
½ cup ground almonds	I tsp instant coffee powder
4 eggs, separated	Confectioners' sugar, to dust

Preheat the oven to 350°F.

Beat the egg yolks and sugar until light and creamy. Mix the walnuts with the almonds, bread crumbs, and cocoa and coffee powders and blend well with the egg yolk mixture. Whisk the egg whites until they are firm and beat 4 tablespoonfuls into the nut mixture to lighten it. Carefully fold in the rest of the egg whites.

Pour the batter into a buttered and breadcrumbed 9 inch springform cake pan and bake immediately. Leave to cool in the pan for 10 minutes before turning out on to a wire rack.

Dust with confectioners' sugar to serve. For more elaborate occasions, brush with strained apricot preserve and cover with a chocolate, vanilla, or caramel frosting and decorate with walnut halves.

Coffee Sponge

An airy, light coffee sponge with a rich alcoholic tang.

MAKES ONE 8 INCH CAKE

5 tsp instant coffee powder

1½ tsp boiling water

4 eggs, separated

Heaped ¼ cup superfine sugar

2 in vanilla bean, split

½ cup ground almonds

2 Tbsp all-purpose flour, sifted

FILLING

⅔ cup heavy or whipping cream

2 Tbsp light cream

2 Tbsp superfine sugar

2 to 3 Tbsp Tia Maria or dark rum

Chocolate-coated coffee beans

Grated chocolate

▣ Preheat oven to 350°F. Butter, flour, and sugar an 8 inch springform cake pan.

▣ Dissolve the coffee powder in the boiling water and leave to cool. Beat the egg yolks and sugar until thick, pale, and creamy. Beat in the seeds of vanilla bean, ground almonds, and about two-thirds of the coffee liquid. Whisk the egg whites until they stand in firm, snowy peaks and fold them into the main mixture in two stages, alternating with siftings of flour.

▣ Pour the batter into prepared pan and bake until well risen and brown. Leave to settle in the pan for 10 minutes before turning out to cool on a wire rack.

▣ Whip the cream to hold soft peaks and beat in the sugar, remaining coffee liquid and liqueur.

▣ Split the cooled cake in half and spread half the cream on the base. Cover with the top layer and smooth over the rest of the cream. Decorate with chocolate coffee beans and grated chocolate. Chill before serving.

Coffee Jelly Roll

This recipe combines coffee, chcocolate, and jelly in a surprisingly tasty way. Delicious served with a good strong cup of coffee.

MAKES 8 SLICES

¼ stick butter	**FILLING**
3 large eggs	6 Tbsp warmed Morello cherry preserve
⅓ cup superfine sugar	
I Tbsp coffee extract	⅔ cup heavy cream
¾ cup all-purpose flour	I Tbsp coffee liqueur
Pinch of salt	I oz coarsely grated semi-sweet chocolate
I Tbsp hot strong coffee	

Preheat oven to 425°F. Butter a 12 × 8 inch jelly roll pan and line with baking parchment.

Put the eggs, sugar, and coffee essence in a large bowl over a pan of hot water and whisk until the mixture is pale and leaves a thick trail. Remove from the heat and sift half the flour and salt over the egg mixture and fold in carefully, using a large metal spoon. Repeat with the remaining flour and add the hot coffee.

Turn the mixture quickly into the prepared pan, tilting it until evenly covered. Bake immediately just above the center of the oven for about 10 minutes or until well risen and springy.

Have ready a sheet of baking parchment drenched with sugar. Turn the sponge cake out onto the paper and roll up the sponge cake at once from the short side, making the first turn firm, then rolling lightly. Cool on a wire rack covered with a clean cloth and with the join of the sponge cake underneath.

When cold, carefully unroll the cake, remove the lining paper and brush with Morello preserve. Whip the cream and liqueur together, spread over the preserve and carefully re-roll the cake. Sprinkle chocolate over the top.

Carrot Cake

A wonderful cake to serve for everyday eating and for special occasions as part of a buffet.

MAKES ONE 9 INCH CAKE

2 cups fine whole wheat flour	**FROSTING**
2 tsp baking powder	1½ sticks softened butter
I tsp baking soda	¾ cup cream cheese
I tsp salt	I tsp vanilla extract
I tsp pumpkin pie spice (optional)	2½ cups confectioners' sugar, sifted
½ cup walnut pieces, finely chopped	
3 large eggs, beaten	
⅔ cup mashed banana (2 medium-sized fruits)	
1½ cups grated carrot	
¾ cup sunflower oil	

Preheat an oven to 350°F then lightly grease a 9 inch, deep round cake pan and line it with baking parchment.

Mix all the dry ingredients together in a large bowl then add the eggs, mashed bananas, and carrots. Pour the oil into the bowl and beat thoroughly to a thick, well-blended batter. Spoon into the prepared cake pan and bake in the center of the preheated oven for about 1 hour, until a toothpick inserted into the cake comes out clean. Remove the cake carefully from the cake pan and allow to cool completely on a wire rack.

Prepare the frosting by beating together the softened butter and cream cheese until blended, then add the vanilla extract and beat again. Sift the confectioners' sugar and beat it gradually into the cheese mixture. Spread the frosting over the cake and decorate, if wished, with finely chopped walnuts or a little extra grated carrot. Serve in thin slices.

Carrot Cake ▶

Polish Honey Cake

<table>
</table>

M ore of a honey spice cake, **Polish Honey Cake** or *Piernik* recipes do not always contain ginger, but a mixture of spices.

4 cups all-purpose flour	**⅓ cup chopped dried figs**
2 tsp baking powder	**⅓ cup chopped angelica**
½ tsp ground ginger	**1⅓ cups honey**
½ tsp ground cinnamon	**¾ cup superfine sugar**
½ tsp ground cloves	**¾ stick butter**
½ tsp ground allspice	**4 egg yolks**
Grated zest ½ orange	**2 tsp instant coffee, dissolved in a little water, or 2 tsp caramel**
⅓ cup chopped hazelnuts or walnuts	
⅓ cup raisins	**4 egg whites**

Preheat the oven to 350°F. Grease a 9 inch cake pan and line with baking parchment.

Sift the flour, baking powder, and spices into a bowl. Stir in the orange zest, nuts, raisins, figs, and angelica. Put the honey, sugar, and butter into a pan and heat until completely melted. Cool slightly.

Add the melted mixture, egg yolks, and coffee or caramel to the flour and mix well. In a bowl, whisk the egg whites until very stiff and then fold into the mixture.

Pour the batter into the cake pan and bake for 1 to 1¼ hours.

If liked, you can slice the cake and sandwich the halves together with thick preserves. You can also decorate the top with chocolate or thick chocolate frosting.

Lime Coconut Layer Cake

Delicious layers of lime-scented sponge with a tangy lime custard topped with classic seven-minute frosting and coconut—a desert island dream.

MAKES ONE DEEP 8 INCH CAKE

1 cup all-purpose flour	**FROSTING**
Pinch of salt	2 egg whites
6 eggs	1½ cups sugar
¾ cup sugar	3 Tbsp cold water
Grated zest of 2 limes	¼ tsp cream of tartar
1 tsp lime juice	1½ tsp light corn syrup
¾ cup shredded coconut	1½ Tbsp lime juice
	1 cup shredded coconut

LIME CUSTARD

2 Tbsp cornstarch

1 cup cold water

2 eggs

Grated zest and juice of 1
  large lime

1 cup sugar

6 Tbsp butter

Preheat oven to 350°F. Lightly grease three 8 inch cake pans. Line the bottom of each with baking parchment; regrease and flour pans. Sift the flour and salt.

Put the eggs in a large heat-proof bowl and set over a saucepan of just simmering water. With an electric mixer, beat until frothy. Gradually beat in the sugar until well-blended. Continue beating until the mixture is doubled in volume and very thick. Remove the bowl from the pan of water and fold in the grated lime zest, and shredded coconut. Sift the flour mixture in three batches, folding in after each addition.

Divide the mixture evenly among the pans. Bake about 30 minutes. Cool for 5 minutes. Unmold on to a wire rack to cool completely.

Prepare the lime custard: Blend the cornstarch with about a tablespoon of the cold water to dissolve. Whisk in the remaining eggs. Put the remaining water, grated zest and lime juice, sugar, and butter in a saucepan and, over medium heat, bring to a boil. Whisk a little of the mixture into the beaten egg mixture, then whisk the egg mixture into the saucepan and return to the heat. Whisk until the mixture boils, about 5 minutes. Pour into a bowl and cool.

Prepare the frosting: Put all the ingredients except the coconut in a heat-proof mixing bowl and set over a saucepan of just simmering water. With an electric mixer, beat for 7 minutes until thick. Remove from the hot water and beat until mixture is at room temperature. Cover with plastic wrap.

Remove the paper from the cake layers. Place a layer on a plate and spread with half the lime custard. Cover with a second layer and the remaining lime custard. Spread the top and side of the cake with the frosting and press some of the shredded coconut on to the side of the cake; sprinkle the remaining coconut over the top.

Chocolate Cakes

Surprise Chocolate Ring

Chocolate and Sour Cream Marble
Cake

Chocolate Decadence

Devil's Food Dream Cake

Chocolate Roulade

Chocolate-almond Zuccotto

Raisin Chocolate Fudge Cake

Chocolate and Almond Sandwich

Family Chocolate Cake

White Chocolate Mousse and
Strawberry Layer Cake

Cooking with Chocolate

Cooking with chocolate as the main ingredient can be quite spectacular, especially when other good quality ingredients are used. To prevent disappointment in your efforts, you must remember to treat chocolate with TLC: tender loving care.

Melting Chocolate

There are several different ways to melt chocolate, but if you wish to avoid ending up with a solid mass there are a few rules which must be observed. Any equipment used must be perfectly dry because any stray drops of water will cause the chocolate to thicken and stiffen. For the same reason, never cover chocolate when it is being, or has already been melted. If you do end up with a solid mass, try stirring in a little vegetable oil and mix very well. Butter or margarine will not do as they contain some water. The second thing to remember is NEVER to rush the melting process. A watched pot never boils and the temptation is to turn up the heat and speed the process. Unfortunately this will ruin the flavor and texture of the chocolate. It is best to grate or chop the chocolate before melting for a smooth result.

Direct Heat Method

This method is only used when the chocolate is combined with butter, sugar, or milk, or similar ingredients, as when making some sweets and sauces. The mixture should always be stirred over a very gentle heat. As soon as the mixture has melted, it should be removed, to prevent the chocolate overcooking and becoming "grainy".

Double Boiler Method

This is probably one of the best and easiest methods of melting chocolate. If you do not possess a double boiler, one can easily be made by placing a heatproof bowl over a saucepan. The bowl should fit securely on the pan so that neither steam nor water can escape. Water in the saucepan should never touch the bottom of the bowl. Place the chocolate in the bowl. Allow the water in the saucepan to come to a boil and place the bowl on top. Turn off the heat under the saucepan and leave to stand for a while until the chocolate is melted.

Oven Method

Chocolate may be melted in an ovenproof bowl in a very low oven (225°F). If the oven has been in use for another purpose and has been turned off, it makes sense to use the lingering heat to melt the chocolate. When the chocolate has almost melted it should be removed and stirred until smooth.

Microwave Oven Method

Microwave ovens are very handy for melting chocolate, especially small quantities, quickly and safely. The chocolate should be broken into small pieces and put into a glass bowl. Microwave, uncovered, until almost melted. The manufacturer's instructions should be followed as the timing and power setting will vary according to the machine.

On average 3 oz chocolate will melt in 1 to 1½ minutes. It is important to stir the chocolate just before the end of the cooking time to see if the chocolate has melted and thus prevent overcooking.

Chocolate for Dipping

Delicious sweetmeats such as marzipan, caramel, fudge, candied or fresh fruits can all be dipped in chocolate. Use either tempered couverture, or semi-sweet chocolate. Heat in a double boiler. The ideal temperature for dipping is 92 to 110°F. The temperature should never exceed 120°F. The chocolate should be in a bowl deep enough for the confection to be totally covered. Using a special dipping fork, fondue fork or thin skewer, lower the confection into the chocolate. Turn it over and then lift out the chocolate, tapping the fork on the edge of the bowl to shake off the excess chocolate. Place the chocolate on a tray lined with non-stick or waxed paper. The dipping fork can be used to decorate the top of the chocolates before they set. Lay the fork on the surface of the chocolate and lift it gently to create ridges.

Storing Chocolate

Chocolate should be kept in a cool dry place. Contrary to popular belief the refrigerator is not the best place to store chocolate other than for short periods during hot weather. When refrigerated, chocolate will absorb odors very easily and also may collect a film of moisture on the surface. So wrap the chocolate in foil, then in a plastic bag if you wish to refrigerate it. Let the chocolate stand at room temperature before unwrapping and using as this should prevent moisture condensing on the surface.

If chocolate is stored in very warm conditions, the cocoa butter or sugar crystals in it may rise to the surface giving a grayish white "bloom." This is completely harmless and although it detracts from the appearance, does not affect the flavor of the chocolate. The "bloom" will also disappear on melting so the chocolate is quite suitable for cooking.

If you wish to keep chocolate for a longer time in hot conditions, then it is best to freeze it. Again, make sure it is tightly wrapped. Remove it from the freezer the night before you need it, and allow it to thaw completely before unwrapping it. The freezer is an especially good place to store chocolate decor-ations such as squares, leaves, etc. These can then be used any time to garnish cakes and desserts and only need a few hours to thaw.

If kept in the correct conditions, semi-sweet chocolate should keep for one year and milk chocolate for about six months.

Making Chocolate Decorations

Chopped Chocolate

Use chocolate at room temperature. Break into small pieces and place on a chopping board. Using a sharp chopping knife, chop into the size required. Chocolate may also be chopped quite successfully in a food processor.

Chocolate Squares, Triangles

Melt semi-sweet chocolate and spread evenly on to waxed paper. Leave to set. Using a ruler, mark into squares or rectangles. Cut with a sharp knife. Cut squares diagonally to form triangles and rectangles diagonally to form wedges.

Chocolate Cups

Use two thicknesses of paper liners or candy cases. If you can obtain foil cases a single layer only is necessary. Melt the chocolate and brush on the bottom and up the sides of the cases. Repeat this process until a thick layer is obtained. Carefully turn upside down on to waxed paper. Chill under hard. Peel paper case away from the chocolate and fill as desired.

Chocolate Scrolls

Melt some semi-sweet chocolate and spread out on a cool work surface to a thickness of about $1/8$ inch. Cool until set, but not hard. Using a long firm knife, hold it at an angle of of 45° under the chocolate and push away from you, scraping off long curls.

Surprise Chocolate Ring

The surprise element of this luxurious cake lies in its rich treasure–trove of hidden contents–cream, fruit, and cherry brandy. It's the cook's secret.

MAKES ONE 8 INCH TUBE CAKE

1¼ cups self-rising flour

¼ cup unsweetened cocoa powder

¾ cup soft margarine

¾ cup superfine sugar

3 eggs

4 Tbsp cherry brandy

1 cup fruit (eg strawberries, raspberries, stoned cherries)

⅔ cup heavy cream

FROSTING

Generous ¼ cup heavy cream

1½ cups semi-sweet chocolate, grated

DECORATION

Chocolate Butterflies (or other chocolate decorations) or Chocolate Dipped Fruits

Preheat oven to 350°F. Grease and flour a 12 cup tube pan.

Sift the flour and cocoa into a mixing bowl. Add the margarine, sugar, and eggs. Beat well together. Spoon mixture into the prepared pan. Bake in the oven for about 35 to 40 minutes. Turn out and cool.

Turn the cake upside down and cut a slice about ¾ inch deep off the flat base of the ring. Lift off the slice carefully and reserve.

With a teaspoon, scoop out the cake in a channel about ¾ inch deep and 1 inch wide. Sprinkle 3 tablespoonfuls of the cherry brandy over the sponge. Chop the fruit and spread in the hollow. Whisk the cream until stiff. Stir in remaining brandy. Spread the cream over the fruit. Place the reserved slice back on the cake. Invert the cake so it is the right way up.

To make the frosting, put the cream into a saucepan and bring just to a boil. Add the chocolate. Stir until the chocolate melts. Cool until the mixture is thick and smooth. Pour over the cake. Put in a cool place until set and decorate with piped chocolate butterflies or chocolate dipped fruit.

Chocolate and Sour Cream Marble Cake

A wholesome classic cake that is always popular, here made in an attractive circular shape.

MAKES ONE LARGE TUBE CAKE

6 oz semi-sweet chocolate	½ tsp almond extract
2 sticks butter	3½ cups self-rising flour
I cup superfine sugar	⅔ cup sour cream
4 eggs	Confectioners' sugar
2 tsp vanilla extract	

Preheat oven to 350°F. Butter and thickly sugar a 9 to 10 inch tube pan.

Melt the chocolate and allow to cool slightly.

Cream together the butter and sugar until light and fluffy. Beat in the eggs one at a time. Add the vanilla and almond essence. Fold in the flour.

Divide the mixture into two. Add the sour cream to one half and the melted chocolate to the other half. Put alternate spoonfuls of the mixtures into the prepared pan. Using a teaspoon, cut down into the mixture and swirl together.

Bake in the oven for about 1 hour or until a toothpick inserted into the center comes out clean. Leave for 5 minutes. Unmold on to a wire rack and cool.

Dredge with confectioners' sugar to serve.

Chocolate Decadence

A very indulgent chocolate treat. The raspberry flavor offsets the chocolate perfectly.

MAKES ONE 9 INCH CAKE

10 oz good-quality bittersweet chocolate, chopped

1 stick unsalted butter

8 eggs, separated

¼ cup raspberry-flavored liqueur

¼ tsp cream of tartar

CHOCOLATE RASPBERRY GANACHE FILLING

12 oz good-quality bittersweet chocolate, chopped

1½ sticks unsalted butter, cut into pieces

½ cup seedless raspberry preserves

¼ cup raspberry-flavored liqueur

CHOCOLATE-RASPBERRY GLAZE

1 cup heavy cream

8 oz good-quality bittersweet chocolate, chopped

2 Tbsp raspberry-flavored liqueur

½ cup fresh raspberries for decoration

Confectioners' sugar for dusting, sifted

Preheat oven to 350°F. Lightly butter two 9 inch springform pans. Line the bottoms with baking parchment and butter again.

Heat the chocolate and butter. Beat the egg yolks then gradually whisk into the melted chocolate. Whisk in the raspberry-flavored liqueur. Beat the egg whites until frothy. Add the cream of tartar and continue beating until soft peaks form. Fold whites into the chocolate-egg mixture.

Divide the mixture evenly between the two pans. Bake for 35 minutes. Remove cakes to a wire rack to cool for 15 minutes. Remove sides of the pans and cool cakes. Invert on to a rack, remove pan bottoms and then peel off the paper.

Heat the chocolate, butter, and half the raspberry preserve for the filling. Remove from the heat and stir in half the raspberry-flavored liqueur. Heat the remaining preserve and liqueur. Spread a thin layer of the preserve mixture over each cake layer.

Place one cake layer in cleaned pan, preserve side up. Spread with filling. Top with second cake layer, preserve-side down against filling. Refrigerate overnight.

Prepare the glaze. Bring the cream to a boil. Remove from heat and add in the chocolate all at once stirring until melted and smooth. Stir in the raspberry-flavored liqueur and set aside to cool. Remove the side of the springform pan. Transfer the cake to a wire rack set over a baking sheet. Pour the glaze over the cake, smooth the top and sides and allow to set. Scrape remaining glaze off the baking sheet back into the bowl and whisk until smooth. Pipe a scroll border around the edge of cake. Decorate with raspberries and dust with confectioners' sugar.

Devil's Food Dream Cake

These rich, dark chocolate layers are filled and frosted with a dark chocolate ganache, a chocolate truffle filling. Truly a wicked dream.

MAKES ONE 9 INCH CAKE

¼ cup unsweetened cocoa powder	3 eggs
2¼ cups cake flour	¾ cup sour cream or buttermilk
2 tsp baking soda	1 tsp vinegar
½ tsp salt	1 cup boiling water
2 oz unsweetened chocolate, chopped	CHOCOLATE GANACHE FROSTING
1 stick unsalted butter, softened	3 cups heavy cream
2½ cups light brown sugar, lightly packed	1½ lb good-quality bittersweet or semi-sweet chocolate, chopped
2 tsp vanilla extract	2 Tbsp butter
	1 Tbsp vanilla extract

Preheat oven to 375°F. Grease two 9 inch cake pans. Line bottoms with baking parchment; regrease and flour pans. Sift together the cocoa powder, cake flour, baking soda, and salt; set aside.

In the top of a double-boiler over low heat, melt the chocolate, stirring frequently until smooth. Cool.

With an electric mixer, beat the butter, brown sugar, and vanilla until light and creamy. Add the eggs, one at a time, beating well after each addition. Add the flour mixture alternately with the sour cream or buttermilk in three batches. Stir in the vinegar and slowly beat in the boiling water. Pour into the pans and bake 20 to 25 minutes. Cool cakes in their pans 5 minutes. Carefully unmold on to a wire rack to cool completely.

Preparing the frosting: Bring the cream to a boil. Remove from the heat and add the chocolate all at once, stirring until melted. Beat in the butter and vanilla. Pour into a bowl and refrigerate until the ganache reaches a spreading consistency.

To assemble: Remove paper from cake bottoms. Slice each cake into two layers. Place one layer, cut side up on a plate and spread with one sixth of ganache. Place second layer on top and frost with another sixth of ganache. Continue layering. Frost the top and sides of cake with remaining ganache.

Chocolate Roulade

The roulade may be made a day in advance but should be filled close to the time of serving.

MAKES 8 TO 10 SLICES

6 oz semi-sweet chocolate	¼ cup unsweetened cocoa powder
5 eggs, separated	2 tsp instant coffee powder
¾ cup superfine sugar	½ tsp vanilla extract
3 Tbsp hot water	
Confectioners' sugar, sifted	DECORATION
	Confectioners' sugar
FILLING	Whipped cream
2 cups heavy cream	Candied violets
½ cup confectioners' sugar, sifted	Angelica leaves

Preheat oven to 350°F. Grease a 9 x 15 inch jelly roll pan and line with baking parchment. Regrease.

Melt the chocolate in a bowl over a pan of hot water.

Put egg yolks into a large bowl. Add the sugar and beat well until pale and fluffy, this is best done with an electric mixer and takes about 10 minutes. Add hot water to the chocolate and stir until smooth. Whisk into the egg mixture. Whisk the egg whites until stiff. Lightly fold into the chocolate mixture. Pour into the prepared jelly roll pan. Cook in the oven for 15 to 20 minutes, until firm.

Remove from the oven. Cover with a sheet of baking parchment sprinkled with confectioners' sugar. Roll up gently leaving the paper in place. Leave until completely cold.

To make the filling put all the ingredients into a bowl. Whisk until thick. Chill. Unroll the roulade and spread the filling over the cake to within 1 inch from the edge. Roll up again using the paper to help.

Place seam side down on a serving plate and chill for one hour. Dredge the roulade with confectioners' sugar. Pipe whipped cream down the center and decorate with violets and angelica leaves.

Chocolate-Almond Zuccotto

An extravagant variation of the cake from the preceding recipe. This Italian specialty could be served as a special cake or dessert.

MAKES 8 TO 10 SLICES

Chocolate Roulade Cake	3 oz semi-sweet chocolate, grated
2 Tbsp almond-flavored liqueur	½ cup chopped almonds, lightly toasted
CHOCOLATE-ALMOND FILLING	CHOCOLATE WHIPPED CREAM
2 cups heavy cream	
1 lb ricotta cheese	10 oz good-quality bittersweet or semi-sweet chocolate, chopped
½ cup sugar	
4 Tbsp almond-flavored liqueur	2 cups heavy cream mixed with 2 Tbsp almond-flavored liqueur
6 oz semi-sweet chocolate, melted	½ cup chopped almonds, lightly toasted

Cool roulade. Cut out an 8-inch circle from cake. Cut remaining long strip of cake into long narrow triangles, 2 inches at base end, and cut any remaining cake into pieces. Sprinkle with liqueur.

Line bowl with plastic wrap, then with the point of each triangle in the center, line with the triangles.

Beat cream into stiff peaks. Beat ricotta with sugar, and liqueur. Stir a spoonful of cream into ricotta, fold in remaining cream. Remove half mixture to "cream" bowl.

Fold melted chocolate into one half of ricotta-cream mixture. Fold grated chocolate and almonds into other half. Spoon this half into cake-lined bowl and spread on base and up sides. Spoon melted chocolate mixture into center.

Top with remaining circle of cake, edging it in to surround the cream. Decorate with chocolate, cream, liqueur and almonds. Chill. Carefully unmold to serve.

Chocolate Roulade ▶

Raisin Chocolate Fudge Cake

A rich chocolate cake full of spicy flavors, nuts, and raisins.

MAKES ONE 8 INCH CAKE

5 Tbsp butter

1¾ cups brown sugar

1 whole egg

2 Tbsp orange juice, sifted

2 tsp orange zest

2 oz semi-sweet chocolate, melted and cooled

¼ cup milk

¼ cup water

Pinch baking soda

1 cup plus 1 Tbsp all-purpose flour, sifted

½ tsp baking powder

½ tsp ground cinnamon

¼ tsp ground cloves

⅓ cup flaked almonds

½ cup raisins

FILLING

¾ stick unsalted butter

3 cups confectioners' sugar

4 Tbsp milk

1½ tsp vanilla extract

½ cup pecan nuts, chopped

¼ cup shredded coconut

½ cup raisins, cut in half

Pecan halves and flaked almonds to decorate

Preheat oven to 350°F. Grease an 8 to 9 inch springform pan and line with baking parchment.

Cream the butter and half the sugar. Beat in the egg, blend well. Add the orange juice and zest. Beat in the rest of the sugar and the chocolate. Combine well. Mix the milk with the water and blend in the baking soda.

Sift together the flour and baking powder with the cinnamon and cloves. Dust the almonds and raisins with some of the flour and set aside.

Beat one-third of the liquid into the mixture followed by one-third of the dry ingredients. Repeat in two further stages. Mix in the raisins and almonds. Turn into the prepared pan. Level the surface. Bake for 1 hour until risen and shrinking away slightly from the edges of the pan. Cool on a wire rack.

Make the filling by beating the butter until light and creamy; sift in the confectioners' sugar, then beat in the milk and vanilla. Mix the pecan nuts, coconut, and raisins and stir into the frosting.

To assemble, split the cake into three layers. Reserve just over one-third of the filling for the outside and use the remainder to sandwich the three chocolate layers together. Smooth the rest on the top and sides of the cake. Decorate with pecans and almond flakes.

The cake should settle for at least a day before it is cut. It will stay fresh for up to a week.

Chocolate and Almond Sandwich

A simple family cake, which is quick and easy to make, but quite delicious.

SERVES 4

1 stick butter

5 Tbsp sugar

1 egg, beaten

6 Tbsp all-purpose flour

6 Tbsp blanched almonds, ground

1 Tbsp cocoa

1 tsp baking powder

¼ tsp salt

3 Tbsp milk

Confectioners' sugar

CHOCOLATE FILLING

4 oz semi-sweet chocolate, grated

1½ Tbsp milk

1 cup confectioners' sugar

6 Tbsp unsalted butter

Dash of almond extract

Preheat the oven to 400°F. Grease two 7 inch pans and bottom-line with baking parchment.

Cream the butter and sugar together. Add the well-beaten egg. In another bowl, sift together the flour, ground almonds, cocoa, baking powder, and salt. Add alternately with the milk to the creamed butter and sugar. Combine thoroughly.

Divide the mixture between the two baking pans and bake for 20 minutes. When cool, sandwich together with the chocolate filling and dredge the top of the cake with confectioners' sugar.

To make the filling, mix the chocolate with the milk and warm over a low heat until the chocolate has melted. Remove from the heat, beat in the confectioners' sugar, then leave until cool. Cream the butter and then add the chocolate mixture and the almond extract; beat until light and creamy. Use to fill the chocolate sandwich.

Family Chocolate Cake

A delicious basic chocolate cake, which will be requested time and time again.

MAKES ONE 7½ INCH CAKE

3 oz semi-sweet chocolate

Approx ¼ cup clear honey

I stick butter or margarine

⅓ cup superfine sugar

2 eggs

I¼ cups self-rising flour

¼ cup unsweetened cocoa powder

I½ tsp baking powder

¼ tsp vanilla extract

⅔ cup milk

FROSTING

2 oz semi-sweet chocolate

3 Tbsp water

2 Tbsp butter

I⅓ cups confectioners' sugar, sifted

1 Preheat the oven to 350°F. Grease and line one 7 to 7½ inch cake pan.

2 Put the chocolate and honey into a small bowl over a pan of hot water. Stir until the chocolate has melted. Cool.

3 Cream together the butter or margarine and sugar until light and fluffy. Beat in the chocolate mixture, then the eggs. Sift together the flour, cocoa powder, and baking powder. Stir in the flour mixture a little at a time, alternately with the vanilla extract and milk.

4 Pour mixture into the cake pan. Bake in the oven for about 45 minutes. Turn on to a wire rack, leaving the lining paper on the cake to form a collar.

5 When the cake is cool, make the frosting. Put the chocolate and water into a small saucepan and melt over a gentle heat. Remove from the heat and stir in the butter. When the butter has melted, beat in the sugar.

6 Spread the frosting over the top of the cake and swirl with a metal spatula. When frosting is firm, remove the lining paper from the cake.

White Chocolate Mousse and Strawberry Layer Cake

Other fresh berries in season can be used in this cake, but ever-popular strawberries look particularly elegant.

MAKES ONE 9 INCH CAKE

4 oz good-quality white chocolate, grated or chopped

½ cup heavy cream

½ cup milk

1 Tbsp rum or vanilla extract

2 cups all-purpose flour

1 tsp baking powder

Pinch of salt

1 stick unsalted butter, softened

¾ cup sugar

3 eggs

1½ lb fresh strawberries, sliced, plus extra for decoration

3 cups heavy cream

2 Tbsp rum or strawberry-flavored liqueur

1 Tbsp confectioners' sugar, sifted

WHITE CHOCOLATE MOUSSE FILLING

10 oz good-quality white chocolate, chopped

1½ cups heavy cream

2 Tbsp rum or strawberry-flavored liqueur

Preheat oven to 350°F. Lightly butter two deep 9 inch cake pans. Line bottoms with baking parchment; regrease and flour pans. Put the white chocolate and cream in a saucepan and stir over low heat until melted and smooth. Stir in the milk and rum or vanilla extract. Cool.

Sift together the flour, baking powder, and salt. Set aside. With an electric mixer, beat the butter and sugar until light and creamy. Add the eggs, one at a time, beating well after each addition.

Add the flour mixture alternately with the melted chocolate mixture in three batches until just blended. Scrape into the prepared pans and bake 20 to 25 minutes or until done. Cool in pans 10 minutes. Unmold on to a wire rack to cool completely.

Prepare the mousse. Process the chopped white chocolate in a food processor 15 to 30 seconds. Bring the cream to a boil. Pour the hot cream through the processor feed tube and process until smooth. Pour into a bowl, stir in the rum or strawberry-flavored liqueur and refrigerate until just set. Whisk until light and mousse-like.

To assemble: Remove the paper from cake bottoms. Slice each cake into two layers. Place on layer, cut-side up, on a cake plate and spread with one third of the mousse mixture. Arrange one third of the sliced strawberries over the mousse. Place a second layer on top and continue layering in this way. Cover with the last cake layer.

Whip the cream with the rum or liqueur and confectioners' sugar until firm peaks form. Spread half over top and sides of cake. Pipe scrolls or rosettes with remaining cream around top edge of cake and in the center. Decorate with remaining strawberries.

C A K E S 161

Fruit Cakes

Raisin Sponge Cushion

Fresh Cherry Cake

Babka

**Whole Wheat Zucchini
and Raisin Cake**

**Pumpkin, Sunflower Seed,
and Raisin Cake**

Gypsy Cake

Raisin and Pineapple Cake

Barm Brack

Irish Tea Brack

Guinness Cake

Raisin Sponge Cushion

The method of preparation and baking is quite unusual and gives a not too sweet, light, and airy cake that is ideal for tea or coffee time.

MAKES ONE 8 INCH TUBE CAKE

¾ stick butter	4 eggs, separated
¾ cup all-purpose flour, sifted	⅓ cup superfine sugar
⅔ cup raisins	Confectioners' sugar, to dust
1 tsp lemon zest	

Preheat the oven to 475°F. Grease and flour an 8 to 9 inch tube pan.

Cut the butter into the flour and blend to a fine crumb texture. Toss in the raisins and lemon zest, making sure that they are well coated with flour. Set aside.

Whisk the egg whites in a large clean bowl until they stand in firm, snowy peaks and beat in half the sugar until the mixture is firm and glossy. Using a large metal spoon or the mixer on very slow, fold in the rest of the sugar and the lightly beaten egg yolks. Very carefully and lightly, fold in the flour and butter mixture in three portions.

Pour the mixture into the prepared pan. Level out and bake immediately in the preheated oven for 5 minutes; then reduce the oven temperature to 425°F for 10 minutes; finally reduce the temperature to 350°F for 30 minutes. The cake puffs up high and turns a rich brown. Lift out of the oven and turn out on a wire rack after 10 minutes to cool. Dust with confectioners' sugar to serve.

Fresh Cherry Cake

Fresh cherry cakes are traditional in south Germany as well as in Switzerland, but are a popular family treat everywhere. This particular version comes from Switzerland.

MAKES ONE 9 INCH CAKE

2 Tbsp toasted bread crumbs	I cup ground almonds
3 small stale bread rolls	½ tsp ground cinnamon
⅔ cup milk	2 lb fresh bing cherries, washed and dried
⅔ cup water	
I stick butter, melted and cooled	Pinch salt
¾ cup superfine sugar	Confectioners' sugar, to dust
4 eggs, separated	Whipped cream, to serve (optional)

Preheat oven to 350°F. Grease a 9 inch springform pan.

Butter well and coat with 2 tablespoonfuls toasted bread crumbs.

Break the bread rolls into pieces and place them in a bowl. Heat the milk with the water and pour the liquid on to the rolls. Leave to soak for about 15 minutes.

Pour the melted butter into a mixing bowl, leaving the sediment behind, mix in the sugar and egg yolks and beat until the mixture is pale and creamy. Beat in the almonds and cinnamon.

Drain the bread rolls, squeezing out any excess moisture by hand. Break them up small with a fork or blend in a food processor bowl for a few seconds. Beat the paste into the main mixture. Stir in the cherries.

Whip up the egg whites with the salt in a clean bowl until they hold firm, snowy peaks. Using a large metal spoon, lightly fold the egg snow into the cherry batter. Pour the batter into the prepared cake pan. Bake until golden, 1 to 1¼ hours.

The cake may be eaten warm or cold. Dredge with confectioners' sugar and serve with whipped cream on the side. It also freezes very well for up to 2 months.

Babka

This is a sponge cake with dried fruit and candied peel.

MAKES 8 TO 10 SLICES

½ stick butter	1½ cups all-purpose flour
Scant 1 cup confectioners' sugar, sifted	1 tsp baking powder
	½ cup raisins
1 tsp natural vanilla extract	3 Tbsp candied peel
3 eggs, separated	Confectioners' sugar to dredge
¼ cup milk	

Base-line and grease a 7½ × 4½ inch loaf pan. Set the oven at 350°F.

Beat the butter in a bowl until very soft, then gradually beat in the confectioners' sugar. Stir in the vanilla and egg yolks, one by one. Slowly add the milk, mixing in the occasional small spoonful of flour to prevent the mixture from curdling. Sift the remaining flour with the baking powder and stir it into the mixture. Stir in the raisins and candied peel.

Whisk the egg whites until stiff and use a metal spoon to fold them in, taking care not to knock out the air. Turn the mixture into the pan and spread it with the back of a metal spoon, hollowing out the middle slightly.

Bake for 40 to 45 minutes, until risen and golden. Turn out the babka to cool on a wire rack. Dredge with confectioners' sugar while still warm.

Whole Wheat Zucchini and Raisin Cake

This cake was inspired by a conventional passion cake made with carrots, but is much more moist. It is excellent eaten plain, but may be spread with butter frosting or cream cheese frosting.

MAKES ONE 9 INCH CAKE

1⅔ cups fine whole wheat flour	1 cup grated zucchini, closely packed
1 tsp baking soda	¾ cup crushed pineapple, drained
2 tsp baking powder	
1 tsp salt	¼ cup grated carrot
1 tsp ground ginger	⅔ cup natural yogurt
1 cup soft brown sugar	3 large eggs, beaten
⅔ cup raisins or golden raisins	⅔ cup corn oil

Preheat an oven to 350°F, and line a 9 inch round cake pan with baking parchment.

Place the flour, baking soda, baking powder, ginger, sugar, and raisins in a bowl then mix in the zucchini, pineapple, and carrot. Add the yogurt with the eggs, then finally add the oil. Mix to a thick batter then beat vigorously for 1 minute.

Pour the mixture into the prepared tin, then bake in the preheated oven for 1 hour, until a toothpick inserted into the mixture comes out clean. Cool slightly, then turn out on to a wire rack and leave until completely cold.

Pumpkin, Sunflower Seed, and Raisin Cake

A moist fruit cake for fall using the seasonal orange pumpkin and nutritious sunflower seeds.

MAKES ONE 8 INCH CAKE

2¼ cups pumpkin	⅓ cup raisins
2¼ cups whole wheat flour	2 eggs
Pinch of salt	2 Tbsp honey
2 tsp baking powder	2 Tbsp molasses
I tsp baking soda	I Tbsp warm water
⅓ cup sunflower seeds, chopped	

Preheat the oven to 375°F. Grease and flour an 8 inch springform cake pan and base line with baking parchment. Peel the pumpkin, cut into smallish pieces and boil until tender. Drain and cut up finely.

Combine flour, salt, baking powder, sunflower seeds, and raisins and mix well.

In another bowl, beat the eggs and stir in the honey and molasses. Add I tablespoon of warm water with the pumpkin and beat well.

Mix all the ingredients together thoroughly and pour into the pan. Bake for 50 to 60 minutes until done. Allow to stand for 10 minutes in the pan, then cool.

Gypsy Cake

This cake is based on a traditional Polish recipe. It is good just as it is but it is also very tempting when sandwiched with plum preserve.

MAKES ABOUT 10 SLICES

6 eggs, separated	⅓ cup chopped dried figs
½ cup superfine sugar	⅓ cup cooking dates, chopped if necessary
I tsp natural vanilla extract	
I cup all-purpose flour	3 Tbsp chopped mixed peel
I tsp baking powder	Confectioners' sugar to dredge
⅓ cup raisins	

Line and grease an 11 x 7 inch pan (a shallow pan is fine, in which case the waxed paper should stand well above the rim. Preheat the oven to 400°F.

Beat the egg yolks and sugar in a bowl until pale and thick. Lightly stir in the vanilla, then fold in the flour and baking powder. Stir in all the fruit. Whisk the egg whites until stiff and stir a couple of spoonfuls into the mixture to lighten it, then fold in the remainder. This is not easy as the mixture is fairly stiff but try not to over-stir while mixing in the whites. Turn the mixture into the pan and spread out.

Bake for about 20 minutes, or until risen, golden and firm to the touch. Cool on a wire rack. Dredge with confectioners' sugar before serving cut into oblong pieces.

Raisin and Pineapple Cake

For those who are not fans of very rich fruit cakes this everyday fruit cake, embellished with unusual dried fruit—raisins and currants would make an excellent Christmas cake.

MAKES ONE 7 INCH CAKE

1 cup mixed fruits (dried pineapple, golden raisins, dried cranberries, etc.)	2 tsp baking powder
	Pinch of salt
½ cup pineapple or orange juice	1 tsp ground ginger
¾ cup margarine or butter	½ cup light brown sugar
2 cups fine whole wheat flour	2 large eggs, beaten

Soak the fruits in the fruit juice for 10 minutes. Preheat an oven to 350°F and lightly grease a 7 inch deep, round cake pan.

Blend the butter into the flour, baking powder, salt, and ginger in a bowl until the mixture resembles fine crumbs. Stir in the sugar, then add the fruits and juice and the beaten eggs. Mix to a soft dropping consistency, adding a little extra fruit juice or milk as required, then spoon the mixture into the prepared cake pan and smooth the top.

Bake for 35 to 40 minutes or until the cake stops "singing"—yes, go on, listen to it—and a toothpick inserted into the center comes out clean.

Cool slightly in the pan then turn out carefully on to a wire rack to cool completely.

Barm Brack

Barm brack means speckled bread, referring to the fruit in the mixture. In Ireland this was a favorite Hallowe'en bake.

MAKES ONE 8 INCH CAKE

Heaped 3 cups all-purpose flour	2 Tbsp sugar
Grated nutmeg	1¼ cups milk
Pinch of salt	2 eggs, beaten
½ stick butter	1½ cups golden raisins
¾ oz yeast	1½ cups currants
	1 cup candied peel

Preheat the oven to 400°F. Sift the flour, nutmeg, and salt together. Cut the butter into the flour.

Cream the yeast in a cup with 1 tsp of the sugar. Add the rest of the sugar to the flour mixture and combine well. Scald the milk; add to the liquid yeast together with all but a little of the well-beaten eggs. Stir into the dry ingredients to produce a stiff but elastic batter. Then carefully fold in the fruit.

Butter an 8 inch round cake pan and pour in the dough. It should come halfway up the pan. Cover with a clean cloth and leave in a warm place to rise—it should double in size in about 1 hour.

Brush the top of the brack with beaten egg to glaze. Bake until a skewer, or thin knife, comes out clean—should be about 1 hour.

Raisin and Pineapple Cake ▶

Irish Tea Brack

Two Irish fruit cakes in which the fruit is soaked in alcohol overnight prior to making the cake. This gives the cake a succulent moistness and a richness of flavor.

MAKES ONE LOAF CAKE

3 cups golden raisins

3 cups raisins

2½ cups brown sugar

2 cups black tea

2 cups Irish whiskey

Heaped 3 cups all-purpose flour, sifted

3 eggs, beaten

1 Tbsp baking powder

2 tsp apple pie spice

Soak the fruit with the sugar in the tea and whiskey overnight to immerse in the flavor.

Preheat the oven to 375°F. Grease a 9 x 5 inch loaf pan or 8 inch cake pan and base-line with baking parchment.

Add the flour, eggs, baking powder, and spice to the fruit mixture.

Mix all the ingredients together well and put into the prepared pan.

Bake for 1 hour. Allow to cool in the pan slightly before turning out to cool fully on a rack.

Guinness Cake

There's a saying in England that "Guinness is good for you," and what better way to enjoy it than in a cake!

MAKES ONE 8 INCH CAKE

⅔ cup raisins, soaked in Guinness overnight

½ cup candied peel, soaked

1⅓ cups golden raisins, soaked

1 stick butter

1 cup brown sugar

3 eggs, beaten

2¼ cups self-rising flour

Pinch of salt

½ tsp apple pie spice

¼ cup candied cherries

⅔ cup Guinness or dark beer

Soak the raisins and peel in Guinness overnight.

Preheat the oven to 350°F. Grease a deep 8 inch cake pan and base-line with baking parchment.

Beat the butter and sugar until the sugar is dissolved. Beat in the eggs. Add the flour, salt, apple pie spice, cherries, and the soaked dried fruit. Finally mix in the Guinness.

Pour the mixture into the prepared pan. Bake for about 2 hours until firm in the center.

Irish Tea Brack ▶

Special Cakes

Chocolate and Whiskey Cake

Irish Coffee Cake

Mocha Gâteau

Black Forest Kirschtorte

Drum Cake

Orange Mousseline Gâteau

Torta Sorentina (Easter Cake)

Sachertorte (Chocolate Cake)

Bouquet Cake

Star Cake

Chocolate and Whiskey Cake

This no cook recipe is from Marlfield House Restaurant in Co. Wexford, Ireland.

MAKES ONE 9 INCH CAKE

½ lb graham crackers	6 Tbsp sugar
8 oz unsweetened cooking chocolate	½ cup candied cherries
	½ cup walnuts
2 sticks butter	⅔ cup Irish whiskey
2 eggs	⅓ cup heavy cream, whipped

Crush the biscuits coarsely and keep them aside.

Melt the chocolate with the butter in a double boiler or saucepan. Cream the eggs and sugar in a bowl until they are pale and thickened, then fold in the chocolate.

To this mixture add three-quarters of the cherries and the walnuts; save the rest for decoration. Fold in all but 1 tablespoon of whiskey.

Oil a 9 inch baking pan, line with the crushed biscuits, then scrape all of the mixture into it. Decorate the top with the remaining cherries and walnuts and place in the refrigerator for several hours or overnight. Take it out of the refrigerator about 30 minutes before serving.

Add the whiskey to the cream. Pipe around the top of the cake and serve.

Irish Coffee Cake

A sophisticated adult cake. Great for a whiskey lover's birthday treat.

MAKES ONE 8 INCH CAKE

1 stick butter	FOR THE SYRUP
½ cup superfine sugar	⅔ cup black coffee
2 eggs	¼ cup superfine sugar
⅔ cup self-rising flour	1 Tbsp Irish whiskey
2 Tbsp black coffee	
	DECORATION
	1¼ cups heavy cream
	Approx 1 Tbsp black coffee or black coffee and whiskey
	¾ cup confectioners' sugar

Preheat the oven to 325°F. Grease two 8 inch springform cake pans.

Cream the butter and sugar together until light and fluffy. Add the eggs, one at a time, adding a little of the flour after each egg. Beat in the coffee, then fold in the rest of the flour.

Divide the mixture in half and place in the two cake pans and bake for about 40 minutes.

To make the syrup, heat the coffee with the sugar until it melts, then add the whiskey. When the cake is almost cool, prick the underside with a fork and drip the syrup all over the cake. Fill the middle with whipped cream and whiskey.

Make a glacé frosting by adding a few drops of coffee to the sifted confectioners' sugar, then beating with a wooden spoon until it becomes glossy and can spread easily with a palette knife. Spread the frosting on the top of the cake.

Mocha Gâteau

This gâteau is prepared a day in advance to allow the flavors to mature.

MAKES ONE 8 INCH CAKE

1 portion Genoese sponge mixture (see page 110)

1 Tbsp instant coffee powder dissolved in ½ tsp boiling water

FILLING AND TOPPING

2¼ cups confectioners' sugar, sifted

3 Tbsp unsweetened cocoa powder, sifted

1¾ sticks butter

1 Tbsp strong black coffee

1 cup toasted slivered almonds

Chocolate coffee beans

Preheat the oven to 350°F. Grease and base-line an 8 inch springform pan.

Prepare the genoese sponge, but mix the coffee liquid into the egg yolk and sugar mixture. Pour into the prepared pan and bake until risen and golden. Cool on a wire rack.

Make the mocha butter frosting. Combine the sifted confectioners' sugar with the cocoa powder. Beat the butter with an electric mixer until light and fluffy. Beat in the sugar, cocoa powder, and coffee.

Split the cake into three layers. Reserve about half the frosting and sandwich the three cake layers together with the remainder. Fit a decorating bag with a small star tip and fill with frosting. Smooth the remainder of the frosting over the top and sides of the cake and press the slivered almonds into the sides. Pipe small mocha butter frosting stars close together in symmetrical lines. Decorate with chocolate coffee beans. Chill for a day before serving.

Black Forest Kirschtorte

There is still no traditional recipe for Black Forest Kirschtorte. It may be made with layers of plain chocolate sponge with or without butter and including nuts, but common to all are cherries, chocolate, cream, and kirsch, and this tempting combination entices so many people that it is probably the youngest but most popular traditional cake in the world today.

MAKES ONE DEEP 8 INCH CAKE

¾ cup unblanched almonds, coarsely ground	**FILLING**
½ cup toasted bread crumbs	2 lb morello or bing cherries, washed and stoned or 1 lb 2 oz canned pitted cherries
1 tsp ground cinnamon	1 cup plus 2 Tbsp red wine
1 tsp ground cloves	1 cup plus 2 Tbsp water
2 Tbsp Kirsch	1 cup granulated sugar
Heaped ½ cup superfine sugar	Cinnamon stick
9 egg yolks	2 tsp orange zest
2 tsp orange zest	⅔ cup Kirsch
4 oz semi-sweet chocolate, melted and cooled	2 cups heavy or whipping cream
6 egg whites	3 Tbsp superfine sugar
	¼ cup grated chocolate and chocolate curls for decoration

Preheat oven to 350°F. Prepare two 8 to 9 inch springform pans: butter, line the base with baking parchment, butter again, dredge with sugar and flour.

Mix together the almonds, bread crumbs, cinnamon and cloves and moisten with Kirsch.

In a separate bowl beat the sugar and egg yolks until thick, pale, and creamy. Mix in the orange zest and chocolate. Lightly combine with the first mixture. Whisk the egg whites separately until they hold firm snowy peaks. Lightly and quickly fold them into the main mixture until just combined.

Divide the mixture equally between the two pans. Smooth the top and tap each pan once to disperse any air pockets. Bake for 30 minutes until well risen and slightly shrinking away from the sides of the pan. Cool on wire racks.

To cook the fresh cherries for the filling, combine the wine, water, and sugar in a pan and heat gently until the sugar has dissolved. Add the cinnamon stick and orange zest, and simmer for about 20 minutes. Drop in the cleaned fruits and poach lightly for 10 minutes. Lift the fruits carefully out of the syrup and drain. Boil the syrup on a high heat for two minutes to reduce and thicken it slightly, cool.

Mix ⅓ cup of cherry syrup with ½ cup Kirsch. Dry the cherries with paper towels. Whisk the cream until softly peaked and beat in the sugar until firm; fold in the remaining Kirsch. Cut both chocolate sponges across the middle. Reserve 3 to 4 tablespoonfuls cream and a few cherries for decoration.

Place a sponge base on a serving plate and sprinkle over about one-third of the Kirsch syrup. Smooth over a quarter of the cream and press in half the cherries. Cover with a second sponge, sprinkle with more syrup, a layer of cream and the rest of the fruit. Place the third sponge on top, sprinkle with the remaining syrup and a layer of whipped cream. Cover with the last sponge layer and coat the top and sides of the whole cake with the rest of the cream. Dust the cake sides with chocolate.

Pipe the reserved cream in large rosettes on the cake surface and dot with cherries. Place a few chocolate curls in the middle to finish. Chill for 3 to 4 hours. Just before serving dredge a little confectioners' sugar on the chocolate curls.

Drum Cake

The caramel can be poured on to waxed paper and cut into triangles. They are then embedded in the chocolate filling, slightly at an angle to create a fan effect.

MAKES ONE 9 INCH CAKE

SPONGE	CHOCOLATE FILLING
6 egg yolks	¼ cup cornstarch
I cup superfine sugar	I½ cups milk
I tsp orange zest	¼ cup sugar
½ cup all-purpose flour	I egg yolk, beaten
½ cup potato flour	2 sticks butter
6 egg whites	I cup mini marshmallows
	2 oz semi-sweet chocolate
	CARAMEL GLAZE
	¾ cup granulated sugar

Preheat the oven to 350°F. Grease and flour a 9 inch springform pan.

Beat the egg yolks and sugar until pale and creamy. Mix in the orange zest. Sift together both the flours to aerate well and add to the egg yolks. Whisk the egg whites in a separate bowl until they are firm and well-peaked. Fold the egg whites into the yolk mixture as lightly and quickly as you can.

This quantity makes six layers. Spread a thin coating of mixture in the bottom of the pan and smooth carefully. Bake immediately for 5 to 8 minutes. (Bake two layers at a time if you have the pans.) When it is colored light gold, remove the cake from the oven and turn out of the tin straight onto a wire rack to cool. Make the remaining layers in the same way.

Assemble the cake as soon as the layers have cooled so that they do not dry out and become crisp.

Make the chocolate filling by mixing a little cornstarch with milk. Heat the rest of the milk with the sugar, add the cornstarch mixture and bring to a boil stirring until thickened. Quickly stir in the egg yolk. Cool. Beat the butter until soft then beat into the cooled custard. Melt the marshmallows and chocolate over a double boiler and beat into the custard. Place in the refrigerator until firm enough to spread.

Set aside the best-looking cake layer and sandwich the rest together with chocolate filling, spreading it over the top and the sides.

Prepare the top layer. Brush any loose crumbs off the cake and lay it on a large sheet of waxed paper. Then take two long knives and lightly grease the blade of one with oil or butter.

Make the caramel glaze by gently heating half of the granulated sugar until golden, then add the rest of the sugar and cook until it has thickened. Quickly pour the caramel straight over the cake layer and smooth it out using the clean knife. Using the greased knife, immediately mark the cake out into 10 sections and cut through the sugar glaze. Leave to cool. Lay the caramel top on top of the filled cake layers.

Do not store in the refrigerator as this spoils the caramel surface.

Torta Sorentina (Easter Cake)

The sparkling lemon flavor balances the richness in this Italian cake.

MAKES ONE TUBE CAKE

2 sticks unsalted butter	**¾ stick unsalted butter**
4 large eggs	**Zest of ½ lemon, grated**
I cup sugar	
2¼ cups self-rising flour	**FROSTING**
rind of ½ lemon, grated	**6 squares semi-sweet chocolate**
LEMON FILLING	**2 Tbsp cream**
I egg white	**2 Tbsp butter**
½ cup confectioners' sugar	**Candied lemon slices**

 Preheat the oven to 350°F. Grease and flour a 3½ pint tube pan.

Melt the butter and leave to cool. Put eggs and sugar into a bowl over a pan of hot water and whisk until they are pale and thick and leave a trail. Gently fold in the flour, zest and butter. Do not overmix.

Pour the mixture into the prepared pan. Bake in the oven for 30 to 40 minutes. Cool slightly, then turn out on to a wire rack.

To make the filling, put the egg white and confectioners' sugar into a bowl over a pan of hot water and whisk until a meringue is formed. Remove from heat and whisk until cool.

Beat the butter until light and fluffy. Beat in the meringue a little at a time. Add the lemon zest.

Split the cake into three layers. Spread the lemon filling between the layers. Chill.

Put the chocolate and cream in a bowl over a pan of hot water. When melted, stir in the butter. Remove from heat and mix until smooth.

Coat the cake with the frosting. Decorate with candied lemon slices. Allow frosting to set.

Sachertorte (Chocolate Cake)

This is usually undecorated, but here chocolate leaves and flakes add interest. To make chocolate leaves, gently melt the chocolate, then drag clean, freshly picked leaves through it. Peel off the leaf when the chocolate has cooled and set.

MAKES ONE 9 INCH CAKE

1 stick plus 2 Tbsp butter	2 drops almond extract
½ cup superfine sugar	¾ cup all-purpose flour, sifted
4 egg yolks	3 egg whites
6 oz semi-sweet chocolate, melted and cooled	Apricot preserve
	8 oz semi-sweet chocolate
1 Tbsp vanilla sugar	

Preheat the oven to 325°F. Grease a 9 inch springform pan.

Beat the butter with the sugar until pale and fluffy. Beat in the egg yolks, one at a time, and the cooled chocolate. Beat in the vanilla sugar and almond extract and continue beating for 15 minutes by electric mixer (25 minutes by hand).

Sift the flour over the mixture and quickly but lightly blend it in without over-beating. Whisk the egg whites until they stand in stiff, creamy peaks and then carefully fold them into the mixture.

Pour the batter into the prepared pan—the mixture should be no more than 1¼ inches deep. Bake for about 1 hour until slightly shrinking from the sides of the pan. Cool on a wire rack.

Brush the cake with strained apricot preserve. Melt the chocolate over a double boiler and spread over the cake. Alternatively a rich chocolate frosting may be used.

CELEBRATION CAKES

There are times when a special cake is called for weddings, anniversaries, and special birthdays for instance and a special effort is always made at Christmas. It is traditional for these to be rich fruit cakes which are commonly decorated with marzipan and royal glaze, or with sugarpaste. However, some people prefer a sponge cake base which is decorated with sugarpaste or maybe a butter frosting. For these cakes, it doesn't matter how good the cake is underneath the frosting, it is the decoration that is on show.

If you are not artistic, then it is best to keep the decoration simple. Mastering a couple of basic shapes with a decorating bag is not very difficult although it does require a bit of practice before you get started. Visit a specialist cake store where they stock a good range of cutters, ribbons, sugar flowers and pre-tinted sugarpaste. You will get a lot of ideas to help you cheat, you might even become inspired.

The instructions here are for a simple celebration cake suitable for a birthday, anniversary, or even wedding, but the basic idea can be adapted for other occasions. We have used pansies in pink, lilac, and purple, but choose your color scheme according to the sugar flowers that you have available.

For a Christmas cake, replace the bouquet with a cut-out angel made from white sugarpaste and placed centrally on the cake which has been lightly dusted with blue decorator's dusting powder. Then, make a small star from yellow sugarpaste and a tiny halo. Replace the angel with other shapes such as a santa, animals, or flowers or even a halloween witch. These figures may look even more effective if simply painted with food coloring and placed on appropriate tinted backgrounds. If the cake is for a man, how about placing a few special chocolates on top or carefully modeling the shape of a beer bottle from brown sugarpaste and laying this on the cake top. The cake shop will have model figures too that are useful for christenings and weddings and other ornaments suitable for Christmas and birthday cakes—once you get started you will be spoilt for choice.

Using a Decorating Tube

The royal glaze needs to be a little thicker than for smooth frosting so beat it for a little longer to thicken. If piping with butter frosting, add a little more confectioners' sugar. Before working on the cake itself, practice with a variety of tips. Try drawing straight and wavy lines with the writing tip, stars, flower petals, and chains with the star tip and shells and scroll borders with the shell tip. While piping, keep the unused frosting covered with a damp cloth to prevent it from drying out.

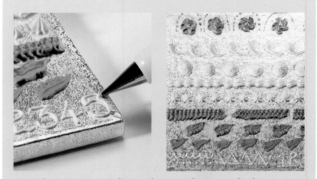

Try drawing straight and wavy lines with the writing tip, stars, flower petals, and chains with the star tip and shells and scroll borders with the shell tip.

Rough Icing

This method is particularly attractive on a Christmas cake. Simply smooth the icing over the cake and work it roughly with a knife.

Smooth the icing over the cake.

Work icing roughly with a knife.

Bouquet Cake

The perfect way to celebrate something special. This cake says "congratulations," but you can alter to suit the occasion.

MAKES ONE 8 INCH CAKE

Bake an 8 inch Christmas Cake (see page 444)

1¾ lb marzipan

5-egg quantity royal glaze

Lemon dusting powder

Lilac food coloring

1½ yards colored ribbon ⅛ inch thick in three toning colors

Purchased sugarpaste pansies

APRICOT GLAZE

1 cup apricot jelly or preserve

2 Tbsp water

To marzipan the cake, cut the top off if domed, then turn upside-down to create a flat surface to work with. If the sides do not sit flat on the board, fill any hollows with marzipan to create a smooth finish on all sides.

Make glaze by melting jelly and water in a pan. Rub through a sieve. Brush over the cake

Measure cake with thread, up one side, across the top and down the other, then roll marzipan about ¼ inch thick Drape marzipan over rolling pin and lay over cake. Smooth out marzipan from center of cake with hands dusted with confectioners' sugar. Trim marzipan around the base. Allow to dry for at least 24 hours and up to 2 weeks before frosting.

Make royal glaze to soft peak consistency. Spoon icing over cake and spread to an even depth of ¼ inch. Remove excess frosting from top edges. The top can be smoothed by dragging a ruler across the surface in one movement. Trim excess from top edges to neaten. To smooth sides, hold a palette knife vertically against icing and rotate cake keeping knife on board to keep sides straight. Repeat until you are happy with the appearance. Allow to dry for 24 hours before decorating. For a lilac tint, dust dried cake with a lilac dusting powder.

Make 1-egg white quantity of royal glaze to hard peak stage. Tint to a pale lilac color with food coloring. Fit a small paper cone or a decorating bag with a shell-shaped tip. Practice on the work surface, then pipe shells all round base of cake. Pipe rows of stars around top of cake. Link with draped lines piped in white. Wrap three bands of ⅛

inch lilac or purple colored ribbon around cake. Write "congratulations" on a piece of card. Lay a sheet of waxed paper over the top and pipe letters over top using a broad writing tip. Leave to dry. Carefully peel off paper and fix message to cake with a little frosting If writing proves too tricky, then purchase message from cake decorator's store. Purchase pink and lilac pansies and arrange on the cake top. Pipe a "ribbon" from scribble of frosting. Attach to the cake with a dab of frosting.

CHILDREN'S BIRTHDAY CAKES

As with celebration cakes, children's birthday cakes are as much about the decoration as the cake. Children often challenge parents to make cakes that reflect their latest craze. If they are very fond of a pet, for instance, then it is appropriate to make a cat or rabbit shape out of a 13 x 9 x 2 inch sponge cake and frost with chocolate frosting or a paler colored butter frosting to match the animal's coloring. Simply draw the shape of the pet on paper, cut out and place on the cake as a template. Cover with frosting and use candies or sugarpaste for the eyes and nose and shoelace licorice for the whiskers. Butterflies work well too. Cut out the shape of the butterfly and cover with colored frosting or marble-colored sugarpaste and decorate with candies.

Football, soccer, and baseball pitches provide another easy option. Use green-tinted frosting and coconut to form the pitches and pipe on the line markings with white or colored frosting. Cake decorator's stores often carry small figures and balls for decoration, or use characters from children's toys. Similarly, a swimming pool can be made by coloring sugarpaste pale blue and draping over the cake. Miniature dolls and accessories to finish the cake can be found in the toy store. Specialist stores carry a great selection of ribbons some of which reflect the latest children's crazes.

Using a shaped cake pan is a great way to create excellent birthday cakes. Number cake pans can be purchased or hired and a star or heart shape is always effective. Draped with sugarpaste or frosted with the child's favorite frosting they can easily be decorated using candies, miniature toys, or piping plus candles. If all else fails, a simple round cake with tasty frosting and generously decorated with candy cannot fail to please.

Star Cake

No child could fail to be thrilled with this fun-shaped, colorful cake.

MAKES ONE 9 INCH CAKE

1 9 inch chocolate or sponge star cake	½ quantity butter frosting
4 Tbsp apricot glaze	Gold or translucent dusting powder
1¾ lb sugarpaste	Moon and star-shaped cookie cutters
Orange food coloring	
12 inch cake board	Egg white
Confectioners' sugar	Candles
1-egg quantity royal glaze or	Candle holders

Brush cake with warmed apricot glaze. Knead sugarpaste until soft, then shape into a flattened ball. Leave white or drop several small drops of food coloring on to sugarpaste and knead until the coloring is streaked throughout the paste.

Do not over knead.

Place cake on board. Generously dust work surface with sugar. Roll out sugarpaste until it is about 3 inches larger than the cake and using rolling pin to support weight, transfer to cake. Use hands coated with sugar to smooth the sugarpaste on top of cake, then flare out corners of star and mold into shape. It is easiest to use the soft part of the palm to gently work the surplus paste into place. Trim sugarpaste around base of cake with a knife.

Color some of the royal glaze or butter frosting bright orange. Pipe stars around base and top edge of cake. Color some surplus sugarpaste solid orange and brush with gold or translucent dusting powder. Cut out star and moon shapes and attach to sides of cake with egg white. Cut a large star shape and, using white frosting, pipe child's name across center using a writing tip. Decorate outer rim of star shape with dots of icing using writing tip. Attach to top of cake with egg white. Insert candles.

Small Cakes

Butterfly Cakes

Iced Mazurek

Mazurek

Almond Cakes

Rocky Mountain Buns

Jaffa Cakes

Eliza Leslie's Ginger Cup Cakes

Chocolate Meringues

Butterfly Cakes

Children love these little cakes which always sell quickly at cake sales.

MAKES 14 TO 16

1 stick butter or margarine

½ cup sugar

2 eggs

1 tsp grated orange zest

½ cup semi-sweet chocolate, finely grated

1 cup plus 2 Tbsp self-rising flour

FROSTING

¾ stick butter or margarine

1 cup confectioners' sugar, sifted

3 oz semi-sweet chocolate, melted

DECORATION

Confectioners' sugar

Seedless raspberry preserve or candied cherries

Preheat oven to 350°F.

Put the butter and sugar into a bowl and cream together until light and fluffy. Beat in the eggs a little at a time. Stir in the orange zest and chocolate. Then fold in the flour.

Arrange cupcake papers in muffin pans. Divide the mixture between the cases. Bake in the oven for about 15 to 20 minutes. Cool.

To make the frosting, beat together the butter and confectioners' sugar. Then gradually beat in the cooled, melted chocolate.

Starting ¼ inch in from the edge, remove the top of each cake by cutting in and slightly down to form a cavity. Pipe a little frosting in the cavity of each cake.

Sprinkle the reserved cake tops with confectioners' sugar and cut each one in half. Place each half, cut side outward, on to the frosting to form wings. Pipe small rosettes of frosting in the center of each cake. Top with a small blob of raspberry preserve or half a candied cherry.

Iced Mazurek

Plain mazurek is a type of shortcake, which may be frosted according to taste. It is usually cut into fingers and is traditionally served at Easter.

MAKES 16 PIECES

2 cups all-purpose flour	**DECORATION**
2 tsp baking powder	7-minute frosting (see page 114)
½ cup butter	
⅔ cup confectioners' sugar, sifted	Candied orange peel, cut into strips
2 egg yolks	About ¼ cup candied cherries, quartered
	About 2 Tbsp slivered almonds, toasted

Sift the flour and baking powder into a bowl. Blend in the butter and mix in the confectioners' sugar. Mix in the egg yolks to make a soft dough. Wrap in plastic wrap and chill for 5 minutes. Meanwhile, base-line and grease an 8 inch square cake pan. Preheat the oven to 350°F.

On a floured surface, roll out the dough into a square. Put it into the pan and press out with your fingers to cover the base of the pan. Make sure the top is smooth and the dough evenly thick.

Bake for about 35 to 40 minutes, until golden and firm. Turn out to cool on a wire rack. Coat with frost and decorate when cool. Cut into fingers to serve.

Mazurek

This improves with keeping for a couple of days before topping with chocolate and eating. The redcurrant jelly together with chocolate make a divinely complementary combination.

MAKES ABOUT 22 PIECES

8 eggs, separated	**DECORATION**
½ cup superfine sugar	1⅓ cup redcurrant jelly
½ cup all-purpose flour	⅔ cup semi-sweet chocolate chips
1¼ cups semi-sweet chocolate chips	
1 cup ground almonds	½ stick unsalted butter

Line and grease an 11 x 7 inch pan (a shallow pan is fine, in which case the waxed paper should stand well above the rim). Preheat the oven to 400°F.

Beat the egg yolks and sugar in a bowl until pale and thick. Lightly fold in the flour. Whisk the egg whites until stiff and fold them into the mixture. Lightly stir in the chocolate and almonds. Turn the mixture into the pan and spread it out evenly.

Bake for 20 to 25 minutes, until firm and lightly browned. Cool the mazurek in the pan for 5 minutes, then turn out on to a wire rack to cool completely.

For the decoration, warm the redcurrant jelly in a bowl over hot water and spread it all over the mazurek. Leave to set completely, then chill for 30 minutes. Melt the chocolate and butter in a bowl over hot water. Leave to cool but do not allow the mixture to thicken. Pour the chocolate all over the mazurek and spread it evenly. Leave to set before cutting into fingers.

Iced Mazurek ▶

Almond Cakes

Easy to make, these little cakes, with their delicate almond flavor, are a mouthwatering treat. For a special occasion, soak the cakes in sherry or freshly squeezed orange juice with a little rum added, then top with whipped cream.

MAKES 16 TO 20

1 cup flaked almonds

Butter for greasing

2 eggs

3 cups sugar

2–3 bitter almonds, grated

1¼ cups all-purpose flour

¾ stick butter, melted

Preheat the oven to 400°F. Toast the flaked almonds lightly, then crumble or chop finely. Leave to cool. Carefully grease 16 to 20 small cake molds or patty pan with soft butter, and scatter them with the chopped almonds.

Whisk the eggs until frothy, add the sugar, and whisk to a fluffy mixture. Mix in the grated almonds, flour, and the cooled butter. Stir gently to prevent the mixture collapsing. Divide the mixture between the molds, and place on a baking sheet. Bake for 15 minutes. Turn out and leave to cool under the upturned molds.

Rocky Mountain Buns

There is a hint of coffee in these fun-to-eat small buns. The marshmallows and raisins give them a "rocky," uneven appearance.

MAKES 12

2½ cups self-rising flour

½ tsp salt

¼ cup polyunsaturated margarine

2 Tbsp superfine sugar

3 Tbsp golden raisins

½ cup mini marshmallows

⅔ cup skim milk

1 Tbsp coffee extract

Confectioners' sugar for dusting

Preheat the oven to 425°F.

Sift the flour and salt into a bowl. Blend in the margarine until the mixture resembles bread crumbs. Stir in the sugar, raisins, and marshmallows.

Mix together the milk and coffee extract and stir into the mixture to form a soft dough. Place 12 equal-sized spoonfuls of mixture on a nonstick baking sheet, spacing slightly apart.

Bake for 20 minutes until risen and golden. Cool on a wire rack, dust with confectioners' sugar, and serve.

Jaffa Cakes

A delicious combination of chocolate and bitter marmalade preserve.

MAKES 18

2 eggs

¼ cup sugar

⅔ cup self-rising flour, sifted

Approx 4 Tbsp marmalade, sieved

4 oz semi-sweet chocolate

Zest of ¼ orange, finely grated

2 tsp corn oil

1 Tbsp water

Preheat oven to 400°F. Grease thoroughly about 18 muffin pans or fluted molds.

Put eggs and sugar into a bowl. Whisk until thick and creamy so that when the whisk is lifted the mixture leaves a trail. If using a hand whisk put the bowl over a pan of hot water. With a metal spoon, fold in the flour.

Spoon the mixture into the muffin pans or molds. Bake for about 10 minutes until golden brown.

Remove and cool on a wire rack.

Spread a little marmalade over each cake.

Put the chocolate, orange zest, oil, and water into a bowl over a pan of hot water. Stir well until melted. Cool until the chocolate starts to thicken and then spoon over the marmalade. Leave to set.

Eliza Leslie's Ginger Cup Cakes

This is a modern interpretation of a recipe in Eliza Leslie's *Seventy-Five Receipts for Pastry, cakes and sweatmeats. By a lady of Philadelphia*, published in 1828.

MAKES 28 CUP CAKES

I stick butter	I tsp ground cloves
½ cup light muscavado or brown sugar	2 tsp ground ginger
¾ cup molasses	I egg
Scant 2 cups all-purpose flour	I egg yolk
I tsp baking soda	4 Tbsp milk
½ tsp ground allspice	

Preheat the oven to 325°F. Gently heat the butter, sugar, and molasses in a pan until the butter has melted and the sugar dissolved. (Do not boil or the cakes will be hard.) Remove from the heat to cool. Sift together two or three times the flour, baking soda, allspice, cloves, and ginger, and finally into a large bowl. Make a well in the middle.

Whisk the egg and egg yolk with about half the milk and pour the mixture into the flour with the cooled syrup. Beat to a smooth batter, adding more milk if necessary.

Use paper cases and fill each no more than half full with the mixture, which rises a lot during baking. Bake for about 30 minutes until well risen. The cakes should feel slightly soft to the touch. Leave to cool on wire racks.

Chocolate Meringues

A delicious treat for chocoholics.

MAKES 6 TO 8

3 egg whites	**FILLING**
⅓ cup superfine sugar	⅔ cup heavy cream
⅔ cup confectioners' sugar, sifted	I Tbsp brown sugar
¼ cup unsweetened cocoa powder, sifted	2 tsp unsweetened cocoa powder

Preheat the oven to 225°F. Beat the egg whites until they form stiff peaks. Gradually whisk in the superfine sugar, a little at a time. Whisk in the confectioners' sugar. Fold in the cocoa powder.

Put the mixture into a decorating bag fitted with a large star tip. Line baking trays with waxed paper. Pipe the mixture into spirals.

Bake in the oven for 2 to 3 hours or until the meringues are dry. Cool on a wire rack.

Whip the cream until stiff. Stir in the sugar and cocoa. Sandwich the meringues together, two at a time, with the chocolate cream.

TIP

Make a batch of plain meringues and a batch of chocolate meringues and alternate them in a pyramid for a spectacular party dessert.

Cheesecakes

New York-style Cheesecake

Coffee Cheesecake

Curd Cake

Low-fat Blueberry Cheesecake

Cheese Placek

**Chilled Sultana and Orange
Cheesecake**

New York-style Cheesecake

Baked cheese recipes can be traced back to the discovery of curd cheese in the Middle East centuries ago. Western cheesecake as we know it is probably a descendant of the Russian Easter pashka, a tall molded dessert of homemade cottage cheese, eggs, sugar, sour cream, butter, and chopped nuts. This dense, smooth, lemony cheesecake is heavenly and makes a perfect dessert.

MAKES 8 TO 10 SERVINGS

1½ **cups crushed graham crackers (20 to 22 squares)**	**SOUR CREAM TOPPING**
½ **teaspoon ground cinnamon**	**1 cup sour cream**
3 **Tbsp butter or margarine, melted**	**2 Tbsp sugar**
1½ **lb cream cheese**	**1 tsp vanilla extract**
¾ **cup sugar**	
Grated zest of 1 lemon	
1 **tsp vanilla extract**	
3 **eggs**	

VARIATION

Strawberry Cheesecake

Prepare the cheesecake as above, but before serving, decorate the edge of cake with strawberries hulled and cut in half lengthwise. In a food processor fitted with a metal blade, process 1 10-ounce package frozen strawberries in light syrup, or 1 pound fresh strawberries, hulled, and 3 tablespoonfuls of sugar to taste. Strain and add a little lemon juice or water to thin if necessary. Serve separately with the cheesecake.

Preheat the oven to 350°F. Lightly butter a 9 inch springform pan. In a medium bowl, combine graham cracker crumbs, cinnamon, and butter or margarine. Press crumbs on to bottom and 1½ inches up sides of the pan. Bake 5 minutes until just set Remove to a wire rack to cool.

In a large bowl, with an electric mixer on medium-low speed, beat cream cheese with sugar until smooth. Add lemon zest and vanilla, then beat in eggs, one at a time, until batter is well blended and smooth.

Carefully pour the filling into the cooled crust. Bake until firm at the edges but still slightly soft in the center, 45 to 50 minutes. Do not allow the cake to brown; it should be puffed and slightly golden. Turn off the oven and leave the cheesecake in the oven with the door closed for 1 hour. (This helps prevent the surface from cracking.) Remove to a wire rack, cool.

Preheat the oven to 425°F. Make the topping. In a small bowl, combine sour cream, sugar, and vanilla. Carefully pour over the top of the cake and return to the oven. Bake 5 minutes. Remove the cake to a wire rack to cool completely. Refrigerate overnight.

To serve, run a sharp knife around the edge of the pan to loosen the edges. Carefully remove the side of the springform pan and place the cake on a serving dish.

Coffee Cheesecake

This no-cook cheesecake is set with gelatin.

SERVES 10 TO 12

1 stick butter	4 eggs, separated
½ cup brown sugar	1 cup brown sugar
2 cups crushed coffee biscuits	2 Tbsp powdered instant coffee dissolved in 1 Tbsp hot water
4 envelopes 1 oz gelatin	
6 Tbsp warm water	1¼ cups heavy cream
2 cups (1 lb) cream cheese	Candied rose petals

Grease a 10 to 12 inch loose-bottomed cake pan. Melt the butter in a saucepan. Stir in the sugar and biscuits. Spoon into the pan and press down firmly with the back of a spoon. Chill.

Dissolve the gelatin in a bowl of warm water over a pan of simmering water. Beat the cream cheese in a bowl until soft and beat in the egg yolks, half the sugar, coffee, and cream. Stir well. Add the gelatin to the coffee mixture and leave until it is on the point of setting.

Whisk the egg whites until stiff and whisk in the remaining sugar. Gently fold into the coffee mixture. Pour on to the chilled biscuit base. Gently tilt and tip the pan to level the surface. Chill for 3 to 4 hours.

Run a heated metal spatula around the edge of the cheesecake and remove from pan. Transfer to a serving plate and decorate the top with the candied rose petals.

Curd Cake

Curd cake is the traditional name for what is now known as cheesecake.

SERVES 10 TO 12

8 oz flour quantity rich pie crust dough (see page 13)	4 Tbsp unsalted butter
2 eggs, separated	Juice and grated zest of 1 lemon
2 cups (1 lb) cottage cheese, pressed through a strainer	Melted strawberry or raspberry preserve, to serve
4 Tbsp sugar	

Preheat the oven to 350°F. Make the pastry dough and chill.

Beat the egg yolks and mix with the cottage cheese, sugar, softened butter, lemon juice, and zest. Combine well. Then, whisk the egg whites until stiff. Fold them into the cottage cheese mixture.

Roll out the dough and line an 8 inch loose-bottomed cake pan. Bake blind until the edge of the pastry begins to color, then fill the pastry shell with the cheese mixture and bake for 30 to 35 minutes.

Serve warm with melted strawberry or raspberry preserve brushed over the surface.

Curd Cake ▶

Low-fat Blueberry Cheesecake

Cheesecake with a delicious granola and dried fig base, in place of the usual cookies and butter, which gives a rich and crunchy base to the soft filling.

SERVES 6

1 cup natural granola

5 oz dried figs

1 tsp vegetarian gelatin

4 Tbsp cold water

½ cup skim evaporated milk

1 egg

6 Tbsp superfine sugar

2 cups (1 lb) low-fat cottage cheese

½ cup blueberries

TOPPING

2 cups blueberries

2 nectarines, pitted and sliced

2 Tbsp honey

Place the granola and dried figs in a food processor and blend together for 30 seconds. Press into the base of a base lined 8 inch springform pan and chill while preparing the filling.

Sprinkle the gelatin on to 4 tablespoonfuls of cold water. Stir until dissolved and heat to boiling point. Boil for 2 minutes. Cool. Place the milk, egg, sugar, and cheese in a food processor and blend until smooth. Stir in the blueberries. Place in a mixing bowl and gradually stir in the dissolved gelatin. Pour the mixture on to the base and chill for 2 hours until set.

Remove the cheesecake from the pan and arrange the fruit for the topping in alternate rings on top. Drizzle the honey over the fruit and serve.

Cheese Placek

T his lattice-topped cheesecake is delicate in flavor with a crisp pastry base.

SERVES 8

BASE	FILLING
2 cups all-purpose flour	2½ cups (1¼ lb) cottage cheese
3 tsp baking powder	½ cup sugar
¾ stick unsalted butter	2 Tbsp all-purpose flour
¼ cup superfine sugar	½ tsp natural vanilla extract
1 egg	Grated zest of 1 lemon
3 Tbsp sour cream	3 eggs, separated
	Confectioners' sugar, to dredge

Grease an 11 x 8 inch loose-based oblong pie dish.

For the pastry, sift the flour and baking powder into a bowl. Blend in the butter, then stir in the sugar. Mix in the egg and sour cream to make a soft dough. Set aside one-third of the dough, then use the rest to line the base and sides of the pan. Prick the base all over, then chill the dough for 30 minutes.

Set the oven at 375°F. Line the dough case with waxed paper and sprinkle with dried peas. Bake blind for 15 minutes. Remove the paper and cool.

For the filling, place the cheese in a double thick piece of cheesecloth and squeeze as much liquid as possible from it. Press the drained cheese through a sieve, then beat in the sugar, flour, vanilla, lemon zest, and egg yolks. Whisk the whites until stiff and fold them into the mixture. Turn the mixture into the prepared base.

Roll out the reserved dough into an oblong about the same size as the pan, then cut it lengthways into ½ inch wide strips. Arrange these in a lattice over the filling, trimming and re-rolling as necessary. Bake for about 35 to 40 minutes, until browned on top and firm. Leave to cool, then dust with a little confectioners' sugar. Cut into squares to serve.

Chilled Sultana and Orange Cheesecake

Although the traditional baked cheesecakes, introduced from Europe, were favored for many years, in recent times America has made the unbaked variation its own, and it has gained worldwide popularity.

SERVES 10 TO 12

½ cup candied orange and lemon peel, chopped	5 Tbsp chopped pistachios
¾ cup golden raisins	⅔ cup sweetened whipped cream
2 Tbsp Grand Marnier or Cointreau	2 Tbsp Grand Marnier or Cointreau
4 envelopes (1 oz) gelatin	Candied orange and lemon peel, to decorate
⅓ cup hot water	Pistachios, to decorate
1½ cups (12 oz) cream cheese	**SYRUP**
⅓ cup superfine sugar	¾ cup granulated sugar
¾ cup lemon preserve	¼ cup water
2 Tbsp orange zest	3 Tbsp Grand Marnier or Cointreau
1½ cups whipping cream, softly whipped	1 cooked fat-free sponge 9 in diameter (see page 110)

Soak the orange and lemon peel and the golden raisins in Grand Marnier or Cointreau for at least 30 minutes. Make a syrup with the sugar and water boiled to thread stage (230°F). Mix in the liqueur. Cool.

Slice the sponge cake horizontally into two layers, of one-third and two-thirds thicknesses. Lightly oil a 9 inch springform pan and line the base with waxed paper. Drop the thicker cake layer into the pan and brush all over with the flavored syrup.

Sprinkle the gelatin powder on to ⅓ cup very hot, but not boiling, water in a cup and stir to dissolve. Leave to cool. The mixture should be transparent and lump-free, if it is not, place the cup in a pan of warm water and heat gently. Cool to room temperature before using. Meanwhile, beat the cream cheese with the sugar, lemon preserve and orange zest until well blended. Gently trickle over the gelatin liquid, beating all the time. Set aside until the mixture is on the point of setting. Using a large metal spoon, lightly fold in the soaked peel and golden raisins, the liqueur, whipped cream, and the pistachios.

Pour the cheese filling on to the sponge cake in the prepared pan and smooth it out. Carefully cut half of the remaining sponge layer into six triangular pieces and evenly space them on top of the filling to create a fan effect.

Flavor ⅔ cup sweetened whipped cream with 2 tablespoons of orange liqueur and pipe rosettes of cream on the cake. Decorate with candied peels and pistachios. Chill for 5 to 6 hours. The cake may be prepared 2 to 3 days ahead of time and kept in the refrigerator.

Dessert Cakes and Puddings

Pumpkin and Lemon Roulade

Cappuccino Sponges

Steamed Coffee Pudding

Banana Choc-chip Pudding

Magic Chocolate Dessert

Date and Ginger Pudding

Danish Apple Dessert Cake

Chocolate Upside-down Pudding

Individual
Sticky Toffee "Pudding" Cakes

Lemon-scented Passover Cake

Pumpkin and Lemon Roulade

Surprisingly light and tangy, this roulade or jelly roll makes a very pleasant change from the more traditional pumpkin pies. An excellent cake for the early days of fall when a little culinary comfort is required.

MAKES 8 SLICES

3 large eggs	**3 Tbsp confectioners' sugar, sifted**
⅓ cup superfine sugar	
½ cup all-purpose flour, sifted twice	**1 cup thick pumpkin purée, fresh or canned**
1 large lemon, grated zest and juice	**⅓ cup seedless raisins**
⅔ cup whipping cream	**Superfine sugar for dredging**

Preheat the oven to 425°F. Line a jelly roll pan 13 x 9 inches with baking parchment.

Whisk the eggs and sugar together until very thick and pale—you should be able to leave a trail of a figure 8 clearly visible in the mixture. Fold the flour and lemon zest quickly into the mixture, then scrape it into the prepared pan and gently level the surface.

Bake in the preheated oven for 8 to 10 minutes, until spongy in texture and golden. Turn the cake on to a wire rack covered with baking parchment and sprinkled with superfine sugar. Trim away the crusts of the cake and make a shallow cut a little way in from one of the short sides, then place another piece of paper over the sponge. Roll it up and leave it, entwined with the paper, until cold.

For the filling, whip the cream until almost stiff, then add the confectioners' sugar and pumpkin. Beat well, then fold in the raisins. Unwrap the cake and remove the inner paper. Spread the cream over the cake, then re-roll it using the sugared paper to help. Transfer the roulade to a plate.

Pierce the cake right through in lots of places with a thin skewer. Squeeze the juice from the lemon, then drizzle it over the roulade. Dredge with more superfine sugar, then leave for 20 minutes or so before serving, to allow the lemon to flavor the sponge.

Cappuccino Sponges

These individual sponge puddings are delicious served with the low-fat coffee sauce. Ideal for dinner parties. they look more delicate and attractive than one large pudding.

SERVES 4

2 Tbsp polyunsaturated margarine

2 Tbsp granulated brown sugar

2 egg whites

½ cup all-purpose flour

¾ tsp baking powder

6 Tbsp skim milk

I tsp coffee extract

½ tsp unsweetened cocoa powder

FOR THE COFFEE SAUCE

1¼ cups skim milk

I Tbsp granulated brown sugar

I tsp coffee extract

I tsp coffee liqueur (optional)

2 Tbsp cornstarch

4 Tbsp cold water

Use non-stick spray to lightly grease 4 x ⅔ cup individual pudding molds. Cream the margarine and sugar together in a bowl and add the egg whites. Sift the flour and baking powder together and fold into the creamed mixture with a metal spoon. Gradually stir in the milk, coffee extract, and cocoa.

Spoon equal amounts of the mixture into the molds. Cover with pleated waxed paper, then foil, and tie securely with string. Place in a double boiler or pan with sufficient boiling water to reach halfway up the sides of the molds. Cover and cook for 30 minutes or until cooked through.

Meanwhile, place the milk, sugar, coffee extract, and coffee liqueur in a pan to make the sauce. Blend the cornstarch with 4 tablespoonfuls of cold water and stir into the pan. Bring to a boil, stirring until thickened. Reduce the heat and cook for a further 2 to 3 minutes.

Carefully remove the cooked puddings from the steamer. Remove the paper and foil and unmold on to individual plates. Spoon the sauce around and serve.

Steamed Coffee Pudding

Use stale cake crumbs as a basis for this dessert.

SERVES 6

2½ cups dry coffee sponge cake

3 oz semi-sweet chocolate

⅔ cup milky coffee

2 Tbsp powdered instant

coffee dissolved in I Tbsp hot water

½ stick butter

2 Tbsp vanilla sugar

2 large eggs, separated

Crumble the cake into fine crumbs. Melt the chocolate in a bowl over a pan of hot, gently simmering, water. When melted, pour over the cake crumbs. Leave to stand for 30 minutes.

Cream the butter and sugar together until light and fluffy; beat in the egg yolks. Then stir in the soaked crumbs and finally the coffee.

Beat the egg whites until stiff and gently fold into the chocolate and coffee mixture. Spoon into a large buttered ovenproof bowl—the mixture should only half fill it. Cover with greased foil or double thickness of waxed paper. Place in a double boiler and steam for 1½ hours. Turn out the pudding on to a serving dish, dust with sugar and serve with English custard, cream, or chocolate sauce.

Banana Choc-chip Pudding

This scrumptious dessert makes a rich and delicious end to a warming winter's dinner.

SERVES 4 TO 5

1 stick butter or margarine	**SAUCE**
½ cup sugar	¼ cup soft brown sugar
2 eggs, beaten	2 Tbsp butter
¼ cup self-rising flour	2 Tbsp corn syrup
¼ cup unsweetened cocoa powder	4 Tbsp half and half
Approx. 2 Tbsp milk	
1 small banana, peeled and chopped	
¼ cup chocolate chips	

Cream the butter or margarine and sugar together until light and fluffy. Gradually add the eggs, beating well between each addition. Sift together the flour and cocoa, and fold into the egg mixture. Add enough milk to give a soft dropping consistency. Stir in the banana and chocolate chips.

Turn the mixture into a greased 3¾ cup ovenproof bowl. Cover with greased waxed paper and foil with a central pleat in each. Secure with string. Steam in a double boiler for about 1½ hours.

To make the sauce, put all the ingredients into a saucepan and bring to a boil, stirring. Turn out pudding and serve with warm sauce.

Magic Chocolate Dessert

The magic in this pudding refers to the delicious sauce that forms at the base of the dessert while it is cooking.

SERVES 4 TO 5

1 cup plus 2 Tbsp self-rising flour, sifted

¼ cup sugar

2 Tbsp unsweetened cocoa powder, sifted

⅓ cup walnuts or pecans, chopped

4 Tbsp butter, melted

⅔ cup milk

A few drops of vanilla extract

SAUCE

⅔ cup soft brown sugar

2 Tbsp unsweetened cocoa powder, sifted

A scant 1 cup boiling water

Vanilla ice cream, to serve

Preheat oven to 350°F.

To make the sponge, put the dry ingredients into a bowl. Add the butter, milk, and vanilla extract and mix to form a thick batter.

Pour the mixture into a well-buttered 7 inch ovenproof dish.

To make the sauce, mix together the brown sugar, cocoa, and boiling water. Pour this sauce over the batter.

Bake in the oven for about 40 minutes. During cooking the chocolate sponge rises to the top, and a chocolate fudge sauce forms underneath. Serve accompanied by vanilla ice cream.

Date and Ginger Pudding

Afavorite winter pudding, sweetened with dates and banana. On a totally decadent day, you could serve this with a toffee or butterscotch sauce, but half and half or ice cream would show a modicum of restraint! It could also be sliced when cold and served as a cake.

SERVES 6 TO 8

⅓ cup stoned dates, chopped roughly

2 pieces preserved ginger, chopped finely

1 banana, mashed

2 Tbsp syrup from the ginger

½ cup margarine or butter

½ cup light brown sugar

2 large eggs, beaten

1½ cups fine whole wheat flour

1½ tsp baking powder

Pinch of salt

2 Tbsp milk

Preheat an oven to 375°F, then lightly grease and line a deep, 7 inch cake pan.

Mix together the dates, ginger, banana, and ginger syrup. Cream the margarine and sugar together until pale and creamy, then beat in the eggs a little at a time. Mix together the flour, baking powder, and salt, then fold them into the mixture. Fold in the date and banana mix, then add a little milk to give a soft, dropping consistency.

Turn into the prepared pan and smooth the top. Bake in the preheated oven for 30 to 35 minutes, until a toothpick inserted into the center comes out clean, and the pudding shrinks away from the sides of the tin. Serve cut into wedges.

Danish Apple Dessert Cake

This crumbly apple pudding is delicious served with whipped cream or ice cream. Sweeten the apples to taste, according to the variety used.

SERVES 4 TO 6

3 cups fresh whole wheat bread crumbs

⅓ cup raw sugar

6 Tbsp butter

4 cups prepared tart green apples, peeled, cored, and sliced

Grated zest and juice of 1 lemon

¼–½ cup sugar

Mix the bread crumbs with the raw sugar. Melt the butter in a large skillet, then add the crumb mixture and fry quickly until the crumbs are crisp, then set them to one side to use later.

Cook the apples with the lemon zest and juice, sugar to taste, and as little water as possible until soft. The apples may be cooked in a microwave because no water at all is required. Allow to cool.

Turn half the apples into a glass dish, then make a layer of half the crumbs over the apples. Repeat the layers, finishing with the remaining crumbs. Allow the pudding to cool, then chill for at least 1 hour before serving.

Date and Ginger Pudding ▶

Chocolate Upside-down Pudding

This perennial pudding is an all-time family favorite. It's always a surprise to find the pineapple rings at the top when the pudding is turned out!

SERVES 6

½ cup brown granulated sugar

½ stick butter

4 pineapple rings

6 walnut halves

2 eggs, separated

2 Tbsp butter, melted

½ cup soft brown sugar

1 cup plus 2 Tbsp self-rising flour

¼ cup unsweetened cocoa powder

Preheat oven to 350°F. Grease an 8 inch cake pan.

Cream together the sugar and butter and spread over the base of the pan. Arrange the pineapple rings on the base, with a walnut in the center of each.

Beat together the egg yolks and butter until creamy. Whisk the egg whites until stiff. fold in the sugar and egg yolks mixture. Sift together the flour and cocoa and fold in carefully.

Pour over the fruit and spread evenly. Bake in the oven for about 30 minutes.

Carefully turn out on to a serving dish and serve with custard sauce or half and half.

Individual Sticky Toffee "Pudding" Cakes

This typical British "pudding" or dessert is like a tiny moist sponge cake with a caramel-toffee sauce—cooked all in one.

SERVES 4

CARAMEL-TOFFEE SAUCE

Melted butter for greasing

5 Tbsp sugar

2 Tbsp water

4 Tbsp heavy cream, heated

PUDDING CAKE

½ cup unsalted butter, softened

½ cup light brown sugar, packed

4 eggs, separated

I cup self-rising flour or I cup all-purpose flour plus I tsp baking powder, sifted

¼ cup chopped dates

Butter for greasing

Prepare the caramel-toffee sauce: Butter four 1¼-cup custard cups or ramekins. Put the sugar in a saucepan and drizzle over the water to moisten. Cook over low heat until sugar dissolves. Boil until a golden caramel forms. Remove from heat and, standing well back, add the warm cream. Return to the heat and stir until all ingredients are melted and smooth.

Prepare the pudding cake: Preheat oven to 350°F. Beat the butter and sugar until fluffy and lightened in color, 2 minutes. Beat in the egg yolks one at a time, beating well after each addition. Fold all but 2 to 3 tablespoonfuls of the flour mixture into the butter-egg yolk mixture.

Beat the egg whites until soft peaks form. Stir a spoonful of whites into the mixture to lighten it, then fold in the remaining whites. Toss the dates in the reserved 2 to 3 tablespoonfuls of the flour mixture and sprinkle over the batter, then gently fold in. Divide equally between the custard cups.

Cover each cup with greased baking parchment. Secure cups then cover with foil. Put cups in a larger roasting pan and pour in enough boiling water to come halfway up sides. Bake 40 minutes. Unmold and spoon over sauce. Serve with custard sauce or whipped cream.

Lemon-Scented Passover Cake

Passover cakes are probably the most uniquely Jewish of all cakes, because they are made with flour substitutes. The most popular substitutes are potatostarch, very fine matzo meal sometimes called cake meal, and ground nuts. The end result is a light, delicate sponge cake, served here with a lemon sauce.

SERVES 6 TO 8

6 eggs, separated	Almond halves or slivered almonds for decoration
I cup sugar	
I cup fine matzo meal (cake meal)	**FOAMY LEMON SAUCE**
	I Tbsp potatostarch
½ cup finely ground blanched almonds or potato flour	⅔ cup sugar
	I½ cups water
¼ tsp ground cinnamon	Grated zest and juice of I lemon
Grated zest and juice of I lemon	2 eggs, separated

Preheat oven to 350°F. Grease an 8½ to 9 inch springform pan. In a large bowl, with an electric mixer, beat egg yolks with half the sugar until thick and lemon colored and mixture forms a "ribbon" when beaters are lifted from the bowl, 3 to 5 minutes.

In another large bowl, with cleaned beaters, beat egg whites until soft peaks form. Gradually beat in remaining sugar, in 3 or 4 batches, beating well after each addition, until whites form stiff peaks.

In a medium bowl, combine matzo meal, ground almonds or potato flour, cinnamon, and lemon zest. Alternately, in 3 batches, fold beaten whites and matzo-almond mixture into the beaten yolks. Fold in lemon juice.

Pour the batter into the prepared pan and press almond halves into the batter at 2-inch intervals or sprinkle with slivered almonds.

Bake until the top is golden and a skewer inserted in the center comes out clean, 45 to 55 minutes. Remove to a wire rack to cool 10 minutes. Carefully run a sharp knife around the edge of the pan to loosen the edges, then unclip the side of the pan and remove. Cool completely; the cake may sink a little.

Prepare Foamy Lemon Sauce. In a medium saucepan, combine potatostarch and sugar. Slowly stir in I½ cups water and lemon zest and juice, until well blended and smooth. Beat in egg yolks.

Over medium-low heat, cook the mixture until slightly thickened, 3 to 4 minutes. Bring to a boil, then remove from the heat.

In a medium bowl, with the electric mixer, beat egg whites until soft peaks form. Slowly fold in the yolk mixture until just blended. Cool, then refrigerate at least I hour or until chilled. Serve cold with the cake.

Cookies

Everyone loves home-baked cookies and this section is packed full of wonderful recipes. There are dropped cookies and rolled cookies, bar cookies and molded cookies. There are old-fashioned gingerbreads and simple shortbreads as well as indulgent new variations on old favorites such as chocolate chip. The only problem with being a good cookie cook is that they disappear so fast that you always have to make more!

INTRODUCTION

Granola cookies, fresh from the oven—light and deliciously crumbly.

Cookies were first introduced to colonial America by the New York Dutch, who brought their Koekjes or "little cakes" from their homeland. Until wood-burning or coal-fired ovens were in general use, cookie baking would have been unreliable at best. By the early 20th century, cookies were so popular that special jars and tins were produced. Since then, there has been no looking back—in the last 10 to 15 years cookies have become so popular that there are now special stores selling fresh baked cookies from every street corner!

Every nation seems to have a special cookie—chocolate chip cookies and brownies from America, tea biscuits like Shrewsbury biscuits from England, shortbread from Scotland—the list is endless.

Cookies are one of life's great treats. Even the strictest of dieters and those who deny having a sweet tooth will splurge and have a cookie with a glass of milk or a cup of tea or coffee. And the bonus is they are almost always easy to make.

The six basic types of cookie are generally determined by the way the dough is shaped.

Drop Cookies

These are usually dropped or pushed from a spoon directly on to a baking sheet, leaving about a 2-inch space between each to allow for spreading.

Molded Cookies

These are usually shaped with the hands into balls, logs, or cylinders before placing on baking sheets; some molded cookies are actually baked in molds. Molded cookies do not usually spread, so less space is required between them.

Refrigerator Cookies

These are made from a rich, stiff, paste-like dough, rolled into log shapes and then sliced as required for baking. Most of these doughs can be refrigerated for several days or frozen for up to 6 months. The advantage with refrigerator cookies is that they can be sliced and baked almost on demand.

Rolled Cookies

These are made from a dough which is rolled out with a rolling pin, then cut into shapes using a knife or cookie cutters, which are popular with children, being available in so many fun shapes. These cookies are often decorated with colored icings.

Pressed Cookies

These are formed by pressing the dough through a cookie press or pastry bag and nozzle on to the baking sheet.

Bar Cookies

These are formed by spreading a soft dough in a shallow pan, with or without a topping, then baking. After cooling they are cut into bars, squares, diamonds or triangles.

Special Cookies

These are usually shaped by one of the above methods, and then either formed into tuiles or tulips, or fried or baked in a waffle iron, to achieve a special effect.

Tips for Successful Cookie Baking

Cookie making is generally easy and requires very little equipment, but always be sure to read the recipe through before you begin. Always assemble the ingredients together before you start to cook, then put them aside or return them to their storage places as you use them, that way you'll never forget an ingredient or include it twice.

Equipment and Pans

Almost all cookie doughs can be made by hand (they all started that way) or with an electric mixer or in a food processor. An electric mixer is probably best, as it gives the baker more of a feel and control over the dough. Use heavy-gauge, flat, shiny aluminum baking sheets. They should be at least 2 inches smaller than the inside of your oven, so that the heat can circulate evenly. (Dark ones may cause overbrowning.) Non-stick pans are ideal for certain cookies, but may cause others to spread too much (this will be indicated in specific recipes). New "Cushionaire" baking sheets are excellent, especially for thin cookies or meringues, which tend to over-brown on the bottom. It is like baking on double baking sheets, but not so cumbersome.

Grease cookie sheets only when indicated, otherwise cookies may spread too much or become too thin. Most butter-rich cookie doughs don't require greased baking sheets, but a very thin layer of butter can be used as a precaution. Use a "baking spray" for the lightest of coatings, or a pastry brush to ensure an even coating.

Evenly space cookies on baking sheets, and do not leave any large gaps. Arrange 2 baking sheets in the lower and upper thirds of the oven; a single baking sheet should always be placed in the center of the oven. Rotate the baking sheets from the bottom shelf to the top and from back to front, half-way through cooking time. If you do not have enough baking sheets, arrange the cookies on sheets of heavy-duty foil, or baking parchment, cut to fit baking sheets. As soon as baked cookies are removed from the oven, slide them off on to a rack, then slide a sheet of foil with the next batch of cookies on to baking sheet and continue to bake immediately. *Never put cookies directly on to a hot baking sheet.* For quick cooling, run back of baking sheet under cold running water and wipe dry.

Mixing and Baking

As with all baking, measure the ingredients carefully. Sweet butter is generally best as it contains less water and impurities, and large eggs. All the recipes have been tested with all-purpose flour although in some recipes cake flour is suitable; it is not essential to sift the flour, but it facilitates the mixing up of the dry ingredients and ensures any lumps are eliminated. Soften the butter and cream well with the sugar, but mix in flour and dry ingredients gently or the dough may toughen.

Preheat the oven to the required temperature (if you are in doubt, double check with an oven thermometer). Use a kitchen timer and check for doneness several minutes before the end of the suggested baking time. Do not overbake cookies or they may be too dry and taste stale. Because they are thin, they continue to bake even when removed from the oven. As soon as they are firm enough, remove cookies to wire racks to cool.

Storing and Freezing

Most cookies can be stored in airtight containers or cookie jars or tins. Store different kinds of cookies separately, as the flavors might blend or moist cookies might soften crisp cookies. Delicate or sticky cookies should be separated by sheets of waxed paper or foil. To recrisp cookies, reheat for 3 to 5 minutes on a baking sheet in a 300°F oven.

Most cookie doughs can be stored in the refrigerator for several days or wrapped tightly in plastic wrap or freezer bags, then frozen. To use frozen dough, thaw, wrapped, at room temperature until soft enough to handle, then shape or slice and bake. Refrigerator cookie dough should be thawed in the refrigerator until just soft enough to slice.

Although cookies are best freshly baked, most baked cookies freeze well and are quick to thaw on short notice. Freeze in small quantities in heavy-duty freezer bags or small airtight containers.

Bar Cookies

Chocolate Brownies

This is the classic chocolate brownie, dense and fudgy with lots of walnuts. A soft chocolate glaze turns the brownies into an elegant treat.

TIP

Mold a sheet of foil over bottom of pan, smoothing evenly around corners. Remove foil and turn pan right side up. Press foil into pan, smoothing into sides and corners. Lightly oil foil.

MAKES ABOUT 2 DOZEN

4 oz unsweetened chocolate, chopped

1½ sticks butter or margarine, cut into pieces

1¾ cups sugar

3 eggs

1 tsp vanilla extract

1½ cups chopped walnuts or pecans

1 cup semi-sweet chocolate chips (optional)

1 cup all-purpose flour

CHOCOLATE GLAZE

6 oz bitter-sweet or semi-sweet chocolate, chopped

½ cup heavy cream

⅛ stick unsalted butter, cut into pieces

1 tsp vanilla extract

24 walnut or pecan halves to decorate

Preheat oven to 350°F. Prepare a 13 x 9 inch baking pan. In a medium saucepan over low heat, melt chocolate and butter or margarine until completely smooth, stirring frequently. Remove from heat, and stir in sugar until blended. Beat in eggs, one at a time, beating well after each addition. Beat in vanilla extract, nuts, and chocolate chips. Stir in flour until just blended; batter will be stiff. Spread in prepared pan.

Bake brownies until a cake tester or toothpick inserted in center comes out with sticky crumbs attached, 30 to 35 minutes. *Do not overbake.* Remove pan to wire rack to cool completely.

In a medium saucepan over low heat, melt chocolate and cream until smooth, stirring frequently. Remove from heat to cool slightly. Whisk in butter and vanilla extract. Dip 24 walnut or pecan halves halfway into chocolate, and place on waxed paper-lined baking sheet to set. Cool remaining glaze until slightly thickened and spreadable.

Using foil as a guide, remove brownies from pan, and invert on to a board or baking sheet. Using a metal palette knife, spread brownies with glaze. Refrigerate until set, at least 1 hour.

Using a long-bladed, sharp knife, cut into 24 squares. Press a walnut or pecan half into center of each brownie square. Store in airtight containers in single layers.

Low Fat Chocolate Brownies

Low fat chocolate brownies? They taste just as good as the real thing but have a slightly different texture. Keep in an airtight container if you can resist them for long enough.

MAKES 16

⅔ cup pitted dried prunes	½ cup all-purpose flour
¾ cup granulated brown sugar	1 tsp baking powder
	3 egg whites
3 Tbsp unsweetened cocoa powder, sifted	Confectioners' sugar for dusting

Grease and line a shallow 7 inch square cake pan.

Place the prunes in a food processor with 3 tablespoons of water and blend to a purée. Transfer the purée to a mixing bowl and stir in the sugar, cocoa, flour, and baking powder. Whisk the egg whites until peaking and fold into the mixture. Pour into the prepared pan and level the surface.

Bake in the oven at 350°F for 1 hour or until cooked through. Let the brownies cool in the pan for 10 minutes, then turn out on to a wire rack and cool completely. Cut into 16 squares, dust with confectioners' sugar and serve.

Flapjacks

This is an easy-to-make, old-fashioned cookie made from dark brown sugar or molasses and oats—sweet and chewy.

MAKES 8 TO 16

½ stick butter	1¼ cups old-fashioned oats
1½ Tbsp dark corn syrup	½ cup chopped walnuts, pecans or hazelnuts
⅓ cup packed dark brown sugar	¼ tsp salt

Preheat oven to 350°F. Line an 8 inch cake pan with non-stick baking parchment or foil, lightly oiled.

In a medium saucepan, cook butter, syrup, and sugar over medium heat until melted and well-blended, 2 to 3 minutes. Remove from the heat, and stir in oats, chopped nuts and salt until blended. Pour into prepared pan, and smooth top.

Bake until crisp and golden brown, 20 to 25 minutes. Remove pan to wire rack to cool slightly, 5 to 10 minutes. Invert on to a board, peel off paper, and, while still warm, cut into 8 or 16 equal wedges. Return to wire rack to cool completely. Store in airtight containers.

Date Flapjack

This is quick to make and bake, looks terrific and tastes delicious. It does, however, contain a lot of calories and should be saved for a treat!

SERVES 8 TO 10

2 cups dried dates, roughly chopped

⅔ cup water

1 tsp vanilla extract

¾ cup butter

2 cups rolled oats

1 cup whole-wheat flour

1 cup light brown sugar

Preheat an oven to 350°F and line a deep 8 inch baking pan.

Place the dates and water in a pan and cook slowly until the dates are soft, the water is slightly reduced, and the mixture can be beaten into a thick purée. Add the vanilla then set the mixture aside until needed.

Melt the butter in a pan then stir in all the remaining ingredients. Press half the mixture into the bottom of the prepared pan, then top it with the date mixture before pressing the remaining oat mixture over the dates. Smooth the top then bake in the preheated oven for 30 minutes.

Mark into portions while still warm then leave to cool completely before slicing. Store in an airtight container.

Pecan-sesame Fingers

The toasted sesame seeds provide an unusual flavor to this chewy bar cookie.

SESAME CRUST

1 stick unsalted butter, softened

½ cup packed brown sugar

1 tsp sesame oil (optional)

1 cup all-purpose flour

½ cup sesame seeds, toasted

PECAN TOPPING

2 eggs

1 cup packed brown sugar

1 tsp vanilla extract

2 Tbsp all-purpose flour

1 tsp baking powder

½ tsp salt

1½ cups chopped pecans

1¼ cups sweetened flaked coconut

2–3 Tbsp sesame seeds for sprinkling

TIP

If bar is difficult to remove from baking pan, cut into bars or squares, and store in baking pan covered with plastic wrap or foil.

Preheat oven to 375°F. Well grease a 13 × 9 inch baking pan. In a large bowl, with electric mixer, beat butter, sugar, and sesame oil, if using, until light and fluffy, 1 to 2 minutes. Beat in flour and sesame seeds until soft dough forms. Push dough evenly on to bottom of prepared pan, smoothing top. Bake 10 minutes.

Meanwhile prepare topping. In a large bowl with electric beater, beat eggs, brown sugar, vanilla extract, flour, baking powder, and salt until light and fluffy, 1 to 2 minutes. Fold in pecans and coconut.

Remove crust to wire rack. Pour over egg–pecan mixture, and sprinkle with sesame seeds. Bake until top is firm and golden, 15 to 20 minutes. Remove baking pan to wire rack, and cool completely.

Run a sharp knife around the sides of the pan to loosen mixture, and then carefully slide on to a board. Cut into 1½-inch bars.

Hermits

In New England the recipes usually contained sour cream; in this Southern version the moisture is provided by the molasses. Use any kind of dried fruits and nuts you like.

1 cup all-purpose flour

1½ tsp baking soda

½ tsp cream of tartar

1 tsp ground cinnamon

½ tsp grated or ground nutmeg

½ tsp ground cloves

¼ tsp ground mace

¼ tsp ground allspice

¾ cup raisins

¾ cup chopped, pitted dates

¾ cup chopped, dried apricots

1 stick butter or margarine, softened

½ cup sugar

2 eggs, lightly beaten

½ cup unsulfured molasses

1 cup chopped walnuts, pecans or hazelnuts

Confectioners' sugar for dusting

Preheat oven to 350°F. Then prepare a 13 × 9 inch baking pan.

Into a medium bowl, sift together flour, baking soda, cream of tartar, cinnamon, nutmeg, cloves, mace, and allspice. Place raisins, dates, and apricots in a small bowl, and toss with a quarter of flour-spice mixture.

In a large bowl with electric mixer, beat butter and sugar until light and fluffy, 1 to 2 minutes. Gradually beat in eggs and molasses until well-blended. On low speed, beat in flour-spice mixture until blended; then stir in flour-coated fruit and nuts.

Spread batter in foil-lined pan. Bake until top is set, 17 to 20 minutes. Remove pan to wire rack to cool completely. Remove cookie mixture to a board, and peel off foil. Cut into bars and dust with confectioners' sugar. Store in airtight containers with waxed paper between layers.

Apricot Granola Bars

A substantial snack or a light meal—these fruit granola bars are satisfying!

MAKES 8

FILLING

1 cup dried apricots, chopped finely

Grated zest and juice of 1 orange

⅓ cup margarine

⅓ cup honey

2 cups granola

½ cup fine whole-wheat flour

Preheat an oven to 375°F and lightly grease a 7 inch square cake pan.

Cook the apricots with the orange zest and juice, simmering slowly until all the orange juice has disappeared. Allow to cool until needed. Melt the margarine in a pan, add the honey, and heat gently until melted into the margarine. Stir in the granola and flour and mix well.

Press half the granola mixture into the prepared cake pan then cover with a layer of apricots. Top with the remaining granola mixture, pressing it down and smoothing the top with a metal spoon. Try to poke any raisins into the mixture so that they do not overcook.

Bake in the preheated oven for 20 to 25 minutes, until lightly browned. Mark into bars and allow to cool in the pan. Cut through then cool completely on a wire rack. Store in an airtight container.

Grasmere Gingerbread

This is an unusual gingerbread containing candied peel. Substitute chopped dried apricots or raisins, if you prefer.

MAKES 12

2 cups self-rising flour

¾ cup sugar

1–2 tsp ground ginger

1 stick butter or hard margarine

1 Tbsp dark corn syrup

2 egg yolks, beaten

¾ cup mixed chopped peel

TOPPING

Egg white

2 Tbsp granulated sugar

Preheat oven to 325°F.

Put the flour, sugar, and ginger into a bowl and mix together. In a pan, melt the butter or margarine and syrup. Take off the heat, cool slightly, and stir the egg yolks into the melted mixture. Gently beat the butter mixture into the flour.

Roll half the dough out to an oblong about 7 × 4 inches on non-stick paper. Sprinkle the peel over the dough. Press the remaining dough over the top.

Lightly whip the egg white and brush the top of the gingerbread with the froth and sprinkle with sugar. Bake the gingerbread for 20 to 30 minutes. When cool cut into small squares and serve.

Houston Gingerbread

Very dark but light and fluffy in texture, this is a sort of gingerbread "brownie."

MAKES ABOUT 24

2 cups all-purpose flour

2 Tbsp unsweetened cocoa powder

2 tsp baking soda

2 tsp ground ginger

2 tsp ground cinnamon

1 stick butter or margarine

¾ cup superfine sugar

2 eggs, separated

1¼ cups molasses

Scant cup buttermilk

FROSTING

7 oz semi-sweet chocolate

Preheat oven to 350°F. Grease and line a 13 × 9 inch cake pan.

Sift the flour, cocoa powder, baking soda, and spices into a bowl. In another larger bowl, cream together the butter or margarine and sugar. Beat in the egg yolks and molasses. Alternately, fold the dry ingredients and buttermilk into the larger bowl. Whisk the egg whites until stiff and fold into the batter.

Spread the batter into the pan and bake for 25 to 30 minutes. Cool the cake slightly before turning out on to a cake rack to cool thoroughly.

Melt the chocolate gently in a bowl over a pan of hot water and spread over the cake. When set, cut the cake into squares to serve.

Caramel Cashew-almond Squares

This is a delicious bar cookie with a rich, sticky topping of caramelized honey and nuts. Not for calorie counters!

PASTRY CRUST	CARAMEL NUT TOPPING
3 cups all-purpose flour	**1¼ sticks sweet butter**
½ cup cornstarch	**½ cup packed dark brown sugar**
½ tsp salt	**½ cup honey**
3 sticks unsalted butter, softened	**2 cups salted cashews, lightly toasted and coarsely chopped**
⅔ cup sugar	**1 cup whole blanched almonds, toasted and coarsely chopped**
Grated zest of 1 lemon	**2½ Tbsp whipping cream**

Prepare a 13 x 9 inch baking pan (see page 219).

Into a medium bowl, sift together flour, cornstarch, and salt. In a large bowl with electric mixer, beat butter, sugar, and lemon zest until light and fluffy, 1 to 2 minutes. On low speed, beat in flour mixture until blended and soft dough forms. Scrape down sides of bowl, and refrigerate dough, 10 minutes.

Turn dough out on to a large sheet of waxed paper, and pat into a rectangle. Cover with another piece of waxed paper, and roll out to 15 x 10 inch rectangle. Slide on to baking sheet, and refrigerate, 10 minutes.

Discard top layer of waxed paper, and carefully invert paste into foil-lined dish. Remove remaining paper, and press paste on to bottom and 1 inch up sides of pan, pressing into corners. Prick bottom of paste with a fork, and bake until paste is lightly colored, about 30 minutes, turning pan halfway through cooking and pricking with fork if paste puffs during baking. Remove pan to wire rack.

In a medium saucepan over medium heat, bring butter, sugar, and honey to a boil, stirring until sugar dissolves. Then boil without stirring until mixture thickens slightly, about 1 minute. Remove from heat and stir in cashews, almonds, and cream until well-mixed.

Pour nut mixture over crust, spreading evenly. Bake until sticky and bubbling, about 20 minutes. Remove to wire rack to cool completely. Using foil as a guide, remove cookie mixture to a board. Peel off foil, and cut into 1½-inch squares. Store in airtight containers in single layers.

Scottish Shortbread

This is the most basic cookie—butter, sugar, and flour—and yet one of the most delicious. Perfect with a cup of tea.

MAKES 16 LARGE WEDGES OR 32 THIN WEDGES

¼ cup confectioners' sugar	1¼ sticks unsalted butter, softened
¼ cup superfine sugar	
¼ tsp salt	2½ cups all-purpose flour

TIP

Scottish Shortbread is sometimes made with part rice flour (about ¼ of the total volume of flour). Rice flour is available at some specialty and health food stores, and can be substituted for part of the flour in the above proportions for an even shorter texture.

Preheat the oven to 275°F. Into a large bowl, sift confectioners' sugar. Add superfine sugar and salt, and mix well. Add butter and, using electric mixer, beat butter and sugars until light and fluffy, 1 to 2 minutes. Stir in flour until blended. On a lightly floured surface, knead dough very lightly to ensure even blending.

Divide dough evenly between two 8 inch cake pans with removable bottoms, and pat on to bottoms in even layers. Using a kitchen fork, press ¾-inch radiating lines around the edge of the dough. Prick the surface lightly with the fork (this helps keep an even surface as well as creating the traditional pattern).

Bake until pale golden (do not brown; shortbread should be very pale), about 1 hour, rotating pans halfway through cooking. Remove the pans to a wire rack to cool, about 10 minutes.

Carefully remove side of each pan, and place pan bottom on to heat-proof surface. Cut each shortbread circle into 8 wide or 16 thin wedges. This must be done while shortbread is warm and soft, or it will break. Return the shortbread wedges on their bases to the wire racks to cool completely. Store in airtight containers.

Chocolate Peanut Butter Bars

This most popular combination of chocolate and peanut butter is wonderful as a glazed brownie filled with chocolate chips and peanuts.

1 cup smooth or chunky peanut butter, softened	GLAZE
¾ stick butter, softened	6 oz semi-sweet chocolate, chopped
1 cup sugar	2 Tbsp smooth peanut butter
3 eggs	2 Tbsp butter
1 tsp vanilla extract	2 Tbsp corn syrup
1 cup all-purpose flour	1 tsp vanilla extract
1 cup semi-sweet chocolate chips	
1 cup salted peanuts, chopped	

Preheat oven to 350°F. Then prepare a 13 x 9 inch baking pan.

In a large bowl, beat peanut butter and butter until creamy and smooth, 30 to 60 seconds. Add sugar, eggs, and vanilla extract. Stir in flour until blended; then stir in chocolate chips and peanuts. Spread batter into prepared pan, smoothing top.

Bake until golden round the edges, 25 to 30 minutes. Remove pan to wire rack to cool completely.

In a medium saucepan over low heat, melt chocolate, peanut butter, butter, corn syrup, and vanilla until smooth, stirring frequently. Remove from heat, and cool until slightly thickened, stirring occasionally.

Using foil as a guide, remove cake from pan, and invert on to a board or baking sheet. Using a metal palette knife, spread glaze over the top. Refrigerate until set, about 1 hour.

Using a long-bladed, sharp knife, cut into 48 1½-inch bars. Store in airtight containers in single layers, or refrigerate in an airtight container with waxed paper between layers.

Coffee Slices

There's something extra special about coffee-flavored bakes. These slices are so simple to make, and very good to eat.

1 stick butter	FROSTING
¼ cup sugar	4 Tbsp confectioners' sugar
1 cup + 2 Tbsp self-rising flour	1 Tbsp instant coffee
1 Tbsp coffee extract	½ stick butter

Preheat oven to 350°F.

Cream together the butter and sugar until light and fluffy. Fold in the flour and coffee extract. Press into a greased jelly roll pan and bake for 15 to 20 minutes.

Place all the frosting ingredients into a saucepan and heat and stir for 2 to 3 minutes until the mixture looks like fudge. Pour the mixture on top of the shortbread. Leave to set and cut into slices.

Lemon Bars

These bar cookies are simple to make and are quite delicious. The combination of buttery shortbread and tart lemon topping is perfect.

MAKES 30

SHORTBREAD CRUST	LEMON TOPPING
1½ cups all-purpose flour	4 eggs
½ cup confectioners' sugar	1½ cups superfine sugar
½ tsp salt	Grated zest of 1 lemon
1½ sticks cold unsalted butter, cut into small pieces	½ cup fresh lemon juice
1 tsp grated lemon zest (optional)	¾ cup heavy cream
	Confectioners' sugar for dusting

Preheat oven to 325°F. Prepare a 13 x 9 inch baking pan (see page 219).

Into a large bowl, sift together flour, sugar, and salt. Sprinkle over cut-up butter with lemon zest, if using, and, using a pastry blender or fingertips, cut in butter until coarse crumbs form and mixture sticks together.

Turn crumbs into the prepared pan, and press firmly into the bottom of the pan to form a level base, smoothing top evenly. Bake until just golden, about 20 minutes. Remove the pan to wire rack to cool slightly.

In a medium bowl, beat eggs and sugar until fluffy, 3 to 5 minutes. Beat in lemon zest and juice until blended.

In another bowl with cleaned beaters, beat cream until soft peaks form. Fold into beaten egg mixture in 2 batches, and pour over base. Return pan to oven, and bake until topping is set, about 40 minutes. Remove the pan to a wire rack to cool completely.

Using the foil as a guide, remove the cookie mixture from the pan, and set on a board. Peel off the foil, and cut into bars. Dust lightly with confectioners' sugar. Store in airtight containers in single layers.

Chocolate Chip Pecan Shortbread

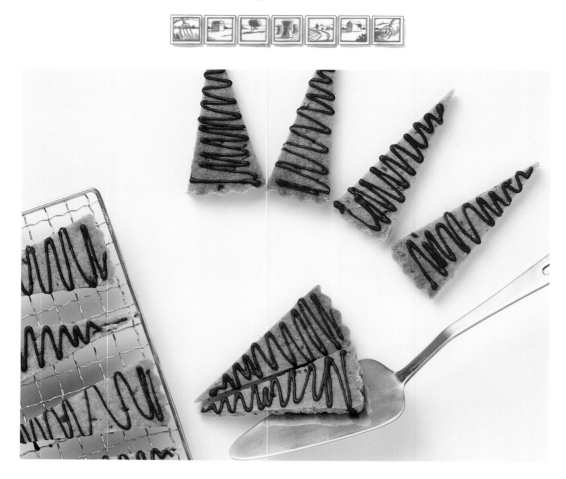

This is a rich shortbread speckled with chocolate chips and finely ground pecans. It will become a favorite cookie and is so easy to make.

MAKES 32 PIECES

1 cup pecans, toasted and cooled	2 sticks unsalted butter, softened
1¾ cups all-purpose flour	1 cup mini semi-sweet chocolate chips
¼ cup cornstarch	
½ cup confectioners' sugar	1½ oz semi-sweet chocolate melted for drizzling
¼ tsp salt	

Preheat oven to 325°F. Lightly grease two 8-inch pie pans with removable bottoms. In a food processor fitted with metal blade, process toasted pecans until very fine crumbs form; do not overprocess or nuts may form a paste and release oil. Pour into a large bowl.

Into ground nuts, sift together flour, cornstarch, confectioners' sugar, and salt, and mix well. Add butter and, using a pastry blender or fingertips, blend well until dough holds together. Stir in chocolate chips.

Divide dough evenly between the pie pans, and pat onto bottom in an even layer. Bake until edges are golden and surface appears slightly puffed, 20 to 25 minutes. Remove pans to wire racks to cool, about 5 minutes.

Carefully remove side of each pan, and place pan bottom with shortbread on heatproof surface. Cut each shortbread circle into 16 thin wedges; this must be done while shortbread is warm and soft, or it will break. Return shortbread wedges on their bases to wire racks to cool completely.

Using a metal palette knife, remove shortbread wedges to wire rack, arranging top-to-toe to fit the wedges close together on rack. Spoon melted chocolate into paper cone or decorator's bag and drizzle wedges evenly. Store in airtight containers with waxed paper between layers.

Maple Macadamia Chewies

Get your teeth into these tasty, chewy morsels, which combine a sweet maple flavor with crunchy nuts.

MAKES ABOUT 2½ DOZEN

MAPLE CRUST	NUT TOPPING
1 stick unsalted butter, softened	1 cup packed dark brown sugar
½ cup sugar	½ stick unsalted butter
1 egg	¼ cup whipping cream
1 tsp natural maple flavor	3 Tbsp corn syrup
1½ cups all-purpose flour	3 Tbsp natural maple syrup
	2 cups unsalted macadamia nuts

Prepare a 13 x 9 inch baking pan (see page 219). In a medium bowl, beat butter and sugar until light and fluffy, 1 to 2 minutes. Beat in egg and maple flavor. On low speed, beat in flour until just blended. Roll out dough between 2 sheets of waxed paper to a 14 x 10 inch rectangle. Slide on to a baking sheet, and refrigerate 10 minutes.

Preheat oven to 350°F. Remove top sheet of waxed paper, and invert dough into prepared pan. Peel off bottom piece of waxed paper. Press paste on to bottom of pan and ½ inch up sides. Prick dough with fork. Line paste with waxed paper or foil, and fill with dried beans or rice. Bake crust for 15 minutes. Remove beans or rice and waxed paper, and bake until top is set and golden, 5 to 7 minutes. Remove pan to wire rack.

In a heavy-bottomed saucepan, whisk together sugar, butter, cream, corn syrup and maple syrup. Over medium heat, bring mixture to a boil, stirring constantly until sugar dissolves; then boil without stirring, 1 minute. Remove from heat; and stir in nuts until well coated. Pour mixture over crust.

Bake until filling is bubbling and thickened, 10 minutes. Remove to a wire rack to cool completely. Using foil as a guide, remove cookie mixture to a board. Peel off foil, and cut into 2 x 1½ inch bars.

Triple Decker Squares

These rich squares are always popular with adults and children alike. They are especially good straight from the refrigerator.

MAKES 16

1 stick butter or margarine	2 Tbsp dark corn syrup
¼ cup sugar	¾ cup can condensed milk
1½ cups all-purpose flour	
	TOPPING
FILLING	6 oz semi-sweet chocolate
1 stick butter or margarine	2 Tbsp milk
⅓ cup sugar	

Preheat oven to 350°F. Cream together the butter or margarine and sugar until light and fluffy. Stir in the flour. Work the dough with your hands and knead well together. Roll out and press into a shallow 8 inch square pan. Prick well with a fork.

Bake in the oven for 25 to 30 minutes. Cool in the pan.

To make the filling, put all the ingredients into a pan and heat gently, stirring until the sugar has dissolved. Bring to a boil and cook, stirring for 5 to 7 minutes until golden.

Pour the caramel over the shortbread base and leave to set.

Melt the chocolate and milk together. Spread it evenly over the caramel. Leave until quite cold before cutting into squares.

Rocky Road Squares

This combination of marshmallows, nuts, and chocolate is a winner. For a delicious dessert, top with store-bought Rocky Road ice cream.

MAKES ABOUT 1 DOZEN

1¾ cups all-purpose flour	1 tsp vanilla extract
¼ cup unsweetened cocoa powder, preferably Dutch-processed	¾ cup sweetened flaked coconut
1 tsp baking soda	3 cups semi-sweet chocolate chips
½ tsp salt	1 cup whole blanched almonds, coarsely chopped
2 sticks unsalted butter, softened	1 cup mini marshmallows
1 cup packed light brown sugar	Confectioners' sugar for dusting
2 eggs, lightly beaten	

Preheat oven to 350°F. Prepare a 13 x 9 inch baking pan (see page 219).

Into a medium bowl, sift together flour, cocoa powder, baking soda, and salt, In a large bowl with electric mixer, beat butter and brown sugar until light and fluffy, 1 to 2 minutes. Beat in eggs and vanilla extract. On low speed, beat in the flour-cocoa mixture until blended, then stir in the coconut, 2 cups of the chocolate chips and the chopped almonds.

Turn dough into a prepared pan, and pat or spread mixture evenly on to the bottom of the pan. Bake until set, but still moist in center, 15 to 17 minutes. Remove pan from oven, and sprinkle the top evenly with remaining chocolate chips and mini marshmallows. Return pan to oven, and bake until chocolate chips and marshmallows begin to soften and blend into each other, about 4 minutes. Remove pan to a wire rack to cool for 10 minutes.

Using the foil as a guide, remove the cookie mixture from the pan and set on a board. Peel off foil and, while still warm, cut into bars or squares. Cool completely on a wire rack. Dust lightly with confectioners' sugar. Store in airtight containers with waxed paper between layers.

Lebkuchen

This is an old German recipe and is equally mouth-watering warm or cold.

MAKES ABOUT 18

2½ cups all-purpose flour

½ tsp baking powder

½ tsp ground ginger

½ tsp ground cinnamon

½ tsp ground cloves

¼ tsp ground nutmeg

1½ cups ground almonds

⅓ cup finely chopped candied orange and lemon peel

2 eggs

½ cup superfine sugar

1 cup honey

6 Tbsp milk

FROSTING

1½ cups confectioners' sugar

½ tsp almond extract

1 tsp lemon juice

Water

Preheat oven to 400°F. Line a jelly roll tin with waxed paper; brush lightly with oil and put aside.

In a bowl, sift the flour, baking powder, and spices together. Stir in the almonds and chopped peel. Break the eggs into another bowl, add the sugar, and whisk until the mixture is light and thick, leaving a trail when the whisk is lifted. Whisk in the honey and milk followed by the flour mixture.

Pour the batter into the prepared tin. Bake for 15 to 20 minutes. Cool on a wire rack for 10 minutes, then turn out. Frost while warm.

To make the frosting, put the confectioners' sugar into a bowl. Add the extract, lemon juice, and enough water to mix to a thick consistency. Brush the frosting over the hot Lebkuchen. Cut into bars to serve.

Drop Cookies

Peanut Butter, White Chocolate,
and Peanut Butter Cookies

Double Chocolate Chip Cookies

Triple Chocolate Chunk Cookies

Spicy Applesauce Cookies

White Chocolate, Cream Cheese
Macadamia Drops

Walnut Cookies

Granola Cookies

Almond Macaroons

Swedish Almond Wafers

Luxury Macaroons

Muesli Cookies

Brownie Cookies

New England-style Jumbles

Low-fat Oat and Orange Cookies

Oatmeal Lace

Peanut Butter, White Chocolate, and Peanut Cookies

These luscious cookies should always be made with a commercially prepared peanut butter, as freshly ground or homemade peanut butters may not react the same way in the recipe.

MAKES ABOUT 18

1 cup freshly shelled peanuts	2 Tbsp sugar
1 cup all-purpose flour	1 egg
½ tsp baking soda	1 tsp vanilla extract
¼ tsp salt	6 oz fine-quality white chocolate, coarsely chopped
½ cup chunky peanut butter	
1 stick unsalted butter	2 oz semi-sweet chocolate, melted
½ cup packed light brown sugar	

In a medium skillet over medium-low heat, toast peanuts until golden and fragrant, about 5 minutes, stirring frequently. Turn on to a plate, and allow to cool.

Preheat oven to 375°F. Into a medium bowl, sift together flour, baking soda, and salt. In a large bowl with an electric mixer, beat peanut butter, butter, and sugars together until light and fluffy, about 2 to 3 minutes. Add egg and continue beating for 2 minutes more; beat in vanilla extract. Stir in flour mixture until well-blended; then stir in white chocolate and toasted peanuts.

Drop heaped tablespoonfuls at least 2 inches apart on 2 large baking sheets. Flatten slightly with the back of a moistened spoon. Bake until golden-brown, about 12 to 15 minutes; do not overbake or the cookies will be dry. Remove baking sheets to wire racks to cool, 3 to 5 minutes. Then, using a metal pancake turner or palette knife, remove cookies to wire racks to cool completely.

Spoon melted semi-sweet chocolate into a paper cone (see below). Drizzle over cookies in a zig-zag pattern. Allow to set; store cookies in airtight containers.

Double Chocolate Chip Cookies

This is a slightly updated version of the classic chocolate chip cookie—more chunky than ever.

MAKES ABOUT 4 DOZEN

2¼ cups all-purpose flour

1 tsp baking soda

¾ tsp salt

2 sticks unsalted butter or margarine, softened

1 cup packed light brown sugar

½ cup sugar

2 eggs

1 tsp vanilla extract

12 oz semi-sweet chocolate chips or semi-sweet chocolate chopped into small pieces

6 oz fine-quality white chocolate chopped into small pieces

1 cup chopped pecans or walnuts

Preheat oven to 375°F. Into a large bowl, sift together flour, baking soda, and salt. In a large bowl, with an electric mixer, beat butter and sugars until light and fluffy. With mixer on low speed, beat in eggs, beating well after each addition, and scraping down the sides of the bowl occasionally. Beat in vanilla extract; then stir in flour mixture until well-mixed. Stir in chocolate chips and nuts.

Drop rounded tablespoonfuls, at least 2 inches apart, on to large ungreased baking sheets. Bake until set and golden-brown, 10 to 13 minutes, rotating baking sheets from top to bottom shelf and front to back halfway through cooking time. Remove baking sheets to wire racks to cool slightly; then using a metal pancake turner or palette knife, remove cookies to wire racks to cool completely. Repeat with remaining cookie dough. Store in airtight containers.

Triple Chocolate Chunk Cookies

These cookies are large and flat, crisp on the edge and soft in the center and filled with chocolate—a chocolate lover's dream. For best results, do not overbake.

MAKES ABOUT 18

9 oz bittersweet or semi-sweet chocolate, chopped

1½ sticks unsalted butter, cut into pieces

3 eggs

¾ cup sugar

⅓ cup packed light brown sugar

2 tsp vanilla extract

½ cup all-purpose flour

6 tbsp cocoa powder, sifted

1½ tsp baking powder

¼ tsp salt

9 oz semi-sweet chocolate, chopped into ¼-in pieces or 1½ cups semi-sweet chocolate chips

6 oz fine-quality milk chocolate, chopped into ¼-in pieces

6 oz fine-quality white chocolate, chopped into ¼-in pieces

1½ cups pecans or walnuts, toasted and chopped

Preheat oven to 325°F. Lightly grease 2 large baking sheets. In a medium saucepan over low heat, melt bittersweet or semi-sweet chocolate and butter, stirring frequently until smooth. Remove from heat to cool slightly.

In a large bowl, with electric mixer, beat eggs and sugars until light and fluffy, about 2 to 3 minutes. On low speed, gradually beat in melted chocolate and vanilla extract until well-blended. Into a small bowl, sift together flour, cocoa powder, baking powder, and salt; then gently stir into chocolate mixture. Stir in unmelted chocolate pieces and nuts.

Drop heaped tablespoons, at least 4 inches apart, on to baking sheets. Moisten the bottom of a drinking glass, and flatten each dough round slightly, trying to make each cookie about 3 inches round; you will only fit 4 to 6 cookies on each baking sheet. Bake 10 minutes until tops are cracked and shiny; do not overbake or cookies will break when removed from baking sheet.

Remove baking sheets to wire racks to cool slightly. Then, using a metal pancake turner or palette knife, remove cookies to wire racks to cool completely. Repeat with remaining dough. Store in airtight containers.

Triple Chocolate Chunk Cookies ▶

Spicy Applesauce Cookies

These soft spicy cookies are delicious. If you don't like nuts, substitute some chopped dates.

MAKES ABOUT 3 DOZEN

1 stick unsalted butter, softened	½ tsp salt
½ cup packed light brown sugar	1 tsp ground cinnamon
⅓ cup sugar	1 tsp ground ginger
1 egg	½ tsp ground cloves
1 cup applesauce	1 cup golden raisins
2 cups all-purpose flour	¾ cup chopped walnuts or pecans
1 tsp baking soda	¾ cup semi-sweet chocolate chips

Preheat the oven to 350°F. Lightly grease 2 large baking sheets. In a large bowl with electric mixer, beat butter until creamy, about 30 seconds. Add sugars, and beat until light and fluffy, 1 to 2 minutes. Beat in egg, and stir in applesauce.

Into a medium bowl, sift together flour, baking soda, salt, cinnamon, ginger, and cloves. Stir into butter-sugar mixture until well-blended; then stir in raisins, walnuts or pecans, and chocolate chips.

Drop tablespoonfuls, about 1½ inches apart, on to baking sheets. Bake until golden, 5 to 7 minutes. Remove baking sheets to wire racks to cool slightly. Using a metal pancake turner or palette knife, remove cookies to wire racks to cool completely. Repeat with the remaining mixture. Store in airtight containers.

White Chocolate, Cream Cheese Macadamia Drops

The combination of white chocolate and macadamia nuts is luscious. Although macadamias are expensive, they are worth it for these cookies.

MAKES ABOUT 4 DOZEN

1 stick unsalted butter, softened

8 oz cream cheese, softened

¾ cup packed light brown sugar

Grated zest of 1 lemon

1½ tsp vanilla extract

1½ cups all-purpose flour

2 tsp baking powder

1 cup coarsely chopped macadamia nuts

4 oz fine-quality white chocolate, coarsely chopped

Confectioners' sugar for dusting

In a large bowl with an electric mixer, beat the butter and cream cheese until creamy, 1 to 2 minutes, scraping the bowl occasionally. Add the sugar and continue beating until light and fluffy, 1 to 2 minutes. Beat in the lemon zest and vanilla extract.

Into a medium bowl, sift together flour and baking powder, and stir into cream cheese mixture. Stir in nuts and chocolate. Chill dough until firm, 1 to 2 hours.

Preheat oven to 400°F. Lightly grease 2 large baking sheets. Drop heaped teaspoonfuls of mixture 2 inches apart on to baking sheets, and flatten slightly. Bake until puffed and golden, 8 to 10 minutes. Remove baking sheets to wire racks to cool, 5 to 8 minutes. Then, using a metal pancake turner or palette knife, remove cookies to wire racks to cool completely. Repeat with remaining mixture.

When cookies are cool, arrange side by side on wire racks, and drizzle over some melted chocolate in a zigzag pattern. Store in air airtight containers.

Walnut Cookies

These cookies are delicious as they are, but could easily be coated with melted chocolate or a chocolate substitute such as carob. Use pecans if you prefer, but the slightly more bitter flavor of walnuts is very good in cookies. Place the cookies far apart on the baking sheets or they may spread into each other.

MAKES ABOUT 30

1 stick butter, slightly softened	1 cup fine whole wheat flour
⅔ cup light brown sugar	1 tsp baking powder
1 large egg, beaten	¾ cup walnut pieces, finely chopped

Preheat an oven to 350°F and then lightly grease 2 or 3 baking sheets.

Beat the butter and sugar together until pale—the mixture will be slightly sticky. Add the egg and mix well, then fold in the flour and baking powder, then finally work in the nuts.

Turn the mixture out on to a lightly floured surface and knead gently to bring the dough together. Roll into a sausage shape about 12 inches long, wrap in plastic wrap, and chill for at least 1 hour, until firm enough to handle.

Cut the dough into thin slices and roll them into balls about the size of a walnut. Place on the prepared baking sheets, flattening the cookies slightly with the palm of your hand. Bake for 12 to 15 minutes, then allow to cool slightly on the baking sheet before transferring to a wire rack to cool completely.

Granola Cookies

These sweet cookies are very quick to make, but they must be chilled before baking or they will spread too much in the oven. The honey binds the mixture together; no egg is used. Work the dough well to produce light cookies.

MAKES ABOUT 20

1 stick butter or margarine	2 cups granola
½ cup light brown sugar	½ cup fine whole wheat flour
¼ cup honey	

Cream the butter and sugar together until pale and fluffy, then add the honey and beat thoroughly again. Work in the granola and flour to give a stiff dough which is only slightly sticky, then turn out on to a lightly floured surface and knead firmly until the dough is easily manageable.

Form into a sausage shape, about 12 inches long, then cover in plastic wrap and chill in the refrigerator for at least 30 minutes.

Preheat an oven to 350°F and lightly grease 2 baking sheets. Cut the cookie dough into 20 pieces, form into balls, then flatten slightly and place on the prepared baking sheets. Bake in the preheated oven for 12 to 15 minutes, until lightly browned. Leave the cookies to cool slightly on the baking sheets until firm enough to transfer to a wire rack to cool completely.

Store in an airtight container or cookie jar.

Almond Macaroons

This is an authentic macaroon, made with almond paste, egg whites, and sugar.

MAKES ABOUT 30

½ lb almond paste, cut into pieces

I cup superfine sugar

3 egg whites, at room temperature

⅓ cup confectioners' sugar

2 Tbsp cake flour

⅛ tsp salt

2 Tbsp chopped blanched almonds

Preheat oven to 300°F. Line 2 baking sheets with rice paper or lightly oiled non-stick parchment paper.

In a food processor fitted with a metal blade, using pulse action, process almond paste. Gradually add sugar and egg whites, and process until smooth. Sprinkle over confectioners' sugar, flour, and salt, and using pulse action, process until well-blended. Scrape into a bowl and chill for 15 minutes to firm slightly.

Drop teaspoonfuls, 2 inches apart, on to prepared baking sheets, and sprinkle a few chopped almonds on to center of each mound. Cover with a clean dish cloth, and allow to sit for 30 minutes. Bake until pale golden and set, allow 20 to 25 minutes.

Dampen 2 dish cloths, and spread over 2 wire racks. Remove the baking sheets from the oven, and slide paper linings on to the damp cloths. Allow to cool completely, then peel the macaroons off the paper.

TIP

Almond paste is a commercially prepared paste of ground almonds and is available at most large supermarkets.

Rice paper is an edible paper available in cookware and specialty shops.

Swedish Almond Wafers

Grinding your own almonds makes all the difference to these rich, buttery, lace-like cookies. Be sure to leave lots of space between the cookies as they really spread. Having extra baking sheets is helpful as it is necessary to bake them in small batches.

MAKES ABOUT 2 DOZEN

¾ cup unblanched almonds

½ cup superfine sugar

I stick unsalted butter, cut into pieces

2 Tbsp all-purpose flour

¼ tsp salt

2 Tbsp light cream

Preheat oven to 350°F. Lightly grease 2 large baking sheets. In a food processor fitted with a metal blade, process almonds until very finely ground. Do not overgrind or they will form a paste. Add a little sugar, and pulse again to be sure they are evenly ground.

Combine almond mixture, remaining sugar, butter, flour, salt, and cream in a heavy-based saucepan, and cook over medium heat until the butter is melted and the batter is smooth. Remove from heat.

Drop scant teaspoonfuls, 3 to 4 inches apart, on to baking sheets (you may only get 5 to 6 on a sheet). Bake 3 to 5 minutes, until lightly brown at the edges, but bubbling in the center. Remove the baking sheet to wire racks to cool slightly.

When the edges are firm enough to lift, use a thin palette knife to remove cookies to wire racks to cool completely. Repeat with the remaining batter, cooling and regreasing baking sheets between each batch. Cookies can be stored in airtight containers with waxed paper between layers. They are very fragile.

Luxury Macaroons

The macadamias are a new addition and go very well with coconut.

MAKES 2 DOZEN

3 cups sweetened, flaked coconut

1 cup unsalted macadamia nuts, chopped

Flavorless vegetable oil for greasing

⅔ cup sweetened condensed milk

1 tsp vanilla extract

2 egg whites

Pinch of salt

6 oz white or semi-sweet chocolate, melted (optional)

Preheat oven to 350°F. Place flaked coconut on 1 large baking sheet and macadamia nuts on another. Toast until lightly golden, 7 to 10 minutes, stirring and shaking frequently. Pour coconut on to one plate and nuts on to another to cool completely.

Line 2 large baking sheets with non-stick baking parchment. Brush very lightly with oil. Into a large bowl, combine condensed milk, vanilla extract, flaked coconut, and macadamia nuts until well-blended.

In a medium bowl with electric mixer on medium speed, beat egg whites until foamy. Add salt and increase mixer speed to high. Continue beating until whites are stiff but not dry. Fold whites into coconut mixture. Drop rounded tablespoonfuls on to prepared baking sheets. Bake until golden around edges, 12 to 14 minutes. Remove baking sheets to wire racks to cool completely, then gently peel off paper.

Line a large baking sheet with waxed paper. Dip macaroon bottoms into melted white or semi-sweet chocolate. Place on lined cookie sheet until chocolate sets, 15 to 20 minutes. Peel off paper and refrigerate in airtight containers with waxed paper between layers.

Muesli Cookies

These chewy cookies are sturdy enough to send in the mail or take on a picnic. They keep well, if they last that long.

MAKES ABOUT 3 DOZEN

2¼ cups all-purpose flour	¼ cup fresh orange juice
2½ tsp baking powder	1 egg
2 tsp ground cinnamon	1 cup natural unsweetened muesli cereal
½ tsp ground nutmeg	
½ tsp baking soda	½ cup raisins
½ tsp salt	½ cup chopped walnuts or almonds
1 stick unsalted butter, softened	½ cup quick-cooking oats
1 cup sugar	

Preheat oven to 250°F. Lightly grease 2 baking sheets. Into a medium bowl, sift together flour, baking powder, cinnamon, nutmeg, baking soda, and salt.

In a large bowl with an electric mixer, beat butter and sugar until light and fluffy, 1 to 2 minutes. Slowly beat in orange juice and egg. Stir in flour mixture until well blended; then stir in muesli cereal, raisins, chopped nuts, and oats.

Drop rounded tablespoonfuls at least 2 inches apart on to prepared baking sheets. Smooth tops slightly with a moistened fingertip. Bake until surface is set and lightly browned, 15 to 18 minutes, rotating baking sheets from top to bottom shelf and front to back halfway through cooking time. Remove baking sheets to wire racks to cool slightly. Then, using a metal pancake turner or palette knife, remove cookies to wire racks to cool completely. Repeat with the remaining dough. Store in airtight containers.

Brownie Cookies

This soft chewy chocolate cookie is like a brownie. Do not overbake or it will be dry.

MAKES ABOUT 3 DOZEN

⅔ cup all-purpose flour	2 eggs, lightly beaten
¼ tsp salt	1 tsp vanilla extract
2 oz unsweetened chocolate, chopped	¾ cup chopped walnuts
1 stick unsalted butter, softened	¾ cup semi-sweet chocolate chips
1 cup sugar	Confectioners' sugar for dusting

Preheat oven to 350°F. Grease 2 baking sheets. Into a small bowl, sift together flour and salt; set aside.

In a heat-proof bowl placed over a saucepan of simmering water, melt chocolate, stirring frequently, until smooth. Remove from heat to cool slightly. In a large bowl with electric mixer, beat butter until creamy, about 30 seconds. Add sugar and beat until light and fluffy, 1 to 2 minutes. Beat in eggs and vanilla extract; then stir in walnuts and chocolate chips. Add flour mixture and stir until just blended.

Drop tablespoonfuls, 2 inches apart, on to greased baking sheets, and bake until tops feel set but centers remain moist, about 10 to 12 minutes. Remove baking sheets to wire racks to cool until cookies have set and become firm enough to move, about 5 minutes. Then, using a metal pancake turner or palette knife, remove cookies to wire racks to cool completely. Repeat with remaining cookie mixture.

Dust the cooled cookies with a little confectioners' sugar. Store in airtight containers with waxed paper between the layers.

New England Style Jumbles

This is a new version of an old-fashioned American cookie which was so called because of the nuts "jumbled" into the dough.

1¼ cups all-purpose flour	1 cup dried cranberries
¾ tsp baking soda	½ cup dried cherries
½ tsp ground cinnamon	1 stick unsalted butter, softened
⅛ tsp salt	
1 cup semi-sweet chocolate chips	¾ cup sugar
	¼ cup packed light brown sugar
¾ cup walnuts, coarsely chopped	
	1 egg
¾ cup hazelnuts, chopped	1 tsp vanilla extract
¾ cup unblanched whole almonds, chopped	

Preheat oven to 375°F. Into a medium bowl, sift together flour, baking soda, cinnamon, and salt. In a large bowl, stir chocolate chips, walnuts, hazelnuts, almonds, cranberries, and cherries.

In a large bowl with an electric mixer, beat the butter until creamy, 30 seconds. Add sugars and beat until light and fluffy, 1 to 2 minutes. Beat in the egg and vanilla extract. On low speed, beat in the flour mixture until blended. Pour into the bowl of nuts and dried fruits, and stir until combined.

Drop rounded tablespoonfuls, 2 inches apart, on 2 large ungreased baking sheets. Bake until golden, 12 to 15 minutes, rotating baking sheets from top to bottom shelf and from front to back halfway through cooking time. Remove baking sheets to wire racks to cool slightly. Then remove cookies to wire racks to cool completely. Repeat with the remaining cookie dough.

TIP

If dough seems soft, refrigerate 15 minutes before dropping on to baking sheets. This will keep batter from spreading too much.

Low-fat Oat and Orange Cookies

These little cookies are hard to resist. Rolled in oatmeal, they have a crunchy outside, and softer inside which has a mild orange flavor.

MAKES 20

3 Tbsp polyunsaturated margarine	Grated rind of 1 orange
¼ cup granulated brown sugar	1¼ cups self-rising flour
1 egg white, lightly beaten	⅓ cup oatmeal
2 Tbsp skim milk	Strips of orange rind to decorate (optional)
3 Tbsp raisins	

Preheat oven to 350°F. Cream the margarine and sugar together until the mixture is light and fluffy. Add the egg white, milk, raisins, and orange rind. Fold in the flour and bring the mixture together to form a dough then roll into 20 equal-sized balls.

Place the oatmeal in a shallow bowl, roll each dough ball in the oatmeal to coat completely, pressing them on gently. Place the cookies on non-stick baking sheets, spacing well apart. Flatten each round slightly.

Bake for 15 minutes or until they are golden. Cool on a wire rack, then decorate the cookies and store any leftovers in an airtight container.

Oatmeal Lace

These beautiful lacy cookies are so thin they are transparent, but simple to make.

MAKES ABOUT 2 DOZEN

- 1½ cups quick-cooking rolled oats
- 1 cup packed light brown sugar
- ½ cup sugar
- 2 Tbsp all-purpose flour
- ¼ tsp salt
- 1 stick plus 2⅔ Tbsp unsalted butter, melted
- 1 egg, lightly beaten
- 1 tsp vanilla extract
- ½ cup mini chocolate chips

Preheat oven to 350°F. In a large bowl, combine oats, sugars, flour, and salt. Make a well in the center. Add the melted butter, egg, and vanilla extract. Stir until blended and in a soft batter-like dough. Stir in chocolate chips.

Drop half-teaspoonfuls, 2½ inches apart, on ungreased baking sheets. Bake 3 to 5 minutes until the edges are lightly browned and centers bubbling; the cookies will spread to large disks. Remove the baking sheets to wire racks to cool slightly.

When the edges are firm enough to lift, use a thin palette knife to remove cookies to wire racks to cool completely. Repeat with remaining batter. Cookies can be stored in airtight containers with waxed paper between the layers. They are crisp and fragile.

Molded Cookies

Chocolate Butter Cookies · Chocolate-dipped Hazelnut Crescents

Chocolate Peanut Butter Cookie-cups · Austrian Crescents

Peanut Butter Cookies · Light and Lemony Madeleines

Mexican Wedding Cakes · Chocolate Madeleines

Grantham Gingerbreads · Almond and Pine Nut Biscotti

Gingernuts · Chinese Almond Cookies

Coconut Macaroons · Poppy Seed Pistachio Puffs

Coffee Macaroons · Kourambiedes

Cinnamon Balls · Rich Cardamom Cookies

Chocolate Butter Cookies

These rich chocolatey butter cookies can also be formed in a cookie press for specific shapes for special occasions.

MAKES ABOUT 3 DOZEN

1½ cups all-purpose flour	1 egg yolk
¼ cup unsweetened cocoa powder (preferably Dutch-processed)	1 tsp almond or vanilla extract
¼ tsp salt	2 oz semi-sweet chocolate
1½ sticks unsalted butter, softened	⅓ cup unblanched chopped almonds, toasted
½ cup superfine sugar	

TIP

Cookies can be shaped into 1½-inch balls, decorated with half a candied cherry, or dusted with sugar.

Preheat oven to 375°F. In a medium bowl, sift together flour, cocoa powder, and salt.

In a large bowl, with electric mixer, beat butter until creamy, 30 seconds. Gradually add sugar and beat until light and fluffy, 1 to 2 minutes. Add egg yolk and almond or vanilla extract, and beat 1 minute more. Gradually stir in flour mixture until well-blended.

Using a teaspoon to scoop dough and also using your palms, form dough into 2-inch logs. Place logs 1 inch apart on greased baking sheets. Bake cookies until just set, 7 to 9 minutes. Remove baking sheets to wire racks to cool slightly. Place cookies on wire racks to cool completely.

Arrange cookie logs on a wire rack placed over a baking sheet to catch any drips. Using a teaspoon or paper cone, drizzle cookies with chocolate in a zigzag pattern; then sprinkle with a few chopped almonds. Allow to set. Store in airtight containers.

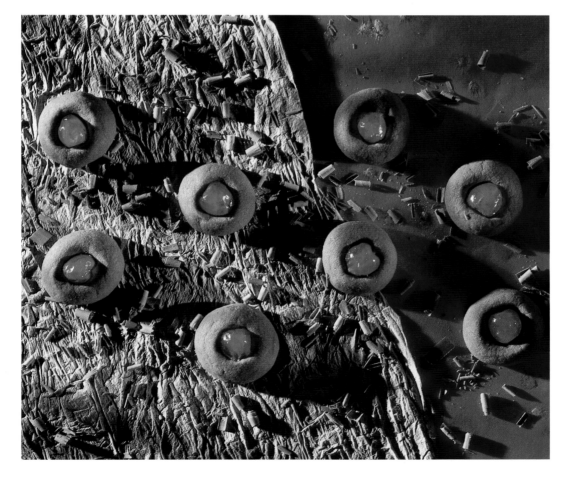

Chocolate Peanut Butter Cookie-cups

T he combination of chocolate and peanut butter is a classic one.

MAKES ABOUT 3 DOZEN

1 cup all-purpose flour	1 egg
1 tsp baking powder	1 tsp vanilla extract
¼ tsp salt	CHOCOLATE FILLING
1 stick unsalted butter, softened	12 oz semi-sweet or bittersweet chocolate, chopped
½ cup packed light brown sugar	¾ stick unsalted butter, softened
¼ cup sugar	
1 cup smooth peanut butter	

Into a small bowl, sift together flour, baking powder, and salt. In a large mixing bowl with an electric mixer, beat butter until creamy, 30 seconds. Add sugars and continue beating until mixture is light and fluffy. Add peanut butter in 3 batches, beating well until mixture is well blended. Beat in egg and vanilla extract. Stir in flour mixture until just mixed. Refrigerate the dough until chilled, 1 hour.

Preheat oven to 375°F. Using a tablespoon, scoop out mixture and, using slightly moistened hands, roll between your palms to form 1-inch balls. Place balls 1½ inches apart on 2 ungreased baking sheets. Using a finger, press down into the center to make a hole. Bake until just set and golden, 10 to 12 minutes. Rotate baking sheets halfway through cooking time. Remove baking sheets to wire racks to cool for about 2 to 3 minutes. Then remove cookies to wire racks to cool completely.

In a medium bowl over a saucepan of simmering water, melt the chocolate until smooth, stirring frequently. Remove from heat, and cool slightly. Gently beat in butter until mixture just thickens. Spoon into a decorating bag fitted with a medium star tip. When cookies are completely cold, pipe a small amount of chocolate ganache into the center of each cookie. Allow to set.

Peanut Butter Cookies

T his is a classic cookie. If you like, add some chopped peanuts for extra crunch.

MAKES 2 DOZEN

1 cup all-purpose flour	1 egg, lightly beaten
½ tsp baking soda	1 tsp vanilla extract
½ tsp salt	1 cup crunchy peanut butter
1 stick unsalted butter, softened	½ cup peanuts, coarsely chopped
¾ cup packed light brown sugar	

> **TIP**
> *Smooth peanut butter can be used instead of crunchy. Be sure to use a commercial, not homemade, peanut butter.*

Into a bowl, sift together flour, baking soda, and salt. In a large bowl with electric mixer, beat butter until creamy, 30 seconds. Add sugar and continue beating, until mixture is light and fluffy, 1 to 2 minutes. Beat in egg and vanilla extract until well-blended. Beat in peanut butter and then, on low speed, beat in flour mixture and peanuts. Refrigerate dough until firm, about 30 minutes.

Preheat oven to 350°F. Lightly grease 2 large baking sheets. Use a teaspoon to scoop out dough and form into 1-inch balls. Place on baking sheets 2 inches apart, and use a 4-tined fork to press flat, making 2½-inch rounds with a crisscross pattern.

Bake until golden, 12 to 15 minutes. Remove baking sheets to wire racks to cool slightly. Then, using a metal pancake turner or palette knife, remove cookies to wire racks to cool completely. Store in airtight containers.

Mexican Wedding Cakes

These melt-in-your-mouth cookies, dusted with several coats of confectioners' sugar, resemble wedding bells and are sometimes called by that name.

MAKES ABOUT 4 DOZEN

¾ cup pecan or walnut halves	1 tsp vanilla extract
¾ cup confectioners' sugar	¼ tsp salt
½ tsp ground cinnamon	2 cups all-purpose flour
2 sticks butter, cut into pieces, softened	Confectioners' sugar for dusting

Preheat oven to 375°F. Place pecans or walnuts on a baking sheet, and toast until golden and fragrant, 7 to 10 minutes, turning and shaking occasionally. Pour on to a plate to cool completely. Turn off the oven.

In a food processor fitted with a metal blade, process toasted pecans or walnuts with confectioners' sugar and cinnamon until fine crumbs form. Add butter to processor, and process until creamy and smooth, scraping sides of the bowl once. Add vanilla extract, and pulse to blend. Add salt and flour, and, using pulse action, process until mixture begins to stick together and form a soft dough. Scrape into a bowl, cover, and refrigerate 1 to 2 hours to firm.

> **TIP**
> If cookies have been stored, re-roll in confectioners' sugar a few hours before serving to ensure they are well coated.

Preheat oven to 375°F. Using a small scoop or tablespoon and lightly floured hands, shape dough into 1-inch balls, rolling between your palms. Place balls 1½ inches apart on 2 large ungreased baking sheets. Bake until cookies are barely golden, 12 to 15 minutes, rotating baking sheets from top to bottom shelf and from front to back halfway through cooking time. Remove baking sheets to wire racks to cool, 2 minutes. Then, using a metal pancake turner or palette knife, remove cookies to wire racks. Repeat with remaining cookie dough.

Place about 1 cup confectioners' sugar in a medium bowl. While cookies are still warm, roll a few at a time in sugar to coat well. Transfer to wire racks to cool completely. Roll again in confectioners' sugar before storing in airtight containers.

Grantham Gingerbreads

These round puffy gingerbread cookies should be "hollow and slightly dome-shaped, with a pleasing fawn tint."

SERVES 8

2 cups plus 2 Tbsp self-rising flour

1 tsp ground ginger

1 stick butter or margarine

1½ cups superfine sugar

1 egg, beaten

Preheat oven to 300°F. In one bowl, sift together the flour and the ginger. In another bowl, beat together the butter or margarine and sugar, then beat in the egg. Stir in the flour mixture and combine well. Roll the dough into walnut-sized balls.

Place the balls on a greased baking tray and bake for about 40 minutes until crisp, hollow, and lightly browned.

Gingernuts

Originally from England, Gingernuts have become a firm favorite all over the world, especially enjoyable when dipped in a cup of tea.

SERVES 4

1 cup self-rising flour	½ stick butter or hard margarine
½ tsp baking soda	
1–2 tsp ground ginger	5 Tbsp dark corn syrup
1 tsp ground cinnamon	1 Tbsp molasses
1 Tbsp superfine sugar	

Preheat oven to 375°F. Sift the flour, baking soda, and spices into a bowl. Stir in the sugar. Melt the butter or margarine, syrup, and molasses together, pour on to the dry ingredients, and combine thoroughly.

Roll the dough into balls. Place on a greased baking tray and flatten slightly with the palm of the hand. Bake for about 15 minutes. Cool and serve.

Coconut Macaroons

These are an easy Passover cookie, and are popular because they store well and taste delicious. Of course, all macaroons are a good way to use extra egg whites.

MAKES ABOUT 30

4 egg whites

¼ teaspoon cream of tartar

1 cup sugar

1 teaspoon lemon juice or distilled white vinegar

1 teaspoon vanilla extract

2½ cups moist, unsweetened shredded coconut

In a large bowl, with electric mixer at medium speed, beat egg whites until frothy. Add cream of tartar and beat on high speed until peaks form. Gradually sprinkle in sugar, 2 tablespoons at a time, beating well after each addition until egg whites form stiff peaks.

Sprinkle lemon juice or vinegar, vanilla, and coconut over egg whites. Gently fold in until just blended.

Preheat oven to 300°F. Line 2 large cookie sheets with non-stick parchment paper or foil. Drop mixture by heaping teaspoonfuls, keeping a cone shape, about 1 inch apart.

Bake 40 to 45 minutes until lightly browned; macaroons should be very slightly soft in the center. Remove macaroons on paper to wire racks to cool slightly. Carefully peel off paper and cool completely. Store in an airtight container.

Coffee Macaroons

The flavor of coffee, the lightness of macaroons, make a perfect combination. These will be eaten in no time at all!

MAKES ABOUT 20

Rice paper	1 Tbsp cornstarch
⅔ cup ground almonds	¼ tsp vanilla extract
¾ cup sugar	1 Tbsp coffee extract
2 egg whites	12 chocolate coffee beans

Preheat oven to 375°F. Line two or three baking trays with rice paper.

Mix the ground almonds, sugar and all but one tablespoon of the egg white together. Stir until all the ingredients are evenly blended. Stir in the cornstarch, vanilla and coffee extract.

Spoon into a decorating bag fitted with a ½ inch plain tube. Pipe the mixture on to the rice paper in large round circles. Top each one with a chocolate coffee bean. Brush with the remaining egg white.

Bake the coffee macaroons for 15 minutes or until lightly browned, risen and slightly cracked.

Cut the rice paper to fit round each coffee macaroon and leave to cool on a wire rack.

Cinnamon Balls

These are a very popular Passover cookie, as they contain no flour.

MAKES ABOUT 20

2 cups finely blanched and ground almonds, walnuts or pecans	2 egg whites
	⅛ tsp cream of tartar
1 cup superfine sugar	½ cup confectioners' sugar
1 tbsp ground cinnamon	1 Tbsp ground cinnamon

TIP
If mixture is too soft, add a little more ground almond or fine matzo meal to stiffen it.

Preheat oven to 325°F. Lightly grease a large non-stick baking sheet. In a medium bowl, combine ground nuts, ½ cup of the sugar and the cinnamon.

In a medium bowl with an electric mixer, beat egg whites until foamy. Add cream of tartar, and continue beating until soft peaks form. Gradually add remaining sugar, a tablespoon at a time, beating well after each addition, until whites are stiff and glossy. Gently fold in nut mixture.

With moistened hands, shape the mixture into walnut-size balls. Place on a baking sheet 1 inch apart. Bake until it is set and golden, about 25 to 30 minutes, rotating from top to bottom shelf and from front to back halfway through the cooking time. Remove the baking sheets to a wire rack to cool slightly.

In a small bowl, combine the confectioners' sugar and the cinnamon. Roll each warm cinnamon ball in the mixture to coat completely; then set on wire racks to cool completely. Roll the balls again when cold. Store in airtight containers.

Chocolate-dipped Hazelnut Crescents

The combination of chocolate and hazelnuts is beautiful, but the cookies are equally delicious on their own.

MAKES ABOUT 36

⅔ cup hazelnuts	flavor liqueur, or water
I cup all-purpose flour	I tsp vanilla extract
I cup cake flour	½ cup grated or finely chopped chocolate
¼ tsp salt	
2 sticks unsalted butter, softened	Confectioners' sugar for dusting
⅓ cup superfine sugar	6 oz semi-sweet chocolate, melted, for dipping
I Tbsp hazelnut or almond-	

Preheat oven to 375°F. Place hazelnuts on a baking sheet, and toast until golden and fragrant, 5 to 7 minutes, turning and shaking frequently. Cool on a plate. Reduce oven temperature to 325°F. Into a medium bowl, sift together the flours and salt.

In a food processor fitted with metal blade, process toasted hazelnuts until finely chopped but not ground; do not overprocess.

In a large bowl with electric mixer, beat butter until creamy, about I minute. Add sugar and beat until mixture is light and fluffy, I to 2 minutes; beat in liqueur or water and vanilla extract. Gently stir in flour until just blended; then fold in chopped hazelnuts and grated or finely chopped chocolate.

Using lightly floured hands, form the dough into I ½-inch balls. Then roll the balls into 2 × ½-inch crescent shapes, and place them 2 inches apart on large ungreased baking sheets. Bake until the edges are set and the cookies are lightly golden, about 20 to 25 minutes, rotating the baking sheets from front to back halfway through cooking time. Remove from baking sheets to wire racks to cool for 10 minutes. Then, using a metal pancake turner or palette knife, carefully remove each cookie on to wire racks to cool completely. Repeat with remaining crescent shapes.

Arrange crescents on a wire rack over a baking sheet to catch drips; then dust with confectioners' sugar. Using kitchen tongs or fingers, dip half of each cookie into melted chocolate. Place on waxed paper-lined baking sheets, and refrigerate until set, 10 to 15 minutes. Store in airtight containers with waxed paper between the layers.

Austrian Crescents

This is a typical Viennese cookie. The addition of ground almonds makes the dough very short and they melt in your mouth.

MAKES ABOUT 3 DOZEN

1 stick unsalted butter, softened	**¼ tsp salt**
¼ cup superfine sugar	**¾ tsp almond extract**
1 cup all-purpose flour	**Confectioners' sugar for dusting**
½ cup slivered blanched almonds, finely ground	

Preheat oven to 325°F. Grease 2 large baking sheets.

In a large bowl, with electric mixer, beat butter until creamy, 30 seconds. On low speed, gradually beat in sugar, flour, ground almonds, salt, and almond extract, until a soft dough forms.

Using a teaspoon, scoop out dough and, using your lightly floured fingers, shape into 1 1/2-inch crescents. Place crescents 1 inch apart on baking sheets. Bake until crescents are firm and just lightly golden (cookies should be pale), about 18 to 20 minutes, rotating from top to bottom shelf and from front to back halfway through cooking time.

Remove baking sheets to wire racks to cool slightly. Then, using a metal pancake turner or palette knife, remove cookies to wire racks to cool completely. Arrange crescents on wire racks, and dust lightly with confectioners' sugar. Store in airtight containers. If you like, redust with confectioners' sugar before serving.

Light and Lemony Madeleines

Madeleines are a French cookie-cake baked in pretty shell-shaped molds. They are delicious with tea or anytime.

MAKES ABOUT 1 DOZEN

2 eggs	1 tsp baking powder
¾ cup confectioners' sugar	¾ stick unsalted butter, melted and cooled
Grated zest of 1 large lemon	
1 Tbsp lemon juice	Confectioners' sugar for dusting
1 cup plus 1 Tbsp all-purpose flour, sifted	

Preheat oven to 375°F. Butter a 12-cup madeleine mold. In a large bowl with an electric mixer, beat eggs and sugar until light and pale and a slowly falling ribbon forms when the beaters are lifted from the bowl, 5 to 7 minutes. Gently fold in lemon zest and juice.

Add baking powder to flour and, beginning and ending with flour, alternately gently fold in flour and butter in 4 or 5 batches. Allow batter to rest for 10 minutes. Spoon batter into prepared molds.

Bake until a toothpick inserted into the center of a madeleine comes out clean, 12 to 15 minutes, rotating the mold from front to back, three-quarters through cooking time. Remove from oven, and turn madeleines out onto wire rack immediately. Allow to cool completely. Dust with confectioners' sugar. Store in airtight containers.

Chocolate Madeleines

This version of the classic madeleine is made with cocoa powder for a rich chocolate flavor.

MAKES 3 DOZEN

4 Tbsp unsweetened cocoa powder (preferably Dutch-processed)	1¼ cups cake flour
	¾ tsp baking powder
3 tbsp hot water	¼ tsp salt
3 eggs	1½ sticks unsalted butter, softened
1 cup superfine sugar	
2 tsp vanilla extract	Confectioners' sugar for dusting

TIP

To cool molds quickly, run back of molds under cold running water to chill. Wipe out and rebutter molds to continue baking.

Preheat oven to 350°F. Butter a 12-cup madeleine mold. In a small bowl, dissolve cocoa powder in hot water, until completely smooth. Set aside to cool; then beat in eggs, sugar, and vanilla extract. Continue beating until mixture is light and creamy, 2 to 3 minutes.

Into a bowl, sift together flour, baking powder, and salt. Add half chocolate-egg mixture and butter, and, on low speed, beat until well blended. Increase speed to medium, and beat 1 minute more until light. Fold in remaining chocolate-egg mixture in 2 batches.

Using a small ladle or large spoon, fill madeleine cup molds almost full. Bake until a toothpick inserted in the center of the madeleine comes out clean, 10 to 12 minutes. Rotate molds from front to back halfway through.

Remove molds to a wire rack and unmold madeleines on to rack immediately. Cool molds, and repeat with remaining batter. Madeleines are best eaten within a day or two of baking, as they tend to dry out on storage. Store in airtight containers. Dust with confectioners' sugar before serving.

Light and Lemony Madeleines ▶

Almond and Pine Nut Biscotti

These dry nutty cookies are an Italian version of the German almond bread, *mandelbrot*. They are delicious with coffee or dunked in a glass of the sweet Italian wine for dessert. They keep for a long time.

ABOUT 4 DOZEN

3 cups all-purpose flour	2 eggs, lightly beaten
½ cup finely ground almonds or fine semolina	1 cup superfine sugar
1 tsp baking soda	½ cup packed light brown sugar
½ tsp salt	½ stick unsalted butter, melted and cooled
½ tsp allspice	1½ tsp almond or vanilla extract
1 tsp cinnamon	
1½ cups blanched almonds, toasted and coarsely chopped	Grated zest of 1 lemon
	Milk for glazing
¾ cup pine nuts, toasted	

Preheat oven to 375°F. Line a large baking sheet with heavy duty foil. In a large bowl, combine flour, ground almonds or semolina, baking soda, salt, allspice, cinnamon, chopped almonds, and pine nuts. In another bowl, whisk eggs until foamy, then whisk in sugars, melted butter, almond or vanilla extract, and lemon zest. Gradually stir flour mixture into egg mixture until a dough forms.

Turn out on to a lightly floured surface, and knead gently just until the nuts are evenly distributed in the dough. Divide dough into quarters, and form into even log-shapes, about 10 inches × 3 inches long.

Using a long metal palette knife, transfer each log, 2 to 3 inches apart, to a prepared baking sheet. Brush each log lightly with a little milk, and bake until golden and a toothpick comes out clean when inserted in the center, 25 to 30 minutes, rotating the baking sheet from front to back halfway through cooking time. Remove the baking sheet to a wire rack to cool, about 10 minutes. Reduce oven temperature to 325°F.

While logs are still warm and soft, with a sharp knife, score logs into ½-inch wide slices. Slide foil on to a wire rack and allow logs to cool until beginning to turn hard. Using a sharp serrated knife, cut through the logs and arrange cut-sides down, on baking sheets. You may need another large baking sheet at this point. Bake biscotti until golden and crisp, 20 to 25 minutes, turning once halfway through cooking time.

Remove on to wire racks to cool completely. Allow to cool thoroughly, about 2 to 3 hours, then store in an airtight container.

Chinese Almond Cookies

These cookies are popular in Chinese restaurants and bakeries. They were originally made with bitter almonds and lard, but you can use half butter and lard or shortening or all butter.

MAKES ABOUT 2 DOZEN

3 cups cake or paste flour	½ cup sugar
¾ tsp baking soda	2 eggs
½ tsp salt	1 tsp almond extract
1 stick plus 2 Tbsp unsalted butter, softened or use 1 stick butter and 2 Tbsp white vegetable shortening	1 egg yolk beaten with 1 Tbsp water
	Blanched almonds for decoration

Into a medium bowl with an electric mixer, beat butter or shortening until creamy, 30 seconds. Add sugar and continue beating until fluffy, 1 to 2 minutes. Beat in eggs and almond extract until blended. On low speed, beat in flour mixture until dough forms. If too soft to handle, refrigerate for 15 minutes. Divide into 4 or 5 pieces.

Preheat oven to 375°F. Lightly oil 2 large baking sheets. On a lightly floured surface, roll each piece of dough into a log shape 1 inch in diameter. Cut off 1-inch pieces and roll into small balls. Place balls on baking sheets, and using back of an oiled spoon, flatten slightly. Brush with the egg and water, then press an almond into center of each cookie.

Bake cookies until lightly colored, 8 to 10 minutes. Remove baking sheets to wire racks to cool slightly. Then, using a metal pancake turner, remove cookies to wire racks to cool completely. Repeat with remaining dough and almonds. Store in airtight containers.

Poppy Seed Pistachio Puffs

These tasty cookies are light as a feather. The flavors of poppy seed and pistachio go very well together.

MAKES ABOUT 3 DOZEN

1½ cups all-purpose flour	2 egg yolks
6 Tbsp poppy seeds	Grated zest from 2 oranges
¼ tsp salt	1½ tsp vanilla extract
2 sticks unsalted butter, softened	1 cup shelled fresh pistachios (or almonds)
¾ cup superfine sugar	

Into a bowl, combine flour, poppy seeds, and salt. In a large bowl, beat butter until creamy, 30 to 60 seconds. Add sugar and continue beating until light and fluffy, 1 to 2 minutes. Beat in egg yolks, orange zest, and vanilla extract. On low speed, gradually beat in flour mixture until soft dough forms. Scrape down sides of the bowl and refrigerate, covered, until firm, about 1 hour.

Preheat oven to 350°F. In a food processor fitted with a metal blade, process pistachios (or almonds) until very fine. (Do not overprocess or paste will form.) Turn into a small bowl. Use a tablespoon to form dough into 1½-inch balls. Drop each ball, as it is formed, into nuts, and roll to coat well. Place the coated balls, 2 inches apart, on 2 large ungreased non-stick baking sheets.

Bake until edges begin to brown, 18 to 20 minutes, rotating baking sheets from top to bottom shelf and front to back, halfway through cooking time. Remove baking sheets to wire racks to cool slightly. Then, using a thin metal palette knife, remove cookies to wire racks to cool completely. Store in airtight containers.

Kourambiedes

These rich, tender almond cookies are served at all festive occasions in Greece. At Christmas, they often bury a whole clove in the cookie to symbolize the gifts the three wise men brought to the Christ-child.

MAKES ABOUT 3 DOZEN

½ cup blanched almonds, lightly toasted and cooled	1 small egg yolk
2 sticks unsalted butter, softened	1 Tbsp brandy or orange-flavor liqueur
2 Tbsp confectioners' sugar	2 cups cake flour, sifted
¼ tsp salt	Confectioners' sugar for dusting

Preheat oven to 450°F. In a food processor fitted with metal blade, process cooled, toasted almonds until very fine crumbs form.

In a medium bowl with an electric mixer, beat butter until creamy, 30 seconds. Gradually add sugar and continue beating until light and fluffy, 1 to 2 minutes. Beat in salt, egg yolk, and brandy. On low speed, gradually beat in cake flour and ground almonds until a soft dough forms. Scrape the bowl and refrigerate until firm, about 1 hour.

Use a tablespoon to scoop out dough, and form into 1-inch balls. Place on ungreased baking sheets, and bake until set and just golden, 15 to 20 minutes. Remove baking sheets to racks to cool slightly. Then, using a metal pancake turner or palette knife, remove cookies to wire racks to cool completely. Dust with confectioners' sugar. Store in airtight containers.

Rich Cardamom Cookies

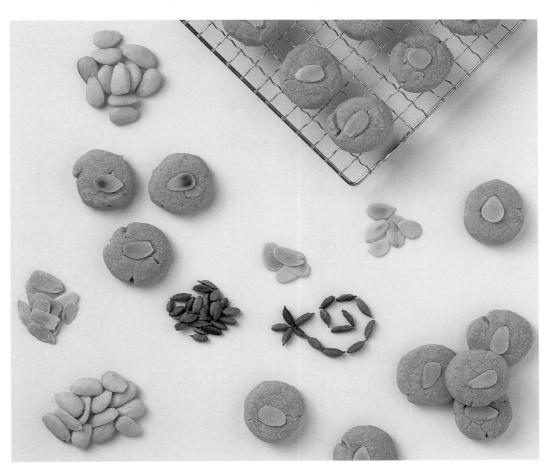

These rich butter cookies are flavored with cardamom, a favorite Scandinavian spice.

MAKES ABOUT 2 DOZEN

2 cups cake flour	½ cup sliced or flaked almonds
4 tsp ground cardamom	
¼ tsp salt	**TO DECORATE**
1½ sticks unsalted butter, softened	⅓ cup confectioners' sugar
	1½ tsp cardamom
½ cup superfine sugar	Sliced or flaked almonds

Preheat oven to 375°F. Grease 2 large baking sheets. Into a medium bowl, sift flour, cardamom, and salt.

In a large bowl with electric mixer, beat butter until creamy, 30 seconds. Gradually add sugar and continue beating until light and fluffy, 1 to 2 minutes. On low speed, gradually beat in flour mixture until well blended; then stir in sliced or flaked almonds.

Into a small bowl, sift together confectioners' sugar and cardamom. Using a tablespoon, scoop out dough and roll into 1½-inch balls. Drop balls one at a time into sugar-spice mixture, rolling to coat well. Place 1½ inches apart on baking sheets. Dip the bottom of a glass into the sugar mixture, and flatten cookies to ½-inch thick rounds. Press 2 or 3 almonds on to tops of cookies.

Bake cookies until golden brown, 12 to 14 minutes, rotating baking sheets from top to bottom shelf and from front to back halfway through cooking time. Remove baking sheets to wire racks to cool, 2 to 3 minutes. Then, using a thin metal palette knife, remove cookies to wire racks to cool completely. Store in airtight containers.

Refrigerator Cookies

Chocolate and Vanilla Pinwheels

Lemon Wafers

Belgian Almond Cookies

Cashew Butter Rounds

Poppy Seed Swirls

Chocolate-ginger Freezer Cookies

Chocolate and Vanilla Pinwheels

Be careful not to overbake these pretty pinwheels or the color contrast could be lost.

MAKES ABOUT 5 DOZEN

3 cups all-purpose flour

½ tsp salt

2 sticks unsalted butter, softened

1 cup superfine sugar

2 eggs, lightly beaten

2 tsp vanilla extract

1 oz unsweetened chocolate, melted and cooled

1 Into a medium bowl, sift together flour and salt, In a large bowl with an electric mixer, beat butter until creamy, 30 to 60 seconds. Add the sugar and continue beating until light and fluffy, 1 to 2 minutes. Beat in the eggs and vanilla extract until blended. On low speed, beat in the flour until well blended.

2 Divide dough in half, and wrap one half in plastic wrap; refrigerate until firm enough to roll. Add melted chocolate to remaining dough in bowl, and mix until completely blended. Wrap chocolate dough in plastic wrap, and refrigerate until firm enough to roll.

3 On a lightly floured surface or between 2 sheets of plastic wrap or waxed paper, roll half the vanilla dough to a ¼-inch thick, 4-inch wide rectangle. Repeat with half the chocolate dough, rolling to the same size.

4 If rolling between sheets of waxed paper, remove the top sheet and turn chocolate dough over on to vanilla dough; roll lightly to seal. Roll up dough, jelly-roll fashion, as tightly as possible. Wrap tightly in plastic wrap, and repeat with remaining doughs. Refrigerate dough rolls for several hours or overnight until firm. (Dough can be prepared ahead up to 5 days or frozen.)

5 Preheat the oven to 375°F. Lightly grease 2 large baking sheets. Using a sharp knife, cut dough rolls into ¼-inch slices, and place 1 inch apart on prepared baking sheets. Bake until just beginning to color, 7 to 10 minutes. Using a metal pancake turner or palette knife, remove cookies to wire racks to cool.

Lemon Wafers

These thin, delicate cookies have a lovely lemon flavor. They are melt-in-the-mouth light and perfect to serve with fruit sorbets.

MAKES ABOUT 50

1½ cups all-purpose flour	1 cup superfine sugar
½ tsp baking powder	½ tsp vanilla extract
½ tsp baking soda	¾ tsp lemon extract
¼ tsp salt	Grated zest and juice of 1 lemon
½ cup white vegetable shortening, softened	Confectioners' sugar for dusting
2 Tbsp unsalted butter, softened	

Into a medium bowl, sift together the flour, baking powder, baking soda, and salt; set aside.

In a large bowl with electric mixer, beat shortening and butter until creamy, 30 to 60 seconds. Gradually add sugar and continue beating until light and fluffy, 1 to 2 minutes. Beat in vanilla and lemon extracts, and grated lemon zest and juice. Stir in flour until soft dough forms.

Scrape dough on to a piece of plastic wrap or waxed paper, and, using this as a guide, form dough into a log about 1½ inches in diameter. Wrap tightly, and refrigerate several hours or overnight until very firm. (Dough can be made up to 5 days ahead or frozen.)

Preheat oven to 350°F. Slice log crosswise into ⅛-inch slices, or as thin as possible, and place dough rounds 2 inches apart on 2 large non-stick baking sheets. Bake until golden around the edges but still pale in the center, about 8 minutes. Remove baking sheets to wire racks to cool slightly. Then, using a metal pancake turner or palette knife, remove cookies to wire racks to cool completely. Before serving dust cookies with confectioners' sugar. Store in airtight containers.

> **TIP**
> *Do not allow cookies to cool on baking sheets or they will be too crisp to remove.*

Belgian Almond Cookies

This is a traditional cookie found in Belgium. The dough log has been rolled in chopped almonds for a prettier effect.

MAKES ABOUT 3 DOZEN

3 Tbsp unsalted butter	¼ tsp salt
¼ cup milk	1 cup grated or very finely chopped blanched almonds
2 Tbsp brandy	
2 cups all-purpose flour	½ cup packed light brown sugar
½ tsp baking powder	
¾ tsp ground cinnamon	1 cup chopped blanched almonds

In a small saucepan over low heat, melt butter. Remove from heat and cool slightly. Stir in milk and brandy; set aside.

Into a large bowl, sift together flour, baking powder, cinnamon, and salt. Stir in grated or finely chopped almonds and sugar. Stir in butter mixture to form a soft dough. (If dough is too soft, add a little more flour.)

Scrape dough on to a piece of plastic wrap or waxed paper, and using wrap or paper as a guide, form dough into a 2-inch roll. Chill dough 5 to 10 minutes. Sprinkle chopped blanched almonds on a work surface, and roll dough log in almonds to coat, pressing almonds into surface. Rewrap log, and refrigerate for several hours or overnight until firm.

Preheat oven to 375°F. Lightly grease 2 large baking sheets. Cut log crosswise into ½-inch slices, and place 1 inch apart on prepared baking sheets. Bake until golden, about 10 minutes. Remove baking sheets to wire racks to cool slightly. Then, using a metal pancake turner or palette knife, remove cookies to wire racks to cool completely. Store in airtight containers.

Cashew Butter Rounds

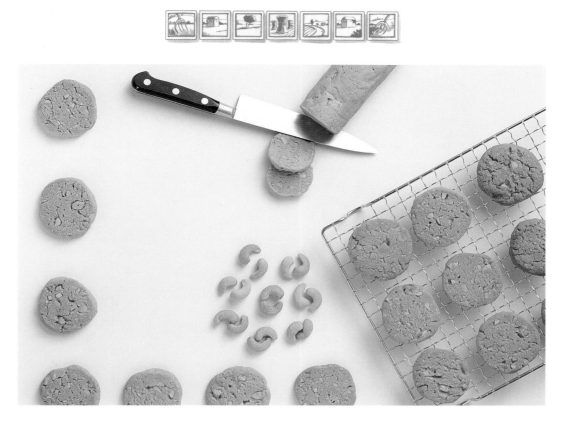

These delicious cookies are enriched by the "cashew butter." A food processor is necessary to make the cashew butter, although it can be bought at some health food stores.

MAKES ABOUT 4½ DOZEN

1 cup unsalted roasted cashews	½ cup packed light or dark brown sugar
2 Tbsp vegetable oil	1 egg
1⅔ cups all-purpose flour	2 Tbsp rum or brandy
1 tsp baking soda	1 tsp vanilla extract
½ tsp salt	1 cup chopped roasted cashews
1 stick unsalted butter, softened	½ cup old-fashioned oats
½ cup sugar	

TIP

Cookie dough can be refrigerated for up to 5 days or frozen. Defrost overnight in refrigerator before using. Cut off as many slices as you require for baking at one time.

In a food processor fitted with a metal blade, process cashews and oil until a thick, smooth paste forms, just like peanut butter. Into a medium bowl, sift together flour, baking soda, and salt; set aside.

In a large bowl with an electric mixer, beat butter until creamy, 30 seconds. Add sugars and beat until light and fluffy, 1 to 2 minutes. Beat in egg, cashew butter, rum or brandy, and vanilla extract until well blended.

On a low speed, gradually beat in the flour mixture until a soft dough is formed. Stir in the chopped nuts and oats. On a lightly floured surface, form the dough into two 2-inch logs. Wrap each log tightly in plastic wrap, and then refrigerate for 4 to 6 hours, or overnight until the dough becomes very firm.

Preheat oven to 350°F. Lightly grease 2 large baking sheets. Cut dough log crosswise into ⅜-inch slices, and place slices 1 inch apart on baking sheets. Bake until golden, 10 to 12 minutes. Remove baking sheets to wire racks to cool slightly. Then, using a metal pancake turner or palette knife, remove to wire racks to cool completely. Repeat with the remaining dough as cookies are required. Store in airtight containers.

Poppy Seed Swirls

Poppy seeds form the basis of the filling in these crisp cookie swirls.

MAKES ABOUT 4 DOZEN

½ cup walnut pieces, finely ground	¾ stick unsalted butter, softened
½ cup poppy seeds	½ cup superfine sugar
⅓ cup honey	I egg, lightly beaten
½ tsp ground cinnamon	I tsp vanilla extract
Grated zest of I orange	I½ cups all-purpose flour

In a small bowl, combine walnuts, poppy seeds, honey, cinnamon, orange zest, and 2 tablespoons of the softened butter until mixture forms a paste. Set aside.

In a large bowl with electric mixer, beat remaining butter and sugar until light and fluffy, 1 to 2 minutes. Beat in egg and vanilla extract until well-blended, then slowly beat in flour until a soft dough forms. Refrigerate dough until firm enough to handle, 15 to 20 minutes.

On a lightly floured sheet of waxed paper or non-stick baking parchment, roll out dough to a 6 x 12 inch rectangle and spread with poppy seed paste. Starting at one short side, roll up dough jelly-roll fashion and wrap tightly. Refrigerate several hours or overnight until firm. (Dough can be refrigerated up to 5 days or frozen.)

Preheat oven to 375°F. Lightly grease 2 large non-stick baking sheets. Slice dough roll crosswise into ¼-inch slices and place ½ inch apart on baking sheets. Bake until golden, about 10 minutes. Remove baking sheets to wire racks to cool slightly. Then, using a metal pancake turner or palette knife, remove cookies to wire racks to cool completely. Repeat with remaining slices. Store in airtight containers.

Chocolate-ginger Freezer Cookies

The combination of chocolate and ginger is a wonderful one. These cookies use fresh ginger root and have a definite zing!

MAKES ABOUT 3 DOZEN

2- to 3-inch pieces of fresh ginger root	2 sticks unsalted butter, softened
1½ cups all-purpose flour	1 cup packed dark brown sugar
2 Tbsp unsweetened cocoa powder (preferably Dutch-processed)	2 egg yolks
	2 tsp vanilla extract
1 cup whole wheat flour	12 oz bittersweet or semi-sweet chocolate, chopped
½ tsp salt	
¼ tsp finely ground black pepper	Crystallized ginger to decorate

Using the small round holes of a box grater, grate ginger root; set aside. Into a medium bowl, sift together all-purpose flour and cocoa powder. Stir in whole wheat flour, salt and pepper.

In a large bowl with electric mixer, beat butter until creamy, 30 seconds. Add brown sugar and continue beating until light and fluffy, 1 to 2 minutes. Beat in egg yolks, vanilla extract, and grated ginger root until the mixture is smooth and well-blended. Stir in the flour mixture until blended.

Scrape out on to a piece of plastic wrap, and, using wrap as a guide, shape dough into a 3-inch log. Wrap tightly and freeze until hard. (Dough can be frozen for up to 2 months.)

Preheat oven to 350°F. Line 2 large baking sheets with non-stick baking parchment. Using a sharp knife, cut frozen dough log into ¼-inch slices, and place 1 inch apart on baking sheets.

Bake until lightly colored, about 15 minutes, rotating baking sheets from top to bottom shelf and from front to back halfway through cooking time. Remove baking sheets to wire rack to cool, about 1 minute. then, using a metal pancake turner or palette knife, carefully remove each cookie to wire racks to cool completely.

Place chopped chocolate in a bowl over a pan of simmering water. Stir until melted and smooth. Remove chocolate from heat, and set aside to cool, stirring occasionally. When chocolate reaches a spreading consistency, use a small palette knife to spread a little on each cookie. Top each cookie with a piece of crystallized ginger, and allow cookies to set. Store cookies in airtight containers with waxed paper between layers.

> **TIP**
>
> *A food processor is ideal for grating or puréeing the fresh ginger root.*

Rolled Cookies

Chocolate-orange Hearts

Shrewsbury Biscuits

Chocolate Macadamia Windmills

Anise-flavor Sugar Hearts

Golden Gingerbread

Gingerbread Men and Women

Chocolate-orange Hearts

These stunning cookies can be made in any shape—you need three cutters of the same shape: about a 3¼-, 2⅛-, and a 1-inch.

MAKES ABOUT 2½ DOZEN

2 oz semi-sweet chocolate, chopped	¾ cup sugar
2¼ cups all-purpose flour	1 egg
1½ tsp baking powder	1 tsp vanilla extract
¼ tsp salt	Grated zest of 1 orange
1½ sticks unsalted butter, softened	1 Tbsp orange juice
	Superfine sugar for sprinkling

In a small bowl over a saucepan of simmering water, melt chocolate until smooth. Set aside to cool.

Into a medium bowl, sift together flour, baking powder, and salt. In a large bowl with electric mixer, beat butter and sugar until light and creamy, 1 to 2 minutes. Beat in egg, vanilla extract, orange zest, and juice until well-blended. On low speed, beat in flour until soft dough forms. Remove half the dough, and wrap tightly in plastic wrap; refrigerate until firm, about 2 hours.

With the mixer on low speed, beat melted, cooled chocolate into the dough remaining in the bowl. Wrap in plastic wrap, and refrigerate until firm.

Grease and flour 2 or more large baking sheets. On a lightly floured surface, using a floured rolling pin, roll out half the orange-flavor dough ⅛ inch thick (keep the remaining dough refrigerated). With a floured, 3¼-inch heart-shaped cutter, cut out as many hearts as possible. Place ½ inch apart on a baking sheet and refrigerate. Repeat with chocolate dough, cutting an equal number of chocolate hearts, and place on another baking sheet. Refrigerate until all cut-outs are firm, about 20 minutes.

Preheat the oven to 350°F. With a 2⅛-inch floured heart-shaped cutter, carefully cut another heart from the center of each 3¼-inch heart. Place smaller orange hearts in larger chocolate hearts and smaller chocolate hearts in larger orange hearts. With a 1-inch heart-shaped cutter, cut small hearts from the center of each cookie, and place small orange hearts into medium chocolate hearts, and small chocolate hearts into medium orange hearts.

Sprinkle cookies with a little superfine sugar. Bake cookies until golden, about 10 minutes. Remove baking sheets to wire racks to cool slightly. Then remove cookies to wire racks to cool completely.

Shrewsbury Biscuits

This traditionally English cookie is flavored with sherry and speckled with dried currants, then dredged with superfine sugar—perfect with tea.

MAKES ABOUT 3 DOZEN

2 sticks unsalted butter, softened	1 tsp caraway seeds, lightly crushed (optional)
1 cup superfine sugar	½ cup dried currants
1 egg, beaten	1 to 1¼ cups all-purpose flour, sifted
¼ cup heavy cream	Superfine sugar for sprinkling
1 Tbsp dry sherry	

In a large bowl with an electric mixer, beat butter and sugar until light and creamy, 1 to 2 minutes. Beat in egg, cream, sherry, caraway seeds if using, and currants. Stir in flour until soft dough forms.

Scrape dough on to a piece of plastic wrap or waxed paper and, using wrap or paper as a guide, shape into flat disk and refrigerate until firm, about 1 hour.

Preheat oven to 350°F. Lightly grease 2 large baking sheets. On a lightly floured surface, using a floured rolling pin, roll dough out ¼ inch thick. With a 2½-inch fluted cutter, cut out as many rounds as possible. If you like, reroll trimmings, and cut out more rounds. Place rounds 1 inch apart on prepared baking sheets.

Brush top of cookies with a little water, and sprinkle with a little superfine sugar. Bake until crisp and golden, 15 to 20 minutes. Remove baking sheets to wire racks to cool slightly. Then, using a metal pancake turner, remove cookies to wire racks to cool completely. Store in airtight containers.

TIP

Cookie dough is easier to handle when chilled. If dough becomes too soft to handle, return it to the refrigerator for a few minutes to firm.

Chocolate Macadamia Windmills

T hese rolled-shaped cookies are rich, yet delicate, and easy to make.

MAKES ABOUT 3 DOZEN

2½ cups all-purpose flour	½ cup superfine sugar
2 tbsp unsweetened cocoa powder	1 egg, lightly beaten
2½ tsp baking powder	2 tbsp light corn syrup
½ tsp salt	½ cup finely chopped macadamia nuts
1 stick unsalted butter, softened	3 oz semi-sweet chocolate, melted

Into a medium bowl, sift together flour, cocoa powder, baking powder, and salt.

In a large bowl with an electric mixer, beat butter and sugar until light and creamy, 1 to 2 minutes. Beat in egg and syrup until blended; then the flour mixture. Turn dough on to lightly floured surface, and knead until smooth. Wrap in plastic wrap or waxed paper, and refrigerate until firm enough to roll, about 30 minutes.

Preheat oven to 350°F. Lightly grease 2 large baking sheets. On a lightly floured surface, using a floured rolling pin, roll out half the dough ⅛-inch thick (keep remaining dough refrigerated). Using a floured 3½-inch round or square cutter, cut as many rounds or squares as possible.

Place cut-outs on baking sheet. Beginning at outside edge, make 4 radial cuts almost to center forming quarters (if a square cutter has been used, cut from each corner). Fold left corner of each quarter to center, and press to seal, forming a windmill shape. Sprinkle center with nuts.

Bake until firm, about 10 minutes. Remove baking sheets to wire racks to cool slightly. Using a metal pancake turner or palette knife, remove cookies to wire racks to cool completely. Repeat with remaining dough and trimmings.

Spoon melted chocolate into paper cone and drizzle chocolate in zig-zag pattern over each windmill cookie. Allow chocolate to set. Store cookies in airtight containers with waxed paper between layers.

Anise-flavor Sugar Hearts

These anise-flavor sugar cookies can be cut into any shape.

MAKES ABOUT 2 DOZEN

3 cups all-purpose flour	I cup sugar
¾ tsp baking powder	I egg
¼ tsp salt	2 Tbsp whipping cream
I½ tsp aniseed, finely chopped	I tsp vanilla extract
2½ sticks unsalted butter, softened	Confectioners' sugar for dusting

> **TIP**
>
> *For a delicious dessert, sandwich two heart cookies with anise-scented whipped cream, and top with a few raspberries or blueberries; dust with confectioners' sugar.*

Into a medium bowl, sift together flour, baking powder, and salt. Stir in chopped aniseed; set aside.

In a large bowl with an electric mixer, beat butter until creamy. Add sugar and continue beating until light and fluffy. Beat in egg, cream, and vanilla extract until blended. Stir in flour mixture, until blended.

Scrape dough on to piece of plastic wrap and, using wrap as guide, shape into flat disk. Wrap tightly, and refrigerate until firm enough to roll out, 30 minutes.

Preheat oven to 350°F. Lightly butter 2 large baking sheets. On a lightly floured surface, using a floured rolling pin, roll out half the dough about ¼-inch thick. Using a 3½- or 4-inch heart-shaped floured cookie cutter, cut out as many cookies as possible. Transfer hearts to prepared baking sheets 1 inch apart.

Bake cookies until they are set and edges are golden, about 8 minutes. Remove baking sheets to wire racks to cool slightly. Then remove cookies to wire racks to cool. Dust cooled cookies with confectioners' sugar.

Golden Gingerbread

If a darker-colored gingerbread is desired, then replace half or all of the syrup with molasses. Be sure to measure the syrup or molasses accurately with measuring spoons or the dough might spread when it is baked.

SERVES 4

3 cups all-purpose flour	I stick butter
2 tsp ground ginger	¾ cup soft brown sugar
I tsp ground cinnamon	4 Tbsp dark corn syrup
½ tsp baking soda	I egg, beaten

Preheat oven to 375°F. Sift the flour, spices, and baking soda into a bowl. Blend in the butter with the fingers until the mixture resembles fine crumbs.

Stir in the sugar. In a saucepan, warm the syrup to make it runny. Add the syrup and the beaten egg to the flour mixture; mix to a soft dough. If it is too sticky, add a little more flour. Knead the dough lightly until smooth.

Roll out as desired. If the dough is rolled out too thinly, a crisp texture will be obtained. If rolled out thickly, a softer texture will result. Most items will take 8 to 10 minutes to cook. Smaller items will need less time and large pieces will take slightly longer.

Gingerbread Men and Women

Everyone loves gingerbread men and women. Keep them plain and simple, or add more detail using glazing.

MINI-PEOPLE GIFT BOX COOKIES

Golden Gingerbread dough

Royal glaze, coating and piping consistency

Red food coloring

Tiny gingerbread people cutters

 Roll out the dough and cut out the mini-people with cutter or template. Carefully remove the excess dough.

Bake for about 8 minutes. Cool completely.

Divide the coating royal glaze in half. Color one half of the coating glaze with red food coloring. Place the cookies on a wire rack.

Coat half the cookies with the red glaze and the other half with the plain white glaze. Allow to dry.

Divide the royal glaze for piping in half. Color one half of the piping glaze with red food coloring. Using a small plain writing tip, pipe features and outline clothes in red glaze on all the white figures. Using white royal glaze, pipe features and outline clothes on all the red people. Let dry.

Pressed and Piped Cookies

Apricot Thumbprints

Vanilla Rings

Viennese Chocolate Cookies

May Day Cookies

Chocolate Amaretti

Florentines

Gingersnaps

Almond Tile Cookies

Pizzelles

Apricot Thumbprints

These classic cookies get their name from the method of using a thumb to create a round depression. The hole can be filled with any preserves you like.

MAKES ABOUT 4½ DOZEN

1½ sticks unsalted butter, softened

½ cup sugar

2 eggs, lightly beaten

1 tsp vanilla extract

½ tsp ground cinnamon

¼ tsp salt

2 cups all-purpose flour

⅔ cup apricot preserves or other favorite preserves or jelly

TIP

For a more colorful selection, use 2 or more different flavor preserves, such as apricot, raspberry, and grape jelly.

Preheat oven to 400°F. In a large bowl with electric mixer, beat butter until creamy, 30 seconds. Add sugar and beat until light and fluffy, 1 to 2 minutes. Gradually beat in eggs, vanilla extract, cinnamon, and salt. Stir in flour until soft dough forms.

Spoon dough into a large decorating bag fitted with a plain ½-inch tip. Pipe 1½-inch rounds, 1 inch apart, on 2 large ungreased baking sheets. Press lightly floured thumb into center of each round, making a deep depression.

Bake cookies until golden, 7 to 10 minutes. Remove baking sheets to wire racks to cool slightly. Then, using a metal pancake turner, remove cookies to wire racks to cool completely.

In a small saucepan over low heat, heat apricot preserves until just beginning to bubble. Using a small teaspoon, spoon a little apricot preserve into each indentation while cookies are still warm. Allow cookies and jelly to set and cool completely. Store in airtight containers in single layers.

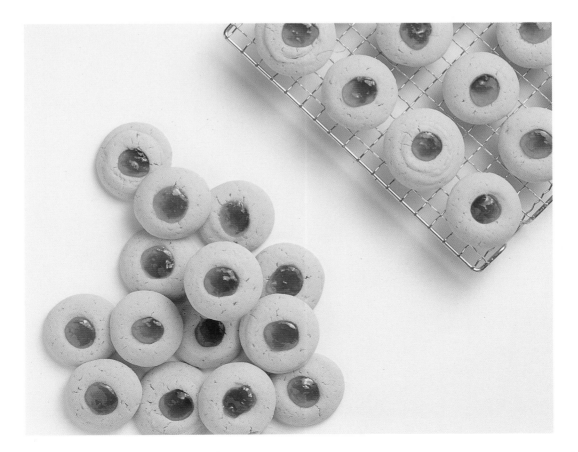

Vanilla Rings

Danish cookies and cakes are both rich and artistic. They deserve the place of honor on the coffee table.

MAKES 20 RINGS

1 cup butter	2 tsp vanilla extract
1 cup sugar	¾ cup ground almonds
1 egg	3 cups flour

Preheat the oven to 350°F. Cream the butter and sugar in a bowl, or use a food processor on a low speed, until light and fluffy. Beat in the egg, then the vanilla extract, almonds, and flour.

Put the paste into a decorating bag fitted with a star-shaped tip. Pipe 2-inch rings on to a greased baking sheet. Bake for 8 to 9 minutes.

Viennese Chocolate Cookies

These elegant little cookies originate from Vienna, where they would be served with tea or coffee.

MAKES ABOUT 20

2 sticks butter or margarine	powder
½ cup confectioners' sugar, sifted	3 Tbsp cornstarch
2⅓ cups all-purpose flour	4 oz plain chocolate
2 Tbsp unsweetened cocoa	Confectioners' sugar

VARIATION

To make chocolate gems pipe mixture into small individual star shapes. Bake for about half the time. Place a chocolate button in the center of each one while still hot.

Preheat oven to 350°F. Cream together the butter or margarine and sugar until light and fluffy. Work in the flour, cocoa powder and cornstarch.

Put the mixture into a decorating bag fitted with a large star tip. Pipe in fingers, or shells, or "s" shapes on to greased baking sheets. Bake in the oven for 20 to 25 minutes. Cool on a wire rack.

Melt the chocolate. Dip half of each cookie into the chocolate and leave to set on non-stick (waxed) paper.

Dust the uncoated halves of the cookies with confectioners' sugar.

May Day Cookies

In Scandinavia May Day is carnival time, which starts on the eve of April 30th. Lots of singing and balloons signal the arrival of spring.

MAKES 20–30

2 eggs	1–2 tsp vanilla extract
2 tsp sugar	1 cup vegetable or coconut oil for frying
1 tsp salt	
1 cup milk	Confectioners' sugar for dusting
3½ cups flour	

Gently mix the eggs and sugar together. Add all the remaining ingredients, and stir until the batter is smooth. Put the batter into a decorating bag fitted with a small tip. Heat the oil in a pan. Squeeze the batter into the pan of hot oil, making a nest-like shape. Use a metal ring in the pan, if possible, to keep the shape better during cooking. Remove the cookies when they are golden brown. Drain and cool on paper towels. When cold, dust the cookies with confectioners' sugar.

Chocolate Amaretti

These delicious macaroon-like cookies combine the flavors of chocolate and almond. They are surprisingly easy to make, and ideal with an espresso coffee!

MAKES ABOUT 2 DOZEN

1 cup blanched whole almonds	2 egg whites
½ cup superfine sugar	⅛ tsp cream of tartar
1 Tbsp unsweetened cocoa powder, preferably Dutch-processed	½ tsp vanilla extract
	½ tsp almond extract
2 tbsp confectioners' sugar	Confectioners' sugar for dusting

Preheat oven to 350°F. Spread almonds on a small baking sheet, and toast until golden and fragrant, 7 to 10 minutes, cool completely. Reduce oven temperature to 325°F. Line a large baking sheet with non-stick baking parchment or lightly greased foil.

In a food processor fitted with metal blade, process almonds with 2 tablespoons of the superfine sugar until finely ground, but not oily. Add cocoa powder and confectioners' sugar, and, using pulse action, process to blend well.

In a medium bowl, beat egg whites, until foamy. Add cream of tartar and continue beating until stiff peaks form. Sprinkle in remaining superfine sugar, a tablespoon at a time, beating well after each addition until whites are stiff and glossy. Beat in vanilla and almond extracts; then gently fold in almond-cocoa mixture until just blended.

Spoon mixture into a large decorating bag fitted with a medium plain ½-inch tip. Pipe 1½-inch mounds 1 inch apart on prepared baking sheets.

Bake until cookies are firm on top when touched with fingertip and surface is slightly crisp, 12 to 15 minutes. Remove baking sheets to wire racks to cool slightly. Then, using a metal pancake turner, remove cookies to wire racks to cool completely. Dust with confectioners' sugar and store in airtight containers.

Florentines

Austrian bakers usually get the credit for inventing these cookies, despite their Italian name. Whatever their origin, they're utterly delicious.

MAKES ABOUT 8–10

½ **stick butter**	**2 Tbsp raisins, chopped**
¼ **cup sugar**	**1½ Tbsp candied cherries, washed and chopped**
4 Tbsp all-purpose flour, sifted	**Zest of ½ lemon, finely grated**
⅓ **cup almonds, blanched and chopped**	**4 oz plain chocolate**
½ **cup candied peel, chopped**	

Preheat oven to 350°F. Then line the baking trays with waxed paper.

Put the butter and sugar into a pan and gently heat them together until melted. Remove the pan from the heat and stir in the flour. Add the almonds, peel, raisins, cherries, and lemon zest. Stir well.

Put teaspoonfuls of the mixture well apart on the baking sheets. Bake in the oven for about 10 minutes or until golden brown.

While still warm press the edges of the cookies back to a neat shape. Leave to cool on the baking sheets until set. Carefully lift florentines on to a wire rack.

Melt the chocolate. Spread over the smooth sides of the florentines. As the chocolate begins to set, mark into wavy lines with a fork. Leave to set.

Gingersnaps

This is a regional variation of the more commonly known "Brandy Snap."

MAKES ABOUT 4 DOZEN

1¼ cups all-purpose flour	½ stick butter
1 tsp ground ginger	⅔ cup dark corn syrup
1 tsp ground cinnamon	3 Tbsp molasses
½ tsp ground mace	2 cups superfine sugar
Grated zest ½ lemon	

Preheat oven to 350°F. Sift the flour and spices into a bowl. Stir in the lemon zest. Melt the butter, syrup, molasses, and sugar together in a pan. Pour the liquid into the flour mixture and blend until it is a soft dropping consistency.

Drop teaspoonfuls of the mixture on to a greased baking sheet. Leave room between the cookies to allow for spreading.

Bake for about 7 to 10 minutes. Allow to cool for 1 to 2 minutes, then loosen with a thin metal palette knife. Roll the still soft "pancakes" around a greased wooden spoon handle. Leave until set, then twist the gingersnaps gently to remove.

If the biscuits cool too much while still on the sheet, return to the oven for a moment to soften them. Serve filled with whipped cream.

Almond Tile Cookies

These are one of the most popular French cookies—tuiles aux amandes—so called because they resemble the curved roof tiles seen all over France.

MAKES ABOUT 2½ DOZEN

½ cup whole blanched almonds, lightly toasted

½ cup superfine sugar

3 Tbsp unsalted butter, softened

2 egg whites

½ tsp almond extract

¼ cup cake flour, sifted

¾ cup flaked almonds

In a food processor fitted with metal blade, process toasted almonds with 2 tablespoons of the sugar until fine crumbs form. Pour into a small bowl; set aside.

Preheat oven to 400°F. Generously butter 2 baking sheets. In a medium bowl with electric mixer, beat butter until creamy, 30 seconds. Add remaining sugar, and beat until light and fluffy, 1 minute. Gradually beat in egg whites and almond extract until well-blended. Sift over already sifted flour, and fold into butter mixture; then fold in reserved almond-sugar mixture.

Begin by working in batches of 4 cookies on each sheet. Drop tablespoonfuls of batter about 6 inches apart on a baking sheet. With the back of a moistened spoon, spread each mound of batter into very thin 3-inch rounds. Each round should be transparent. If you make a few holes, the batter will spread and fill them in. Sprinkle tops with some flaked almonds.

Bake, one sheet at a time, until the edges are browned and centers just golden, 4 to 5 minutes. Remove the baking sheet to a wire rack and, working quickly, use a thin-bladed metal palette knife to loosen the edge of a hot cookie and transfer to a rolling pin or glass tumbler. Gently press sides down to shape each cookie.

If cookies become too firm to transfer, return the baking sheet to the oven for 30 seconds to soften, then proceed as above. When cool, transfer immediately to airtight containers in single layers. These cookies are fragile.

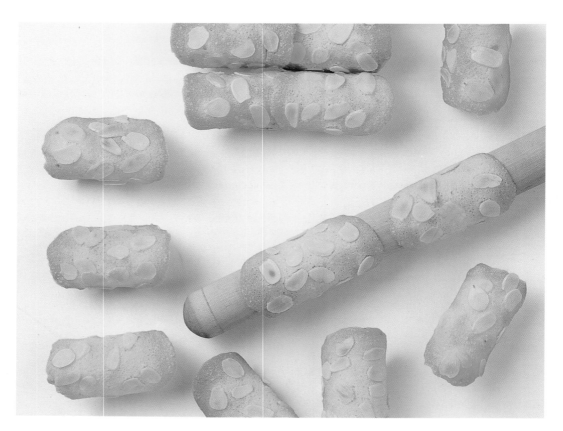

Pizzelles

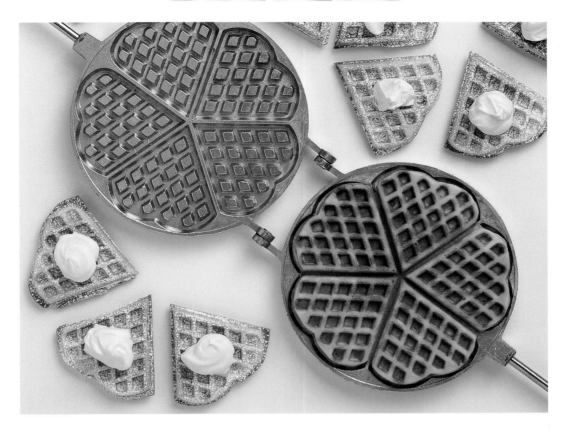

T hese Italian cookies are really like little waffles. Use any shape waffle iron you like, but heart shape is prettiest.

MAKES ABOUT 4 DOZEN

1¾ cups all-purpose flour	1 stick unsalted butter, melted
2 tsp baking powder	
½ tsp salt	2 Tbsp anise flavor or vanilla extract
3 eggs, lightly beaten	
¾ cup sugar	Confectioners' sugar for dusting

Preheat a 7-inch electric pizzelle or other waffle iron as the manufacturer directs. Into a large bowl, sift together the flour, baking powder, and salt.

Make a well in the center of flour mixture, and pour in eggs, sugar, melted butter, and anise flavor or vanilla extract. With an electric mixer on low speed, beat liquid ingredients until blended, then slowly incorporate flour from edge of well until it is all blended and mixture is smooth. (If batter is too thick, thin with a little milk or water.)

Using a small ladle, pour about 2 tablespoons of batter into the center of the pizzelle iron. Pull down the cover and allow to bake, without lifting the cover, for manufacturers' specified time.

Lift cover, and use a metal palette knife or fork to lift edge of pizzelle. Slide on to wire rack to cool completely. Repeat with remaining batter. Dust pizzelles with confectioners' sugar. Store in airtight containers. Alternatively, keep pizzelles warm in a 250°F oven, and serve dusted with confectioners' sugar and with a little preserve or maple syrup.

TIP

Pizzelle irons and waffle irons are available in electric and non-electric models and in different shapes and sizes. Be sure to follow each manufacturers' instructions for use and cooking times.

Meringues and Soufflés

This section is about the wonderful baking properties of whisked egg whites. Meringues combine the egg white with sugar to make a powdery light cookie or a foamy topping for tarts, deceptively simple but wickedly good. Some believe that soufflés are difficult to make, but once the principles are explained, they are easily mastered. They make excellent family meals or equally may be served to impress at dinner parties.

INTRODUCTION

Egg Whites

The chief joy of the egg white is that it will hold amazing quantities of air (8 times its own volume) when whisked. As it is practically tasteless, it is the ideal for both sweet and non-sweet dishes.

Whisking and Folding

The best method of getting the maximum volume of air into egg whites is to use a steel balloon whisk in a copper bowl. The copper reacts with the egg white (especially if a little vinegar or lemon juice is added—which is why copper bowls are often wiped out with a cut lemon before whisking) and a mass of chains or tunnels of small stable air bubbles are produced. An electric whisk works faster, but produces bigger bubbles that burst and disintegrate faster. But the difference is not vital—perfectly good whisked egg white can be produced by machine, and in commercial kitchens today copper bowls are not used as much as chefs and catering colleges

would have us believe. Apart from being very hard work, copper bowls have another disadvantage—the egg white frequently discolors as a result of the contact with the copper, and even when the bowl is assiduously cleaned beforehand the egg whites will often look greenish gray. But this color disappears on cooking, and is nothing to worry about.

If using an electric machine, hand whisk or mixer, a metal bowl with the machine running at half pace produces the best results. Rapidly whisked white produced in a glass or ceramic bowl will be the least voluminous, and the least likely to hold their air for any length of time. But even whites whisked like this, if they are immediately incorporated into soufflés, cakes, or mousses, are perfectly adequate.

Raw egg whites are used in cooking at all stages from un-whisked to whisked until stiff and dry.
Un-whisked As they come from the shell. Used to paint rose or geranium petals if making crystallized petals. The egg white must not be at all frothy or the coating will be bubbly. Perfect dry fresh petals are painted on both sides with the egg white. The petal

Frothy egg whites—the first stage of the whisking process.

Egg whites whisked until soft peaks form.

is then dusted lightly on both sides with superfine sugar and left on a sheet of waxed paper in a warm room (or above the boiler or heater) for about 24 hours until dry and brittle, when they can be stored in an airtight container or used at once for cake or pudding decoration. They must be fully dried out before storing or they will soften and go moldy.

Frothy Whisked, usually with a fork, just enough to mix them and prevent them plopping out of the jug separately. This makes them easier to add gradually to mixtures.

Soft peak Whisked until the egg white will just hold its shape when the whisk is lifted, the points that are dragged up by the rising action are flopping over softly. Used to add to fairly liquid mixtures such as batters or whipped cream.

Medium peak Whisked until the egg white will stand in peaks when the whisk is lifted, but with the tips of the peaks just flopping over like wilted leaves. For incorporating in soft mixtures such as soufflés, creams, and sorbets. The idea is to have the two mixtures combining as close to each other in consistency as possible. It can be difficult to add over-whisked (too stiff and too dry) egg whites to a very soft chocolate mousse mixture—the egg whites break up into islands of foam and by the time the cook has stirred and struggled to get the mixture mixed most of that carefully incorporated air has been knocked out.

Stiff peak Whisked until the egg white will stand up in rigid peaks (not floppy) peaks when the whisk is lifted. Used mainly for meringues, at which point the sugar is added.

Holding egg whites If stiffly-whisked, egg whites must be left before being folded into the mixture, liquefication can be delayed by excluding the air which causes the disintegration, either by wrapping plastic across the bowl or turning the bowl right over on the surface (the whisked whites will stick to the bowl). Alternatively, if sugar is to form part of the mixture, as in meringue or sweet puddings, some, or all of it folded into the whites will keep them stable for 15 minutes or so.

The Technique of Folding

Egg whites, and other mixtures into which air has been carefully incorporated (such as sifted flour, creamed sugar-and-butter mixtures, whipped cream) are often "folded" into something else. The difference between folding and simple mixing is that, with folding, great care is taken to preserve the trapped air in the mixture. Simple stirring or vigorous beating could easily break the bubbles and let out the air. The technique of folding is easier to learn than to describe, but the essential points are laid out below:

Folding Techniques

● **Use a bowl rather than a flat-bottomed container. Make sure the bowl is large enough to hold the completed mixture comfortably. (Working in a small bowl is awkward and leads to lumps of egg white spilling out.) Add first a spoon of egg white to the base mixture, beating it in to soften the mixture. Then tip in the rest of the egg whites and fold.**

● **Use a large metal cook's spoon, not a wooden spoon and not an ordinary tablespoon. It should be metal because that will cut neatly and cleanly through the mixture with as little disturbance of the air bubbles as possible. A wooden spoon is too clumsy, does not cut through cleanly, and has not a big enough head to lift sufficient mixture.**

● **Hold the spoon near the head, not halfway up the handle.**

● **Do not stir round and round but using the spoon edge like a knife, cut down to the bottom of the bowl, then turn the spoon to lift up the maximum amount of mixture from the bottom and bring it to the top. Turn the spoon over to drop the mixture when it comes to the top, and repeat the action in various parts of the bowl, always lifting the mass, bottom to top. Many cooks develop a "figure of eight" motion, and it is helpful to use the non-folding hand to turn the bowl.**

● **Do not overbeat. As the mixture is tipped into a soufflé dish or bowl, patches can be broken up with spatula or spoon.**

Meringue

Meringue is whisked egg white with sugar added (to the proportion of ½ cup sugar to each egg white). Sometimes a few drops of vinegar are added to encourage volume on whisking. It is used in countless ways, and there are three main types of meringue, folded into various mousses, ice creams, and desserts, or baked in the oven as pie-toppings or crisp meringue.

Swiss Meringue

Swiss Meringue is probably the nicest to eat of the meringues—light, airy, crumbly and crisp. It also makes the lightest meringue topping for pies etc.

- **Whisk the egg whites to stiff peaks but take care not to overbeat as the whites can break down and lose their volume.**
- **Fold in 1 teaspoon sugar per egg white and whisk again until the eggs have become rather shiny. Half the sugar can be beaten in using a strong electric machine, but beating whites and sugar to the correct solid consistency by hand is almost impossible. The mixture at this point should not be at all runny and should form a solid bridge between whisk and bowl if the whisk is held 1 to 2 inches above the mixture.**
- **Then fold the rest of the sugar into the mixture until combined. Do not let it stand about because, after about 15 minutes it will begin to "weep."**
- **Swiss meringue can take 3 hours in a cool oven to cook and ends up pale cookie-colored with a slightly toffee-like center.**
- **A good variation of Swiss meringue is made by substituting brown sugar for half of the superfine sugar. The resulting meringue is caramel flavored.**

The Soufflé

There is a certain amount of myth and mystique about soufflés but in truth, they are easy things to make. They are satisfyingly untemperamental. They rise because the air inside them expands but will sink fast if the mixture cools while still uncooked. To stay up permanently they must be rigid and overcooked. Chefs have solved this problem. They overcook the soufflé, then serve a sauce with it.

To Make a Perfect Soufflé

Make the base: this can be done in advance, but should be warmed before folding in the egg whites or it will be too stiff. It should be of not-quite-

The final stage of the whisking process.

Brush out the soufflé dish with melted butter and dust with breadcrumbs before adding the soufflé mixture.

A super-light coffee soufflé, one of the many varieties you can try.

pouring consistency. If it is too solid it will take too vigorous stirring, as opposed to light folding, to incorporate the whites and much air will be lost resulting in a too-heavy soufflé. If it is too liquid the mixture will rise unevenly, not dry out satisfactorily and sink. Soufflé bases almost always include egg yolks, so stir the base over a low heat when reheating to prevent scrambling. Stop when the mixture is warm and soft. Season and flavor the base very well.

Preheat the oven. Most soufflés are cooked at 375˚F. Put a baking sheet on the middle shelf to heat too. When the soufflé is put on this will give the bottom a good burst of heat. Make sure there is no shelf above the one to be used.

Brush out the soufflé dish with butter and dust with dried breadcrumbs. This helps the mixture glide easily up the sides and gives a crisp crust at the finish. For an impressively straight-sided soufflé tie a collar of waxed paper round the dish and grease

that too. It is not strictly necessary—a well made soufflé will rise above the rim anyway, but it helps even rising if the oven is at all uneven or draughty. Whisk the whites to medium peak.

If necessary, briskly stir a single spoonful of the whites into the base to further loosen and soften it. Using a spatula scrape all the egg white into the base mixture and fold in with a metal spoon. Pour the mixture into the soufflé dish. It should not be more than three-quarters full. Smooth the top. Give the whole dish a sharp crack on the table top. This will burst any over-large air bubbles.

Bake, without opening the door until 5 minutes before the estimated end of the cooking time. Test for "doneness" by giving the dish a sharp shove. If the soufflé wobbles easily it should be left in the oven. If it is rock solid, it is too dry. A slight tremble is best—it means a just moist center. Remove the paper collar. Serve as fast as feasible.

Chocolate-Nut Meringue

This is a delicious combination of meringue and nut layers (almonds or hazelnuts), with chocolate frosting. It makes a lovely after-dinner dessert and may be frozen for up to 2 months.

SERVES 4–6

2¼ cups ground toasted hazelnuts	½ cup sugar
1¼ cups superfine sugar	2 oz semi-sweet chocolate
2 Tbsp all-purpose flour	1 Tbsp milk
6 egg whites	½ tsp vanilla extract
2 Tbsp vanilla sugar	2 cups confectioners' sugar
FILLING	1 whole toasted hazelnut for decoration
¾ stick butter	

Preheat oven to 300°F. Prepare three baking sheets with waxed paper. Draw the chosen shape on each.

Mix together ⅔ of the hazelnuts and half the sugar and the flour; set aside. Whisk the egg whites in a large, spotlessly clean bowl until they hold firm, snowy peaks. Beat in the rest of the sugar and vanilla sugar until the mixture is firm and glossy. Using a large metal spoon, lightly fold in the nut, sugar, and flour mixture.

Divide the mixture evenly between the three baking sheets and level out, taking care not to break down the delicate aerated structure. Because of the nut content the meringue bases rise little.

Bake them in the oven until lightly colored; they will feel slightly soft to the touch while warm but become crisp and brittle as they cool. Leave on the papers to cool on wire racks.

To make the filling melt over a low heat the butter, sugar, and chocolate. Stir in the milk and vanilla. Add the confectioners' sugar and beat until the frosting is of spreading consistency.

To assemble the cake trim the meringue bases to the same size. Place one on a wire rack. Spread one-third of the frosting over it and cover with the second layer. Smooth over half the remaining frosting and place the last meringue on top. Cover the top and sides of the cake with the remaining frosting. Press the last of the hazelnuts all round the side of the cake. Place one whole hazelnut in the center. Transfer to a serving dish and chill for at least 3 to 4 hours or, if possible, overnight.

The top may be piped with a chocolate frosting decoration if wished.

Lemon Meringue Pie

Lemon meringue pie is a great classic, loved by many. It has that unbeatable contrast of textures, and sweet and tangy flavors.

SERVES 4

8–9 in sweet pie shell, baked blind

LEMON CURD

Zest and juice of 3 lemons

1½ cups granulated sugar

1½ sticks unsalted butter, chilled and cubed

2 eggs

3 egg whites

¼ tsp cream of tartar

6 Tbsp superfine sugar

Superfine sugar to dredge

Using a wooden spoon, crush the lemon zest and sugar in a heat-proof bowl. Strain in the lemon juice and add the butter cubes. Set the bowl over a pan of simmering water and leave the butter to melt and the sugar to dissolve. Meanwhile whisk the 2 eggs in a separate bowl until frothy and strain them into the lemon mixture. Blend all the ingredients carefully and cook slowly, stirring often, until the mixture thickens to a creamy consistency. Take off the heat, lightly rub a little butter over the surface to prevent a skin forming and set aside to allow it to cool.

Preheat oven to 350°F. Pour the lemon curd into the cooled pastry shell and level out. Place the flan in the heated oven to warm and set the filling.

Reduce the temperature to 300°F. Make the meringue. Beat the egg whites and cream of tartar until foamy. Beat in sugar, 1 tablespoon at a time; continue beating until stiff and glossy. Lift the flan out of the oven and reduce the temperature of the oven. Quickly spoon the meringue on to the lemon filling and dredge with superfine sugar. Replace the pie in the oven and bake until the meringue peaks are crisp and have turned a golden brown color. Serve warm or cold.

Mocha Meringue Stars

These unusual meringue cookies are made with cocoa and coffee powders for a sophisticated mocha flavor.

MAKES ABOUT 3½ DOZEN

2¼ cups confectioners' sugar, sifted

1½ tsp unsweetened cocoa powder, preferably Dutch-processed

1 tsp instant espresso powder (not granules)

4 egg whites

¼ tsp cream of tartar

1 tsp vanilla extract

TIP

For even-sized stars, use a star-cutter as a guide; place cutter on foil and gently make a mark at each tip in rows on the foil.

Line 2 large baking sheets with foil. Into a small bowl, sift together ¼ cup of the confectioners' sugar, and the cocoa and espresso powders; set aside.

Preheat oven to 200°F. In a large bowl with electric mixer, beat egg whites on low speed until foamy. Add cream of tartar and continue beating until soft peaks form. Gradually add remaining confectioners' sugar, a tablespoon at a time, beating well after each addition, until whites are stiff and glossy, 10 to 14 minutes. Beat in vanilla extract. Add sugar-cocoa mixture, and fold into whites until just blended.

Spoon meringue mixture into a large decorating bag fitted with medium star tip. Pipe 2½-inch star shapes, 1½ inches apart, on to prepared baking sheets. Bake cookies 1 hour. Turn off oven, but leave meringues in oven 1 hour more to continue drying. Remove baking sheets from oven and peel foil off meringues. Cool completely on wire racks. Store in airtight containers.

Meringue Swirls

The grated chocolate cuts the sweetness of these lovely speckled meringues. Dipping in chocolate adds a sophisticated effect.

MAKES ABOUT 3½ DOZEN

2 oz unsweetened chocolate, chopped

⅓ cup confectioners' sugar, sifted

4 egg whites

¼ tsp cream of tartar

1¼ cups superfine sugar

1 tsp vanilla extract

Cocoa for dusting

Line 2 large baking sheets with foil. In a food processor fitted with metal blade, process chocolate with confectioners' sugar very finely. Pour into a small bowl and refrigerate until ready to add to meringues.

In a large bowl with electric mixer on low speed, beat egg whites until foamy. Add cream of tartar, and beat on high speed until soft peaks form. Gradually add superfine sugar, a tablespoon at a time, beating well after each addition until whites are stiff and glossy, 10 to 15 minutes. Gently fold in chocolate mixture until just blended.

Preheat oven to 200°F. Spoon mixture into a large decorating bag fitted with a medium star tip. Pipe 3-inch "S" shapes 1½ inches apart on prepared baking sheets.

Bake meringues 1 hour. Turn off oven but do not remove meringues. Leave meringues in oven 1 hour more. Remove baking sheets from oven and peel off foil. Arrange meringues on wire racks to cool completely. Dust with cocoa if you like.

In a small bowl set over a saucepan of simmering water, melt chocolate until smooth, stirring frequently. Remove from heat. Dip one end of each cookie into melted chocolate and place on waxed paper-lined baking sheet. Allow to set until firm, about 1 hour. Store in airtight containers with waxed paper between layers.

Meringue Swirls ▶

Chocolate-nut Divinity

Although these meringues may not be technically "cookies," they are always great in a box of Christmas cookies.

MAKES ABOUT 2 DOZEN

4 egg whites, at room temperature

¼ tsp cream of tartar

1 cup superfine sugar

1 tsp cornstarch

2 tsp vanilla extract

1 cup hazelnuts, toasted and coarsely chopped

1 cup semi-sweet chocolate chips

Preheat oven to 225°F. Line 2 large baking sheets with foil, shiny side up.

In a large bowl with electric mixer, beat egg whites on low speed until foamy. Add cream of tartar, increase speed to medium-high, and continue beating until whites are stiff. Combine 2 tablespoons sugar with cornstarch; set aside. Add remaining sugar to egg whites a tablespoon at a time, beating well after each addition, until sugar is completely dissolved and whites are stiff and glossy, 15 to 20 minutes. Fold in reserved sugar-cornstarch mixture; then fold in vanilla extract, nuts, and chocolate chips.

Using a tablespoon, scoop up a mound of meringue; then use another tablespoon to scrape mound off on to baking sheets. Make each meringue with tall rough peaks to form a large spectacular shape.

Bake meringues 2 hours, rotating baking sheets from top to bottom shelf and front to back halfway through cooking time. Turn off heat, but do not open oven for 1 hour. Meringues should be completely dry, but not colored. Remove baking sheets from oven, and peel meringues off foil. Store in airtight containers in single layers to avoid breaking any sharp peaks.

Chewy Nutty-lemon Bites

These meringue-like cookies are crisp on the outside but nutty and chewy on the inside.

MAKES ABOUT 16

4 egg whites, at room temperature	⅔ cup diced candied citron (lemon peel)
¾ cup superfine sugar	Candied citron to decorate
2 cups chopped hazelnuts	

Preheat oven to 250°F. Line a large baking sheet with rice paper. Place egg whites and sugar in top of a double boiler, or in a heat-proof bowl over a saucepan of simmering water.

With a hand-held electric mixer, beat whites until stiff and glossy, 4 to 6 minutes. Remove top of double boiler or bowl from water, and continue beating until meringue mixture is completely cold. Fold in chopped nuts and diced citron.

Using a teaspoon, scoop up balls of meringue and push them off with another teaspoon on to the baking sheet, 2 inches apart. Press a piece of candied citron on to top of each mound. Bake until meringue is set, but pale, 12 to 15 minutes; cookies should remain white. Remove baking sheets to wire rack to cool then slide paper with cookies on to rack to cool completely. When cool, gently peel off cookies from paper. Store in airtight containers.

TIP

Rice paper is an edible paper which is available in cookware and specialty stores. If you cannot find it, use non-stick baking parchment, brushed very lightly with a flavorless vegetable oil.

Tropical Slice

Juicy fresh pineapple and shredded coconut make this meringue dish a truly tropical treat.

SERVES 8

4 egg whites	⅔ cup heavy cream
1 cup sugar	1 small fresh pineapple, peeled, cored, and chopped into pieces
2 Tbsp powdered instant coffee	
⅔ cup ground almonds	½ cup shredded coconut
¼ cup slivered toasted almonds	

Preheat oven to 200°F. Draw two rectangles 12 × 4 inches on to sheets of waxed paper. Place upside down on baking sheets.

Beat the egg whites until stiff and whisk in 4 tablespoons of sugar and the coffee. Continue whisking until the meringue forms stiff peaks. Fold in the remaining sugar and ground almonds.

Spoon the meringue into a decorating bag fitted with a ½ inch plain tip. Pipe in lines across the width of each rectangle. Sprinkle one rectangle with the toasted almonds. Bake for 2 hours and leave to cool.

Whip the cream until thick and soft, spread over the meringue base without almonds. Cover with the pineapple pieces and sprinkle over the coconut. Top with the second meringue layer. Refrigerate for 2 hours.

Meringue Mushrooms

Thee little cookies never fail to please. In France they are used to decorate the Christmas log, *Buche de Noël*.

MAKES ABOUT 3 DOZEN

3 egg whites

⅛ tsp cream of tartar

1¼ cups confectioners' sugar

2 oz semi-sweet chocolate, melted

Unsweetened cocoa powder for dusting

Line a large baking sheet with foil. In a large bowl with electric mixer on low speed, beat egg whites until foamy. Add cream of tartar, increase speed, and beat until soft peaks form. Gradually add sugar, a tablespoon at a time and beat well until stiff and glossy.

Spoon into a large decorating bag fitted with a ½-inch plain tip. Pipe about 30 1½-inch rounds, resembling mushroom caps, 1½ inches apart on prepared baking sheets. Pipe remaining mixture between rounds into an equal number of ¾- to 1-inch high cone shapes. Allow to sit 1 hour to dry slightly.

Preheat oven to 200°F. Bake meringues 1 hour, rotating baking sheet from front to back halfway through cooking time. Turn off oven, but leave meringues in oven 1 hour more to continue drying. Remove baking sheet to wire rack and peel foil off mushroom caps and stems. With tip of small sharp knife, make a small hole in underside of each cap.

With a small palette knife or round-bladed kitchen knife, spread a little melted chocolate on the underside of a "mushroom cap," and gently push the pointed end of a cone shape into the hole to form the stem. Allow to set at least 1 hour. Dust tops with cocoa powder.

Coffee and Almond Pavlova

My Mom's favorite dessert, a marshmallowy meringue topped with coffee and toasted almond cream, then drizzled with chocolate. The best pavlovas are crisp on the outside and sticky in the middle. I don't add sugar to the cream as the meringue base is very sweet, but you may sweeten it slightly if you wish.

SERVES 8 TO 10

1⅓ cups superfine sugar, plus extra for sprinkling	1 tsp white wine vinegar
⅓ cup ground almonds	2 Tbsp coarsely ground high roast coffee
1 tsp cream of tartar	⅓ cup hot water
1 Tbsp cornstarch	¼ cup blanched almonds
4 egg whites	1¼ cups heavy cream
Pinch of salt	⅓ cup roughly chopped bittersweet chocolate
½ tsp almond extract	

Preheat the oven to 300°F. Cover a cookie sheet with baking parchment and mark out a 10-inch circle. Scatter a little superfine sugar over the parchment to prevent the pavlova from sticking to the paper.

Toast the ground almonds under a medium broiler until golden, stirring them once or twice, then allow to cool. Mix together the sugar, cream of tartar and cornstarch in a small bowl.

Whisk the egg whites with the salt until stiff. The mixture should remain firm in the bowl when tipped upside down. Add the almond extract and whisk again. Gradually add the sugar mixture, and stop whisking as soon as it is combined. Quickly fold in the vinegar and the cold toasted almonds using a wire whisk. (Do not attempt to add the almonds with an electric whisk as the fat from them will oil the mixture and the meringue will collapse.)

Pile the meringue on to the cookie sheet, spreading it lightly over the marked circle, then fork up the edges into soft peaks. Bake the meringue in the preheated oven for 2 hours, until crisp on the outside and a pale golden color.

Prepare the coffee while the meringue is cooking. Pour the hot water over the grounds then leave for 15 minutes. Strain through a fine sieve, then leave until completely cold. Toast the blanched almonds for 3 to 4 minutes under a medium broiler until browned, stirring and turning them once or twice, then leave them to cool. Chop the almonds roughly.

Turn off the oven and leave the cooked meringue to stand for about 10 minutes, then lift it carefully on to a wire rack and leave until completely cold.

Whip the cream until thick and soft, then add the cold coffee—you should have 3 to 4 tablespoons. Continue whipping until soft peaks form, then fold in the chopped toasted almonds. Carefully peel away the paper from the meringue base, then gently place it on a large serving plate. Spoon the coffee and almond cream on to the meringue. Spread it over the center and fork it up gently into tiny peaks.

Melt the chocolate pieces in a bowl over a pan of hot water, or in a microwave. Spoon the melted chocolate into a waxed paper piping bag, snip off the end, then drizzle the chocolate over the pavlova. Leave for a few minutes before serving, to allow the chocolate to set.

Spinach Soufflé

Cheese and spinach make a great, nutritious, combination. The addition of mustard and cayenne brings out the flavors.

SERVES 4

4 oz sorrel	**Pinch of cayenne**
12 oz spinach	**½ tsp mustard**
Salt and pepper	**½ cup grated strong Cheddar or Gruyère cheese**
½ stick butter	
Dried white breadcrumbs	**4 eggs**
½ cup all-purpose flour	**I Tbsp grated Parmesan cheese**
1¼ cups milk	

To prepare the sorrel and spinach, remove the stalks and wash the leaves very carefully. Place in a pan of boiling salted water for 2 minutes. Drain very well, squeezing water out through a colander or sieve or between two plates. Chop finely.

Preheat the oven to 400°F. Lightly butter a 6 inch soufflé dish or 4 large ramekins. Coat the sides lightly with breadcrumbs.

Melt the butter in a pan and stir in the flour. Add the milk and bring to a boil, stirring continuously. Boil for one minute. Take the sauce off the heat, stir in the salt and pepper, cayenne, mustard, cheese, spinach, and sorrel. Cool slightly.

Separate the eggs, adding the yolks to the spinach mixture. Whisk the egg whites until stiff but not dry, and mix a spoonful thoroughly into the spinach mixture. Then gently fold in the rest. Spoon into the dish and bake for about 40 minutes, until set.

Serve with a tomato sauce or with anchovy butter, and sprinkle with grated Parmesan.

Coffee Soufflé

wonderfully light soufflé, ideal to serve after a
heavy main course or on a summer's evening
in the garden with a glass of chilled dessert wine.

SERVES 8

⅔ cup hot water

4 Tbsp coarsely ground high
   roast coffee

4 eggs, separated

½ cup superfine sugar

I Tbsp powdered gelatin

3 Tbsp boiling water

1¼ cups heavy cream,
   whisked until thick

DECORATION

⅔ cup heavy cream

10 to 12 coffee beans, or
   chocolate-coated coffee
   beans

Pour the hot water over the ground coffee then leave
to infuse for 10 to 15 minutes. Meanwhile, place a 1½ pint
soufflé dish on a cookie sheet (which makes it easier to
handle) and tie a double thickness collar of waxed paper
or baking parchment around the dish, to stand about
1½ inches above the top.

Strain the coffee through a fine sieve into a large
bowl, then add the egg yolks and sugar. Whisk in a food
processor for about 10 minutes, until very thick, and the
beaters leave a ribbon trail when lifted. If whisking by hand,
place the bowl over a pan of hot water as the heat will
help to thicken the mixture.

Sprinkle the gelatin over the boiling water in a small
bowl and stir, then leave to stand for 2 to 3 minutes. Stir
again to make certain that the gelatin has dissolved. If
necessary, heat the bowl for 30 to 60 seconds in a shallow
pan of hot water or in the microwave, until the gelatin has
completely dissolved.

Stir a spoonful of the coffee mixture into the gelatin,
then whisk it all into the mixture, and fold in the whipped
cream. Chill in the refrigerator for 20 minutes, or until
starting to set and thicken around the edges of the bowl.

Whisk the egg whites until stiff, then fold them into
the soufflé mixture using a wire whisk. Turn into the
prepared soufflé dish, then chill in the refrigerator for 2 to
3 hours.

To decorate the soufflé carefully loosen the paper
from the top with a sharp, thin-bladed knife and peel away
from around the dish. Whip the cream until stiff, then pipe
it into rosettes either around the top of the soufflé or
around the base of the dish on a serving plate. Top each
rosette with a coffee bean.

Twice-Baked Soufflé

hese tasty individual soufflés are baked once, then turned upside down, sprinkled with cheese, and baked again before serving.

SERVES 4

1¼ cups milk	1½ cups grated strong Cheddar cheese
Slice of onion	
Pinch of nutmeg	4 eggs plus 1 entire egg white
Knob of butter	
½ stick butter	Salt and freshly ground black pepper
½ cup flour	1½ cups half and half
Pinch of dry English mustard	

Heat the milk slowly with the onion and nutmeg.

Preheat the oven to 350°F. Butter 6 small teacups.

Melt the butter, add the flour and mustard. Cook for 30 seconds. Remove from the heat and leave to cool for one minute. Strain in the milk. Stir well and return to the heat. Bring gradually up to a boil and simmer, stirring continuously for 30 seconds. Then add three quarters of the cheese.

Separate each of the eggs. Add the egg yolks to the cheese sauce. Taste and season as necessary.

Whisk the egg whites until stiff: put the egg whites into a clean, dry bowl and with a large dry balloon whisk, whisk the whites until stiff but not dry. Whisk slowly to begin with and gradually build up speed. Do not stop whisking or leave the whites sitting around—they will liquefy and not re-whisk.

Fold the egg whites into the soufflé base mixture: mix a spoonful of the egg whites into the base. Mix it in thoroughly, to "loosen" the mixture. With a large metal spoon held near the bowl, not at the end, fold the remaining egg whites in. Be gentle but firm to ensure that they are completely incorporated without knocking out all the air. Think of it as drawing a three dimensional figure of eight as you cut and fold. Do not forget to take your spoon right down to the bottom of the bowl.

Spoon into the cups, which the mixture should fill to two thirds at the most. Stand the cups in a roasting pan of boiling water and bake for 15 minutes or until the mixture is risen and set. Allow to sink and cool.

Butter a shallow ovenproof serving dish. Run a knife round the soufflés to loosen them. Turn them out on to your hand, giving the cups a sharp jerk. Put them, upside down, on the dish.

Twenty minutes before supper, set the oven to 425°F. Sprinkle the remaining cheese on top of the soufflés.

Season the cream with the salt and pepper and pour all over the soufflés, coating them completely. Bake for 10 minutes until a pale gold. Serve at once.

> **TIP**
>
> *If egg and cheese soufflés soaked in double cream seems excessively rich, a simple béchamel sauce can be used instead of the cream, or cream and béchamel could be mixed together.*

Spiced Pumpkin Soufflé

Many people worry about preparing soufflés, but they are actually very easy to make—it's just that they don't stay all light, puffy and fluffy for very long, so rounding up your guests at the appropriate time is actually more important than your cooking technique!

SERVES 3

2 Tbsp butter	1 cup thick pumpkin purée, canned or homemade
1 Tbsp fine whole-wheat flour	1 tsp Dijon mustard
1 tsp ground cumin	3 large eggs, separated
1 tsp ground ginger	Salt and freshly ground black pepper
⅔ cup milk	

Preheat the oven to 350°F, and lightly butter a 6—7 inch soufflé dish.

Heat the butter in a small pan, then stir in the flour with the spices, salt, and pepper, and cook briefly for 1 minute, stirring all the time. Gradually beat in the milk, off the heat, then bring slowly to a boil, stirring all the time. Cook for 1 minute, then stir in the spiced pumpkin, mustard, and egg yolks and blend well.

Whisk the egg whites until stiff then fold them into the pumpkin mixture. Scrape the soufflé into the prepared dish, then bake in the hot oven for 30 to 40 minutes, until set. Serve immediately with a salad garnish.

Batter

A simple batter can be transformed into pancakes, crêpes, waffles, or even baked into a rugged Toad in the Hole. Batters are versatile—griddle pancakes and sour-cream waffles make excellent breakfast foods, Persian pancakes, latkes, and apple pancakes are brilliant snacks, while stuffed crêpes accompanied by a side salad make the perfect dinner dish.

INTRODUCTION

Batter has many uses and is very versatile.

Batter is a versatile mixture of flour and liquid— *usually milk and sometimes beaten egg—used to make pancakes, dropped biscuits, and waffles, and also to give a protective coating to many foods which are deep fried.*

Pancakes

Thin Pancakes

Thin pancakes, or French crêpes, are made by pouring a thin layer of pancake batter into a hot greased skillet about 8 inches in diameter, tipping to spread the batter evenly and pouring out the excess. The pancake is cooked fast to brown one side, turned to brown the other and when ready, wrapped around sweet or non-sweet fillings, or eaten simply with sugar and lemon juice.

Batter for Thicker Pancakes

Batter for thicker pancakes, sometimes called griddle cakes or dropped biscuits, is mixed with baking powder or yeast. The rising agent causes the butter to rise in the pan to form thickish pancakes which spread out only a little as they are fried on a greased hot griddle or in a large skillet. They are best eaten warm with plenty of butter. Blinis are an example of a yeasted batter.

Waffles

Waffles are also made from raised batter and cooked in a special iron device which holds the batter and gives the cooked waffles a thin, flat, indented shape on both sides. The waffle iron is heated over a gas flame if of the hand-held variety, or electrically if a table-top one, before the batter is poured in. This ensures that the waffles are crisp on the outside and soft on the inside, while the raised batter makes them light. As with the coating on deep fried foods, waffles must be eaten quickly.

Making Batter

The following recipes are examples of the main uses of batters. If the cook successfully manages these, no batter recipe should really present any problems in the future.

- **Sift the flour into a large, wide bowl ensuring the absence of lumps. Sprinkle the salt (or sugar or other dry ingredients) on top.**
- **Using either a wooden spoon or your hand, make a well in the flour to expose the bottom of the bowl. The hole should be wide enough to mix in liquid ingredients (say, two eggs and a little milk) without bringing in too much of the surrounding flour.**
- **Using a fork, whisk, wooden spoon, or the fingertips of one hand, mix and stir the central liquid ingredients to a smooth paste.**
- **Gradually incorporate the surrounding flour. With practice, the stirring action flips the liquid over the banks of flour and; as it runs back into the central well, it brings with it a thin film of flour. Pour more liquid into the center as the batter gets thicker. The idea is to keep it at the consistency of heavy cream—easier to keep lump-free than a runny mixture. Once all the flour is incorporated and the batter is absolutely smooth, beat in the remaining liquid.**
- **Leave for 30 minutes, if possible, to allow time for the starch cells to swell, giving a less doughy final product. If the mixture is left for more than an hour it might separate, but it is easily remixed. Do not make batter more than 12 hours in advance. It ferments easily.**

Food Processor Method

With a food processor, batter making takes much less effort. Put any eggs and other liquid ingredients into a processor fitted with the metal blade, and spoon the flour and other dry ingredients on top. Turn on the machine for a second or two—just enough to blend them without creating too many bubbles.

Crêpes with Lemon

This is the classic French pancake made with the thinnest of batters.

MAKES ABOUT 12

1 cup all-purpose flour	1¼ cups milk or milk and water mixed
Pinch of salt	
1 egg	1 Tbsp oil
1 egg yolk	Oil for frying
	Superfine sugar
	Lemon juice

Sift the flour and salt into a bowl and make a well in the center exposing the bottom of the bowl. Into this well place the egg and egg yolk with a little of the milk.

Using a wooden spoon or whisk mix the egg and milk and then gradually draw in the flour from the sides as you mix.

When the mixture reaches the consistency of thick cream beat well and stir in the oil. Add the rest of the milk—the consistency should now be that of thin cream. (Batter can also be made by placing all the ingredients together in a blender for a few seconds, but take care not to over-whizz or the mixture will be bubbly.)

Cover the bowl and refrigerate for about 30 minutes. This is done so that the starch cells will swell, giving a lighter result.

Prepare a crêpe pan or skillet by heating well and wiping out with oil. Crêpes are not fried in fat like most foods—the purpose of the oil is simply to prevent sticking. When the pan is ready, pour in about 1 tablespoon batter and swirl about the pan until evenly spread across the bottom. Place over heat and, after 1 minute, using a thin palette knife and your fingers, turn the crêpe over and cook again until brown. (Crêpes should be extremely thin, so if the first one is too thick, add a little extra milk. The first crêpe is unlikely to be perfect, and is often discarded.)

Make up all the crêpes, turning them out on to a plate. Lay the crêpes spotty side (the second side to be fried) up, sprinkle them with a little sugar and lemon juice and roll up. Serve warm.

NOTE
Crêpes can be kept warm in a folded cloth, on a plate over a saucepan of simmering water, in the oven, or in a warmer. They freeze well, but should be separated by pieces of waxed paper. They may also be refrigerated.

Toad in the Hole

This unattractively named dish is one of the most delicious of inexpensive English family recipes. It is particularly good if served with meat gravy so is traditionally cooked the day after a roast dinner, when a little leftover gravy is available.

SERVES 8

1 lb pork sausages	**BATTER**
4 Tbsp lard, meat fat, or sunflower oil	1 cup all-purpose flour
	Good pinch of salt
	2 eggs
	⅔ cup water mixed together with ⅔ cup milk

Sift the flour and salt into a large wide bowl. Make a well or hollow in the center of the flour and break the eggs into it.

With a whisk or wooden spoon mix the eggs to a paste and very gradually draw in the surrounding flour, adding just enough milk and water to the eggs to keep the central mixture a fairly thin paste. When all the flour is incorporated, stir in the rest of the liquid. The batter can more speedily be made by putting all the ingredients together in a blender or food processor for a few seconds, but take care not to overwhisk or the mixture will be bubbly. Leave to "rest" at room temperature for 30 minutes before use. This allows the starch cells to swell, giving a lighter, less doughy final product.

Preheat the oven to 425°F. Heat 1 tablespoon fat or sunflower oil in a skillet and in it fry the sausages until evenly browned all over, but do not cook them through.

Heat the rest of the fat or oil in an ovenproof shallow metal dish or roasting pan until smoking hot, either in the oven or over direct heat. Add the sausages to it and pour in the batter. Bake for 40 minutes or until the Toad in the Hole is risen and brown. Serve with hot gravy.

Banana Fritters

Bananas and batter are made for each other. Try this recipe once and you'll be hooked for life!

MAKES 8

8 small bananas	**BATTER**
Oil for shallow frying	1 cup plus 1 Tbsp all-purpose flour
Confectioners' sugar	Pinch of salt
	2 eggs
	1¼ cups milk
	1 Tbsp oil
	¼ cup sugar

> **NOTE**
> This batter can be speedily made in a blender. Simply put all the ingredients, except the egg white, into the machine and then whizz briefly.

Sift the flour with the salt into a bowl. Make a well in the center, exposing the bottom of the bowl. Put one whole egg and one yolk into the well and mix with a wooden spoon or whisk until smooth, gradually incorporating the surrounding flour and the milk. A thick creamy consistency should be reached. As the mixture thickens gradually add the milk to retain the creamy consistency. Add the oil and sugar. Allow to rest for 30 minutes.

Whisk the egg white and fold into the batter with a metal spoon just before using.

Peel the bananas and cut in half lengthwise and dip immediately into the prepared batter.

Heat ¼ inch of oil in a skillet and when hot fry the fritters for about 2 minutes on each side until golden brown. Drain well and dredge with confectioners' sugar.

Waffles

This is a thick batter with plenty of rising agent (baking soda) so that it will puff up. The outside cooks to crispness, while the inside remains soft. Waffles can be served with maple syrup, preserves, or honey, with or without cream or topped with crispy grilled bacon or fried egg. Here they are served with a heavy dusting of confectioners' sugar.

MAKES 10

2 eggs	1¼ cups milk
1½ cups all-purpose flour	½ stick butter, melted
Pinch of salt	Vanilla extract
3 tsp baking powder	Extra melted butter
2 Tbsp superfine sugar	Confectioners' sugar

Separate the eggs. Sift the flour, salt, baking powder, and sugar together. Make a well in the center and drop in the egg yolks. Stir the yolks, gradually drawing in the flour from the edges and adding the milk and melted butter until you have a thin batter. Add the vanilla extract.

Grease a waffle iron and heat it up.

Whisk the egg whites until stiff but not dry and fold into the batter.

Add a little melted butter to the hot waffle iron, pour in about 4 tablespoons of the mixture, close and cook for 1 minute per side. Do not worry if the first waffle sticks to the iron. It always does. Throw it away. The second one will come away cleanly. Serve the waffles heavily dredged with confectioners' sugar.

Sour Cream Waffles

In the past, many families owned special irons made and embossed by the local blacksmiths with individual patterns. However, these waffles are just as delicious when made with a modern waffle iron.

SERVES 6

5 eggs	¾ cup sour cream
½ cup sugar	½ stick butter
1 cup flour	
1 tsp ground cardamom or ginger	

Mix the eggs and sugar for about 5 minutes until fluffy. Whisk in the flour, cardamom or ginger, and sour cream. Whisk until smooth and creamy. Melt the butter, and stir it into the mixture. Set aside for 10 minutes.

Cook in a waffle iron according to the manufacturers' instructions. Serve with preserves, cream, or sugar.

Sour Cream Waffles ▶

Potato Cakes 1

There are many versions of potato cakes in Ireland. Here are two.

SERVES 4 – 6

¾ stick butter	A little milk
1½ cups self-rising flour	Butter
Salt and pepper	Bacon
1½ cups freshly mashed potatoes	

Preheat the oven to 425°F. Cut the butter into the flour, with a pinch of salt and pepper. Mix with the mashed potato and enough milk to make a soft dough.

Roll out on to a floured board and cut into circles or triangles. Place on a lightly oiled tray and bake for 25 minutes. Serve hot split with butter and bacon.

Potato Cakes 2

This slightly more plain version is no less delicious, served hot and dripping with butter.

SERVES 4 – 6

½ stick butter	½ tsp baking powder
Scant 1 cup all-purpose flour	3 cups freshly mashed potatoes
½ tsp salt	Butter

Cut the butter into the flour. Add the salt and baking powder and mix well. Mix in the potatoes and knead for a few minutes.

Roll out on to a well-floured board with a floured rolling pin. Cook on a dry griddle or skillet until brown on both sides. Serve hot, dripping with butter.

Cheese Blintzes with Strawberries

Blintzes are a symbol of Jewish cooking around the world, with the name coming from the Yiddish for pancake. It is a simple crêpe or pancake filled with cheese or fruits or fillings such as potato and mushroom, chicken livers, or meat.

SERVES 6 TO 8

3 large eggs	**FILLING**
½ tsp salt	1 16-oz container creamed cottage cheese
½ tsp sugar	
2 Tbsp butter or margarine, melted	2 3-oz package cream cheese, softened
1½ cups milk or water	¼ cup sugar
⅔ cup all-purpose flour	1 tsp vanilla extract
Butter or margarine for baking or frying, melted	1 lb strawberries, thawed if frozen
	Sugar
	Juice and grated zest of 1 lemon

In a large bowl, beat eggs,. salt, sugar, melted butter or margarine and milk or water until well blended.

Into a medium bowl, sift flour; make a well in center. Using a wire whisk, gradually stir beaten egg mixture into flour, drawing in flour from edges of well until all egg mixture is added. Whisk until smooth. Strain into a 4-cup measure. Cover and refrigerate about 1 hour. (Batter may thicken; add milk or water to thin if necessary.)

Over medium heat, heat a 7-inch crêpe pan or skillet. Brush bottom of pan with a little melted butter. Pour 3 to 4 tablespoons (about ¼ cup) batter into crêpe pan, tipping pan to coat bottom with batter. Cook until top looks set and bottom is lightly browned, about 2 minutes. Using a metal pancake turner, loosen edges and flip crêpe, then cook 10 seconds. Slip cooked blintze on to a piece of waxed paper. Repeat until all batter is used, stacking blintzes between sheets of waxed paper. (Blintzes can be used immediately or stored in the refrigerator or frozen.)

Preheat oven to 350°F. Brush a 15½ x 10½ inch jelly-roll pan with melted butter or margarine.

Make filling. In a medium bowl, with a mixer at medium speed, beat cottage cheese, cream cheese, sugar, and vanilla until smooth.

NOTE

For Passover, the blintze batter can be made with potato flour and water. The mixture will be slightly thinner and will make a crisper blintze.

On a clean work surface, spread 1 heaped tablespoon of cheese mixture down center of each blintze. Fold sides toward center, so each side covers about half the filling. Beginning at bottom edge, roll up blintze. Arrange seam-side down on buttered pan. Brush each folded blintze with a little butter and bake about 10 minutes.

Reserve 6 to 8 strawberries and hull the remainder. Slice each in half lengthwise and set aside. Into a food processor, fitted with a metal blade, place half the remaining strawberries. Add sugar to taste and lemon juice and grated zest. Process until smooth and pour into a small bowl. Chop remaining strawberries and add to the purée. Add more sugar if necessary.

To serve, place 2 blintzes on a plate, spoon over a little strawberry sauce and garnish with a strawberry half.

Blinis with Smoked Salmon and Sour Cream

Blinis are Russian pancakes made with buckwheat flour. They have a nutty flavor which is enhanced by smoked salmon or lox and sour cream. A less extravagant presentation can be offered with chopped radishes and cucumber, scallions, and capers. Blinis make a wonderful brunch, light lunch, or supper dish.

SERVES 6

¼ cup lukewarm water	¼ lb smoked salmon or lox, thinly sliced
1½ tsp active-dry yeast	4 scallions, thinly sliced on the diagonal
½ cup all-purpose flour	2 Tbsp sour cream
¾ cup buckwheat flour	Snipped fresh chives for garnish
½ tsp salt	
1 cup milk	
2 eggs, separated	
½ stick butter or margarine	
½ cup sour cream	

Into a small bowl, pour lukewarm water and sprinkle yeast over water. Leave to stand until yeast becomes foamy and bubbly, 5 minutes.

Into a large bowl, sift all-purpose flour, buckwheat flour and salt; make a well in center. Heat ¾ cup of the milk to lukewarm and add it to well with yeast mixture, stirring with a wire whisk and drawing in flour little by little to form a smooth batter. Cover bowl with a clean dish towel and leave in a warm place until the batter becomes light and bubbly, 2 to 3 hours.

Beat remaining ¼ cup milk into batter; beat egg yolks and stir into batter with half the butter, melted, and the sour cream.

In another bowl, with a hand-held mixer at medium speed, beat egg whites until stiff peaks form (do not overbeat). Fold them into blini batter until just blended. (Do not overblend; a few white lumps will cook out.)

In a large skillet or on a griddle, over medium-high heat, melt remaining butter. Using a small ladle, pour batter into pan or griddle to form small pancakes. Cook until undersides are lightly browned and tops are covered with bubbles, about 2 minutes. Turn blinis over and cook 1 to 2 minutes longer. Continue until all batter is used, adding more butter if necessary. (Keep blinis warm in a 300°F oven if necessary.)

Arrange blinis on individual plates or on a large serving dish. Divide smoked salmon or lox slices equally on to blinis. Top each blini with a few sliced scallions and a spoonful of sour cream. Sprinkle with chives and serve.

Orange-flavored French Toast

Challah bread is used in this recipe, but any good white bread could be used. Serve with maple syrup or dust with confectioners' sugar.

SERVES 6

4 eggs, well beaten	12 slices challah bread, each about ¾ inch thick
½ tsp salt	Butter for frying, melted
2 Tbsp sugar	Maple syrup or confectioners' sugar for serving
1 cup orange juice	Orange slices for garnish (optional)
½ tsp vanilla extract	
½ to 1 cup milk	

In a large shallow baking dish, beat eggs with salt, sugar, orange juice, vanilla, and ½ cup milk. (Depending on the size of the bread, you may need to add a little more milk.)

Lay slices of bread in egg mixture and leave to stand 2 minutes. Turn bread slices over and leave to soak until egg mixture is completely absorbed, about 5 minutes longer.

In a large skillet or on a griddle, over medium heat, melt 3 tablespoons butter. Add slices of soaked bread and cook until underside is golden. Using a metal pancake turner, turn slices until brown. Serve immediately.

Blinis with Smoked Salmon and Sour Cream ▶

Potato Latkes

Latkes are a well-known and well-loved vegetable dish in the Jewish repertoire. Cooked in oil, these potato pancakes are traditional at Hanukah because they symbolize the miracle of the oil which lasted eight days. They are delicious with poultry, but can also be eaten on their own sprinkled with sugar or topped with applesauce or sour cream.

SERVES 6 TO 8

6 medium potatoes, peeled	1 tsp salt
1 onion	Pinch ground white pepper
2 eggs, lightly beaten	Vegetable oil for frying
½ cup fine matzo meal, or all-purpose flour	Applesauce or sour cream for serving

In a food processor fitted with grater attachment, grate potatoes and onion. Drain in a colander, pressing to squeeze out as much liquid as possible. Place in a large bowl and beat in remaining ingredients except oil and accompaniments. (Work as quickly as possible so potatoes do not turn brown.)

In a large heavy skillet, over medium-high heat, heat about 1 inch vegetable oil or just enough to cover pancakes. Drop batter by tablespoonfuls into hot oil and cook until underside is browned, 2 minutes. Turn and cook until second side is browned, 1 to 2 minutes longer.

Remove to a serving platter and keep warm in a 300°F oven. Continue until all batter is used, adding a little more oil if necessary. Serve immediately with applesauce or sour cream.

Persian Pancakes with Yogurt

These delicious "green" pancakes are like a fritter. They can be eaten on their own with yogurt or cream cheese, or as an accompaniment to spicy curries.

SERVES 4

4 cups chopped spinach, Swiss chard or watercress

2 large sprigs each fresh coriander, parsley, and dill

2 small leeks, or 4 large scallions, thinly sliced

6 eggs, beaten

Salt

Freshly ground black pepper

¼ tsp grated nutmeg

1 cup matzo meal

Vegetable oil for frying

Yogurt, sour cream, or cream cheese for serving

Fresh cilantro or dill for garnish

In a food processor fitted with metal blade, process spinach, Swiss chard or watercress, herbs, and leeks or scallions until smooth. Turn into a large bowl. Add beaten eggs, salt, and pepper to taste and nutmeg. Stir in matzo meal. Batter should be quite thick but pourable.

In a large skillet, over high heat, heat 2 tablespoons oil. Drop batter by heaping tablespoonfuls into a pan. Cook until undersides are lightly browned, about 2 minutes, then turn over and cook 2 minutes longer. Remove to paper towels to drain; keep warm. Continue until all the batter is used, adding more oil to the skillet as needed. (Keep warm in a 300°F oven until all batter is used.) Serve hot with yogurt, sour cream, or cream cheese, garnished with cilantro or dill.

Baking with Yeast

Home baked breads are a real treat.
Although they take hours to make, most of
that time they need simply to sit in a warm
place while you get on with other things,
and the results are definitely worth the
effort. Whether it be a simple bread, a
special breakfast bake, a fruit bread, or a
bagel, you will find the recipes in this
section along with a comprehensive
introduction that will dispel all the mysteries
of this wonderful substance, yeast.

INTRODUCTION

All types of bread supply carbohydrate, protein and B vitamins to the diet.

Whole-wheat and brown breads provide more dietary fiber than white bread. Bread also supplies calcium, phosphorus and iron. Flour with an extraction rate of 80 per cent or less of the bran and wheatgerm is fortified with the B vitamins thiamine (B1) and nicotinic acid and iron to compensate for milling losses. Brown and white flours also contain added calcium. The varieties of bread are numerous and display a wide spectrum of textures and flavors, plain and enriched, sweet and savory. The home baker is able to cater for special requirements such as salt-free bread, gluten-free bread, milk- and wheat-free breads and breads, buns, and fruit loaves free of artificial coloring and flavoring as indicated in hyperkinetic diets. There is a growing consumer preference today for whole-wheat breads, in fact some 25 per cent ofthe bread consumed in English-speaking countries is now non-white.

Bread-Making Ingredients

Flour

The flour most commonly used in bread-making is wheat. Bread may be made from a single flour or a mixture of two or more flours, but wheat is prized for its fine baking qualities. There are three main types of wheaten flour: whole-wheat containing the whole of the wheat grain with nothing added or taken away, an extraction rate of 100 per cent; graham flour containing about 85 per cent of the wheat grain; and white containing about 75 per cent of the wheat grain. Most of the bran (ie the outer fibrous layers of the grain) and the wheat germ are removed in the milling process. The term stoneground, sometimes applied to flours, means that the flour is ground between two stones instead of being milled by the modern steel-roller-mill process.

Gluten is composed of insoluble proteins which absorb water and produce a fine network of elastic strands. Carbon dioxide is produced by yeast fermentation and this raises the bread. The gluten stretches to give the loaf its bold volume. Flour used in yeast cookery should be all-purpose and not the chemically aerated self-rising type. The so-called hard or bread flour gives the best bread-making results because of its higher gluten content. The texture of loaves made from whole-wheat and brown flours is closer than that of white bread. The volume is also usually less in the whole-wheat and brown bread types because of the effect of the higher bran content on gluten elasticity.

As whole-wheat and rye flours produce a very heavy result, it is best to mix them with all-purpose flour, but remember that even the same brand of flour can vary from region to region, or from season to season, depending on the level of humidity and how long it has been stored, so the amount of liquid needed in the dough may vary.

Liquids Used in Dough-Making

The liquid in a dough usually consists of water or milk (which may be skimmed or whole, dried, or fresh). Some baking-powder breads utilize sour milk and buttermilk which react with the rising agent for a lighter dough. Less commonly, wort (a yeasty liquid made from hops), beer, and even blood provide the liquid ingredient as in some Scandinavian breads, for instance. Liquids for yeast doughs are usually added when lukewarm.

Eggs

Eggs are added to doughs to enrich them nutritionally. They also improve the keeping properties and color of the baked product.

Rising Agents

Fresh yeast is moist, and gray-cream in color.

Compressed baker's yeast consists of unicellular organisms which, under suitable conditions of temperature, moisture, and food supply, break down the sugar in dough, forming carbon dioxide and alcohol. Fresh yeast is moist, gray-cream in color and free from a dry, brown, covering of dead cells. Yeast works best at blood heat (body temperature). Blend the fresh yeast with dough liquid at 100°F. It is unnecessary to add sugar when blending compressed yeast with liquid. Cold temperatures slow down yeast activity as do doughs containing a lot of fat, sugar, and salt. Slow rising is often desirable, as it improves the flavor and texture of the bread; it may be achieved by placing the dough in a refrigerator for several hours at a time. Suitably wrapped fresh yeast (in amounts most frequently used) may be stored in the refrigerator for about three weeks or in a freezer for up to six weeks. If too much yeast is used in a dough, it produces a sour, yeasty flavor and a smell of alcohol. The bread becomes stale quickly and is crumbly in texture. Compressed yeast is usually sold in cakes weighing 1 ounce.

Active-Dry Yeast

Active-dry yeast is convenient to store—up to four months in an airtight container. Check the date stamp when purchasing it. Dried yeast has a shelf life of 4 to 6 months. Reconstituted dried yeast with some of the warm dough liquid (at 100°F) and a small quantity of "starter" sugar or follow manufacturer's instructions if they are different. Leave in a warm place until the yeast dissolves and the mixture becomes frothy. Easy blend dried yeast is mixed directly with the flour. The package instructions will also tell you how much dried yeast will raise what amount of flour. Follow manufacturer's instructions if these conflict with the recipe.

The Sponge Batter Technique

This method is applied to enrich yeast doughs where the amounts of fat, eggs, and sugar slow down the fermentation process. The use of a sponge batter helps to overcome the slowness.

Prepare the sponge batter by adding the yeast (and a little sugar in the case of dried yeast) to warm liquid. Stir in a small amount of the flour to make a batter. If dried yeast is used, allow some 5 to 10 minutes for the yeast to foam before flour is added.

Set the batter aside in a warm place for about 20 minutes to enable the yeast to ferment. The fat, eggs, and sugar are then added to the foaming batter and mixed to a soft dough.

Sourdough

Sourdough is a fermentation agent seldom used in home-baking today. It is made from dough which has been allowed to lie and ferment naturally, thereby producing yeast cells and lactic acid bacteria. The final product flavor results from normal yeast activity combined with the sour lactic acid taste. Nowadays, even in the San Francisco area, sourdough starter is usually made under laboratory conditions, to prevent impurities entering the bread.

Chemical Substances

Chemical substances used to lighten doughs include baking soda which needs to combine with an acidic ingredient such as sour milk or buttermilk, as in Irish soda bread.

Baking Equipment

Measuring cups in various sizes.

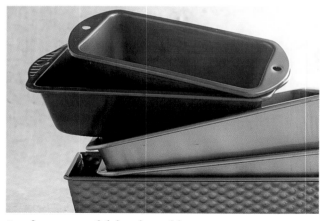

Loaf pans—useful for shaped loaves.

Sieve, rolling pin, wooden spoons, whisk, and baking sheet.

The equipment for baking consists of a large glass, porcelain, or stainless steel bowl, a wooden fork and mixing spoon, a rubber or plastic spatula, a rolling pin, plastic sheets, 2 pastry brushes, oven cloths or gloves, wire racks and baking sheets, loaf pans, measuring cups and a set of measuring spoons, a sieve for confectioners' sugar, weighing scales, and a grater for citrus zests.

Loaf pans and flowerpots are useful for shaped loaves. They should be prepared before use to prevent sticking. Grease pans and baking sheets with shortening or dust thoroughly with flour. The greased pans may also be dusted with cracked wheat, semolina or bran flakes. Non-stick pans are ready for use without greasing.

Earthenware (not plastic) flowerpots need to be washed thoroughly and dried. Coat them with shortening, inside and out, and then bake in a hot oven for 5 to 10 minutes. Allow to cool and repeat the process 3 or 4 times. The pots are then ready for use. Grease prior to half-filling with dough. Wipe with damp paper towels after use. Electric food mixers with a dough hook accessory are available on the market to facilitate dough-kneading.

Storage

Breads vary in their keeping properties. Crusty loaves are best eaten freshly baked. Enriched breads, milk, malt, and rye breads keep fresh for several days. The storage life depends on the recipe formula and the storage conditions.

Unwrapped bread is best stored at room temperature in a clean, airy, dry container such as a bread crock or bin. The container should not be airtight. Bins and crocks should be cleaned and dried weekly, or crusts and crumbs may promote mold growth. Unsliced bread may be put into a clean, dry, plastic bag for storage. Wrapped bread should be left in its wrapper. Leave the wrapper loosely folded.

Bread can stale rapidly if refrigerated, since moisture may be lost. Freezer storage of wrapped bread is very successful. Plain breads may be kept in a freezer for about 6 months, enriched loaves for 4 months. Crusty loaves (French or Vienna) may shed their crusts after a few days. Frozen bread may be thawed in a microwave oven and sliced bread may be toasted directly from the freezer.

Stale bread loaves and rolls may be refreshed by wrapping in foil and heating for 5 to 10 minutes in a preheated oven at 450°F. Allow to cool in the foil. Crusty varieties should not be covered but placed in a hot oven for 5 to 10 minutes. Stale bread is better than fresh bread for use in cooking.

Baking Techniques and Methods

Fermented Doughs

Cream the yeast, fresh or dried, with the warm dough liquid. Add the yeast liquid to the flour and mix by hand or with a wooden dough fork.

Kneading

Knead the dough with the heel of the right hand on a lightly floured board, folding the dough in half toward you, then pushing it down and away from you. Using the fingertips of the left hand, give the dough a quarter turn and repeat the folding and pushing movements with the heel of the right hand. The soft, sticky dough gradually becomes smooth and elastic and loses its stickiness. White doughs require about 10 minutes' kneading, whole-wheat and brown doughs only about 4 minutes (even less for quick brown doughs).

Kneading may also be done using a food mixer or processor according to the manufacturer's instructions. If the dough is very soft, beat it with a wooden spatula, or in a food mixer, until smooth and elastic.

The kneaded dough is allowed to rise until doubled in size. Normally the dough is allowed to rise twice, first after kneading and then after shaping. Quick methods of bread-making cut out this first rising stage and reduce the overall time to 1¾ hours. The method involves the use of vitamin C in the dough, 25 mg vitamin C is added to 1½ lb all-purpose flour. It is added to the dough liquid. Dough which is left to rise must be covered. The traditional floured cloth is replaced nowadays with oiled plastic. The dough may be placed in a large, oiled plastic bag or the dough bowl may be covered with a sheet of oiled plastic. The speed at which the dough rises depends upon the surrounding temperature. Suitable places include a warm place such as a kitchen or hot cupboard to the cool of the refrigerator. Dough may need only one hour to rise in a warm place (up to 90°F), 1½ to 2 hours at room temperature (65 to 70°F), 3½ to 4 hours in cool conditions and up to 12 hours in a refrigerator. Reduce by half the quantity of yeast used if rising takes place in the refrigerator or the dough will be difficult to handle and the product will taste yeasty when served. However warm the environment, if the atmosphere is too damp this can affect the rising.

Before the final stages of dough-handling, ensure that the oven is preheated to the correct temperature. Plain doughs require an oven temperature of 450°F and enriched doughs 400°F.

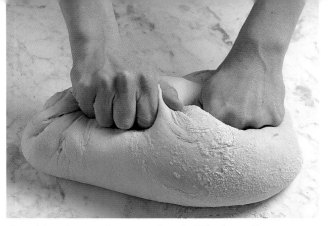

Punching down—the second part of the kneading process.

Knead the dough with the heel of your right hand.

Punching Down

The second kneading process is known as punching down. The aim is to obtain a product with good, even texture. Punching down ensures that large air bubbles are broken up and the air redistributed. Nutrients for the yeast cells are also redistributed and made more readily available. Knead the dough as before and then shape into loaves or rolls, as required.

The shaped items (on baking sheets, in baking pans or even flowerpots) are lightly covered with oiled heavy plastic sheeting and set aside to prove for ½ to 1 hour (according to the volume of the items to be baked). The dough becomes light and doubles in size.

Baking

Bake in a very hot oven in order to kill the yeast cells. The loaves, rolls or buns should rise well, look brown and crisp and feel light. Loaves tapped on the base should sound hollow. Bread may be tested by inserting a skewer into it. If the skewer is dry when withdrawn, the bread is baked. Loaves may be removed from their pans some 5 minutes before the end of baking if crisp results are needed.

Ready Mixes

Products for preparing yeasted wheaten doughs (including pizza-base mixes) and soda breads, using both white and whole-wheat flours, are obtainable. When purchasing wheaten dough powder, check the label to see if it includes yeast. If not, this must be bought separately. Follow the instructions on the package.

Prepared doughs of various kinds are obtainable deep-frozen, ready to put into the oven. They may even be ready meals, deep-frozen or chilled, such as pizzas, with a yeast dough base. Thawing may be carried out in a microwave oven, but baking results are usually best using an ordinary domestic oven.

Handy Hints for Yeast Breads and Cakes for Coffee

- **Prepare pans in advance.**
- **Use a thermometer to check liquids before adding yeast; choose a warm place for rising dough.**
- **Check bread for doneness by tapping the bottom of the loaf with your knuckles; it should sound hollow.**
- **Dough textures vary, and can range from soft and slightly sticky to firm, smooth doughs. Doughs for firm, chewy bread should be very firm, while medium-firm doughs are fine for savory breads. Most cakes for coffee and sweet-yeast bread doughs are soft and some can even be quite sticky.**
- **For kneading, fold the dough, then push down and away from you with the heel of your hand, slightly curving your fingers over the edge. Turn the dough and repeat.**
- **For rising the dough, place in an oiled bowl, and turn to coat the dough with oil; this prevents a crust from forming over the surface. Alternatively, slide the dough in its bowl into a large, plastic bag, and seal tightly, allowing room for expansion.**
- **To check if the dough has doubled in volume, press a finger into the dough. If the hole remains, the dough is ready to be punched down.**
- **To punch down the dough, push your first into the center of the dough, pulling the edges to the center, knead once or twice. Alternatively, turn the dough on to a lightly floured surface; it will automatically deflate. Knead once or twice.**

Bread Machines

Using a bread machine, baking bread becomes one of the easiest tasks in the kitchen, yet it produces spectacular results. You don't have to worry that water will be too cold to activate yeast, or so hot that it kills it: the bread machine regulates the temperature. You won't be kneading dough until your muscles ache: the bread machine will do all the kneading for you.

With a bread machine, you can create an infinite variety of loaves to suit your tastes, your store cupboard and the season. Substitute dried cranberries for raisins in a Christmas bread, add cracked wheat to a favorite bread to give it more fiber, or decorate a plaited loaf with the slivered almonds left over from another baking project. You no longer have to settle for ordinary bread.

Mastering bread-machine baking is like getting to know the quirks and idiosyncracies of any new piece of equipment. Some machines knead longer than others or allow longer rising time. Some bread pans have different capacities than others, although they are labeled as the same size. Some models require a little more liquid or yeast than others. Flour absorbs varying amounts of liquid depending on the weather. The dough reacts differently to water that is highly acidic or alkaline.

To get accustomed to a new machine, start with a simple recipe, such as basic white bread, and see how it comes out. With a little experience you will soon be able to adapt conventional recipes for use in the machine.

Before you start, assemble all the ingredients. Be sure that the yeast is fresh. All ingredients should be at room temperature. Cold liquids and butter can be heated in the microwave.

Be sure the kneading paddle is well seated in the bottom of the pan. Add the ingredients in the order suggested by the manufacturer's instructions. This may vary from one machine to the next. If you are using a timer, the order may change. Fix the bread pan securely into the bread machine. Select settings on the control panel according to the manufacturer's instructions and press Start.

To check the dough while the bread is kneading, look for it to form a fairly smooth ball that is a bit tacky to the touch and settles only slightly when the paddle stops kneading. If, after the ingredients are mixed, the imprint of the

The kneading paddle should be well seated in the bottom of the bread pan.

Add ingredients in the order suggested by the manufacturer.

The bread pan should be securely seated inside the machine.

paddle remains in the dough and the edges look a little jagged, add more liquid. Start with one tablespoon, then add additional liquid one teaspoon at a time, giving the dough time to absorb the liquid before adding more. If the dough is so soft that it loses its shape as soon as the paddle pauses, add more flour, one tablespoon at a time. Although these instructions fit most breads, some breads are designed to have dough that is a little stiffer or softer.

Don't be shy about keeping the lid up and watching at this stage. It is only when the bread is in the rising and baking stages that an open lid will interfere with temperature controls.

When the bread is done, remove it from the machine and the baking pan immediately. Otherwise, the steam released by the bread will condense in the pan, making the bread soggy on the outside. The bread should be allowed to cool for 20 to 30 minutes before you slice into it.

Instead of putting the dough into a bread pan it may be shaped in various ways as loaves or rolls.

Round Loaf

Shape the dough into a large ball. Flatten it slightly and place on a greased baking sheet. Slash the top of the dough with a sharp knife to make a cross. Cover and allow to rise for about 45 minutes in a warm place. Bake for 30 to 40 minutes.

Rolls

Baking time for rolls is 10 to 15 minutes after shaping, rising and glazing.

Cottage Rolls

Cut off one-third of each 2 oz piece of dough. Shape each piece into a ball. Place the large ball on a baking sheet and put the smaller one on top. Push a floured wooden spoon handle through both pieces of dough.

Dinner Rolls

Shape each 2 oz dough piece into a ball or sausage shape. Place on a baking sheet.

Clover Leaf Rolls

Divide each 2 oz piece of dough into 3 equal parts. Shape into 3 balls. Place on the baking sheet in the shape of a clover leaf and press lightly together.

Knot Rolls

Roll 2 oz pieces of dough into a thick 6 inch strand. Tie into a simple knot.

Braid

Divide the dough into three equal pieces. Roll each piece into a strand 12 to 14 inches long. Pinch together one end of the three strands and then braid them. Pinch the remaining ends together and lift the braid on to a greased baking sheet. Cover, allow to rise, and glaze. Decorate with poppy seeds, if desired. Bake for 25 to 30 minutes.

Three-Strand Braided Rolls

Cut off 2 oz pieces of risen dough. Divide and roll each piece into three 4 inch strands. Braid as above.

Two-Strand Braided Rolls

Divide the 2 oz dough pieces in half. Roll each piece into a strand 8 inches long. Place the strands in the form of a cross on the work surface. Take the two ends of the lower strand and cross them over the middle of the upper strand so that they lie side by side. Repeat this with the remaining strand and repeat alternately until all the dough has been used. Pinch the ends firmly together. Place on the baking sheet, glaze and decorate, cover, rise, and bake.

Braided Loaf

1 Cut dough into 3 equal pieces. Roll each piece to a long sausage shape, tapering the ends. Lie the shapes next to each other. Beginning in the center and working towards one end, braid shapes together.

2 Pinch the ends together and tuck them under the braid. Turn dough and continue braiding the other end, pinching ends and tucking under. Transfer to a baking tray, keeping ends tucked under.

The finished braided loaf.

Simple Yeast Breads

White Bread · Lemon Poppyseed Braid

Quick White Bread · Pumpernickel

Whole-wheat Bread · Potato Bread

Oatmeal Bread · Muesli Bread

Old-fashioned Rye Bread · Seed Bread

Challah · Sourdough Starter

Cheese Bread · San Francisco Sourdough Bread

Onion Bread · Milk Bread

Foccacio ·

White Bread

This recipe is the cornerstone of yeast baking.

1 cake (1 oz) compressed yeast or 2 Tbsp active-dry yeast and 1 tsp sugar	2 to 3 tsp salt
	1 Tbsp sugar
3¾ cups warm water	½ stick butter or margarine
12 cups bread or all-purpose flour	

BREAD MACHINE METHOD—MAKES 1lb LOAF

½ cup water	1 tsp salt
¼ cup milk	2 cups bread flour
1 Tbsp butter	2 tsp yeast
1 Tbsp sugar	

● Put all ingredients in bread pan in order suggested by your bread machine instructions. Set for white bread, medium crust. Press start.

Grease three large bread pans. Stir the yeast with a few tablespoons of the water adding the teaspoon of sugar if dried yeast is used. Put the bowl of dried yeast liquid aside for 10 minutes until frothy.

Mix the flour and salt together. Add the sugar, blend in the fat, stir in the yeast liquid and the rest of the warm water to make a soft dough. Turn the dough on to a lightly floured board and knead until it becomes smooth, elastic and non-sticky. Return the dough to the bowl, cover it with oiled plastic and allow to rise until doubled in size, about 1¼ hours.

Punch back the dough and divide it into 3 portions. Knead and shape into loaves to fit into the three bread pans. Cover the bread pans with oiled plastic. Allow to rise until doubled in size, about 45 minutes. Remove plastic and bake loaves for 45 to 50 minutes. Cool on a wire rack.

Quick White Bread

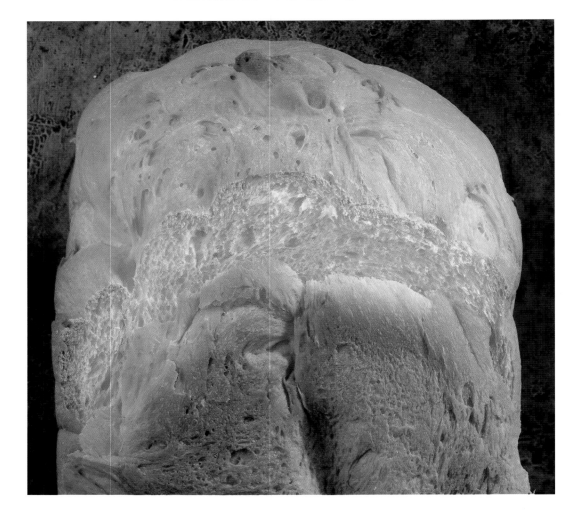

A quick bread because the rising process is accelerated by the addition of citric acid in the form of vitamin C.

MAKES 2 LARGE (OR 4 SMALL) LOAVES

2 cakes (2 oz) fresh compressed yeast or 4 Tbsp active-dry yeast and ½ tsp sugar	12 cups bread or all-purpose flour
	2 tsp salt
3¾ cups warm water	2 Tbsp sugar
2 25 mg pills vitamin C	½ stick butter or margarine

Grease two large (or four small) bread pans. Mix the yeast with a few tablespoons of the water adding the teaspoon of sugar if dried yeast is used. Set the dried yeast liquid aside for 10 minutes until frothy. Crush the vitamin C pills in a little water and add to the yeast liquid.

Mix the flour and salt together in a large warm bowl. Add the sugar and blend in the fat. Stir in the yeast liquid and the rest of the warm water and mix to a soft dough. Turn on to a lightly floured board and knead the dough until it is smooth, elastic and non-sticky. Divide the dough in half, shape into 2 or 4 loaves and put them into the bread pans. Cover the pans with oiled plastic and allow to rise until doubled in size, about 1 hour.

Preheat oven to 450°F. Remove the plastic and bake the loaves for about 45 minutes (30 to 35 minutes for small loaves). Cool the bread on a wire rack.

Whole-wheat Bread

This bread has a dense texture as it uses only whole-wheat flour. To lighten use half all-purpose and half whole-wheat flours.

MAKES 3 LARGE LOAVES

1½ cakes (½ oz) fresh compressed yeast or 3 Tbsp active-dry yeast and 1 tsp sugar

3¾ cups warm water

12 cups whole-wheat flour

2 to 3 tsp salt

1 Tbsp sugar

½ stick butter or margarine or 4 Tbsp vegetable oil

Beaten egg, milk, or salted water for glazing

Cracked wheat, bran, or buckwheat for decorating (optional)

TIP

The rising takes some 15 to 30 minutes longer if carried out at room temperature.

Grease three large 9 x 5 inch bread pans. Stir the yeast into a few tablespoons of warm water, adding the teaspoon of sugar if dried yeast is used. Set the dried yeast liquid aside for 10 minutes until frothy. Put the whole-wheat flour into a large mixing bowl and add the salt and sugar. Blend in the fat and stir in the yeast liquid and the rest of the warm water. Mix well and turn on to a floured board. Knead the dough until it is non-sticky. Return the dough to the bowl, cover it with oiled plastic and leave it to rise in a warm place for about 1¼ hours, until doubled in size.

Punch down the dough. Divide it into 3 portions and shape into loaves to fit into the bread pans. Cover the bread pans with oiled plastic and allow them to rise in a warm place for about 40 to 45 minutes, until doubled in size.

Preheat oven to 450°F. Remove the plastic and brush the tops of the loaves with the selected glaze. Sprinkle the loaves with grain if desired.

Bake for 45 to 59 minutes. Cool on a wire rack.

Oatmeal Bread

A delicious home-baked bread with a distinctive nutty flavor.

MAKES 2 SMALL LOAVES

1 cake (1 oz) compressed yeast or 1 package (1 Tbsp) active-dry yeast and 1 tsp brown sugar	(½ whole-wheat, ½ white flour)
	2 cups fine oatmeal
2¼ cups warm water	4 Tbsp wheatgerm
2 Tbsp brown sugar	4 Tbsp soya flour
4¾ cups mixed flour	2 Tbsp vegetable oil
	1½ tsp salt

BREAD MACHINE METHOD—MAKES 1 lb LOAF

½ cup rolled oats (not quick oatmeal)	1 tsp salt
⅓ cup very hot water	½ tsp baking soda
⅝ cup buttermilk	2 Tbsp wheat germ
1 Tbsp butter	1¾ cups bread flour
2 Tbsp sugar	1½ tsp yeast

● Put oats in a bread pan. Pour very hot or boiling water over the oats and stir. Let sit at least 15 minutes. Put remaining ingredients in bread pan in order suggested by your bread machine instructions. Set for white bread, medium crust. Press Start.

Grease two small bread pans. Put the yeast into a bowl (with the sugar, if dried yeast is used) and stir with ½ cup of the warm water. Set aside for up to 10 minutes until foamy. Add the sugar and half the mixed flours to the rest of the water and beat well for 5 minutes. Add the yeast liquid and beat thoroughly. Stir in the rolled oats and set the mixture aside in a warm place for about 30 minutes to make a sponge batter.

Add the wheatgerm, soya flour, oil, salt, and the rest of the mixed flours to the sponge batter. Turn out on to a floured board and knead well until smooth. Return the dough to the bowl and cover with oiled plastic. Set aside in a warm place until doubled in size, about 30 minutes.

Punch down the dough on a floured board and divide into 2 pieces. Shape into loaves and place them in the bread pans. Cover with oiled plastic and allow to rise until double in size once again. Bake for about 1 hour. Cool on a wire rack.

Old-fashioned Rye Bread

Rye flour is very low in gluten, so white flour is needed to lighten the texture and give the bread more body. It does make the dough more difficult to work with, so an electric mixer is helpful unless you are an expert bread maker.

MAKES 2 LOAVES

5 cups all-purpose flour	2 Tbsp caraway seeds
3 cups rue flour	⅓ cup vegetable oil
2 tsp salt	2½ cups lukewarm water
2 packages (2 Tbsp) active dry yeast	I egg, beaten or 2 Tbsp butter or margarine, melted, for glaze
2 tsp sugar	

BREAD MACHINE METHOD—MAKES I lb LOAF

¾ cup water	2 tsp caraway seeds
I Tbsp vegetable oil	I½ cups bread flour
4 tsp molasses	¾ cup rye flour
I tsp salt	2 tsp yeast

● Put all ingredients in bread pan in order suggested by your bread machine instructions. Set for whole-wheat bread, medium crust. Press start.

● For oven-baked bread, set machine for dough stage. When dough is ready, remove it from the machine and press down. Shape it into a large ball and flatten it slightly. Or roll it into a fat baguette. Place it on a baking sheet and cover the bread loosely, set it in a warm place, and let it rise until doubled in volume, about I hour.

● Make a wash of I egg lightly beaten with I tablespoon of milk. Gently brush the egg wash over the top and sides of the loaf. Bake the bread in a preheated 375°F oven until the top and bottom are crusty and sound hollow when thumped— about 35 minutes.

In a large bowl, combine flours and salt. Set aside. In bowl of an electric mixer fitted with the dough hook, combine yeast, sugar, and caraway seeds. Add oil and I cup lukewarm water and stir; sprinkle with a little flour. Cover bowl with a clean dish towel and leave until mixture looks slightly foamy and bubbly, 10 to 12 minutes.

With mixer on low speed, pour in I½ cups lukewarm water and beat until combined. Gradually add flours; when completely incorporated dough will be sticky. You may have some flour mixture left over.

Increase mixer to medium speed and knead dough until it forms a soft ball around the dough hook and leaves side of bowl, 5 to 7 minutes. If dough remains very sticky, add a little more all-purpose flour and continue to knead

2 minutes longer. (Do not add too much more flour or bread will be tough.)

Lightly grease a bowl and place dough in it; turn dough to coat with oil. (This prevents a crust from forming on surface.) Cover bowl with dish towel and leave to rise until doubled in bulk, I½ to 2 hours, in a warm draft-free place.

Lightly grease a large cookie sheet. Turn out dough on to lightly floured work surface and knead gently to knock air out of dough. Knead lightly and cut dough in half and shape each half into a smooth round ball. Place each loaf on opposite corners of cookie sheet, flatten slightly and cover with a towel. Let loaves rise until almost doubled in bulk, I hour.

Preheat oven to 350°F. Brush loaves with egg glaze or melted butter or margarine. With a sharp knife, slash top of each loaf 2 or 3 times. Bake until loaves are well browned and sound hollow when tapped on bottom, 35 to 40 minutes. Remove to a wire rack to cool.

Challah

Challah is the traditional, braided egg bread served on the Sabbath and other Jewish holidays. It is usually braided, except at Rosh Hashana when a special spiral loaf is prepared to symbolize reaching for heaven in the hope of a Happy New Year. This is the most popular egg bread in the United States and one of the most versatile because its soft, yellow, cake-like crumb suits most foods very well.

MAKES 2 LOAVES

1 package (1 Tbsp) active-dry yeast	3 eggs, lightly beaten
1 Tbsp sugar	4¼ cups all-purpose flour, sifted
⅓ cup lukewarm water	1 egg, beaten with a pinch of salt and pinch of sugar, for glazing
1 tsp salt	
1 cup milk, scalded	Sesame or poppy seeds
6 Tbsp vegetable oil	

BREAD MACHINE METHOD—MAKES 1 lb LOAF

	GLAZE
2 eggs	1 egg yolk
¼ cup water	1 tsp water
1 Tbsp butter	1 to 2 tsp poppy seeds
2 Tbsp sugar	
1 tsp salt	
2 cups bread flour	
2 tsp yeast	

● Put ingredients in bread pan in order suggested by your bread machine instructions. Set for white bread, dough stage. Press start.

● When dough is ready, remove and punch down. Cut dough into three equal parts. Roll each piece into a rope about 12 inches long. Braid the three ropes together. Pinch the ends together and turn them under. Cover the loaf and set it in a warm place to rise until doubled in volume, 45 minutes to 1 hour.

● Preheat the oven to 350°F. Make glaze by beating egg yolk and water with fork. Brush lightly over loaf. Sprinkle top with poppy seeds.

● Bake until top is nicely browned, 30 to 35 minutes.

VARIATION

To form the traditional Rosh Hashana spiral loaf, prepare dough as above but roll each dough half into 1 long sausage shape about 24 inches long and 1 inch in diameter. Hold one end against the surface and using it as the center, begin coiling the spiral. Place on upper left-hand corner of baking sheet and tuck one end under loaf. Repeat with second piece and bake as for braided loaves.

In the bowl of an electric mixer with dough hook fitted, combine yeast and sugar. Stir in water. Sprinkle with a little flour to cover. Cover with a clean dish towel and leave until mixture looks slightly foamy and bubbly, 10 to 12 minutes.

With mixer on low speed, beat in salt, milk, oil, and eggs until well mixed. Gradually add flour; when completely incorporated dough will be slightly sticky. Increase mixer to medium speed and knead dough until dough forms a ball around the dough hook and leaves sides of bowl, 5 to 7 minutes. If dough remains sticky, add a little more flour and continue to knead 2 minutes longer. (Do not add too much flour; a softer dough yields a moister loaf.)

Lightly grease a large bowl. Place dough in it, turn dough to coat with oiled plastic. Cover with a clean dish towel and leave to rise until doubled in bulk, 1½ to 2 hours, in a moderately warm, draft-free place; do not leave to rise in too warm a place or texture may be uneven.

Turn out dough on to lightly floured work surface and knead gently. Return dough to bowl, cover tightly and refrigerate 6 to 8 hours or overnight to let dough rise slowly a second time. (Allowing dough to rise slowly provides a light, even texture.)

Turn out dough on to a lightly floured work surface and knead gently. Shape into a ball and cut into 2 equal-size pieces.

Lightly grease a large baking sheet. Working with one half at a time, cut dough half into 3 equal-size pieces; roll into balls. Roll each ball into long sausage shapes about 18 inches long and 1 inch wide. Braid the 3 sausage shapes together and place on one side of baking sheet, tucking ends neatly underneath loaf. Repeat with remaining dough to form second loaf.

Cover loaves with clean dish towel and leave in a warm place to rise until almost doubled in size, 1 hour. Preheat oven to 375°F.

Brush each risen loaf with egg glaze and sprinkle with sesame or poppy seeds. Bake 40 minutes until loaves are well browned and sound hollow when tapped on the bottom. Remove to a wire rack to cool.

Cheese Bread

Perfect to accompany soups or salads. The dough may also be used as a pizza base.

½ cake (½ oz) compressed yeast or 1 package (1 Tbsp) active-dry yeast and ½ tsp sugar	½ tsp dry mustard powder or 2 tsp creamed horseradish
1¼ cups warm water	1 Tbsp butter or margarine
4 cups all-purpose flour	1 cup finely grated Cheddar cheese
1 tsp salt	Beaten egg or milk for glazing
¼ tsp cayenne pepper	1 to 2 Tbsp grated cheese for decorating (optional)
2 Tbsp chives	

Grease one large or two small bread pans. Stir the yeast into the warm water, adding sugar if dried yeast is used. Stand the dried yeast liquid for 10 minutes to become frothy.

Put the flour, salt, cayenne pepper, mustard, and chives into a bowl and blend in the fat. Stir in the cheese and then the yeast liquid (and horseradish if used). Work together to make a dough. Turn the dough on to a floured board and knead until smooth and non-sticky.

Return to the bowl, cover with oiled plastic and leave to rise for 1 hour until doubled in size. Punch down the dough and shape into 1 large or 2 small loaves. Place the

---

BREAD MACHINE METHOD—MAKES 1 lb LOAF

⅔ cup water	⅓ cup crumbled feta cheese
2 Tbsp olive oil	¼ cup coarsely chopped green olives
1 Tbsp sugar	2 Tbsp chopped sun-dried tomatoes
½ tsp dried thyme	
1 tsp salt	2 Tbsp bread flour
2 cups bread flour	2 Tbsp cornmeal
1½ tsp yeast	

● Put first seven ingredients in bread pan in order suggested by your bread machine instructions. Set for white bread, medium crust. Press start. Toss remaining ingredients with flour, then add them to the dough after first kneading or at the beeper.

● To bake in the oven, set the bread machine for dough stage. When dough is ready, remove and punch down. Shape into a round loaf. Put on a baking sheet that has been sprinkled with cornmeal. Cover loosely and put in a warm place to rise until doubled in volume. Brush the surface with a glaze of 1 egg mixed with 1 tablespoon water, and bake in a preheated 350°F oven until golden, about 25 minutes.

---

shaped dough in the pan(s). Brush the dough with beaten egg or milk. Cover the pan(s) with oiled plastic and leave to rise in a warm place for about 45 minutes.

Sprinkle the bread dough with grated cheese if desired. Bake for about 40 minutes until brown. Turn out and cool the bread on a wire rack.

Onion Bread

Serve this tasty bread hot or cold.

One quarter of the Quick White Bread dough (see page 328)	⅔ cup milk
2 cups onions, sliced	¼ tsp salt or garlic salt
½ stick butter or margarine	Pinch freshly ground black pepper
2 Tbsp all-purpose or bread flour	1 tsp poppy or sesame seeds

Grease and flour an 8 inch round cake pan. Roll out the dough to fit the pan. Put the dough into the pan, cover with oiled plastic and allow to rise until doubled in size, about 30 minutes.

Preheat oven to 375°F. Cook the onions in the fat in a heavy pan until transparent and softened. Stir in the flour and cook for a couple of minutes. Add the milk, stirring constantly. Bring to a boil and simmer for another minute. Add the salt and pepper. Spread the onion mixture over the dough and sprinkle with the seeds. Bake for 30 minutes.

Foccacio

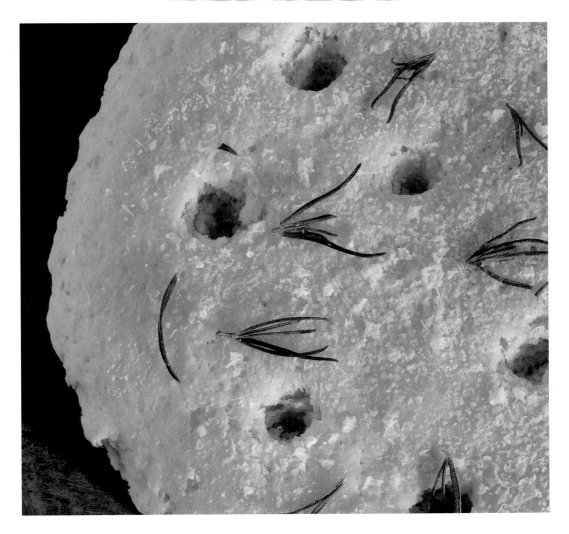

Serve wedges of this hearty bread as an hors d'oeuvre or with a meal instead of garlic bread. Instead of butter, dip pieces in high-quality olive oil. This bread is best served warm.

BREAD MACHINE RECIPE—MAKES 1 lb LOAF

⅔ cup water	1 or 2 minced garlic cloves
2 Tbsp olive oil	1 tsp dried rosemary
1 tsp salt	1 tsp coarse salt
2 cups bread flour	2 Tbsp olive oil
1¼ tsp yeast	2 tsp grated Parmesan

Put first five ingredients in a bread pan in order suggested by your bread machine instructions. Set for white bread, dough stage. Press Start.

Preheat oven to 400°F. Lightly sprinkle cornmeal on a baking sheet.

Remove dough and punch down. Let dough rest about 5 minutes. On a lightly floured surface, roll dough into a round, about ½ inch thick. Place dough on baking sheet. Sprinkle the garlic, rosemary, and coarse salt over the top, then lightly press it into the dough. With your fingertips, poke shallow indentations all over the top of the round. Pour the remaining olive oil over the top, letting it pool in the indentations. Sprinkle Parmesan over the top.

Bake bread until lightly browned, about 20 minutes.

Lemon Poppyseed Braid

Slightly sweet, flavored with lemon, and full of poppy seeds, this braided bread, easily made in a bread machine, makes an impressive appearance at brunch or tea.

BREAD MACHINE RECIPE—MAKES 1 lb LOAF

1 egg	1 tsp salt
½ cup lemon yogurt	2 cups bread flour
3 Tbsp butter	1½ tsp yeast
3 Tbsp sugar	
3 Tbsp poppy seeds	**GLAZE**
2 tsp grated lemon peel	1 egg white beaten with 2 tsp water

Put all dough ingredients in bread machine pan. Set for white or sweet bread, dough stage. Press Start.

When dough is ready, remove from pan and punch down. Cut into three equal pieces. Let it rest 5 minutes. Butter a baking sheet. Roll each piece of dough into a rope, about 14 inches long. Braid three ropes together and tuck ends under. Cover dough and put in a warm place to rise until doubled, 45 minutes to 1 hour.

Brush dough with egg-water wash. Bake bread in a preheated 350°F oven until golden, 25 to 30 minutes.

Pumpernickel

Pumpernickel is an eastern European bread which keeps well. Serve with butter and cheese or cured meats.

MAKES 2 LARGE LOAVES

1 cake (1 oz) compressed yeast or 2 packages (2 Tbsp) active-dry yeast and 1 tsp brown sugar	⅔ cup buckwheat flour
	⅓ cup cornmeal
5 cups warm water	2 tsp salt
6 cups whole-wheat flour	1 cup cooked, mashed potato
1 Tbsp molasses	1 tsp caraway seeds
1 cup dark rye flour	1 cup whole-wheat flour (if needed)

Grease two large bread pans. Stir the yeast into one cup of the warm water, adding the brown sugar in the case of dried yeast. Set the dried yeast liquid aside for 10 minutes until frothy.

Mix the whole-wheat flour, molasses, yeast liquid, and the rest of the warm water to make a very wet dough. Beat well, knead in the bowl until it becomes smooth and less sticky. Add the rest of the ingredients and mix well. Turn on to a floured board knead, working in the last cup of whole-wheat flour if required. Knead until the dough is smooth and elastic. Return it to the bowl and cover with a sheet of oiled plastic. Leave to rise in a warm place until doubled in size, 1¼ to 1½ hours.

BREAD MACHINE METHOD—MAKES 1lb LOAF

¾ cup milk	2 tsp caraway seeds
1 Tbsp vegetable oil	⅓ cup bread flour
2 Tbsp molasses	1 cup rye flour
½ tsp salt	½ cup whole-wheat flour
2 Tbsp unsweetened cocoa powder	2 Tbsp cornmeal
	2 tsp yeast

● Put ingredients in bread pan in order suggested by your bread machine instructions. Set for whole-wheat bread, medium crust. Press Start.

● Alternatively, to make baguettes, remove dough from bread machine after first kneading and punch down. Cut dough in two equal parts. Roll each part into a thick rope, about 8 inches long. Put baguettes on a baking sheet that ha`s been sprinkled with cornmeal. Put in a warm place and cover loosely. Let rise until doubled in volume. Bake in a preheated oven 350°F oven about 25 minutes, or until loaves are crusty and sound hollow.

Punch down the dough, divide it into 2 pieces. Shape into loaves and put the dough into the bread pans. Cover the pans with oiled plastic and allow to rise until doubled in size, about 1 hour.

Preheat oven to 375°F. Bake for 1 hour, remove the loaves from the pans and bake for a further 10 to 15 minutes. Cool the bread on a wire rack. Keep the bread for 1 to 2 days before slicing.

Potato Bread

This is a nutritious bread containing potato, egg, and sour cream. It is delicious toasted with preserves.

MAKES 3 LOAVES

1 (8–9oz) large raw potato, peeled	8 cups flour
2 cups milk	2 tsp salt
1 cake (1 oz) compressed fresh yeast or package (1 Tbsp) active-dry yeast and 1 tsp sugar	1 egg
	3 Tbsp sour cream

Grease three small bread pans. Grate peeled potato finely. Bring milk to a boil and pour over potato in a bowl. Cool until lukewarm and add fresh yeast. If dried yeast is used stir it, with the sugar, into 3 tablespoons warm milk or water. Leave for 8 to 10 minutes until frothy. Add dried yeast mixture to potato–milk mix. Beat in half the flour until well mixed. Add salt, egg, sour cream, and rest of flour. Beat thoroughly.

Cover the bowl with oiled plastic and set aside in a warm place for 2 to 2½ hours. Knead thoroughly. Divide between 3 bread pans. Allow to rise again, covered, for 40 minutes. Preheat oven to 350°F and bake for 45 minutes.

Muesli Bread

This recipe calls for unsweetened muesli so the only sweetness comes from the raisins. The texture is nutty and oaty making this the ideal breakfast bread.

MAKES 3 LARGE LOAVES

Cracked wheat or bran for decoration	6 cups all-purpose or bread flour
1 cake (½ oz) compressed yeast or 1 package (1 Tbsp) active-dry yeast and 1 tsp sugar or honey	4 cups whole-wheat flour
	2 tsp salt
	¼ cup margarine
3¾ cups warm water	2 cups unsweetened muesli

BREAD MACHINE METHOD—MAKES 1 lb LOAF

½ cup water	1⅓ cups bread flour
¼ cup milk	⅔ cup whole-wheat flour
2 Tbsp vegetable oil	1½ tsp yeast
2 Tbsp honey	½ cup trail mix
1 tsp salt	

● Put all ingredients except trail mix in bread pan in order suggested by your bread machine instructions. Set for whole-wheat bread, medium crust. Press Start. Add trail mix at the beeper or after first kneading.

● If the only trail mix you fan find is a mix of raisins and sunflower seeds, doctor it with dates, dried apricots, dried cherries, pecans, or cashews. Coarsely chop whole nuts such as almonds. Avoid using chocolate in the trail mix as it tends to turn in a bread machine.

Grease three large flowerpots or three large bread pans and sprinkle them with cracked wheat or bran.

Stir the yeast into the water, adding the sugar or honey if dried yeast is used. Set aside for about 10 minutes to become frothy. Mix the white and whole-wheat flours together with the salt (and sugar, if used). Blend in the margarine. Pour in the yeast liquid and mix thoroughly. Turn the dough on to a floured board and knead until smooth and elastic. Cover the dough in the bowl using a sheet of oiled plastic and allow to rise in a warm place until doubled in size (1 to 1¼ hours). Turn the dough on to the floured board and punch down after working in the muesli.

Divide the dough into 3 portions and shape them to fit the flowerpots or bread pans. Brush the dough with milk and cover with oiled plastic. Allow to rise for 40 to 50 minutes until doubled in size.

Preheat oven to 425°F. Bake for about 45 to 50 minutes. Cool on wire racks.

Seed Bread

The seeds in this loaf add flavor and texture to the bread. Easy to eat, it is divided into six portions which are simply broken off for serving.

MAKES 1 LOAF

1 package (1 Tbsp) active-dry yeast	2 Tbsp polyunsaturated margarine
4 cups whole-wheat flour	2 tsp fennel seeds
2 tsp fine granulated sugar	2 tsp sesame seeds
2 tsp salt	1 egg white
2 tsp caraway seeds	

BREAD MACHINE METHOD—MAKES 1lb LOAF

½ cup buttermilk	½ cup whole-wheat flour
⅓ cup water	1½ cups bread flour
1 Tbsp vegetable oil	1½ tsp yeast
1 Tbsp sugar	3 Tbsp raw, shelled
¼ tsp baking soda	sunflower seeds
1 tsp salt	1 Tbsp toasted sesame
2 Tbsp toasted wheat germ	seeds

● Put all ingredients except seeds in bread pan in order suggested by your bread machine instructions. Set for whole-wheat bread, medium crust. Press Start. Add seeds after first kneading or when machine beeps to add nuts.
● To toast wheat germ and sesame seeds, put each in a small, ungreased skillet over medium heat. Shake the pan occasionally so seeds do not scorch. Cook until they are lightly brown. Let seeds or wheat germ cool before adding them to the dough.

Place the yeast, flour, sugar, and salt in a large bowl. Rub in the margarine and add half of each of the seeds. Stir in 1¼ cups warm water and mix well. Bring the mixture together to form a soft dough. Knead the dough for 5 minutes on a lightly floured surface and break into six equal pieces.

Lightly grease a deep 6 inch round cake pan. Shape each of the dough pieces into a round. Place five pieces around the edge of the pan and one in the center. Cover and allow to rise in a warm place for 1 hour or until doubled in size.

Whisk the egg white and brush over the top of the dough. Sprinkle the remaining seeds on to the top of the dough, alternating the different types on each section of the loaf.

Bake in the oven at 400°F for 30 minutes or until cooked through. The loaf should sound hollow when tapped on the base. Cool slightly and serve.

Sourdough Starter

Sourdough is the product of fermentation in dough that has been allowed to sit out for days and gather wild yeasts from the air. In ancient times, it was the only leavening known to bread bakers, and much effort was made to disguise its sour taste. It came back into common usage in mining camps during the California Gold Rush of 1849, then hit a new wave of popularity in the middle of the 20th century.

Making and maintaining your own sourdough starter is not difficult. A pot of starter takes at least a few days to ferment and develop a sour flavor before you add it to the first loaf, but after that, it can be used and replenished daily.

1 cup low-fat milk, scalded	2¼ tsp active-dry yeast
1 cup hot water	2½ cups all-purpose flour or bread flour
1 Tbsp sugar	

Mix the milk, water, and sugar. When the temperature has cooled to between 105°F and 115°F, add the yeast. Allow the yeast to develop a foamy head, about 5 to 10 minutes. Then add it to the flour and mix well.

Put the bowl in a warm place, between 80°F and 100°F, like the back of the stove. Loosely cover the bowl so that air will still circulate and the starter will gather airborne yeasts. Within 24 hours, it should be bubbly and have the beginnings of a sour smell. Stir it once or twice a day. The starter may separate into a thick, curd-like mixture on the bottom and gray watery liquids on the top. That's normal, as long as it doesn't turn green or pink. (If it does, throw it out and start again.) The mixture is ready to use when it develops a good sour smell, usually 3 to 5 days.

To bake sourdough bread, you need to prepare a sponge at least six hours in advance. Mix some starter with a portion of flour and liquid, as directed by the recipe. Replenish the starter with amounts of flour and water equal to the amount you removed. For instance, if the recipe calls for ½ cup of sourdough starter, replenish the starter with ½ cup water and ½ cup flour. Both the sponge and the replenished starter should be put in a warm place, covered loosely, and left to ferment at least 6 hours, until bubbly.

If you use the sourdough on an almost daily basis, you can leave the starter pot at the back of the stove, replenishing it after each use. If you are only an occasional baker, replenish it, let it sit out for 6 to 24 hours, then put the starter in the refrigerator. The starter pot should be tightly covered when it is in the refrigerator. If you do not bake at least once a week, refresh the starter every week or two. Remove 1 cup of starter and discard the rest. Add 1 cup of water and 1 cup of flour and return it to the refrigerator.

San Francisco Sourdough Bread

There are almost as many versions of this bread as there are bakeries in San Francisco.

MAKES 2 LOAVES

1 package (1 Tbsp) active-dry yeast	½ tsp salt
1 Tbsp sugar	2 Tbsp vinegar
1½ cups warm water	5½ cups all-purpose or bread flour
1 cup sourdough starter	½ tsp baking soda

Stir the yeast and sugar into the water and set aside for 15 minutes, or until foamy. Stir in the starter, salt, and vinegar and 3 cups of the flour. Cover with oiled plastic and allow to ruse until doubled in size.

Punch down the dough and combine with remaining flour and baking soda. Knead on a floured surface until smooth, elastic, and non-sticky. Divide the mixture in two and form into long loaves. Place on large greased and floured baking sheets. Cover with oiled plastic and allow to rise until doubled in size, about 1 hour.

Preheat oven to 450°F. Place a tray of water in the oven. Spray the loaf with water and bake for 10 minutes. Reduce heat to 400°, remove the water and bake for a further 35 minutes misting the loaves with water twice more to ensure a hard crust. Turn out on to a wire rack.

Milk Bread

Using milk instead of water gives this bread additional richness of flavor.

MAKES 3 SMALL LOAVES OR 1 LARGE
AND 1 SMALL LOAF

½ cake (½ oz) compressed yeast or 1 package (1 Tbsp) active-dry yeast and ½ tsp sugar	6 cups all-purpose or bread flour
	1½ tsp salt
2 cups warm skim milk or whole milk and water mixed	1½ tsp sugar
	¾ stick butter or margarine
	Beaten egg or milk for glazing

VARIATION: OLIVE BREAD

Omit the 1½ tsp sugar and stir in 5 to 6 tablespoons olive oil instead of blending in the butter or margarine. Add 1½ cups pitted, sliced black olives to the dough with the dough liquid. The olive loaves may be shaped into 2 or 3 rounds and baked on greased baking sheets instead of being baked in bread pans if preferred.

Grease three small bread pans (or 1 large and 1 small). Stir the yeast into the liquid, adding sugar if dried yeast is used. Allow 15 minutes in a warm place for dried yeast to become frothy.

Mix the flour, salt, and sugar and blend in the butter or margarine. Stir in the yeast liquid and mix to a soft dough. Turn the dough on to a lightly floured board and knead until it becomes smooth and loses its stickiness. Return the dough to the warm mixing bowl and cover it with oiled plastic. Leave to rise until doubled in size, about 1½ hours.

Punch down the dough, divide it into three (or 1 large and 1 small piece) and shape to fit the bread pans. Brush the loaves with beaten egg or milk. Cover the pans with oiled plastic and allow to rise until doubled in size, about 1 hour.

Preheat oven to 400°F and bake for about 50 minutes. Cool on a wire rack.

Pizza

Basic Pizza Dough

Basic pizza dough goes well with just about any topping you like. This is the recipe for the classic Italian base.

MAKES 2 12 INCH THIN CRUST PIZZAS
OR 1 DEEP PAN PIZZA

1 package (1 Tbsp) active-dry yeast	5 cups all-purpose flour
	2 Tbsp olive oil
1 cup warm water	½ tsp salt

Combine the yeast, warm water, and 3 cups of the flour. Mix well to blend. Add the oil, salt, and remaining flour and stir until the dough sticks together (1).

Place the dough on a lightly floured surface. Dust your hands with flour and knead the dough until it is smooth and elastic, above 5 minutes. If the dough gets sticky, sprinkle it with a little flour (2).

Roll the dough into a ball. Cover with a cloth and set in a warm, but not hot, place to rise until doubled in volume, about 1 hour (3).

When the dough has risen, roll it into a ball to make one deep pan pizza or divide it in two balls to make two 12 inch thin crust pizzas. Before rolling out and topping the pizza, allow the dough to rest for 20 minutes (4).

When ready to bake, place dough in center of lightly oiled baking sheet.

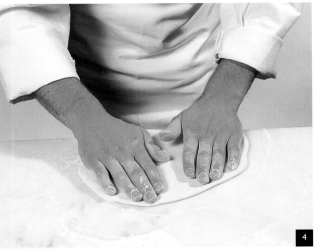

Whole-wheat Pizza Dough

Whole-wheat flour adds robust flavor to the dough, but this recipe also calls for all-purpose flour. On its own, whole-wheat flour is too heavy to make a proper crust. It, too, goes well with most toppings.

MAKES 2 12 INCH THIN CRUST PIZZAS
OR 1 DEEP PAN PIZZA

1 package (1 Tbsp) active-dry yeast	2 Tbsp olive oil
1 cup warm water	½ tsp salt
2¾ cups all-purpose flour	1¼ cups whole-wheat flour

In a large bowl, combine the yeast, warm water, and white flour. Mix well to blend. Add the oil, salt, and whole-wheat flour and stir until the dough sticks together. Place the dough on a lightly floured surface. Dust your hands with flour and then knead the dough until it is smooth and elastic, about 5 minutes. If the dough gets sticky, sprinkle it with a little more flour.

Roll the dough into a ball and place it in a lightly oiled bowl. Cover the bowl with a cloth and set in a warm, not hot, place to rise until doubled in volume, about 1 hour.

When the dough has risen, roll it into a ball to make one 12 inch deep pan crust pizza or divide it in two balls to make two thin crust 12 inch pizzas. Before rolling out and topping the pizza, allow the dough to rest for 20 minutes.

When ready to bake, place dough in center of lightly oiled pan. Roll outward toward the edges with the palm of your hand until the dough fills the pan evenly.

VARIATION

To make Whole-wheat Cheese Pizza Dough, follow instructions as for Whole-wheat Pizza Dough, but add ½ cup grated Parmesan cheese to the oil and salt which will then be added to the yeast mixture.

Corn Bread Pizza Dough

Cornmeal makes an interesting variation on ordinary flour. It complements tomato-based sauces such as Creole, jambalaya, or Mexican-style toppings. It also goes well with cheeses.

MAKES 1 12 INCH THIN CRUST PIZZA

1 cup warm water	1⅓ cups yellow cornmeal
1 package (1 Tbsp) active-dry yeast	¼ tsp salt
3¼ cups all-purpose flour	1 tsp sugar
	2 Tbsp corn oil

In a large bowl, combine the warm water, yeast, 2 cups of white flour, and half of the cornmeal. Stir to mix thoroughly. Add the remaining ingredients, stirring with a wooden spoon until mixed. Place the dough on a floured surface. Dust your hands with white flour and knead the dough for 5 minutes, dusting with additional flour if necessary to keep it from sticking. Dough should be smooth and elastic.

Place the dough in a clean bowl, cover with cloth, and set in a warm place to rise for about 1 hour or until doubled in size.

When dough is ready, roll into a ball and set aside to rest for 20 minutes before topping and baking.

Pizza Primavera

"**S**infully rich" is how this pizza can be described with its sauce made of cream and cheese. But it's also loaded with healthy fresh vegetables.

MAKES 1 12 INCH DEEP PAN PIZZA

1 batch Whole-wheat Pizza Dough (see page 346)	2 scallions, chopped
	½ cup Parmesan cheese
3 tsp olive oil	8 oz fresh asparagus, chopped
3 tsp flour	
1 cup heavy cream	½ large red bell pepper
1 handful basil leaves, finely chopped	1 small onion
	1 small zucchini
2 cloves garlic, crushed	

Preheat oven to 500°F. Bake the pizza dough for 3 minutes and remove from oven.

To make the sauce, heat the olive oil in a pan and add the flour, stirring to blend. Allow to cook for 2 or 3 minutes until bubbling. Slowly add the cream, stirring to mix. When the flour mixture is smooth, add the basil, garlic, and scallions. Bring to a boil and then simmer over low heat for 5 minutes, stirring frequently. Remove from the heat and stir in the Parmesan cheese.

Wash the asparagus and snap off the ends, and then chop on the diagonal into 2 inch pieces. Seed and chop the bell pepper into 2 inch squares. Chop the onion and zucchini into fairly small pieces. Toss the vegetables in a bowl and mix.

To assemble the pizza, spread the vegetables on the prebaked base. Pour the sauce over the vegetables, spreading it with a back of a spoon if necessary. Bake for 7 to 8 minutes.

Pizza with Caramelized Onions

Caramelized onions are cooked slowly in oil until they are golden brown and very soft. They have a wonderful flavor that goes well on a pizza. Make them ahead of time and store them in the refrigerator until ready to use.

MAKES 1 12 INCH DEEP PAN PIZZA

1 batch Basic or Whole-wheat Pizza Dough (see page 346)	½ tsp salt
	2 tsp red wine vinegar
2 large onions	1½ cups grated fontina cheese
3 Tbsp olive oil	

SAUCE

1 28-oz can puréed tomatoes	1 tsp basil
1 bay leaf	1 tsp thyme
1 tsp oregano	½ tsp marjoram

Slice both ends off the onions but do not peel. Cut the onions in quarters. Place them skin side down in a roasting pan. Liberally brush each onion with 1 tablespoon of oil and sprinkle with salt. Cover the pan with foil and bake for 30 minutes, remove the foil and brush the onion with the remaining oil. Sprinkle with vinegar. Turn onion quarters on one side and return to the oven for one hour. Occasionally turn the onions and baste with the oil from the pan. When done, allow to cool or store in refrigerator for later use.

Preheat oven to 500°F.

To make the sauce, place ingredients in a pan and bring to a boil. Reduce heat, cover loosely to keep from spattering, and simmer for 30 minutes, stirring occasionally.

When ready to assemble the pizza, slice the onion quarters into strips. Spread the pizza sauce over the pizza dough. Spread sliced onion over the sauce and top with cheese. Bake for 10 minutes.

Deep Pan Creole Pizza

Creole dishes tend to be spicy tomato and vegetable mixtures, and this pizza is no exception. Okra is available from most markets. It exudes a sticky mucus when cut, which adds a viscous texture to the topping.

MAKES 1 9 X 13 INCH DEEP PAN PIZZA

1 batch Basic Whole-wheat Pizza Dough (see page 346)	1 tsp thyme
2 cups okra	½ tsp basil
2 14-oz cans chopped tomatoes	½ tsp cayenne pepper
1 tsp oregano	2 cloves garlic, crushed
	2 stalks celery, chopped
	1 small onion, chopped

Preheat oven to 500°F.

Place the dough in the center of a lightly oiled 13 x 9 x 2 inch pan.

Using your fingers, gently spread the dough until it covers the bottom of the pan evenly and goes halfway up the sides.

Boil the okra until tender then chop. Put the tomatoes into a colander and drain and discard the liquid but retain the thick sauce. Place the tomatoes and sauce in a bowl. Add the spices and garlic. Chop the celery and onion into small pieces and add them to the bowl. Finally, add the okra and stir gently to mix.

To assemble, spread the tomato and okra mixture on to the pizza dough and bake for 20 minutes.

Sweet Breads and Yeasted Cakes for Coffee

Spicy Sweet-potato Bread

In a small saucepan over low heat, heat the water and 1 tablespoon of the sugar until very warm (120°F to 130°F). Pour into the bowl of a heavy-duty electric mixer, and sprinkle over the yeast and 1 tablespoon of the flour. Allow to stand until foamy, about 15 minutes.

Fit the mixer with the dough hook and beat in the salt, 2 teaspoons of the pumpkin-pie spice, the dry milk, mashed sweet potato or pumpkin, ½ cup of the sugar, half the butter, the grated orange zest, and 2 cups of the flour until well blended.

On low speed, gradually beat in the remaining flour; continue to beat on medium speed until a rough dough forms. Turn dough on to a lightly floured surface and knead until smooth, 10 to 12 times. Place the dough in a greased bowl, turning to grease the top. Cover with a clean dish towel and let rise in a warm place (80°F to 85°F) until doubled in volume, about 1 to 1½ hours.

Punch down the dough and turn on to a lightly floured surface; knead lightly 2 to 3 times. Cut the dough into 3 equal pieces, and roll each into a cylinder about 18 inches long. Cut each cylinder into 18 pieces, and roll each piece into a ball.

Generously grease a 10 inch Bundt or tube pan. Combine the remaining sugar and pumpkin-pie spice in a small bowl. Roll the dough balls in the remaining butter and then into the sugar mixture. Arrange the balls in the bottom of the prepared pan, and sprinkle over half of the chopped nuts. Arrange the remaining balls over the first layer, pushing into the creases and pressing together to fit. Sprinkle over the remaining nuts. Cover with the dish towel and leave in a warm place until just doubled, about 45 minutes.

Preheat the oven to 350°F. Bake until risen and well colored, about 1 hour. Remove to a wire rack to cool, for 10 to 15 minutes, then unmold on to the wire rack to cool, top-side up, until just warm. Serve with a flavored butter, if you like.

This mellow, well-colored bread is like an old-fashioned sweet-potato pie—warm and spicy. It is perfect for a winter brunch or coffee morning.

MAKES 12 TO 14 SERVINGS

1 cup water	1 cup sweet potato or pumpkin, mashed, cooked, or canned
1¼ cups sugar	
2 packages (2 Tbsp) active-dry yeast	1 stick butter, melted and cooled
5½ cups all-purpose flour	Grated zest of 1 orange
1 tsp salt	½ cup chopped walnuts or pecans
4 tsp pumpkin-pie spice	
½ cup instant, non-fat dry milk	

Malt Bread

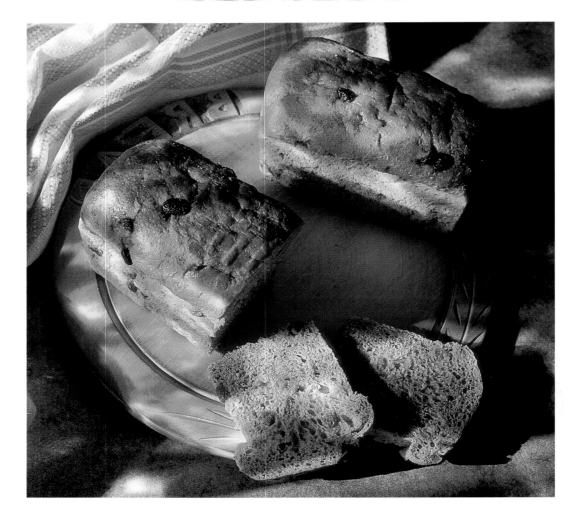

This sticky bread studded with golden raisins is excellent for breakfast spread with honey.

MAKES 2 SMALL LOAVES

1 cake (1 oz) compressed yeast or 2 tsp active-dry yeast and 1 tsp sugar	1 Tbsp honey or corn syrup
	2 Tbsp vegetable oil
2½ cups warm water	1 cup golden raisins
1 tsp salt	4 cups whole-wheat flour
2 Tbsp malt	Honey or syrup for glazing

Grease two small bread pans. Mix the yeast (and sugar) in the warm water.

Add the malt, honey, oil, and golden raisins to the warmed flour. Stir in the yeast liquid and mix thoroughly. Put the mixture into the two bread pans.

Set aside for 1 hour in a warm place, covered with oiled plastic. Preheat oven to 400°F. Bake for 15 minutes then lower the temperature to 350°F and bake for a further 20 minutes until cooked. A skewer inserted into the center of the loaf should emerge clean.

Place the loaves on a wire rack. Warm a little honey or syrup and brush the tops of the loaves while they are still hot.

Swedish Limpa

For an even richer flavor use half syrup and half molasses.

2 cakes (2 oz) compressed yeast or 4 Tbsp active-dry yeast and 1 tsp sugar

2¼ cups warm milk

½ to ¾ stick butter, melted and cooled

1 tsp salt

3½ to 7 Tbsp dark corn syrup

2 to 4 tsp ground aniseed or fennel or 2 tsp ground aniseed, 2 tsp ground fennel, and 1 tsp bitter orange rind, finely chopped

5½ cups rye flour

1¾ cups all-purpose flour

BREAD MACHINE METHOD—MAKES 1 lb LOAF

¾ cup water

1 Tbsp vegetable oil

2 Tbsp honey

1 tsp salt

½ tsp anise seed

½ tsp caraway seeds

1 Tbsp grated orange zest

1½ cups bread flour

¾ cup rye flour

1½ tsp yeast

● Put ingredients in bread pan in order suggested by your bread machine instructions. Set for whole-wheat bread, medium crust. Press Start.

Grease a large baking sheet. Put the yeast into a mixing bowl and beat it with a little of the milk. Add the teaspoon of sugar if dried yeast is used and set it aside for 10 minutes until frothy. Mix the melted fat with the milk, pour it on to the yeast and add the salt, corn syrup, and spices. Stir in half the rye flour. Add the rest by degrees and the white flour.

Work the dough until smooth. Cover it with oiled plastic and leave to rise until doubled in size, 40 to 50 minutes.

Punch it down then put it on a lightly floured board and knead thoroughly. Divide the dough into 3 and roll into smooth loaves. Put them side by side on the baking sheet with a piece of oiled foil between loaves. Cover the loaves with oiled plastic and leave to rise.

Preheat oven to 400°F. Prick the loaves with a skewer. Bake for about 30 minutes. Brush them with water twice during and after baking. Wrap the loaves in a clean towel and cool on a rack.

Kubaneh

This Yemenite sweet bread is eaten on the Sabbath. It is a soft, semi-steamed bread which can be eaten with preserves or jams or as the Yemenites do, with a hot chutney-type relish or zhoug, a chili-paste dip. Kubaneh can be baked in the oven or on top of the stove in a very heavy-bottomed saucepan.

SERVES 8

1 package (1 Tbsp) active-dry yeast	1 tsp salt
6 Tbsp sugar	½ tsp ground cinnamon or ginger
2 cups lukewarm water	Margarine or butter, softened, for greasing
4 cups all-purpose flour	

In the bowl of an electric mixer fitted with dough hook, combine yeast, 1 teaspoonful sugar and ½ cup lukewarm water. Stir until yeast is almost dissolved, 1 to 2 minutes. Leave yeast mixture to stand until it looks bubbly and foamy on surface, 5 to 7 minutes.

In a large bowl, combine flour, salt and cinnamon or ginger. With mixer on low speed, beat in 1½ cups lukewarm water until well blended.

With machine on low speed, gradually add flour mixture and beat until mixture forms a soft dough. If mixture is very sticky, add a little more flour, but dough should be soft. Increase mixer speed to medium and knead until dough is very smooth but still soft, 5 to 7 minutes.

Lightly oil a bowl. Place dough in bowl and turn to coat with oil. Cover with a clean dish towel and leave in a warm place to rise until doubled in bulk, 1½ to 2 hours.

Turn out dough on to a lightly floured surface and knead lightly to knock out air. Return to bowl, re-cover and leave to rise again in a warm place, about 1 hour longer.

Preheat oven to 325°F. Heavily coat a 10-inch tube pan with 3 to 4 tablespoonfuls softened margarine or butter. Turn out dough on to lightly floured surface and knead lightly to knock air out. Divide dough into 8 pieces. Roll each piece into a ball. Place balls into pan bottom just touching each other. Cover pan and leave in a warm place to rise again until balls form a ring, 30 minutes.

Heavily grease a piece of foil large enough to cover pan; cover pan tightly. Bake until bread comes away from side of pan, 1¼ to 1½ hours. Carefully remove foil, lifting an edge facing away from you to allow steam to escape. If you like, continue baking, uncovered, to brown top, 15 to 20 minutes. Serve warm.

Bara Brith

T his Welsh currant bread has an attractive
speckled appearance.

MAKES 1 LARGE LOAF

1 cake (1 oz) compressed yeast or 1 package (1 Tbsp) active-dry yeast plus 1 tsp sugar	¾ stick butter or margarine
	⅓ cup soft brown sugar
1 cup warm milk	1 egg, beaten
4 cups all-purpose or bread flour	3 cups mixed dried fruit (currants, golden raisins, raisins, candied citrus peel)
1 tsp salt	Warm milk and honey for glazing
1 tsp mixed spice	

Stir the yeast into the warm milk. If the yeast is dried, add the sugar and set aside for about 10 minutes until foaming. Add ½ cup of the flour and beat well. Set the bowl aside in a warm place for 20 minutes to produce a foamy batter.

Mix together the rest of the flour with the salt and spice. Blend in the fat and add the brown sugar. Add the flour mixture and the beaten egg to the yeast batter and knead the dough, first in the bowl and then turned on to a floured board. Knead until the dough is smooth. Return the dough to the bowl. Cover it with a sheet of oiled plastic and allow to rise for 1½ hours in a warm place.

Work the dried fruit into the dough, knead and shape to fit into the bread pan. Brush the dough with warm milk and honey and cover with oiled plastic. Allow to rise for a further 1 to 1¼ hours, until the dough is doubled in size.

Preheat oven to 425°F. Bake for 15 minutes. Reduce the heat to 350°F, then bake for a further 45 minutes at the lower temperature. Turn the loaf on to a wire rack to cool. Serve with butter.

Sally Lunn

These little cakes are named after Sally Lunn, an 18th century English woman who first made them in Bath, England.

MAKES 2 CAKES

½ cake (½ oz) compressed yeast or 2 tsp active-dry yeast and 1 tsp sugar

1¼ cups warm milk

4 cups all-purpose flour

1 tsp salt

2 eggs, beaten

½ stick butter or margarine, melted and cooled

TO GLAZE

2 Tbsp sugar

2 Tbsp water

BREAD MACHINE METHOD—MAKES 1 lb LOAF

⅓ cup milk

2 eggs

½ stick butter

3 Tbsp sugar

½ tsp salt

2 cups bread flour

1½ tsp yeast

● Put ingredients in bread pan in order suggested by your bread machine instructions. Set for whole-wheat bread, medium crust. Press Start.

Grease two 6 inch cake pans. Stir the fresh yeast (or dried yeast and sugar) into the warm milk. If dried yeast is used, set the bowl aside for 10 minutes until foamy.

Mix in 1 cup of the flour and leave in a warm place for about 20 minutes until the yeast batter is frothy.

Mix the remaining flour with the salt and stir into the yeast with the eggs and melted butter. Beat well until a smooth batter is produced. Pour the batter into the cake tins, cover them with oiled plastic and leave in a warm place for about 1½ hours until doubled in size.

Bake for about 20 minutes until nicely browned. Turn the cakes on to a wire rack and brush them with the hot glaze made by boiling the sugar and water together. Allow to cool a little before serving warm with whipped cream or butter.

Swedish Saffron Bread

This bread is served for the Santa Lucia festival in Sweden (December 13).

MAKES 2 OR 3 SAFFRON LOAVES

2 cakes (2 oz) compressed yeast or 4 Tbsp active-dry yeast and 1 tsp sugar

2¼ cups warm milk

1½ sticks butter or margarine, melted and cooled

1 tsp powdered saffron

½ tsp salt

1 cup sugar

6½ cups all-purpose or bread flour

1 egg

½ cup almonds, blanched and chopped

⅔ cup raisins

½ cup mixed candied citrus peel, chopped

Egg for glazing

Crushed sugar cubes and chopped almonds or raisins for decorating

Grease two baking sheets. Put the yeast into a mixing bowl with a few tablespoons of the warm milk. If dried yeast is used add the teaspoon of sugar and set aside in a warm place for 10 minutes until frothy.

Add the fat and the rest of the milk to the yeast liquid. Stir in the saffron, salt, sugar, half the flour, the egg, nuts, and dried fruit. Add the rest of the flour by degrees and work the dough until it becomes non-sticky, smooth and shiny. Cover the dough with oiled plastic and set aside to rise until doubled in size, about 1 hour. Knead the dough in the bowl then turn it on to a lightly floured board and knead thoroughly until smooth.

Divide the dough into 2 or 3 rounds and place them on the baking sheets. Cover with oiled plastic and allow to rise, about 40 minutes. Brush with egg and sprinkle with sugar and almonds or decorate with raisins.

Preheat oven to 400°F. Bake for 20 to 25 minutes. Cool on a wire rack.

Lemony Brioche Loaf

Rich and buttery, classic French brioche is a favorite breakfast treat. It can be baked in a loaf pan, but use the traditional molds if you like; be sure to start the dough the night before you want the loaf.

MAKES I LARGE LOAF OR I2 BUNS

2 Tbsp sugar	¼ tsp salt
3 Tbsp water	Grated zest of I lemon
I package (I Tbsp) active-dry yeast	¾ stick unsalted butter, cut into small pieces, softened
2 eggs, lightly beaten	I egg yolk beaten with I Tbsp water for glazing
I to I½ cups all-purpose flour	

Put I tablespoon of the sugar in a small saucepan with the water, and heat over low heat until very warm, 120°F to 130°F, stirring to dissolve the sugar. Sprinkle over the yeast and allow to stand until yeast is foamy, about 5 to 10 minutes. Stir to dissolve, then beat in the eggs.

Put the flour, salt, grated lemon zest, and remaining sugar in a food processor fitted with a metal blade, and blend. With the machine running, slowly pour the yeast-egg mixture through the feed tube; a dough will form immediately. Scrape down the side of the bowl, and process the dough until very well kneaded, 2 to 3 minutes. Sprinkle over the softened butter pieces, and pulse in the butter until just blended, about 12 times.

Scrape the dough into a large, greased bowl, turning to grease the top. Cover with a clean dish towel and let rise in a warm place (80°F to 85°F) until dough doubles in volume, about I½ hours. (At this point the dough can be refrigerated overnight to rise very slowly.)

Butter a 9 x 5-inch loaf pan. Punch down the dough and turn on to a lightly floured surface; knead lightly 2 to 3 times. Divide the dough into 8 or 9 pieces, and shape into balls. Arrange the dough balls in the pan, pushing them together to fit. Cover and leave to rise in a warm place until just doubled in volume, about 40 minutes.

Preheat the oven to 400°F. Brush the top of the risen loaf with the egg glaze and bake until well risen and deep-golden brown, about 30 minutes. Remove to a wire rack, and unmold immediately, top-side up, to cool. Serve warm with butter and preserves, if desired.

Savarin

Is it a cake, a bread, or a dessert? Whenever you choose to serve it, savarin is delicious soaked as it is in syrup and fruit.

MAKES 1 SAVARIN

½ cake (½ oz) compressed yeast or 1 package (1 Tbsp) active-dry yeast and ½ tsp sugar	**SYRUP**
	6 Tbsp honey
5 Tbsp warm milk	6 Tbsp dark corn syrup
1½ cups all-purpose or bread flour	⅔ cup water
¼ tsp salt	3 Tbsp rum
1 Tbsp superfine sugar	
¾ stick butter	
3 eggs, beaten	

Grease an 8 inch tube pan. Stir the yeast into the warm milk, adding the sugar if dried yeast is used. Stand the dried yeast mixture in a warm place for 5 to 10 minutes until frothy. Add 4 tablespoonfuls of the flour to the yeast liquid and set aside in a warm place for 20 to 25 minutes until the batter is foamy. Mix together the rest of the flour with the salt and sugar. Blend in the butter. Stir this mixture into the eggs and yeast batter. Beat thoroughly with a wooden spoon or fork.

Put the savarin mixture into the pan. Cover with oiled plastic and allow to rise in a warm place for 30 to 40 minutes.

Preheat the oven to 400°F. Uncover the pan, place it on a baking sheet and bake for 20 minutes until nicely browned and cooked. Turn the savarin on to a wire rack standing on a large plate.

Combine the syrup ingredients in a saucepan and heat them. Prick the savarin with a thin skewer or toothpick. Pour the hot syrup over the savarin. Serve with whipped cream. Fruit may be piled into the center of the savarin if you like.

Swedish Tea Ring

T his tea ring is moist and delicious, a perfect, refreshing accompaniment to a cup of tea at tea-time.

MAKES ONE RING CAKE

½ cake (½ oz) compressed yeast or 1 package (1 Tbsp) active-dry yeast and ½ tsp sugar	1 Tbsp melted butter
6 Tbsp warm milk	4 Tbsp coarse sugar crystals or coffee sugar mixed with 2 tsp ground cinnamon or 4 Tbsp sweetened apple sauce and 1 Tbsp slivered almonds
2 cups all-purpose or bread flour	1 cup confectioners' sugar
½ tsp salt	2 Tbsp water
2 Tbsp sugar	A few red and green candied cherries
2 Tbsp butter or margarine	
1 egg, beaten	

Grease a baking sheet. Stir the yeast (and sugar if dried yeast is used) into the warm milk. Set aside the dried yeast for 10 minutes until frothy. Add one-quarter of the flour to the yeast liquid and leave in a warm place for about 20 minutes.

Mix the rest of the flour with the salt and sugar and rub in the fat. Add the egg and stir the mixture into the yeast batter to make a soft dough. Turn the dough on to a floured board and knead until smooth, elastic, and non-sticky. Return the dough to the warm bowl. Cover with oiled plastic and allow to rise for about 1 hour, until doubled in size.

Roll out the lightly kneaded dough on a floured board into a rectangular strip 10 x 15 inches. Brush the dough with the melted butter and sprinkle the cinnamon sugar over the dough (or spread the apple sauce over the dough and sprinkle on the flaked almonds). Roll up the dough like a jelly roll, starting at the longer side. Transfer the roll to the baking sheet and form into a circle. Moisten the ends of the dough with milk and pinch them together. Clip the dough with scissors at 1 inch intervals but without cutting right through. Turn the corners backward and bend them downward to make a decorative pattern. Cover the ring with oiled plastic and allow to rise for about 45 minutes.

Preheat oven to 400°F. Uncover and bake for 20 to 25 minutes. Transfer the ring to a wire rack to cool.

Mix the confectioners' sugar and water and frost the ring. Decorate with cherries.

Honey-walnut Bread

This dense, nutty, slightly sweet bread is delicious for breakfast, especially when eaten with soft cheeses.

MAKES 1 LOAF

1½ cups water	1 package (1 Tbsp) active-dry yeast
1 Tbsp sugar	
2 cups whole-wheat flour	1 cup walnut halves, chopped, plus extra walnut halves for decoration (optional)
1½ cups all-purpose flour	
2½ tsp salt	
2 Tbsp honey	1 egg, lightly beaten for glazing
Water	

In a small saucepan over low heat, heat the water and sugar until very warm (120°F to 130°F). In a large bowl, stir the whole-wheat flour, all-purpose flour, and salt together until well blended, and make a well in the center. Stir the honey into warm water and pour into the well. Sprinkle the yeast over it and allow to stand until foamy, about 15 minutes.

Pour in the remaining water, and slowly incorporate the flour from the edge of the well into the liquid with an electric mixer on low speed or a wooden spoon, mixing to form a smooth dough. If the dough is very sticky, sprinkle in a little more flour.

Turn dough on to a lightly floured surface, and knead until smooth and elastic, about 5 minutes. Place the dough in a greased bowl, turning to grease the top. Cover with a clean dish towel or plastic bag and let rise in a warm place (80°F to 85°F) until doubled in volume, about 1½ hours.

Grease a large baking sheet. Punch down the dough and turn on to a lightly floured surface. Sprinkle over the chopped walnuts, and knead into the dough until evenly distributed. Shape the dough into a round or oval, and place on the baking sheet. Cover with a dish towel and leave in a warm place to rise again until just doubled in volume, about ½ hour.

Preheat the oven to 425°F. Brush the loaf with the egg glaze. With a sharp knife, slash the top of the dough in 3 to 4 places and bake for 15 minutes. Reduce the oven temperature to 375°F, and bake until the loaf is deep-golden brown, about 40 minutes more. Remove to a wire rack, sliding the loaf on to the rack to cool completely.

Plum Cake

You can use other plums and you can layer them on a sweet shortcrust pastry base; you can also scatter a streussel crumb mixture on top; and you can even serve it with whipped cream. But the genuine traditional German "Zwetschkenkuchen" should be made of a yeast dough base with fresh ripe plums baked in a large rectangular pan.

MAKES 1 X 12 INCH CAKE

¾ cake (¾ oz) compressed yeast or 1½ Tbsp active-dry yeast plus 1½ tsp sugar	2 eggs
	2 tsp lemon zest
	Pinch salt
⅔ cup warm milk	2 lb plums
⅓ cup superfine sugar	2 Tbsp ground hazelnuts or almonds or toasted bread crumbs
2¾ cups all-purpose or bread flour	
5 Tbsp butter	

Crumble the yeast into the warm milk, add a teaspoon of sugar and 1 cup flour taken from the main quantity. Beat well. Cover and leave to ferment for 10 minutes.

Beat the butter and sugar until pale and fluffy, mix in the eggs one at a time. Then add the lemon zest. Sift the flour and salt two or three times, finally into a large bowl. Make a well in the center and put in the egg mixture, scatter over a little of the flour, then add the yeast batter. Combine well, then knead hard in the bowl or on a floured work-top until the dough starts to roll cleanly off the sides of the bowl or board and becomes very elastic and forms air bubbles. Replace in the bowl and cover with oiled plastic. Allow the dough to rise in a warm place until it has doubled in bulk.

Grease two cake trays about 8 x 12 x 1½ inches, and dust with flour. Divide the dough in two. Keep one half covered and roll out the other half on a floured board to fit the cake pan approximately. Use to line the pan, gently easing it into place and pushing the dough up the sides a little. Stand it uncovered in a warm place for about 20 minutes to rise again. Repeat with the remaining dough.

Prepare the fruits; wash, dry, and split almost in half. Remove the stones. Lightly brush the risen dough with melted butter and scatter over the ground nuts or toasted bread crumbs. Pack in the prepared fruits close together in straight rows; they should not be opened out but left closed so that the layer of fruit is rich and juicy when it is baked.

Preheat oven to 400°F and bake for 35 minutes. Plum cake tastes best while it is still slightly warm. Dredge the slices generously with superfine sugar as you serve them.

Crumb Cake

Like Plum Cake (see page 362), this is a German classic. Here the yeast dough base is covered with a thick cinnamon and almond crumb covering. Streussel is made like pastry, and here are two simple ways of making it.

MAKES 1 X 12 INCH CAKE

DOUGH	STREUSSEL
(see Plum Cake, opposite)	2¼ sticks unsalted butter
	11 oz all-purpose flour, sifted
	1 cup ground almonds
	2 tsp cinnamon powder
	1 tsp lemon zest
	1 cup plus 3 Tbsp sugar
	Confectioners' sugar to serve

Prepare the yeast dough and line two baking pans as for Plum Cake. Leave to rise.

Using a food processor. Gently melt the butter and leave to cool. Drop the flour, almonds, cinnamon, lemon zest, and sugar into the processor bowl and switch on for 2 to 3 seconds to mix well. Then quickly pour the cooled butter through the tube on to the mixture with the machine switched on. Stop the motor as soon as a crumb texture is reached.

By hand. Cut the chilled butter pieces into the sifted flour and blend to fine crumbs. Use a knife to blend in the rest of the ingredients and make a coarse crumb texture. Roll into a ball, wrap, and chill for 1 hour until hardened. Rub the dough through a coarse grater and dust lightly with flour to prevent it from sticking together.

Preheat oven to 400°F. Finish the cakes by brushing the risen dough with melted butter; scatter the crumb mixture generously on top. Bake until well risen and golden, about 35 minutes. Cool in the pans, set on a wire rack. Dust with confectioners' sugar before serving and cut in slices.

Currant Loaf

A simple fruit bread, which is good with butter, and especially good toasted.

MAKES 2 LOAVES

1 cake (1 oz) compressed yeast or 1 package active-dry yeast and 1 tsp sugar	2 Tbsp sugar
	1 tsp salt
1¼ cups warm skimmed milk (or warm milk and water)	¼ stick butter or margarine
	⅔ cup currants
4 cups all-purpose flour	Warm honey for glazing

Grease two small loaf pans. Stir the yeast into the warm milk (add the spoonful of sugar if the yeast is dried). Leave until frothy, about 10 minutes in the case of dry yeast. Mix the flour, sugar, and salt together and blend in the butter. Add the currants and pour on the yeast liquid. Work to a firm dough which no longer clings to the bowl.

Turn the dough on to a lightly floured board and knead until it is smooth and elastic, about 5 minutes.

Put the dough back into the bowl, cover it with oiled plastic and allow to rise for about 45 minutes or more, until doubled in size.

Punch down the dough on a lightly floured board. Divide the dough into 2 halves. Roll out each piece into an oblong shape, then roll it up jelly roll fashion. Place each roll into a loaf pan. Cover them with oiled plastic, then leave to rise for 1 to 1¼ hours until doubled in size. Bake the uncovered loaves for 40 to 45 minutes.

Turn the loaves out on to a wire rack and brush the tops of the bread with warmed honey. Cool and then serve with butter.

Chocolate Poppy-seed Braid

This sweet-yeast dough is filled with a rich, poppy-seed and chocolate-chip mixture before being braided. It makes a beautiful addition to any breakfast or brunch table.

MAKES 1 LARGE LOAF

¼ cup water	**CHOCOLATE POPPY-SEED FILLING**
¼ cup sugar	
1 package (1 Tbsp) active-dry yeast	¼ cup poppy seeds
	¼ cup sugar
¼ cup lukewarm milk	¼ cup raisins
½ tsp salt	½ tsp ground cinnamon
1 egg, lightly beaten	Grated zest of ½ orange
½ stick butter, softened	¼ cup sour cream
3 to 3½ cups all-purpose flour	1 Tbsp marmalade or apricot preserve
1 egg yolk, beaten with 1 Tbsp milk for glazing	½ cup semi-sweet chocolate chips

In a small saucepan over low heat, heat the water and 1 tablespoonful sugar until very warm (120°F to 130°F). Pour into the bowl of a heavy-duty electric mixer, and sprinkle over the yeast. Allow to stand until foamy, about 15 minutes.

Fit the mixer with the dough hook and beat in the warm milk, remaining sugar, salt, egg, and butter. On low speed, gradually beat in 3 cups of the flour until a soft dough forms. If the dough is sticky, add more flour. Beat until the dough comes together and becomes elastic.

Turn the dough on to a lightly floured surface, and knead until smooth and elastic, 2 to 3 minutes, adding a little more flour if necessary. Place the dough in a greased bowl, turning to grease the top. Cover with a clean dish towel, and let rise in a warm place (80°F to 85°F) until doubled in volume, about 1½ hours.

Meanwhile, prepare the filling. Put all the ingredients except the chocolate chips in the bowl of a food processor fitted with the metal blade, and process using the pulse button, until just well blended, but not completely smooth. Grease a large baking sheet.

Punch down the dough and turn on to a lightly floured surface, kneading 2 to 3 times. With a lightly floured rolling pin, roll into a rectangle about 15 × 10 inches. To transfer to the baking sheet, roll the dough around the rolling pin and carefully unroll on to the baking sheet, stretching gently to keep the shape. Spread the filling down the center third of the dough, to within about 2 inches from each end.

With a sharp knife, cut 8 to 10 diagonal slashes from both sides of the filling to both edges of the dough, cutting about ½ inch from the filling. Beginning at one end, fold the end over the bottom edge of the filling, then fold over all the strips from alternate sides, and tuck the ends of the strips under the braid. Cover with the dish towel. Leave in a warm place to rise again until almost doubled in size.

Preheat the oven to 375°F. Brush the braid with the egg glaze, and bake until golden and well browned, about 30 minutes. Remove the baking sheet to a wire rack to cool, 15 to 20 minutes, then carefully transfer the braid on to the rack to cool until just warm.

Butter Kuchen

Kuchen, Austrian-German-style cakes for coffee, were taken to the United States by German immigrants, the best ones are still the ones found in old German-Jewish bakeries.

SERVES 10 TO 12

2 packages (2 Tbsp) active-dry yeast

¾ cup sugar

¼ cup lukewarm milk

1½ sticks unsalted butter or margarine, softened

3 eggs, lightly beaten

1 cup sour cream

Grated zest of 1 lemon

1 tsp vanilla extract

5½ cups flour

1 tsp salt

FILLING

3 Tbsp butter or margarine, melted

1 tbsp ground cinnamon

¾ cup sugar

1 cup golden raisins

½ cup candied lemon peel

GLAZE

3 to 4 Tbsp confectioners' sugar

2 Tbsp water

1 to 2 tsp lemon juice

In a small bowl, combine yeast, 2 tablespoonfuls sugar and lukewarm milk. Stir until yeast begins to dissolve, 1 minute. Leave to stand until bubbles form on the surface and mixture looks foamy, 7 to 10 minutes.

In bowl of an electric mixer fitted with beaters, cream butter or margarine and remaining sugar until well blended and smooth, 2 to 3 minutes. Beat in eggs, sour cream, lemon zest, vanilla, and yeast mixture.

Scrape beaters and replace with dough hook. On low speed, slowly add flour and salt and beat until well blended and a soft dough forms. Increase speed to medium and knead dough until dough is smooth and elastic, 5 to 7 minutes.

Lightly grease bowl. Place dough in bowl and turn to coat. (This prevents dough from forming a crust.) Cover bowl with a damp dish towel and leave in a warm place until doubled in bulk, 2 to 2½ hours. (Alternatively, cover bowl with dish towel and refrigerate overnight to allow dough to rise very slowly.)

Lightly grease a large cookie sheet. Turn out dough on to lightly floured surface and roll dough ½ inch thick into a rectangle at least 24 inches long; brush with melted butter for filling. In a small bowl, combine cinnamon and sugar, then sprinkle over dough. Sprinkle with raisins and candied lemon peel.

Starting at one long end, roll up dough jelly-roll fashion and bring ends together. Pinch ends to form a ring and place on cookie sheet. With a sharp knife or scissors, slash ring diagonally from outer edge halfway to center edge at 3-inch intervals. (This allows dough to rise more evenly, shows filling and forms a decorative shape.) Cover with dish towel and leave in warm place until ring doubles in bulk, 1½ to 2 hours.

Preheat oven to 375°F. Bake until golden brown, 40 to 45 minutes. Remove kuchen to wire rack to cool.

Into a small bowl, sift confectioners' sugar. Stir in 2 tablespoonfuls water and lemon juice to form a glaze. Thin with a little more water if necessary. Drizzle over warm kuchen and slide on to serving plate. Serve warm.

Small Yeast Bakes

Crisp Breadsticks : Whole-wheat Morning Rolls

Soft Breadsticks · Whole-wheat Cheese Burger Rolls

Cinnamon Sticky Buns . Hamburger Buns and Hot Dog Rolls

Almond Croissants : Garlic Herb Monkey Bread

Chocolate Croissants · English Muffins

Danish Pastries . Doughnuts

Hot Cross Buns : Chelsea Buns

Crumpets · Brioche

Swiss Buns · Pita

Bagels : Naan

Carnival Buns :

Crisp Breadsticks

These thin breadsticks, made in the bread machine, will keep for several days if they are stored in an airtight container.

BREAD MACHNE RECIPE—MAKES 24

⅔ cup water	2 tsp yeast
¼ cup vegetable oil	About 2 Tbsp vegetable oil
2 tsp sugar	1 egg white
1 tsp salt	2 Tbsp water
2 cups bread flour	Sesame or poppy seeds or coarse salt, optional

Put all but last three ingredients in bread pan in order suggested by your bread machine instructions. Set for white bread, dough stage. Press Start.

Grease 2 or 3 baking sheets.

When dough is ready, remove from bread pan and punch down. Cut into 24 pieces. Roll each piece between your palms to form a very skinny rope, about 8 inches long. Place bread sticks 1 inch apart on baking sheets. Brush lightly with oil. Cover loosely and set in a warm place to rise 20 to 25 minutes.

Preheat oven to 350°F. Make wash of egg white and 2 tablespoonfuls water. Brush egg wash lightly on bread sticks. Sprinkle with seeds or salt, if desired. Bake until golden brown, about 25 minutes.

Soft Breadsticks

These soft breadsticks do not keep well, but they are delicious still warm from the oven. Sprinkle them with sesame with poppy seeds or coarse salt.

BREAD MACHINE RECIPE—MAKES 20

1 egg, separated	2 cups bread flour
10 Tbsp water	1½ tsp yeast
2 Tbsp vegetable oil	2 Tbsp water
2 tsp sugar	Sesame or poppy seeds or coarse salt, optional
1 tsp salt	

Separate the egg and put the yolk in the bread pan. Save the white for glazing. Put remaining ingredients except last 2 tablespoonfuls water and seeds in bread pan in order suggested by your bread machine instructions. Set for white bread, dough stage. Press Start.

Grease 2 or 3 baking sheets. Make a wash of the egg white and 2 tablespoons water. Preheat oven to 350°F.

When dough is ready, remove from bread machine and punch down. Cut the dough into 20 pieces. Roll each piece between your palms to form a rope about 6 inches long. Place breadsticks on baking sheet about 1½ inches apart. Brush with egg wash. Sprinkle with seeds or salt, if desired.

Bake breadsticks until golden, 20 to 25 minutes.

Cinnamon Sticky Buns

These sweet, sticky buns can be assembled in advance and refrigerated overnight. In the morning, they will have to finish their second rising before you bake them.

BREAD MACHINE RECIPE—MAKES 15

½ cup milk	**FILLING**
1 egg	⅓ cup brown sugar
3 Tbsp butter	1 tsp cinnamon
¼ cup sugar	2 Tbsp very soft butter
½ tsp salt	
2 cups bread flour	**SYRUP**
2 tsp yeast	3 Tbsp butter
	½ cup brown sugar
	2 Tbsp water
	30 pecan halves

Put dough ingredients in bread pan in order suggested by your bread machine instructions. Set for white or sweet bread, dough stage. Press Start.

Remove the dough from the bread machine and punch down. Let it rest for 5 minutes to make it easier to roll out. While dough is relaxing, mix brown sugar and cinnamon to make filling. Roll dough into a rectangle 7 to 8 inches wide and about 16 inches long. Spread the soft butter over the surface of the dough. Thickly sprinkle brown sugar and cinnamon over the surface, spreading to edges. Roll dough into a long cylinder. Slicing crosswise through the cylinder, cut into 15 pieces.

The rolls can be baked together in baking pans or separately in muffin pans. The muffin-pan rolls are neater and crusty on the outside. If you cook them in baking pans, they will be softer. An 8 inch square baking pan is the perfect size for nine rolls; a 9 x 13 inch pan should easily hold 15 rolls.

Make the syrup by combining butter, brown sugar, and water in a small pan. Heat until butter is melted and sugar is dissolved. Stir well, then pour syrup into the bottoms of the baking pan or muffin-pan cups. Place two pecan halves in the bottom of each muffin-pan cup, or on the top of each roll if you are using a baking pan. Place rolls in muffin cups, or turn them upside down (so pecans are on the bottom) in a baking pan. Cover rolls loosely, set them in a warm place, and then let them rise until doubled, 45 minutes to 1 hour.

Bake rolls in a preheated 350°F oven until they are nicely browned, 17 to 22 minutes in a muffin pan, 20 to 25 minutes in a baking pan. The rolls must be removed from the pan immediately, or the sugar syrup will harden. Keeping in mind that excess sugar syrup will run off, invert the pan or muffin pan over a large plate or baking sheet. Remember to let them cool slightly, otherwise the hot sugar will burn your mouth.

Almond Croissants

These tender, flaky croissants are filled with a homemade almond paste for an extra-luxurious treat. Making them is well worth the effort.

MAKES 24 CROISSANTS

1⅓ cups milk	**ALMOND PASTE**
2 Tbsp sugar	⅔ cup blanched almonds
1 package (1 Tbsp) active-dry yeast	1 Tbsp all-purpose flour
3 to 3½ cups all-purpose flour	1 Tbsp cornstarch
1½ tsp salt	½ cup sugar
2 sticks unsalted butter	¼ stick unsalted butter, cut into pieces, softened
1 egg, with 1 tsp water for glazing	1 egg
Slivered almonds for sprinkling	1 egg yolk
Confectioners' sugar for dusting (optional)	½ tsp almond extract

In a small saucepan, heat the milk and half of the sugar over low heat until very warm (120°F to 130°F). Pour into the bowl of an electric mixer, and sprinkle over the yeast and 1 tablespoonful of the flour. Allow to stand until foamy, about 15 minutes. With a hand whisk, beat in 1 cup of the flour, the salt, and the remaining sugar.

Fit the mixer with the dough hook, and gradually beat in 2 cups of flour on low speed. Beat on high until the dough comes together and begins to pull away from the side of the bowl; if the dough is very wet, sprinkle in a little more flour. Beat until smooth. Scrape the dough into a greased bowl. Cover and let rise in a warm place (80°F to 85°F) until dough doubles in volume, about 1½ hours.

Punch down the dough and turn on to a lightly floured surface; knead lightly until smooth, 4 to 5 times. Wrap in a dish towel and refrigerate about 10 minutes, while preparing the butter.

Put the butter between 2 sheets of plastic wrap, and roll the butter into a rectangular shape. Fold the butter in half and roll out again. Repeat until butter is smooth and pliable, but still cold. Flatten to form a 6 x 4-inch rectangle.

Roll the dough to an 18 x 8-inch rectangle on a lightly floured surface, keeping the center third thicker than the two outer ends. Put the butter rectangle on the thicker center of the dough, and fold the bottom third of the dough over the butter. Fold the top third of the dough over the bottom to enclose the butter; with the rolling pin press down the "open edges" to seal the dough and create a neat dough "package."

Turn the dough "package" so that the short "open edge" faces you, the folded edge is on the left and it resembles a closed book. Gently roll the dough to a rectangle about 18 inches long, keeping the edges straight; do not press out the butter. Fold the rectangle in thirds, as for enclosing the butter, and press down the edges to seal. Press your index finger into one corner to mark the first turn clearly. Wrap the dough in plastic wrap, and refrigerate for 30 minutes.

Repeat the rolling and folding, or "turns," twice more, wrapping, marking, and chilling the dough between each turn. After the third turn, wrap and refrigerate the dough for at least 2 hours.

Meanwhile, prepare the almond paste. Put the blanched almonds, flour, cornstarch, and sugar in the bowl of a food processor, and process until very fine crumbs form. Sprinkle over the butter, the egg, egg yolk, and almond extract, and process until a smooth paste forms. If not using immediately, cover and refrigerate.

Lightly spray 2 large baking sheets. Soften the dough at room temperature, 5 to 10 minutes, for easier rolling. Roll the dough to a ⅛-inch thick rectangle about 13 inches wide on a lightly floured surface. Trim the edges straight. Cut the rectangle in half to form 2 long, narrow strips. Cut each strip into triangles, 6 inches high and 4 inches wide at the base. Using the rolling pin, roll gently from the base to the point, stretching each triangle lengthwise.

Place a tablespoonful of almond paste about 1 inch up from the base of each triangle. Pulling the base slightly to widen it, roll up the dough from the base to the point. Arrange point-side down on the baking sheets, curving the ends to form a crescent shape. Brush each croissant with a little egg glaze; cover and let rise in a warm place until almost tripled in volume, about 2 hours. (At this point, the formed croissants can be refrigerated overnight and baked the next day.) Refrigerate the egg glaze until ready to bake the croissants.

Preheat the oven to 475°F. Brush each croissant again with the egg glaze. Sprinkle each with a few flaked almonds. Bake for 2 minutes, then reduce the oven temperature to 375°F and bake until golden, about 10 minutes more. Remove to a wire rack and transfer the croissants to the wire rack to cool. Dust lightly with confectioners' sugar, and serve warm.

TIP

In Step 6, if the butter squeezes out of the package, or the dough becomes sticky at any time, slide it on to a baking sheet and chill until easier to handle.

Chocolate Croissants

A variation on the preceding recipe, chocolate croissants make a wonderful sweet treat.

MAKES ABOUT 24

1 quantity Croissants (see preceding recipe)	**1 egg, beaten**
	2 tsp water
1 cup chocolate chips	**1 tsp sugar**

Make the croissants as in the previous recipe.

At the base end of each triangle put a little pile of chocolate chips.

Beat together the egg, water, and sugar. Brush over the edges of each croissant.

Roll up each croissant loosely starting at the base and finishing with the tip underneath.

Put on to a baking sheet and shape as in the previous recipe. Cover and leave to rise for 20 to 30 minutes. Brush with glaze.

Preheat oven to 475°F and bake for 2 minutes, then reduce the oven temperature to 375°F and bake until golden. Cool on a wire rack and serve warm.

Danish Pastries

A breakfast classic. Danish pastries can be filled with a variety of ingredients from cream cheese to spiced nuts. Here, almonds and chocolate are used.

MAKES ABOUT 16

1½ cakes (1½ oz) compressed yeast

⅔ cup tepid water

4½ cups all-purpose flour

A pinch of salt

4 Tbsp shortening

2 tbsp sugar

2 eggs, beaten

2½ sticks butter

FILLING

½ stick butter

¾ cup confectioners' sugar, sifted

3 oz semi-sweet chocolate, melted

1½ Tbsp toasted almonds, finely chopped

A few drops of almond extract

GLAZE

1 egg, beaten

Honey

Blend the yeast and water together. Sift flour and salt into a bowl and blend in the shortening. Stir in the sugar. Add the yeast liquid and eggs to the flour and mix to a smooth elastic dough. Knead lightly until smooth. Put into a lightly-oiled bowl and cover with oiled plastic. Chill for 10 minutes.

Soften the butter and shape into a flat oblong on waxed paper. Roll out the dough on a floured surface to a rectangle three times the size of the butter. Place the butter in the center of the dough and fold the dough over to enclose it. Press the rolling pin firmly along the open sides. Give the dough a quarter turn and roll out to a rectangle three times as long as it is wide. Fold into three. Wrap in plastic wrap and chill for 10 minutes. Repeat the rolling and folding three more times.

To make the filling, beat together the butter and confectioners' sugar. Beat in the chocolate, almonds, and extract. Chill.

Roll out the dough thinly and cut into 3-inch squares. Put a rounded teaspoonful of filling on to the center of each square. Bring two opposite corners of the dough to the center. Either seal with beaten egg or insert a wooden toothpick through.

Place on a greased baking sheet. Cover with greased plastic wrap and leave to rise for about 30 minutes.

Preheat oven to 425°F. Brush with beaten egg. Bake for about 20 minutes. Brush with a little honey whilst still warm.

Hot Cross Buns

Hot Cross Buns, an English tradition, are eaten on Good Friday. Without the cross, they make delicious breakfast rolls year-round.

BREAD MACHINE RECIPE—MAKES 12 TO 16

1 egg	½ tsp salt
½ cup milk	2 cups bread flour
½ stick butter	2 tsp yeast
¼ cup sugar	¼ cup currants or raisins
1 tsp grated lemon zest	GLAZE
½ tsp cinnamon	½ cup confectioners' sugar
¼ tsp nutmeg	1 Tbsp milk or cream
⅛ tsp ground cloves	½ tsp lemon juice

Put all ingredients except currants or raisins in bread pan in order suggested by your bread machine instructions. Set for white bread, dough stage. Press Start. Add the currants and raisins after the first kneading or when the machine signals it's time to add fruit.

Lightly oil a 9 inch square pan or a 10 inch round pan.

When the dough is ready, remove from bread machine and punch down. Cut into 12 to 16 equal pieces. Roll each piece into a ball. Place balls about ½ inch apart in baking pan. Cover loosely and set in a warm place to rise until doubled, 45 minutes to 1 hour.

Preheat oven to 375°F. With a sharp knife or razor blade, cut a cross in the top of each roll. Bake 12 to 15 minutes, until a skewer inserted in roll comes out clean.

Make glaze, adding sugar or milk if needed to give it a consistency that will allow you to drizzle it over the rolls but is not runny. Let rolls cool slightly but not completely. Drizzle icing in a cross, following the cuts in the top.

Crumpets

These griddle cakes are full of tiny holes into which melted butter drips when served hot.

MAKES ABOUT 20 CRUMPETS

½ cake (½ oz) compressed yeast or 1 package (1 Tbsp) active-dry yeast and ½ tsp sugar	1 tsp salt
	½ tsp baking soda
1¼ cups warm water	Up to 1 cup warm milk (more, if required, to make a pouring batter)
3 cups all-purpose flour	

Heat a greased griddle or skillet. When ready to cook the batter, grease egg-poaching rings or plain cookie cutters 3 inches in diameter. Stir the yeast into the water, adding the sugar if dried yeast is used.

Let the dried yeast liquid stand for 5 to 10 minutes until frothy. Mix in half the flour and beat well. Set the batter aside in a warm place for about 30 minutes until it becomes foamy.

Add the rest of the ingredients to the batter, stirring thoroughly. Beat well, adjusting the milk quantity if necessary.

Place the crumpet rings on the heated griddle and pour 2 tablespoonfuls of the batter into each ring. Cook until set underneath and holes appear on the upper surface. Take away the rings and turn the crumpets with a palette knife. Lightly cook the second side. Cool the crumpets stacked on a wire rack. Serve freshly made with butter or toast them on both sides, serving them hot with butter, later on.

Swiss Buns

These simple, colorful, little buns are, not surprisingly, very popular with children.

MAKES 8 BUNS

½ cake (½ oz) compressed yeast or 1 package (1 Tbsp active-dry) yeast and 1 tsp sugar

⅔ cup warm milk

2 cups all-purpose flour

2 tsp sugar

½ tsp salt

¼ stick butter or margarine

GLACÉ FROSTING

1½ cups confectioners' sugar

3 Tbsp water

Coloring (optional)

Grease one large or two small baking sheets. Stir the yeast with the milk, adding 1 teaspoonful of sugar in the case of the dried yeast. If the latter, allow the yeast liquid to stand for 10 minutes or so until frothy.

Mix the flour with the sugar and salt and blend in the fat. Stir in the yeast liquid and mix to a soft dough. Turn on to a lightly floured board and knead thoroughly until the dough loses its stickiness and become smooth. Return the dough to the warm bowl, cover with oiled plastic and allow to rise until doubled in size, about 1 hour.

Punch down the dough, divide it into 8 pieces and shape each piece into an oblong 5 inches long.

Place the buns on the greased baking sheet(s). Cover with oiled plastic and allow to rise in a warm place for about 20 minutes.

Preheat oven to 425°F. Uncover the buns and bake for about 15 minutes until browned. Lift on to a wire rack to cool. Combine the frosting ingredients and use to frost the buns.

Bagels

Dense and chewy, bagels are a delight when they are split and toasted and served with butter or cream cheese. They also made delicious sandwiches. You can experiment by adding chopped sautéed onions, or raisins and cinnamon, to the dough.

BREAD MACHINE RECIPE—MAKES 8 TO 10

1 egg	2 tsp yeast
½ cup milk	1 Tbsp sugar
1 Tbsp vegetable oil	1 egg white
2 tsp sugar	2 tsp water
½ tsp salt	Sesame or poppy seeds or coarse salt
2 cups bread flour	

Put all but last four ingredients in bread pan in order suggested by your bread machine instructions. Set for white bread, dough stage. Press Start.

When dough is ready, remove from bread machine and punch down. Cut into 8 to 10 equal pieces. Roll each piece between your palms to form a thin rope, about 8 inches long with tapered ends. Bring ends together to form a circle, with the tapered ends overlapping. With moistened fingers, pinch or lightly knead the joined ends so the circle is securely fastened.

Set the bagels in a warm place to rise and cover them loosely. They should rise for 15 minutes. Preheat oven to 400°F. While they are rising, bring about 2 quarts of water to boil in a saucepan.

Add 1 tablespoonful sugar. When the bagels have risen for 15 minutes, drop one or two at a time into the boiling water, handling them as gently as possible so they do not deflate. They will rise to the surface of the water and swell up. Let them cook 1 minute, then turn them over and let them cook 3 minutes longer.

Remove bagels, let drain over the water, and place on an ungreased baking sheet. Beat egg white with water and brush over bagels. Sprinkle with sesame or poppy seeds or coarse salt. Bake until golden, 20 to 25 minutes.

VARIATIONS

Poppy Seed Bagels: Sprinkle the bagels generously with poppy seeds after they have been glazed.

Sesame Seed Bagels: Sprinkle the bagels generously with sesame seeds after they have been glazed.

Onion Bagels: Heat 3 tablespoonfuls vegetable oil in a large skillet and add 2 large finely chopped onions. Cook for about 10 minutes or until golden brown. Drain. Place a little of the fried onion on the top of the bagels after they have been glazed.

Cinnamon and Raisin Bagels: Substitute 1 cup of the strong plain flour with whole-wheat flour and add 3/4 cup raisins and 1 Tbsp ground cinnamon to the dry ingredients. Stir well and continue following the recipe.

Carnival Buns

On the Monday before Shrove Tuesday, Danish children wake up their parents early by traditionally beating them with birchwood twigs. In the afternoon they play a game called "beating a cat off the barrel," and dress up for a party afterward, when these buns are served.

MAKES 8 TO 10

1 package (1 Tbsp) active-dry yeast	**4 sticks butter**
¼ cup tepid water	**¾ cup milk**
2 Tbsp sugar	**4 cups flour, sifted**
1 egg	
1 egg yolk	**FILLING**
½ tsp salt	**¼ lb finely chopped marzipan (almond paste)**
1 tsp ground cardamom	**2 Tbsp candied citrus peel**
	Confectioners' sugar, to dust

Dissolve the yeast in the tepid water. Mix the sugar, egg, egg yolk, salt, cardamom, and ⅔ stick of the butter. Add to the dissolved yeast. Warm the milk. Add the lukewarm milk to the mixture. Mix in the flour and the rest of the butter. Knead the dough until smooth and pliable. Add the marzipan and citrus peel. Chill for 10 minutes.

Roll out the chilled dough to ¼-inch thickness. Then cut into 2 to 3 inch squares, and put on to a greased baking tray.

Cover with oiled plastic and leave to rise until doubled in size. Preheat the oven to 425°F. Bake for 12 minutes, until golden brown. Sprinkle with sifted confectioners' sugar.

Whole-wheat Morning Rolls

This is an overnight dough to make creamy, soft rolls in time for breakfast. There is nothing better than waking up to the smell of freshly baking bread—a great way to impress your guests.

MAKES 18

OVERNIGHT DOUGH

2½ cups warm water

3 cups whole-wheat bread flour

1 Tbsp salt

1 package (1 Tbsp) easy-blend yeast

MORNING DOUGH

1 package (1 Tbsp) easy-blend dry yeast

¾ cup warm water

3½ cups whole-wheat bread flour

½ stick margarine, at room temperature

1 tsp light brown sugar

BREAD MACHINE METHOD—MAKES 12–16

½ cup mashed potatoes	1 tsp salt
1 egg	1⅓ cups bread flour
¼ cup milk	⅔ cup whole-wheat flour
1 Tbsp vegetable oil	2 tsp yeast
1 Tbsp sugar	About 3 Tbsp melted butter

● Put all the ingredients except melted butter in bread pan in order suggested by your bread machine instructions. Set for whole-wheat bread, dough stage. Press Start.
● Lightly oil 12 to 16 muffin cups.
● When dough is ready, remove from bread machine and punch down. Cut into 12 to 16 equal pieces. Cut each piece into thirds. Roll each piece into a tiny ball and dip in the melted butter. Place three tiny balls in each muffin cup. Cover loosely and set in a warm place to rise until doubled, 45 minutes to 1 hour.
● Preheat oven to 375°F. Lightly brush tops of rolls with remaining melted butter. Bake 15 to 20 minutes, until tops are golden brown.

Place the water for the overnight dough in a large bowl. Add the flour, salt, and yeast and mix lightly—do not beat or knead. Cover with oiled plastic and leave overnight at room temperature.

In the morning, add all the remaining ingredients to the bowl and mix to a manageable dough; the margarine will be incorporated during the mixing. Turn out on to a floured surface and knead well for about 10 minutes until smooth and elastic.

Divide the dough into 18 pieces and shape them into rolls. Place them on lightly greased baking sheets, quite close together so that they grow into each other and form a broken crust. Cover with oiled plastic and leave in a warm place for 30 minutes to rise.

Preheat an oven to 425°F. Bake the rolls for about 20 minutes. The bases will sound hollow when tapped, but the tops will only brown slightly and remain soft. Cool on a wire rack.

Whole-wheat Cheese Burger Rolls

Burger rolls or baps are almost inextricably linked with hamburgers—a soft roll of the perfect shape for serving with meat and salad. They do, however, also make excellent sandwich rolls, being soft in texture and able to take more filling than the typical bread roll. Add some white flour to this mixture, which should make the dough soft and silky.

MAKES 8

¼ cup shortening	1 cup warm milk and water, mixed
2½ cups whole-wheat bread flour	¼ cup sunflower seeds
1 cup flour	½ cup grated Cheddar cheese
1 tsp salt	
1 package easy-blend dried yeast	

Blend the shortening into the flours and salt in a large bowl. Stir in the yeast then mix to a manageable dough with the warm liquid, adding a little extra if necessary. Knead thoroughly on a lightly floured surface until soft and elastic, then return the dough to the bowl, cover, and leave in a warm place for about 1½ hours, until doubled in size.

Punch the dough down. Add the sunflower seeds and knead it lightly to incorporate the seeds, then divide the dough into 8 balls. Shape into rolls, then roll out until half an inch thick. Place the baps on lightly greased baking sheets, then cover with oiled plastic and leave in a warm place for a further 30 to 40 minutes.

Preheat an oven to 400°F. Scatter the cheese over the baps then bake in the preheated oven for 15 to 20 minutes. Transfer to a wire rack to cool.

Hamburger Buns and Hot Dog Rolls

Baking your own hamburger buns or hot dog rolls in the bread machine is as easy as making simple dinner rolls.

BREAD MACHINE RECIPE—MAKES 6

1 egg	2 cups bread flour
½ cup milk	2 tsp yeast
3 Tbsp butter	2 Tbsp milk
2 Tbsp sugar	Sesame seeds, optional
½ tsp salt	

Put all ingredients except 2 or 3 tablespoonfuls milk and sesame seeds in bread pan in order suggested by your bread machine instructions. Set for white bread, dough stage. Press Start.

When dough is ready, remove from bread machine and punch down. Cut into 6 equal pieces. Let dough rest 5 minutes while you butter one or two baking sheets. For hamburger buns, roll each piece into a ball and flatten it to form a patty about 3 inches wide and ½ inch thick. For hot dog buns, roll each piece into a 6-inch rope and flatten to ½ inch thickness. Place rolls on baking sheet. Cover loosely and set in a warm place to rise for 20 minutes. Preheat oven to 400°F.

Lightly brush tops of rolls with milk and sprinkle with sesame seeds, if desired. Bake for 12 to 15 minutes, until a skewer inserted in roll comes out clean.

Garlic Herb Monkey Bread

This savory pull-apart bread is a variation on the traditional sweet monkey bread. Small balls of garlic-flavored dough are dipped in melted butter seasoned with garlic and herbs, and layered in a baking pan. Unlike sweet monkey bread, which tastes good hot or cold, garlic-herb monkey bread loses its charm when cold, so time the making of the bread to make sure it comes out of the oven 5 minutes before meal time.

BREAD MACHINE RECIPE—MAKES A 1 lb LOAF

¾ cup milk	1½ tsp yeast
2 Tbsp vegetable oil	½ stick butter
1 tsp sugar	2 cloves garlic, pressed
1 tsp salt	¼ tsp dried sage
1 clove garlic, pressed	¼ tsp dried rosemary, crushed
1½ cups bread flour	½ tsp dried basil
½ cup whole-wheat flour	

Put first eight ingredients in bread pan in order suggested by your bread machine instructions. Set for whole-wheat bread, dough stage. Press Start.

A few minutes before dough is ready, melt butter in small skillet. Add garlic and herbs. Sauté for 2 minutes. If the garlic or herbs brown too quickly, remove the pan from the heat and let the mixture continue cooking in its own heat. The garlic will give the bread a bitter flavor if it burns. Lightly oil baking dish.

Remove the dough from the bread machine and punch down. Roll dough into a thick log and cut out into 20 to 24 pieces. Roll pieces of dough into balls (they do not need to be perfectly round). Dip each ball in butter-herb mixture and layer in baking pan. The pieces in the first layer should be close but not touching to give them room to rise. On each succeeding layer, place balls so they overlap empty spaces on the layer beneath. Drizzle any remaining butter over the dough in the pan.

Cover dough loosely and put it in a warm place to rise. When bread has doubled in volume, about 30 to 40 minutes, put it in preheated 350°F oven. Bake until bread is lightly browned and a skewer inserted comes out clean, about 25 to 30 minutes. Invert bread on serving plate, remove baking pan, and serve.

If you need more time to coincide the baking with serving a meal, you can slow down the rising by putting the assembled bread in the refrigerator, then letting it return to room temperature before baking. Monkey bread is traditionally baked in a tube pan, 7 or 8 inches across. However, it looks impressive and tastes just as good when baked in round casserole dishes, about 1 inch smaller in diameter than the tube pan.

English Muffins

These English muffins are a bit crisper than the soft, store-bought kind, but they have a fresher flavor. The easiest way to make them is with a 3-inch round cookie cutter and a griddle, but you can use a clean tuna or pineapple can and a large skillet.

BREAD MACHINE RECIPE—MAKES 10 TO 12

½ **Tbsp baking soda**	½ **tsp salt**
¼ **cup water**	**2 cups bread flour**
½ **cup milk**	**2 tsp yeast**
2 Tbsp vegetable oil	**Cornmeal**
2 tsp sugar	

Dissolve the baking soda in the water. Put the water and remaining ingredients except cornmeal in bread pan in order suggested by your bread machine instructions. Set for white bread, dough stage. Press Start.

Sprinkle cornmeal on a baking sheet or large platter. White cornmeal is more esthetically pleasing on English muffins, but yellow will do the job just fine. When dough is ready, remove it and punch it down and cut it in half. Let it rest for 5 minutes. Then on a lightly floured surface, roll out the first half to ⅜ inch thick. With the cookie cutter, cut out 3-inch rounds. Put the rounds on the cornmeal-covered baking sheet, then turn to coat both sides. Repeat with the second half. If you wish, you may roll up the scraps, knead them a little, let the dough rest a few minutes, then roll it out and cut a few more muffins. Don't reroll yet again—the muffins will be tough.

Cover muffins and let them rise 45 minutes.

If you have a griddle, set it for moderate heat. If not, place a skillet—preferably one with a non-stick finish—over moderate heat. If the griddle or pan is well-seasoned, it will not require oil. If not, use just the barest trace of oil to cook. Cook until muffin bottoms are nicely browned, then turn and cook the other side. Cooking time will vary from 6 to 10 minutes per side according to the temperature of your stove.

Doughnuts

W**ho can live without doughnuts? This recipe is the real thing.**

MAKES 28 DOUGHNUTS

1 cake (½ oz) compressed yeast	2 egg yolks, lightly beaten
1 cup milk, warmed to blood heat	¾ stick butter
3½ cups all-purpose flour, sifted	½ tsp salt
	Raspberry jelly for the filling
2 Tbsp sugar	Vegetable oil for deep frying
	Superfine sugar for dredging

BREAD MACHINE METHOD

½ cup milk	CHOICE OF SUGAR COATINGS
1 egg	Confectioners' sugar
2 Tbsp butter	Granulated cinnamon and
¼ cup sugar	sugar
½ tsp salt	Sugar glaze (see below)
2 cups bread flour	SUGAR GLAZE
1½ tsp yeast	¾ cup confectioners' sugar
Oil for frying	½ tsp vanilla
	1 Tbsp warm milk

● Put all the ingredients except oil and sugar coating in bread pan in order suggested by your bread machine instructions. Set for white bread, dough stage. Press Start.

● When dough is ready, punch down. Let it rest about 5 minutes. Then, on a lightly floured surface, roll dough into a rectangle about ⅜ inch thick. Using a doughnut cutter or a 3-inch cookie cutter, cut out doughnuts. If you are not using a doughnut cutter, cut out a ½-inch hole in the center. Knead scraps together and let rest 5 minutes. Reroll the dough and cut out more doughnuts. Place the doughnuts on ungreased baking sheets. Cover loosely and put them in a warm place to rise 45 minutes to 1 hour, until doubled in bulk.

● About 15 minutes before doughnuts finish rising, pour oil at least 3 inches deep into a deep skillet, wok, or saucepan. Heat oil to 365°F. Watch the oil temperature carefully, as it can climb quickly. Slide two or three doughnuts into the hot oil. Do not crowd them. Cook until golden on the bottom, 1½ to 2½ minutes. Then turn and cook the other side.

● When doughnuts are golden, remove them from the oil, letting them drain for a few moments over the oil. Then put them on several layers of paper towels. Make sure the oil temperature returns to 365°F before you add the next batch of doughnuts.

● Put confectioners' sugar on a mixture of cinnamon and granulated sugar in a paper bag with two doughnuts. Shake until they are coated. Remove and repeat until all doughnuts are coated.

● Alternatively, mix the ingredients for the sugar glaze together and drizzle it over the tops of the doughnuts.

Mix the yeast with ⅓ cup milk, 1 cup flour, and 1 teaspoonful of sugar. Beat well. Set aside to froth. Mix half the remaining milk with the egg yolks and set aside. Melt the butter in the rest of the milk. Cool to lukewarm.

Sift together the rest of the flour with the salt into a large bowl and make a well in the center. Stir in the rest of the sugar, the yeast, and the milk mixture. Blend all together and beat well until the dough thickens and continue beating until the dough is smooth and shiny. It should drop off a spoon. Take out half the mixture and cover the bowl with a warm dishcloth while you prepare the first batch of doughnuts.

Dust the worktop well with flour and drop the mixture on to it. Dredge with just a little flour and gently roll it out to about ½ inch thick. Using a floured glass or cookie cutter about 2 inches in diameter, lightly press circles into half the dough, but do not actually cut it. Place a small teaspoonful of jelly in the center of each. Cut out the same number of circles from the other half of the dough, and turn the top, unfloured sides over on to the jellied circles.

Stick the doughnut edges well together (the jelly must not leak out as they cook) and gently press around the edges with the end of a teaspoon handle. Cut out each pastry with a slightly smaller cutter. Turn over the finished doughnuts and place them well apart on a floured board, covering lightly with a dishcloth. Leave the doughnuts to rise in a warm place and turn them over when they have risen on one side so that the other side may rise. Assemble the left-over scraps and beat them into the remaining dough with 2 spoonfuls of warm milk and finish in the same way.

A light and well-risen doughnut should have a pale ring around its middle, and the wider the ring, the lighter the pastry will be. Cook only four or five pastries at a time and always start by cooking the side that has risen first.

Heat the vegetable oil to 330 to 350°F. Using a large slotted spoon, gently lower each doughnut into the hot oil at 4-second intervals. Watch them all the time as they brown very quickly. As soon as they have colored well, which takes about 2 minutes, flip each one over and cook the other side until it is golden brown.

Lift the doughnuts out of the oil, drain on paper towels for a minute or two and roll them in superfine sugar. Serve the doughnuts while they are still warm.

Chelsea Buns

An old-fashioned sticky cake, tangy, chewy, and delicious.

MAKES 9 BUNS

1 cake (½ oz) compressed yeast or 1 tsp dried yeast and ½ tsp sugar	1 egg, beaten
⅓ cup warm milk	¼ stick butter, melted
2 cups all-purpose flour	½ cup currants or raisins
½ tsp salt	3 Tbsp mixed candied citrus peel
2 Tbsp margarine	¼ cup soft brown sugar
	Warm honey

Grease a 7 inch square baking pan. Stir the fresh yeast into the warm milk. If dried yeast is used, also add the sugar and set aside for 10 minutes in a warm place until frothy.

Put one-quarter of the flour into a warmed bowl, stir in the yeast mixture and leave in a warm place for about 20 minutes until the batter is foamy.

Mix the remaining flour with the salt. Blend in the margarine. Stir this flour mixture and the egg into the yeast batter and mix to a soft dough. Turn on to a lightly floured board and knead until smooth. Place the dough in a bowl, cover with a lightly oiled sheet of plastic wrap or a plastic bag and leave in a warm place until double in size, about 1½ hours.

Roll out to an oblong strip 12 x 9 inches. Brush the dough with melted butter and sprinkle with the dried fruit, candied peel, and brown sugar. Starting from the longer side, roll up the dough like a jelly roll. Cut into nine slices and place them close together, cut side down, in the baking pan. Cover and leave for about 40 minutes until the buns have doubled in size and joined together.

Preheat oven to 425°F. Bake for about 25 minutes, until golden brown. Transfer the buns to a wire rack and brush with warm honey while they are hot. Separate the buns when cool.

Brioche

These light egg-based buns have a delicate texture.

MAKES 12 SMALL BRIOCHES

½ cake (½ oz) compressed yeast or 1 package (1 Tbsp) active-dry yeast and ½ tsp sugar	1 tsp sugar
	½ tsp salt
3 Tbsp warm milk	½ stick butter
1¼ cups white flour	2 eggs, beaten

BREAD MACHINE METHOD—MAKES 1 lb LOAF

¼ cup water	½ tsp salt
2 eggs	2 cups bread flour
¾ stick butter	1½ tsp yeast
1 Tbsp sugar	

● Put ingredients in bread pan in order suggested by your bread machine instructions. It is crucial that the butter is softened to room temperature—not melted—when it is added to the other ingredients. Set for white bread, medium crust. Press Start.

Grease 12 brioche pans 3 inches in diameter.

Stir the yeast into the milk, adding the sugar if dried yeast is used. Let the dried yeast stand in a warm place for about 5 minutes.

Stir in ¼ cup flour and the teaspoon of sugar and leave the batter in a warm place for about 20 minutes.

Mix together the rest of the flour with the salt and blend in the butter. Beat the eggs into the yeast batter. Stir in the dry flour mixture and mix to a soft dough. Turn on to a lightly floured board and knead until smooth and non-sticky. Return the dough to the warm bowl, cover with oiled plastic and leave to rise until doubled in size, 1 to 1½ hours.

Punch down the risen dough. Divide the dough into 12 pieces. Cut off a quarter of each piece. Shape the larger part of each piece into a ball and place it into brioche pans. Press the center of each ball to make a hole into which the small piece of dough is placed like a marble. Brush the tops with beaten egg. Cover the 12 tins with oiled plastic and set aside to rise for about 40 minutes. Bake for about 20 minutes and cool on a wire rack.

Pita

Pita bread is of Middle Eastern origin and readily available in many food stores nowadays. Pita may be made from white flour or from whole-wheat. Serve pita hot.

BREAD MACHINE METHOD—MAKES 6

¾ cup water	1⅓ cups bread flour
1 Tbsp olive oil	⅔ cup whole-wheat flour
1 tsp sugar	1½ tsp yeast
1 tsp salt	1 Tbsp cornmeal

● Put ingredients in bread pan in order suggested by your bread machine instructions and set for whole-wheat, dough stage. Press Start.

● Punch down dough and cut into 6 equal pieces. Roll each piece between your hands to form a ball. Flatten slightly and let dough rest about 10 minutes. This will let the dough relax so it will stretch more readily when you roll it out, rather than bouncing back. On a lightly floured surface, roll out each circle of dough to a diameter of about 6 inches. Use flour sparingly, as too much flour will interfere with the moisture that creates steam and causes the dough to puff up. Cover the dough with plastic wrap or a barely damp towel, and let the dough rise about 30 minutes, until it is puffy.

● Preheat oven to 475°F. Lightly sprinkle cornmeal on a baking sheet. When dough is ready, carefully transfer rounds to the baking sheet. Bake until dough puffs up and is lightly browned, 5 to 6 minutes, then turn and bake until other side is lightly browned, about 2 minutes.

MAKES 8 PITA BREADS

½ cake (½ oz) compressed yeast or 1 package (1 Tbsp) active-dry yeast and ½ tsp sugar	1¼ cups warm water
	1 tsp salt
	4 cups all-purpose flour

Grease two baking sheets. Stir the yeast into the warm water, adding the sugar if dried yeast is used. Leave dried yeast for about 10 minutes in a warm place to become frothy.

Stir the salt into the flour and mix to a dough with the yeast liquid. Knead thoroughly on a lightly floured board for about 10 minutes until the dough is smooth, elastic, and non-sticky. Return the dough to the warm bowl and cover with oiled plastic. Leave to rise in a warm place until doubled in size, about 1¼ hours.

Punch back the dough. When thoroughly kneaded, divide the dough into 8 pieces. Roll each portion into an oval shape 10 x 5 inches. Put the 8 pitas on baking sheets. Cover with oiled plastic and set aside to rest for 5 to 8 minutes. Bake for 6 to 8 minutes. (Do not overbrown as, if not eaten freshly baked, the pitas are reheated before serving.) Wrap the pitas in a clean dish towel to cool to make them soft and pliable.

Naan

This Indian bread is served with tandoori (oven-baked) dishes. As with pita, naan is a yeast-risen flatbread which puffs up on cooking under a very hot broiler, because this creates an air pocket inside the bread.

MAKES 6 NAAN

1 cake (½ oz) compressed fresh yeast or 1 package dried yeast and ½ tsp sugar	½ tsp salt
	1½ tsp sugar
	1 tsp baking powder
Scant cup warm milk	2 Tbsp vegetable oil
4 cups all-purpose flour	4 Tbsp plain yogurt

Stir the yeast into the warm milk, adding sugar if the yeast is dried. Leave dried yeast mixture about 10 minutes in a warm place to become frothy.

Mix the remaining dry ingredients in a large bowl. Stir in the oil, yogurt, and yeast liquid. Work into a dough. Turn out on to a lightly floured board and knead for about 10 minutes until the dough is smooth, elastic, and non-sticky. Return the dough to the warm bowl, cover with oiled plastic and leave to rise for about 1 hour in a warm place, until doubled in size. Punch down the dough and, when thoroughly kneaded, divide the dough into 6 pieces. Roll into oval shapes 10 x 4 inches and place them on the baking sheets.

Preheat the broiler a few minutes before baking the naan. Grease two baking sheets.

Cook each naan bread under the hot broiler, 2 to 3 minutes on each side, until brown and well puffed.

Quick Breads,
No-yeast Cakes for Coffee, Muffins, and Biscuits

This section contains a range of breads that requires no rising, from cornbreads and soda breads to the ethnic specialties such as Mexican tortillas and Indian chapatis. There are delicious cakes for coffee featuring such delights as blueberries, apples, and polenta. Finally a wonderful range of muffins and biscuits featuring chocolate, oranges, cranberries, and even Parmesan, Roquefort, and goat cheese.

INTRODUCTION

Equipment

Most of the recipes in this book can be produced with the basic baking utensils found in the average kitchen. If you like muffins, it is worth investing in the newer, nonstick bakeware on the market as only minimal greasing is required. It is best to use a vegetable cooking spray, as it is quick and easy. Alternatively, use a pastry brush to butter or grease the bakeware. Paper and foil liners also eliminate fussy clean-up, and using various colors and designs will make pretty "packaging."

Most tea breads are baked in 9 x 5 x 3-inch or 8 x 4 x 2½-inch loaf pans; non-stick pans are a good choice. Cushion-air baking sheets are excellent for breads and cakes for coffee, since they prevent the bottoms from burning before the bread has a chance to bake through.

Paper liners eliminate fussy clean-up

Methods

Quick breads are quick and easy to prepare.

Preheat Oven

Always preheat the oven as indicated. Most baked goods and breads require a quick blast of heat at the start of the rising action; the temperature can be reduced for recipes that require longer baking times. For even results, bake on the middle-oven shelf. Prepare any bakeware as directed before you start so the batter or dough can be baked immediately, then assemble all the ingredients and prepare any that need it beforehand.

Measuring

As with all baking, accurate measuring is essential. The "scoop-and-sweep" method for dry ingredients such as flour, sugar, cocoa powder, and confectioners' sugar is recommended. Lightly spoon the dry ingredients into a metal or plastic measure from a measuring set, then, with the back of a knife blade or other straight edge, sweep off the excess. Brown sugars should be packed firmly into the indicated measure until level with the top. For baking powder, baking soda, salt, and spices, use tablespoon and teaspoon measures, not a spoon from your kitchen drawer; fill and sweep off the excess as for dry ingredients. Use a clean cup measure for liquids, and check the amount at eye level for accuracy.

Mixing

Combining the ingredients for all baked goods is very important, as it determines the texture of the end result. Muffins and quick breads should be mixed lightly only until the flour is just incorporated. Although the consistency of different batters might vary, the texture should be slightly lumpy. If over-mixed until completely smooth, the texture will be slightly dry and tough. Scones should never be over-mixed or over-kneaded, as they will be dense and tough-textured. Mix the dough until it just holds together, and then knead lightly until the dough is well combined, but not smooth and elastic.

Filling the Pans

Batter should be spooned lightly into muffin-pan cups and loaf pans; let the mixture drop gently from the spoon, or scoop it into the cups or pan, and remember not to pat down or smooth the tops of the muffins. Try to spoon quick bread mixtures evenly into pans so the tops do not require much handling. Most baking should be done in single layers on the middle-oven shelf, as this allows for the air to circulate evenly. Baking times are a guide; it is a good idea to begin checking to see if it is done after the minimum time.

Doneness

Doneness can be judged in many ways; usually the baked goods will smell, and will have just begun to shrink from the side of the pan. For plain mixtures, a cake tester or wooden toothpick inserted into the

It's worth investing in non-stick bakeware

center of the muffin, loaf, or cake will come out clean. Other mixtures may have ingredients that will contain moisture or solid ingredients such as dried or chopped fresh fruits, or vegetables, which make testing more difficult. These are best tested by pressing with a fingertip. If the surface springs back lightly, it should be done; however, it is preferable to underbake slightly than overbake, and baked goods will generally continue to cook for a few minutes after being removed from the oven. Rolls and cakes for coffee are usually fully done when risen and golden.

Most muffins and quick breads can be unmolded or removed from the pan very quickly after baking. Muffins and quick breads will become damp and soggy if left in their pan too long. Muffins can be removed immediately, although leaving them to cool for about two minutes will ensure that they are set. Quick breads should be left for a few minutes before unmolding. Some cakes for coffee can be treated like quick breads, but because many have toppings, they are best cooled in their pans, or as directed, before careful unmolding.

Muffins, scones, and biscuits are best when eaten immediately or on the same day. Most quick breads benefit from complete cooling and storing overnight; this helps to develop their flavor, and makes for easier slicing. Before storing, cool all baked goods, then wrap them in plastic wrap or foil. To freeze, place in freezer bags, label, and store in freezer. To thaw, transfer to the refrigerator for several hours before serving, or thaw for 2 to 3 hours at room temperature. For really quick, "freezer-to-table" muffins, line a muffin pan with paper or foil liners.

Fill with the batter and freeze immediately. When frozen, remove the filled cups to a plastic freezer bag or container, label them, and mark the baking time and temperature. When ready to bake, just drop the frozen muffins into the pan and bake, adding about five minutes to the baking time.

Hot Tips for Quick Breads, Cakes for Coffee, and Muffins

Remember the following tips to help you make successful muffins, scones, biscuits, and quick breads every time:

- **DO NOT OVERMIX—This tip cannot be overemphasized. If you stir until the batter is smooth, you will get a tough, dry result with tunnels or holes. Stir wet and dry ingredients together just until combined; the batter *should* be slightly lumpy.**
- **Unless specified, have all your ingredients ready and at room temperature before you start, especially butter and eggs.**
- **Shiny baking pans reflect heat, while dark, dull pans absorb it. If using a dark, non-stick pan, first reduce the heat by 25°F, and then put a bowl of water on the bottom of the oven for moisture. Bake all cakes and breads in a single layer on the middle oven-shelf or rack.**
- **For an evenly rounded muffin top, only grease the bottom and ½ inch up the side of the cup.**
- **Bake muffins and quick breads as soon as they are mixed, since both baking powder and soda begin to rise as soon as they are moistened.**
- **To avoid soggy sides and bottoms, remove the muffins from the pan almost immediately after removing them from the oven. Cool quick breads for slightly longer.**
- **Begin checking for doneness after the minimum baking time indicated.**
- **Day-old muffins, scones, and biscuits can be split and toasted, then served with butter or preserves for a delicious breakfast treat.**
- **For "instant muffins," mix the dry ingredients and wet ingredients separately (wet ingredients should not be mixed more than 2 to 3 hours ahead) and grease the pan. When ready, preheat the oven, mix, and bake.**
- **Never over-knead biscuit or scone dough. Lightly folding and pressing between 8 to 12 times is enough to distribute the ingredients.**
- **For soft-sided biscuits, bake close together. Arrange the shapes at least 2 inches apart for a crisper, crustier finish.**

Quick Breads

Cranberry-apricot-banana Bread	Oatcakes
Chocolate-chip and Peanut Butter Bread	Whole-wheat Soya Bread with Orange and Prunes
Bran Teabread	Eliopita
Banana-pecan-chocolate Chip Loaf	Whole-wheat Coffee Bread
Cornbread	Whole-wheat Drop Scones
Fiesta Buttermilk Cornbread	Quick Onion and Nut Loaf
Light Cornbread	Low-fat Raisin and Honey Bread
Almond Bread	Corn Tortillas
Yogurt Bread	Flour Tortillas
Pumpkin-oatmeal-nut Loaf	Norwegian Flatbread
Brown Soda Bread	Crispbread
Irish Soda Bread	Chapatis

Cranberry-apricot-banana Bread
with cranberry-apricot compote

The flavors of this moist, delicious tea bread are accentuated by the Cranberry-apricot Compote, a quick, warm preserve.

MAKES I MEDIUM LOAF

1¼ cups all-purpose flour	2 eggs
1½ tsp baking powder	½ cup sunflower or vegetable oil
½ tsp freshly grated or ground nutmeg	1 tsp vanilla extract
½ cup old-fashioned oats	2 ripe bananas, mashed
1 cup firmly packed, light-brown sugar	**FOR GLAZE** (OPTIONAL)
½ cup dried cranberries	¼ cup confectioners' sugar
½ cup dried apricots, chopped	2 to 3 Tbsp lemon juice or water

Preheat the oven to 350°F. Lightly grease and flour an 8 x 4 inch loaf pan. Sift the flour, baking powder, and nutmeg into a bowl. Stir in the oats, brown sugar, cranberries, and apricots until well blended, and make a well in the center.

Using an electric mixer in a medium bowl, beat the eggs, oil, vanilla extract, and mashed bananas until well blended. Pour into the well and stir until combined. Scrape the batter into the prepared pan, finishing by smoothing the top evenly.

Bake until well risen and golden brown, and a cake tester inserted in the center comes out with just a crumb or two attached, about 1 hour. Remove to a wire rack to cool, about 10 minutes, then unmold top-side up on to the rack to cool completely.

If glazing, in a small bowl, stir the confectioners' sugar and 2 to 3 tablespoons lemon juice until it reaches a pouring consistency. Add a little more lemon juice or water if necessary. Drizzle over the top of the tea bread and allow to set. Alternatively, dust with confectioners' sugar. Serve slices with the Cranberry-apricot Compote.

Cranberry-apricot Compote

MAKES ABOUT 2 CUPS

½ cup fresh or frozen cranberries	1 cinnamon stick
½ cup dried cranberries	Grated zest and juice of 1 orange
10 to 12 oz dried, "no-soak" apricots, chopped	2 Tbsp ruby port or marsala wine
½ cup sugar	1 tsp vanilla extract

Put the dried fruits, sugar, cinnamon stick, grated orange zest and juice in a medium heavy-based, noncorrosive saucepan. Add enough water to cover the fruit. Place over medium heat, and bring to a boil. Simmer over low heat until the cranberries pop, the fruits are tender, and almost all the liquid is absorbed. Remove from the heat, discard the cinnamon stick, and stir in the port or marsala and vanilla. Pour into a bowl and serve warm, or refrigerate, covered, until ready to serve.

Chocolate-chip and Peanut Butter Bread

This is a moist, dense bread with a good,
peanutty flavor. The chocolate-crumb topping
is similar to a famous chocolate peanut-butter candy.

MAKES 1 LARGE LOAF

2 cups all-purpose flour	1 tsp vanilla extract
2 tsp baking powder	FOR THE CHOCOLATE-CRUMB TOPPING
¼ tsp salt	
1 cup semi-sweet chocolate chips	½ cup sugar
¼ cup smooth or chunky peanut butter, at room temperature	¼ cup unsweetened cocoa powder
1 Tbsp sugar	3 Tbsp unsalted butter, cut into pieces
1 egg, lightly beaten	2 Tbsp finely chopped, dry-roasted peanuts
1 cup milk	

Preheat the oven to 350°F. Lightly grease or spray a 9 × 5 inch loaf pan. Sift the flour, baking powder, and salt into a large bowl. Stir in the chocolate chips, and make a well in the center.

Put the peanut butter in another bowl, and beat with an electric mixer to break up and soften. Gradually beat in the sugar, the egg, milk, and vanilla extract. Pour into the well, and lightly stir with a fork until combined.

Combine the crumb-topping ingredients in a small bowl. Spoon half the batter into the prepared pan and smooth, sprinkling with half of the crumb mixture. Spoon the remaining batter into the pan and gently smooth the top. Sprinkle with the remaining crumb mixture. Using a round-bladed knife or spoon handle, gently draw through the batter in a zigzag to marbelize the mixture slightly.

Bake until risen and golden, and a cake tester inserted in the center comes out moist, but with no uncooked crumbs attached, 50 to 55 minutes. Remove to a wire rack to cool, about 25 minutes, then carefully unmold onto a wire rack, top-side up. Cool completely, then wrap and keep for 1 day before serving, if possible.

Bran Teabread

A teabread is a moist, semi-sweet loaf that is
usually served sliced and buttered, although
seldom with preserves or honey. For extra
moistness, soak the fruits, although this is not
essential. The mixture is very wet when it goes into
the oven and is usually frothing. Don't worry—this
is how it should be!

MAKES 1 LOAF

1 cup mixed dried fruit	1 tsp baking powder
1 cup cold tea	1 tsp baking soda
½ cup light brown sugar	1 tsp pumpkin pie spice
½ stick margarine	Pinch of salt
¼ cup orange marmalade	1 cup bran cereal
1 cup fine whole-wheat flour	1 egg, beaten

Preheat an oven to 350°F and lightly grease a large loaf pan. Place the cake fruits, tea, sugar, margarine, and marmalade in a pan and heat gently until the sugar has dissolved and the margarine melted, then leave to cool.

Mix the dry ingredients together in a large bowl and make a well in the center. Beat the egg and add it to the fruit mixture, then pour into the dry ingredients and mix thoroughly and quickly. Pour immediately into the prepared loaf pan. Bake in the preheated oven for 50 to 60 minutes, until a toothpick inserted into the loaf comes out clean.

Cool the teabread on a wire rack. Serve sliced and lightly buttered.

Banana-pecan-chocolate Chip Loaf

This delicious quick bread is great while the chocolate is still soft and melty, but keeps really well wrapped in plastic wrap or foil.

MAKES 1 LARGE LOAF

⅔ cup all-purpose flour	2 eggs, lightly beaten
1 tsp baking soda	5 Tbsp just boiling water
½ tsp salt	1 cup chopped pecans
1 tsp ground cinnamon	1 cup semi-sweet chocolate chips
½ tsp ground ginger	
⅔ cup whole-wheat flour	**FOR THE GLAZE**
1 stick butter, softened	½ cup confectioners' sugar
⅔ cup sugar	2 to 3 Tbsp lemon juice
2 large ripe bananas, mashed	

Preheat the oven to 325°F. Grease and flour a 9 x 5 inch loaf pan. Sift the flour, baking soda, salt, cinnamon, and ginger into a medium bowl and stir in the whole-wheat flour; set aside.

In a large bowl with an electric mixer, beat the butter until light and creamy, 1 to 2 minutes. Gradually beat in the sugar until light and fluffy. On low speed, beat in the mashed bananas and then the eggs; do not worry if the mixture looks curdled. Stir in the flour alternately in batches with the hot water until just combined. Stir in the pecans and chocolate chips.

Scrape the batter into the prepared pan, smoothing the top evenly. Bake until well risen and dark-golden brown, about 1 hour 10 minutes. Because this is a very moist quick bread, a cake tester or skewer will not come out clean. Remove pan to a wire rack to cool about ½ hour, then unmold on to the rack top-side up. To glaze, stir the confectioners' sugar and lemon juice together until smooth. Drizzle over the loaf and allow to set completely.

Cornbread

This basic cornbread is a staple in the south and it is very simple to prepare.

MAKES 16 2 INCH SQUARES

I cup whole-wheat flour	1½ cups buttermilk or half yogurt, half skim milk
I cup cornmeal	3 Tbsp sunflower oil
½ tsp salt	2 eggs beaten
I tsp baking soda	I Tbsp brown sugar or honey
¾ tsp cream of tartar	

Preheat the oven to 425°F. Grease an 8 inch square cake pan.

Mix together the flour, cornmeal, salt, baking soda, and cream of tartar. Stir the buttermilk with the oil, eggs, and sugar or honey. Pour the liquid ingredients into the dry mixture and stir together.

Put the batter into the pan and bake for about 35 minutes. Cut into 2 inch squares and serve warm.

Light Cornbread

This lighter version is also delicious, and ideal for calorie-counting.

MAKES 9 SQUARES

I cup rice flour	I cup yellow cornmeal
¼ cup sugar	2 medium eggs, lightly beaten
4 tsp baking powder	½ stick margarine, softened
½ tsp salt	I cup skim milk

Preheat the oven to 425°F. Grease a 9 inch square cake pan.

Sift together the rice flour, sugar, baking powder, and salt. Stir in the cornmeal. Mix together the eggs and softened margarine. Stir in the milk and add the liquid mixture to the dry ingredients. Beat them together thoroughly.

Pour the batter into the prepared pan and bake for 20 minutes. Cool on a wire rack and cool in the pan for 5 minutes.

Cut the cornbread into 3 inch squares—it can be served either warm or cold.

Fiesta Buttermilk Cornbread

This delicious cornbread is flecked with colorful green onions, red pepper, corn kernels, and even fresh chiles. A delicious accompaniment to Chili con Carne and other Tex-Mex-style dishes.

MAKES 8 SERVINGS

¾ stick unsalted butter	1 cup buttermilk
1 cup cornmeal	2 to 3 scallions, finely chopped
1 cup all-purpose flour	1 small red bell pepper, deseeded and chopped
1½ tsp baking powder	
½ tsp baking soda	1 cup fresh, frozen (thawed) or canned corn kernels, drained
2 Tbsp sugar	
½ tsp crumbled sage or dried oregano	1 small green chile, deseeded and chopped (or to taste)
2 eggs	

Preheat the oven to 400°F. Put the butter in a 9-inch black iron skillet or heavy 9 inch cake pan and place pan on the middle rack of the oven until butter is melted. Keep pan warm.

In a large bowl, stir together the cornmeal, flour, baking powder, baking soda, sugar, and sage or oregano, and make a well in the center.

In a small bowl using a fork, beat the eggs with the buttermilk until well blended. Pour into the well, add all but 2 tablespoons of the melted butter from the pan, and stir lightly until just combined. Fold in the scallions, bell pepper, corn kernels, and chile, until just blended.

Pour batter into the hot pan and spread evenly. Bake until risen and golden, and a cake tester inserted into the center comes out with just a few crumbs attached, about 30 minutes. (Do not overbake or cornbread will be dry.) Remove to a wire rack and cool in the pan, 10 minutes. Serve hot or warm from the pan with lots of butter, on its own, or as an accompaniment to Chili con Carne.

Almond Bread

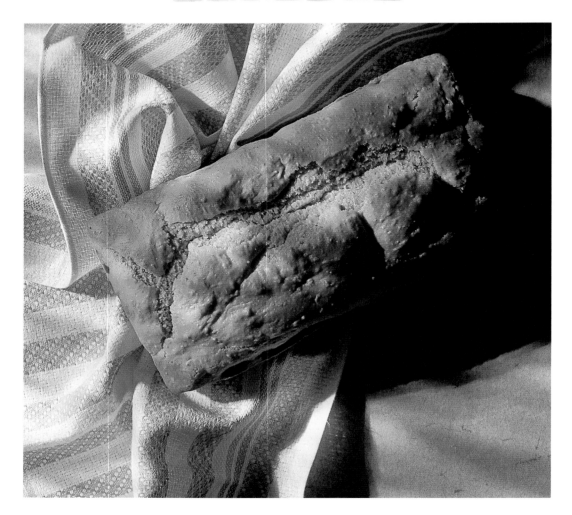

T his delicious quick bread has the tang of citrus as well as the crunchy nutritious quality of the almonds.

MAKES 42 TO 48 SLICES

3 cups all-purpose flour	5 to 6 Tbsp honey or brown sugar
2 tsp baking powder	2 tsp grated orange or tangerine zest
¼ tsp salt	
2 large eggs	2 tsp almond extract
½ cup sunflower oil	¾ cup chopped almonds

Pre-heat the oven to 350°F. Sift together the flour, baking powder, and salt. Beat together in an electric blender or a bowl the eggs, oil, honey, citrus zest, and almond extract. Transfer the mixture into a large bowl and beat in the flour mixture a little at a time.

Stir the almonds into the stiff dough then divide it into six oblong rolls about 2 inches wide. Place the rolls well apart on a foil covered baking sheet and bake for 20 minutes. Lift out the baking sheet and cut each roll into seven or eight slices ½ inch thick. Return the slices to the oven on the baking sheet and bake for a further 15 to 20 minutes until brown. Cool on a wire rack, then store in an airtight container.

Yogurt Bread

This is a classic bread, which is quick and easy to prepare. It goes well with sweet or savory accompaniments.

MAKES 1 LARGE LOAF

3½ cups of two or more mixed flours (wheat, rye, barley, millet)	1 tsp baking powder
	1 cup plain yogurt
3 Tbsp wheat germ	1 cup skim milk or water
2 tsp baking soda	1 tsp salt
	½ cup honey

Preheat the oven to 300°F. Grease a large loaf pan. Mix all the ingredients in a large cool bowl. Scrape the mixture into the prepared pan. Bake slowly for about 1 hour 40 minutes.

Cool the loaf on a wire rack.

Pumpkin-oatmeal-nut Loaf
with orange-lemon butter

This teabread has a sweet, natural flavor and lots of texture. Serve with Orange-lemon Butter, or on its own.

3¼ cups all-purpose flour

2 tsp baking soda

1 tsp ground cinnamon

½ tsp ground ginger

½ tsp freshly grated or ground nutmeg

¼ tsp ground cloves

½ tsp salt

¼ cup old-fashioned oats

1 cup chopped walnuts or pecans, lightly toasted

One 15- to 16-oz can natural, solid-pack pumpkin

3 eggs, lightly beaten

1½ cups sugar

1½ cups firmly packed, light-brown sugar

½ cup sunflower or vegetable oil

½ cup milk

½ cup evaporated milk

Preheat the oven to 350°F. Grease and flour two 9 × 5 inch loaf pans. Sift the flour, baking soda, cinnamon, ginger, nutmeg, cloves, and salt into a large bowl. Stir in the oats and chopped nuts into the mixture.

Put the pumpkin in a large bowl and beat to break up with an electric mixer on low speed. Gradually beat in the eggs until smooth. Beat in the sugars, oil, and milks until smooth. On low speed, beat the flour mixture into the pumpkin-egg mixture until just blended.

Divide the batter equally between the two pans, smoothing the tops evenly. Bake until risen, dark golden, and a cake tester inserted in the center comes out clean. Remove pans to a wire rack to cool, about 15 minutes, then unmold, top-side up on to the wire rack to cool completely. Wrap well, and let stand overnight for flavors to develop. Serve with Orange-lemon Butter

Orange-lemon Butter

MAKES ABOUT 1 CUP

2 sticks unsalted butter, softened

Grated zest of 1 orange

1 to 2 Tbsp orange juice

Grated zest of 1 lemon

1 Tbsp lemon juice

½ tsp vanilla extract

⅓ cup superfine sugar (or to taste)

Beat all the ingredients together in a medium bowl, using an electric mixer, until light and fluffy. Scrape on to a piece of plastic wrap or waxed paper, and shape into a log. Wrap tightly and refrigerate until firm, about 1 to 2 hours. Slice into rounds and serve.

Brown Soda Bread

W**ith soda bread, there is no waiting for it to rise, nor does it involve endless kneading. The less soda bread is handled the better it will be.**

MAKES 2 LARGE LOAVES

6 cups whole-wheat flour

3 cups all-purpose or bread flour

1 heaped tsp baking soda

Good pinch of salt

2 eggs

Approx 2½ cups plain yogurt mixed with the water to the consistency of buttermilk

Preheat the oven to 375°F. Place all the dry ingredients in a large mixing bowl. Combine well using your fingers.

In another bowl mix the eggs with the yogurt and water.

Make a well in the dry mixture and slowly pour on the yogurt and water. Mix with your hands until you get a nice soft dough—to too wet. A dough that is too wet or too stiff will result in a hard and heavy bread.

Lightly flour a worktop or pastry board. Divide the dough in half. Make 2 flat rounds of bread on the board.

Cut a deep cross in the middle of each loaf. Place in the preheated oven for 10 minutes, then reduce the heat to 350°F. Bake until the bottom of the bread sounds hollow when knocked. This takes about 30 minutes.

Irish Soda Bread

Irish soda bread is one of the best breads in the world. Many women in Ireland still make it every day. It is traditionally baked with a cross scored on the top, which people believed would scare away the devil.

VARIATION

You can use plain milk instead of buttermilk, but if you do, double the quantity of cream of tartar.

MAKES 1 LARGE LOAF

4 cups all-purpose flour	1½ tsp cream of tartar
1 tsp salt	2 Tbsp shortening
2 tsp baking soda	1¼ cups buttermilk

Preheat the oven to 425°F. Sift the flour, salt, baking soda and cream of tartar into a bowl. Rub in the shortening and add enough buttermilk to make a soft dough. Turn the mixture on to a lightly floured board and knead for a minute. Shape into a round and place on the baking sheet. Mark with the traditional cross, cutting deep into the dough.

Bake for 40 to 50 minutes, until lightly browned and firm when tapped on the base. Then cool the bread on a wire rack.

Oatcakes

These oatcakes make a satisfying, nutritious snack, and are delicious with cheese.

MAKES 12

¾ cup oatmeal	1 Tbsp melted bacon fat
Pinch of salt	Hot water
Pinch of baking soda	¼ cup all-purpose flour

Mix the dry ingredients in a bowl, make a well in the center and pour in the melted fat. Add enough hot water to make a stiff paste.

Scatter your work surface or board liberally with rolled oats and transfer the paste to the board, pressing with the hands. (Cover your hands with flour as the oatmeal is very sticky at this stage.)

Roll to about ¼ inch thickness and cut into 8 inch circles. Sprinkle with more rolled oats, then cut into quarters.

Place on a hot griddle—a heavy skillet will do—and cook until the edges curl a little. Then turn them over and cook on the other side, or finish them under a warm broiler.

They may also be baked in a medium oven (350°F) for about 20 minutes.

Whole-wheat Soya Bread with Orange and Prunes

This soya bread is brimming over with good things—oranges and prunes give it a really dense, chewy texture.

MAKES I LARGE LOAF

1½ cups whole-wheat flour	1 Tbsp grated orange zest
½ cup soya flour, sifted	¾ cup cooked, chopped, pitted prunes
2 tsp baking powder	½ cup chopped hazelnuts
¼ tsp salt	1 large egg, beaten
½ cup brown sugar	¾ cup milk
½ tsp ground aniseed	
2 Tbsp margarine	

Preheat the oven to 350°F. Grease a 9 × 5 × 3 inch loaf pan.

Mix together the flours, baking powder, salt, sugar, and aniseed. Rub the margarine into the dry mix. Add the orange zest, prunes, and nuts. Beat the egg and milk together and add to the flour mixture. Turn into the prepared pan.

Bake for about 1 hour until a skewer comes out clean. Place the pan on a wire rack and turn out the loaf after 10 minutes. Allow to cool before slicing.

Eliopita

This Cypriot olive-batter bread is scented with rosemary and studded with olives.

MAKES I LOAF

3 cups all-purpose flour	**½ cup extra-virgin olive oil**
½ cup whole-wheat flour	**I cup warm water**
I tsp baking soda	**I onion, chopped**
I Tbsp dried-mint leaves	**Approximately 20 olives, pitted and cut into quarters or small pieces**
I Tbsp fresh rosemary, chopped	

Combine the two flours with the baking soda and the mint, and set aside.

Combine the rosemary, olive oil, and warm water, and stir into the flour mixture, then stir in the onion and olives. Work only until the mixture has the consistency of a thick batter.

Pour the batter into a lightly oiled, 9 x 13 inch or 12 x 15 inch baking pan, and bake at 350°F for 30 to 40 minutes, or until evenly browned and firm. Though it is traditionally served hot, it is also excellent cool after it has set a while. When hot, it has a tendency to be a bit squishy inside.

Whole-wheat Coffee Bread

The taste of coffee is great in a cake, so why not in a bread? Try it, and be converted!

MAKES I LOAF

I¼ cups all-purpose flour	**½ cup dark corn syrup**
I cup whole-wheat flour	**½ cup molasses**
3 Tbsp dark brown sugar	**I tsp baking soda**
3 Tbsp golden raisins	**I¼ cups strong milky coffee**
⅓ cup chopped candied peel	**I egg, beaten**
2 Tbsp coffee extract	**2 Tbsp chopped hazelnuts**
I stick butter	

Preheat oven to 350°F. Grease and line a 6 x 9 inch oblong pan.

Mix together the plain flour, whole-wheat flour, dark brown sugar, golden raisins, and candied peel. In a large pan, melt together the coffee extract, butter, dark corn syrup and molasses. Add to the flour and beat well.

Dissolve the baking soda in the milky coffee and beat in the egg.

Pour into the prepared mixture and beat to form a smooth batter. Pour the mixture into the pan. Scatter the hazelnuts over the top.

Bake in the center of a moderate oven for 40 to 45 minutes until well risen and springy to the touch.

Leave to cool for 15 minutes and turn out to cool further on a wire rack. When cold, wrap in foil without removing the lining paper.

Whole-wheat Drop Scones

Sometimes called Scotch pancakes, these are quick to make and delicious served with butter and preserve or honey. Serve them cold or keep them warm in a clean dish towel while cooking the remaining mixture. Whole-wheat drop scones are more substantial than those made with white flour.

MAKES ABOUT 12

⅔ cup fine whole-wheat flour

1 tsp baking powder

Pinch of salt

1 large egg, beaten

⅔ cup milk, or milk and water mixed

Mix the flour, baking powder, and salt together in a bowl and make a well in the center. Beat the egg with the milk, add it to the flour, and beat to a smooth, thick batter.

Heat a heavy skillet until evenly hot then drop dessertspoonfuls of the mixture on to the surface, allowing room for them to spread slightly. Turn the scones after a minute or so, when bubbles begin to rise to the surface. Cook for a further 1 to 2 minutes then serve.

Quick Onion and Nut Loaf

Quick breads are often very like scone doughs but this one, being more highly seasoned than most, makes a very good loaf to serve with soups and chowders—a Saturday lunchtime bread. It may also be baked in a flat, round pan, in which case reduce the cooking time to about 30 minutes.

MAKES 1 LOAF

2 cups fine whole-wheat flour

2 tsp baking powder

½ tsp salt

1 Tbsp margarine

2 Tbsp roughly chopped parsley

½ cup coarsely grated onion

½ cup pecan nuts, chopped roughly

1 large egg, beaten

1 tsp Dijon or yellow mustard

1 cup milk

Preheat an oven to 375°F and lightly grease a small loaf pan.

Mix all the dry ingredients together in a bowl, then blend in the margarine. Stir in the parsley, onion, and pecans. Beat the egg with the mustard then add to the milk. Pour the liquid into the flour and mix to a stiff, wet batter. Pile the mixture into the prepared loaf pan—it will almost fill it—and smooth the top.

Bake in the preheated oven for 45 to 50 minutes, until set and lightly browned. Cool for a few minutes in the pan then turn out on to a wire rack to cool.

Low-fat Raisin and Honey Bread

This loaf contains a high proportion of yogurt which gives it a white, light center.

MAKES 1 LOAF

2¼ cups all-purpose flour	2 egg whites
1½ tsp baking powder	⅓ cup raisins
½ tsp baking soda	2 Tbsp honey
½ tsp salt	Polyunsaturated margarine for greasing
1¾ cups low-fat plain yogurt	

Mix the flour, baking powder, baking soda, and salt in a large bowl. Whisk together the yogurt and egg whites and fold into the flour mixture with the raisins and honey.

Grease a large loaf pan and spoon in the mixture. Bake in the oven at 425°F for 20 minutes until golden. Cool slightly and turn out of the pan. Serve warm.

Corn Tortillas
Tortillas de Maiz

Mexican tortillas are the cornerstone of Mexican and Texmex cooking. They are eaten as a staple or integrated into many of their cooked dishes.

MAKES ABOUT 30 TORTILLAS

4 cups maize flour	2½ cups hot water
1½ cups all-purpose flour	

Mix the maize and all-purpose flours together. Slowly add the hot water. Knead as you would for bread for 10 to 15 minutes, alternatively knead in the food processor for 2 minutes. If you place a small ball of the dough into a glass of cold water and it does not dissolve, the dough is the right consistency. Flours vary, so if the mixture is too wet, add a little more flour, if too dry, add more water.

Take one heaped tablespoon of the dough and roll it into a small ball. Place the ball inside a new plastic food bag which has been split down one side and, using a tortilla press, press down hard. If you do not have a tortilla press, roll out using a rolling pin, although you will not get such a thin tortilla.

Cook on a hot griddle or a skillet for a few seconds until they are speckled golden brown and puff up. Store in a clean damp cloth in the refrigerator and warm when needed by returning to the hot griddle or pan for 30 seconds on each side.

Flour Tortillas
Tortillas de Harina

Flour Tortillas are lighter than their corn cousins, and used in enchalladas and buritos.

MAKES ABOUT 10 TO 15 TORTILLAS

1 Tbsp salt	⅓ cup lard or shortening
1 lb all-purpose flour	1¼ cups warm water

Sieve salt and flour together and blend in the fat until it resembles crumbs as you would for pastry. Slowly add the warm water until you have a manageable dough like that resembles pastry in texture.

On a well floured surface, knead the dough until it is no longer sticky. Keep the dough covered with a damp cloth or with plastic wrap.

Take a golfball-sized piece of dough and knead individually for about a minute. Roll into a ball and roll out with a well floured rolling pin until the dough is almost transparent. Cut around a 9 inch plate.

Heat the griddle or skillet so that a drop of water sizzles. Then cook the tortilla for 30 seconds on each side.

To store the tortillas, put a sheet of waxed paper in-between each one and wrap in a dry cloth or plastic wrap and refrigerate.

Reheat the tortilla on a hot griddle or skillet for about 30 seconds on each side, alternatively, fry in a little maize or sunflower oil and leave to cool. Great for dips.

Flour Tortillas (Tortillas de Harina) ▶

Norwegian Flatbread

Two crisp breads from Scandinavia. Both are great with dips and soft cheeses.

MAKES 20 FLATBREADS

2 cups fine oatmeal flour	2 cups all-purpose flour
2 cups barley flour	½ tsp salt
2 cups rye flour	¾ pint water

Lightly grease a griddle or hot plate. Mix the flours and salt well together. Add the water and work into a pliable dough. Roll out the dough very thin, cut into oblong pieces and cook until crisp on a well-heated griddle. Pile on a wire rack and store in a box or foil-wrapped in a cool place.

Crispbread

Healthy and light, you can vary this crispbread by sprinkling the rolled-out dough with sesame seeds or cumin.

MAKES 20 PIECES CRISPBREAD

2¾ cups 80% extraction flour	¼ stick unsalted butter
I cup whole-wheat flour	Approx. I cup boiling water
2 tsp salt	

Grease two baking sheets. Put the flours and salt into mixing bowl. Add the butter in pats, pour the boiling water into the mixture and stir vigorously to make a firm dough, adding more water if required. Allow the dough to get cold, put it into the refrigerator and chill for 20 minutes. Knead thoroughly. Divide into 20 pieces and roll each one out thinly. Place on the baking sheets and bake for about 15 minutes. The bread should be dry but not browned. It will keep indefinitely in a dry place.

Chapatis

An unleavened whole-wheat bread, the traditional accompaniment to curries and various vegetable dishes in India and Pakistan.

MAKES 15 CHAPATIS

3 cups whole-wheat flour	2 Tbsp vegetable oil
1 tsp salt	1 cup water

Heat a lightly-greased griddle or large skillet. Mix the flour and salt in a bowl. Add the oil and sufficient water to make a soft dough. Knead the dough on a lightly floured board until smooth and pliable, 5 to 10 minutes. Put the dough into a lightly oiled plastic bag and let it rest for an hour. Divide the dough into about 15 pieces. Roll out each piece into paper-thin circles of about 7 inches in diameter. Put each chapati in the plastic bag as soon as it is ready, to prevent drying out.

Use a pastry brush to remove surplus flour from the chapatis. Cook the chapatis on the griddle for about ½ minute on the first side, and 1½ to 2 minutes on the reverse side, until lightly browned. Turn the chapati back to the first side and cook for a further minute. The chapati should puff up.

Pile the chapatis in a stack, wrapped in a clean, dry dish towel. Serve hot, each one folded in four.

No-yeast Cakes for Coffee

Lemon-yogurt-crumble Coffee Cake

"Jewish" Applecake

Prune Coffee Cake

Blueberry-cream-cheese Streusel Coffee Cake

Sweet Polenta Cake

Rhubarb Streusel Cake

Lemon-yogurt-crumble Coffee Cake

This moist cake has a rich, lemony flavor, with a crumbly swirl and topping.

MAKES 10 TO 12 SERVINGS

CRUMBLE TOPPING

½ cup sugar

¼ cup all-purpose flour

Grated zest of 1 lemon

3 Tbsp butter, cut into small pieces

CAKE

2 cups all-purpose flour

1½ tsp baking powder

½ tsp baking soda

¼ tsp salt

¼ cup finely chopped, candied lemon-peel

1 stick unsalted butter

¼ cup sugar

1 cup plain yogurt or buttermilk

2 eggs, lightly beaten

Grated zest of 1 lemon

1 tsp vanilla extract

Preheat the oven to 350°F. Grease and lightly flour a 9 x 5 inch loaf pan. Combine the crumble topping ingredients in a small bowl and rub in the butter using your fingertips, until the mixture resembles coarse crumbs; set aside.

Sift the flour, baking powder, baking soda, and salt into a large bowl. Stir in the candied lemon peel and make a well in the center.

Put the butter in a saucepan and set over low heat until melted, stirring occasionally. Remove from heat and whisk in the sugar, yogurt, eggs, grated lemon zest, and vanilla extract. Pour into the well and stir with a fork until just blended.

Spoon half the batter into the prepared pan, smoothing the top and pushing into the corners. Sprinkle over half the crumb topping. Drop spoonfuls of the remaining batter over the topping, and spread as evenly as possible, then sprinkle with the remaining topping.

Bake until the cake is risen and golden, and a cake tester inserted in the center comes out clean, about 1 hour. Remove to a wire rack to cool for at least 30 minutes. Run a thin-bladed knife between the cake and the sides of the pan to loosen it, then carefully unmold on to the rack, top-side up, to cool. This cake is best made a day ahead, wrapped tightly until ready to serve.

"Jewish" Applecake

Applecake made with oil is a popular choice for a Hanukkah cake because the oil symbolizes the holiday's miracle. These layers of tangy apples baked in a moist, sweet, lemon-scented batter will make this a favorite recipe.

MAKES 16 TO 20 SLICES

APPLE FILLING

2 lb tart cooking apples, peeled, cored and thinly sliced

4 Tbsp sugar

1 tsp ground cinnamon

Grated zest and juice of 1 lemon

CAKE

4 eggs

1 cup superfine sugar

1 cup vegetable oil

2 cups self-rising cake flour, or 2 cups cake flour plus 2 tsp baking powder

1 tsp vanilla extract

Sugar for sprinkling

1 Preheat the oven to 350°F. Grease a 9 x 13 inch cake pan. In a large bowl, toss apple slices with sugar, cinnamon, lemon zest and juice.

2 In a large bowl, with electric mixer at medium speed, beat eggs with sugar until thick and lemon colored and mixture forms a "ribbon" when beaters are lifted from bowl, 3 to 5 minutes. Beat in oil until well blended. Stir in flour and vanilla just until well mixed and smooth.

3 Pour half the batter into prepared pan. Spoon half the apple slices over batter. Cover apple slices with remaining batter; top with remaining apple mixture. Sprinkle with about 2 tablespoonfuls sugar.

4 Bake until apples are tender and cake is golden brown and puffed and top springs back when gently pressed with a finger, 1¼ to 1½ hours. Cover with foil during baking if top colors too quickly. Remove to wire rack to cool. Cut cake into squares and serve at room temperature.

Prune Coffee Cake

My Polish neighbors serve this cake with mid-morning coffee. The chocolate glaze makes this cake extra special.

MAKES 10 TO 12 SLICES

3 cups all-purpose flour

1½ tsp baking soda

1 tsp baking powder

2 sticks unsalted butter, cut into pieces

Grated zest of 1 orange

2 cups sugar

1 Tbsp vanilla or rum extract

¼ tsp salt

2 cups sour cream

3 eggs, lightly beaten

¾ cup prune purée*

½ cup chopped walnuts or pecans

2 Tbsp unsweetened cocoa powder, sifted

1 tsp ground cinnamon

CHOCOLATE-HONEY GLAZE

3 oz bittersweet or semi-sweet chocolate, chopped

3 Tbsp unsalted butter

1½ Tbsp honey

Preheat oven to 350°F. Grease and flour a heavy 10-inch Bundt or tube pan (preferably nonstick). Sift the flour, baking soda, and baking powder.

Melt the butter in a saucepan. Stir in the orange zest and remove from heat. Immediately stir in the sugar, vanilla or rum extract, salt, sour cream, and eggs, then beat in all the flour mixture until blended.

Spoon about half the batter into the pan. Stir the prune purée and drop heaped tablespoonfuls over the center of the batter. Sprinkle the walnuts or pecans, cocoa powder, and ground cinnamon over the top of the prune purée.

Spoon the remaining batter over the prune purée and nut mixture and smooth the top evenly. Draw a palette knife through the mixture creating a swirling pattern. Bake 50 minutes. Cool in the pan 10 minutes.

Invert the cake on to a wire rack to cool completely. Melt the chocolate, butter, and honey. Drizzle the glaze over the cake and allow to set.

NOTE

*Prune purée, sometimes called lekvar, is used in Eastern European and Jewish baking. It can be found in large supermarkets or delicatessens or specialty stores. To make your own, simmer 1 cup dried prunes with ½ cup water, a little grated orange zest, and about 2 tablespoonfuls orange juice until all the liquid is absorbed and the prunes form a mushy purée. Blend in a food processor. Store, covered, in the refrigerator.

Blueberry-cream-cheese Streusel Coffee Cake

This luscious coffee cake is a cross between a blueberry muffin and old-fashioned cheesecake—perfect for a brunch, or anytime.

MAKES 10 TO 12 SLICES

STREUSEL TOPPING

1 stick unsalted butter, softened

⅔ cup sugar

¼ cup firmly packed, brown sugar

⅔ cup all-purpose flour

½ cup chopped, toasted hazelnuts

1½ tsp ground cinnamon

½ tsp ground nutmeg

¼ tsp salt

CREAM-CHEESE FILLING

12 oz cream cheese

⅓ cup sugar

1 egg

Grated zest of 1 lemon

1 Tbsp lemon juice

1 tsp almond extract

CAKE

4 cups all-purpose flour

4 tsp baking powder

1 tsp salt

1 stick unsalted butter, softened

1¼ cups sugar

2 eggs, lightly beaten

1 tsp almond extract

1¼ cups milk

3 cups fresh blueberries

TIP

Be sure to use an ovenproof glass dish, as the blueberries could react with metal. (A porcelain dish would not allow the cake to cook completely.)

Preheat the oven to 375°F. Generously butter a 13 × 9 inch glass baking dish. To prepare the topping, rub together all the ingredients with fingertips or a pastry blender in a medium bowl, until well blended, and large crumbs form. Set aside.

To prepare the filling: Soften the cream cheese and beat with the sugar until creamy in a medium bowl using an electric mixer, scraping down the side of the bowl occasionally. Beat in the egg, grated lemon zest and juice, and almond extract until smooth. Set aside.

To prepare the cake: Sift the flour, baking powder, and salt into a bowl. In another bowl, with an electric mixer, beat the butter and sugar until light and fluffy, about 2 to 3 minutes. Gradually beat in the eggs until very light and smooth. Beat in the almond extract. Beat in the flour mixture on low speed, alternating with the milk, and ending with the flour mixture, until well blended. If batter is too stiff, add a little more milk. Gently fold in the washed and dried blueberries.

Spread slightly less than half the cake mixture on the bottom of the dish, smoothing the surface and pushing into corners. Gently spread the cream-cheese filling over the cake batter, and lightly sprinkle about one quarter of the streusel topping over the filling. Drop spoonfuls of the remaining batter over the top and spread evenly, trying not to mix the layers. Sprinkle the remaining topping evenly over the surface.

Bake until the topping is crunchy and golden brown, and a skewer inserted into the center comes out with just a few crumbs attached, about 1 hour. Remove to a wire rack and cool until the cake is just warm. Cut into squares, and serve slightly warm or at room temperature.

Sweet Polenta Cake
with caramelized apples

This cake is a slightly more upmarket version of a sweet cornbread—there are many versions found all over Italy.

MAKES 6 TO 8 SERVINGS

¾ cup all-purpose flour

½ cup polenta or yellow cornmeal

1 tsp baking powder

Grated zest of 1 lemon

¼ tsp salt

2 eggs

¾ cup sugar

⅓ cup milk

½ tsp almond extract

¼ cup currants or raisins, soaked in hot water for 20 minutes, and well drained

¾ stick unsalted butter, softened

2 dessert apples, peeled, cored, and thinly sliced

¼ cup slivered almonds

3 to 4 Tbsp apricot preserve

1 to 2 Tbsp water

Whipped cream, sour cream, or ice cream to serve (optional)

TIP

Be sure to stir or sift together the dry ingredients (including any grated or ground spices) until they are completely well blended. Most wet ingredients can be beaten until well blended with a hand whisk or fork. Heavier mixtures that include mashed bananas, pumpkin, or sweet potato might require a hand-held electric mixer.

Preheat the oven to 375°F. Generously butter a 9 inch springform pan, then dust the pan lightly with flour. Stir the flour, polenta or cornmeal, baking powder, grated lemon zest, and salt together in a large bowl.

Beat the eggs and ½ cup of the sugar in another bowl with an electric mixer until foamy; gradually beat in the milk and almond extract. Stir in the drained currants or raisins. Beat in the dry ingredients on low speed, adding 4 tablespoons of the softened butter.

Spoon into the prepared pan and smooth the top evenly. Arrange the apple slices in concentric circles over the top, and sprinkle with the slivered almonds. In a small saucepan, melt the remaining 2 tablespoonfuls of butter over low heat, and drizzle over the apples. Sprinkle with the remaining sugar.

Bake until the cake is puffed and golden, and the apples are lightly caramelized, about 45 minutes. Remove to a wire rack to cool, about 20 minutes. Run a thin knife blade between the cake edge and pan side, then unclip the pan side and carefully remove. Heat the apricot preserves with 1 to 2 tablespoonfuls of water in a small saucepan until melted and smooth. Carefully brush or spoon over the top of the apples to glaze. Allow to cool to room temperature, and serve with whipped cream, sour cream, or ice cream, as preferred.

Rhubarb Streusel Cake

This may be served as either a cake or a pudding, or cold as a cake. The crumb topping gives a delicious crunch in contrast to the rhubarb, which softens into the cake mix. Apples and gooseberries are good alternatives to the rhubarb.

MAKES I LARGE CAKE

STREUSEL TOPPING

¾ **stick butter**

I **cup fine whole-wheat flour**

½ **tsp baking powder**

½ **cup raw sugar**

CAKE

I **stick butter or margarine**

⅔ **cup light brown sugar**

2 **large eggs, beaten**

I **cup fine whole-wheat flour**

I **tsp baking powder**

½ **tsp ground cinnamon**

I **Tbsp milk**

2 **cups rhubarb pieces, in 2-inch lengths, fresh or canned**

Preheat an oven to 350°F, then line an 8 inch deep, round cake pan with baking parchment.

First prepare the topping. Blend the butter into the flour, baking powder, and sugar until evenly distributed, then set aside. Cream the butter and sugar together until pale and fluffy then gradually add the beaten eggs. Mix the flour, baking powder, and cinnamon together, then fold it into the mixture, adding the milk to give a soft dropping consistency.

Spoon the cake mixture into the prepared pan and roughly smooth the top. Arrange the rhubarb over the sponge then cover with the topping mixture, spreading it evenly.

Bake the cake in the oven for I hour, or until a toothpick inserted into the cake comes out clean. Leave in the pan for 2 to 3 minutes, then remove the cake carefully, peel off the paper, and allow to cool completely on a wire rack.

Muffins and Biscuits

Sour Cream and Cherry Muffins

Double Chocolate-chip Muffins

Gingery Pear-and-pecan Muffins

Warm Orange Muffins

Very Blue-blueberry Muffins

Parmesan and Pine Nut Mini Muffins

Cheese and Bacon Muffins

Oatmeal-raisin Muffins

Cheese and Walnut Scone Round

English-style Scones

Cranberry-orange Biscuits

Goat Cheese and Sun-dried Tomato Biscuits

Sesame Roquefort Crescents

Sweet-potato Pinwheels

Sour Cream and Cherry Muffins

with cherry compote

These delicious muffins are moist, crumbly, and delicately flavored, and are enhanced by the intense flavor of the cherry compote. A spectacular brunch or dessert recipe.

MAKES 12 MUFFINS

½ cup semi-dried Montgomery or other cherries	½ tsp ground cardamom
1¾ cups all-purpose flour	½ cup sugar
1 tsp baking powder	1 egg
½ tsp baking soda	1 cup sour cream
½ tsp salt	½ tsp vanilla extract

Put the cherries in a small bowl, and pour over enough boiling water to cover them. Allow to stand for about 15 minutes to soften. Drain and pat dry with paper towels.

Preheat the oven to 400°F. Grease or spray a 12-cup muffin pan or line with paper liners. Sift the flour, baking powder, baking soda, salt, and ground cardamom into a large bowl. Stir in the sugar, then the cherries, being sure they are coated with the flour mixture, and make a well in the center.

Beat the egg and sour cream in another bowl until well blended; beat in the vanilla. Pour into the well and stir lightly until just combined. Do not overmix; the batter should be slightly lumpy.

Spoon the batter into the prepared cups, filling each about ¾ full. Bake until risen and golden, about 20 minutes. Remove pan to a wire rack to cool, about 2 minutes, then remove muffins to the wire rack to cool until just warm. Serve with the Cherry Compote.

Cherry Compote

MAKES ABOUT 6 CUPS

1 lb fresh black or red cherries, pitted	½ cup sugar
8 oz dried cherries	1 tsp cornstarch or arrowroot, dissolved in 2 tsp cold water
1 vanilla bean, split	
4 to 6 cardamom pods, crushed	

Put the first five ingredients in a large, noncorrosive saucepan, and add just enough water to cover the fruit. Place over medium heat and bring to a boil, stirring to dissolve the sugar. Simmer for about 5 minutes, until the cherries are just tender. Stir the dissolved cornstarch or arrowroot, and then stir into the simmering cherry liquid. Bring to a boil, and cook for 1 to 2 minutes, until the juices are thickened and clear. Remove from the heat to cool, stirring occasionally. Pour into a bowl and refrigerate, covered, until ready to serve.

Double Chocolate-chip Muffins

These rich, chocolate muffins make a great morning snack with a cup of *cappuccino* or a glass of cold milk.

MAKES 10 MUFFINS

1¾ cups all-purpose flour

¼ cup unsweetened cocoa powder

1 Tbsp baking powder

½ tsp salt

½ cup sugar

½ cup semi-sweet chocolate chips and ¼ cup white-chocolate chips

2 eggs

½ cup sunflower or vegetable oil

1 cup milk

1 tsp vanilla extract

Preheat the oven to 400°F. Line 10 muffin pan cups with foil or double-paper liners. Half fill any remaining empty cups in the muffin pan with water to prevent them from scorching. Sift the flour, cocoa powder, baking powder, and salt into a large bowl. Stir in the sugar and chocolate chips, and make a well in the center.

In another bowl or 4-cup measure, beat the eggs with the oil until foamy. Gradually beat in the milk and vanilla extract. Pour into the well and stir until just combined. Do not overmix; the batter should be slightly lumpy.

Spoon the batter into the prepared cups, filling each about ¾ full. Bake until risen, golden, and springy when pressed with your fingertip, about 20 minutes. Remove pan to a wire rack to cool, about 2 minutes, then remove muffins to the wire rack to cool. Serve warm or at room temperature.

Gingery Pear-and-pecan Muffins

Ginger and pear go well together, and the combination of tangy, fresh gingerroot and sweet, candied ginger create a "hot-and-spicy" sensation.

MAKES 18 MUFFINS

2 cups all-purpose flour	½ cup sunflower or other vegetable oil
2 tsp baking powder	2 Tbsp milk
½ tsp salt	1 tsp grated gingerroot
¼ tsp ground cinnamon	1½ cups peeled, cored, and chopped pears
¼ cup sugar	¼ cup chopped pecans
2 eggs	Candied ginger, chopped

Preheat the oven to 375°F. Lightly grease or spray 18 muffin pan cups or line each cup with a paper liner. Sift the flour, baking powder, salt, and ground cinnamon into a large bowl, then stir in the sugar, and make a well in the center.

Beat the eggs, oil, milk, and grated gingerroot in another bowl until well blended. Pour into the well. Using a fork, lightly stir until just combined. Do not overmix; the batter should be slightly lumpy. Gently fold in the pears, pecans, and candied ginger.

Spoon the batter into the prepared muffin cups, filling each just over ⅔ full. Bake until risen and golden, and a cake tester inserted in the center comes out clean, 20 to 25 minutes. Remove muffins to the wire rack to cool, about 2 minutes. Serve warm with the Honey-and-ginger Butter.

Honey-and-ginger Butter

MAKES ABOUT 1 CUP

2 sticks unsalted butter, softened	½ tsp ground ginger
	¼ tsp ground cinnamon
1 to 2 Tbsp honey	

Beat the butter in a medium-sized bowl until light and creamy, about 1 to 2 minutes. Add the honey, ginger, and cinnamon, and beat until well blended. Spoon into a bowl and refrigerate, covered, until ready to serve. Soften for a few minutes at room temperature for easier spreading.

TIP

Chopped nuts, fruit, or even chocolate chips can be added at various stages. Tossing them in the dry ingredients before mixing with the liquids helps to even out their distribution, but they can be folded in just before the batter is completed.

Warm Orange Muffins

with winter dried-fruit salad

These warm, delicate muffins make a perfect accompaniment to a "winter salad" of dried fruits. Serve with fresh whipped cream or crème fraîche for a brunch, snack, dessert or treat.

MAKES 12 MUFFINS

1¼ cups all-purpose flour	I egg
2 tsp baking powder	Grated zest of I orange
½ tsp salt	½ tsp vanilla extract
½ cup sugar	I cup buttermilk
½ cup candied orange peel, chopped	½ stick butter or margarine, melted and cooled

Preheat the oven to 400°F. Grease or spray a 12-cup muffin pan or line with paper liners. Sift the flour, baking powder, and salt into a large bowl, then stir in the sugar and chopped orange peel, and make a well in the center.

Beat the egg, orange zest, and vanilla extract in another bowl or 4-cup measure until foamy. Beat in the buttermilk, and melted butter. Pour into the well, and lightly stir until just combined. Do not overmix; the batter should be slightly lumpy.

Spoon the batter into the prepared cups, filling each about ¾ full. Bake until risen and golden, and a cake tester inserted in the center comes out clean, about 20 minutes. Remove pan to a wire rack to cool, about 2 minutes, then remove muffins to the wire rack to cool slightly. Serve warm with the Winter Dried-Fruit Salad.

Winter Dried-Fruit Salad

2 cups large, pitted prunes	I orange
1½ cups dried, no-soak apricots	I tsp vanilla extract
1½ cups dried, no-soak pears	I cinnamon stick
¾ cup dried, no-soak peaches	2 to 3 cloves
½ cup golden or seedless raisins	2 to 3 Tbsp sugar or honey, or to taste
	Boiling water

Put the prunes, apricots, pears, and peaches in a large bowl, then sprinkle in the raisins. Using a swivel-bladed vegetable peeler, peel the orange zest in long, thin strips, and add to the fruit. Cut the orange in half and squeeze the juice over the fruit, removing any seeds. Add the vanilla extract, cinnamon stick, cloves, and the sugar or honey to taste. Pour over enough boiling water to cover the fruit by I inch, then cover and allow to stand for at least I hour until the fruit is plump and tender. Stir to blend in the flavors (remove the cinnamon stick and cloves if you like), and serve at room temperature or refrigerate in order to serve chilled.

Very Blue-blueberry Muffins

Thse muffins are bursting with blueberries; mashing some of the berries releases more flavor into the batter.

MAKES 12 MUFFINS

2 cups all-purpose flour

2½ tsp baking powder

½ tsp salt

¼ tsp freshly grated or ground nutmeg

¼ cup sugar

2 eggs

¼ cup milk

1 stick butter or margarine, melted and cooled

Grated zest of ½ orange

1 tsp vanilla extract

½ cup fresh blueberries, mashed

2 cups fresh blueberries

¼ cup coarse sugar, mixed with ¼ tsp freshly grated nutmeg for sprinkling

TIP

Muffin pan cups can vary in size, depending on the manufacturer. Your batter may not completely fill each cup; if so, it doesn't really matter. Whatever the size, make sure to fill the cups about ¼ full.

Preheat the oven to 375°F. Lightly grease or spray a 12-cup muffin pan or line each cup with a paper liner. Sift the flour, baking powder, salt, and nutmeg into a large bowl; stir in the sugar, and make a well in the center.

In another bowl, beat the eggs, milk, melted butter or margarine, grated orange zest, and vanilla extract; then stir in the mashed blueberries. Pour into the well and lightly stir using a fork, until blended in. Do not overmix. Lightly fold in the remaining blueberries.

Spoon the batter into the prepared muffin cups, filling each to almost full. Sprinkle each with the sugar-nutmeg mixture, and bake until risen and golden (a cake tester or toothpick inserted in the center should come out with a few crumbs attached), 25 to 30 minutes. Remove pan to a wire rack to cool, about 2 minutes, then remove muffins to the wire rack to cool. Serve warm or at room temperature.

Parmesan and Pine Nut Mini-muffins
with sun-dried tomato butter

These delicious mini-muffins have an unusual, versatile flavor. Served with a tangy sun-dried tomato butter, they make a great savory snack or *hors d'oeuvre*; with a sweetened honey or cinnamon butter, they have a much sweeter taste. Try them both ways.

MAKES 24 MINI-MUFFINS

1½ cups all-purpose flour

2 tsp baking powder

¼ tsp salt

½ tsp dried basil leaves, crumbled

⅓ cup sugar

½ cup golden raisins

½ cup pine nuts, lightly toasted, plus extra for sprinkling

½ cup freshly grated Parmesan cheese

1 egg

¾ cup milk

½ stick butter, melted and cooled

Preheat the oven to 375°F. Grease or spray 24 mini-muffin pan cups or line with mini-paper or foil liners. Sift the flour, baking powder, and salt into a large bowl. Stir in the dried basil, sugar, raisins, pine nuts, and Parmesan until well mixed, and make a well in the center.

Whisk the egg with the milk in another bowl until well blended and foamy, then whisk in the melted butter. Pour into the well and lightly fold together until combined. Do not overmix; the batter should be slightly lumpy.

Spoon batter into the prepared cups, filling each to almost full. Sprinkle each with a few pine nuts. Bake until risen, golden, and springy when pressed, about 15 minutes. Remove to a wire rack to cool, 1 to 2 minutes, then remove muffins to the wire rack to cool until just warm. Serve warm with the Sun-dried Tomato Butter. Alternatively, cool to room temperature, then split each muffin crosswise, spread the bottom halves with the butter, and close with the sandwich tops.

Sun-dried Tomato Butter

MAKES 1½ CUPS

1½ sticks unsalted butter, softened

½ cup sun-dried tomatoes, packed in oil, drained and chopped

Freshly ground black pepper

In a medium bowl, beat the butter until smooth and creamy. Add the sun-dried tomatoes and season with pepper to taste. Stir gently until well blended. Scrape into a serving bowl, and refrigerate, covered, until ready to serve. Soften for a few minutes at room temperature for easier spreading.

> **TIP**
>
> *If you prefer a larger muffin, bake the batter in a 12-cup muffin pan prepared as above for about 20 minutes.*

Cheese and Bacon Muffins

These savory muffins are delicious as a brunch dish or with scrambled eggs. Vary the cheese to your taste.

MAKES 12 MUFFINS

6 slices bacon

Vegetable oil

1½ cups all-purpose flour

2 tsp baking powder

½ tsp salt

2 tsp sugar

1 cup grated Swiss, Gruyère, or other cheese

3 to 4 green onions, finely chopped

1 egg

¼ cup milk

1 Tbsp Dijon-style mustard

Preheat the oven to 400°F. Grease or spray 12 muffin pan cups, or line each with paper liners. Put the bacon slices in a large skillet and fry over medium heat, turning once, until crisp and brown on both sides. Drain on paper towels, and pour remaining fat into a cup. Add extra oil, if necessary, to make ¼ cup. When cool, crumble the bacon into small pieces.

Meanwhile, sift the flour, baking powder, and salt into a large bowl. Stir in the sugar, cheese, and green onions, tossing lightly to mix. Add the crumbled bacon and mix again, and make a well in the center.

Beat the egg with the milk in another bowl until well blended. Beat in the mustard and the reserved bacon fat. Pour into the well and stir lightly until just combined. Do not overmix; the batter should be slightly lumpy.

Spoon the mixture into the prepared muffin pan cups, and bake until risen, golden, and springy when pressed, 15 to 20 minutes. Remove to a wire rack to cool, about 2 minutes, then remove muffins to the rack to cool until just warm. Serve warm with butter or cream cheese.

Oatmeal-raisin Muffins

Oatmeal adds a chewy texture to these dark, moist muffins. Substitute dried cranberries for raisins, if you like.

MAKES 12 MUFFINS

1 cup old-fashioned oats	2 eggs
1 cup all-purpose flour	¼ cup firmly packed dark-brown sugar
2 tsp baking powder	
½ tsp ground cinnamon	¼ cup milk
½ tsp salt	½ stick butter or margarine, melted and cooled
½ cup raisins	
½ cup whole-wheat flour	½ tsp vanilla extract

Preheat the oven to 400°F. Grease or spray a 12-cup muffin pan or line with double-paper liners. Put the oats in a large bowl and sift in the all-purpose flour, baking powder, cinnamon, and salt. Stir in the raisins and whole-wheat flour, and make a well in the center.

Using an electric mixer, beat the eggs and brown sugar in another bowl until foamy. Gradually beat in the milk, melted butter or margarine, and vanilla extract until well blended. Pour into the well, and stir until combined. Do not overmix; the batter should be slightly lumpy.

Spoon the batter into the prepared cups, filling each about ¾ full. Bake until risen, golden, and springy when pressed with your fingertip, about 20 minutes. Remove pan to a wire rack to cool, then remove muffins to the rack, about 2 minutes. If you like, serve them with salted butter or a flavored butter.

Cheese and Walnut Biscuit Round

Biscuits are quick and easy to prepare and cook, the perfect accompaniment to soups, stews, or a bedtime drink. This mixture is baked in one large round, cutting the preparation time to an absolute minimum.

SERVES 4 TO 8

1 stick butter	½ cup walnuts, roughly chopped
2 cups fine whole-wheat flour	
2 tsp baking powder	1 cup grated Cheddar cheese
Pinch of salt	1 large egg, beaten
	½ cup milk

Preheat an oven to 425°F and lightly oil a baking sheet.

Blend the butter into the flour, baking powder, and salt, then stir in the nuts and cheese. Beat the egg with the milk then use to mix to a soft but manageable dough.

Turn on to a lightly floured surface then knead lightly until smooth. Shape the dough into a round about 1 inch thick, and mark into eight. Bake on the baking sheet for 20 to 25 minutes. Cool for at least 10 minutes before eating to avoid indigestion!

English-style Scones

This is a classic English-style treat for tea-time. Often made with heavy cream, this recipe uses buttermilk, which makes the scones soft and fluffy, with a smooth texture.

MAKES ABOUT 15 SCONES

3 cups all-purpose flour

1½ tsp baking soda

½ tsp salt

3 Tbsp sugar

¾ stick unsalted butter, cut into pieces

⅓ cup seedless currants or raisins

1 egg, lightly beaten

1¼ cups buttermilk

2 Tbsp milk

Clotted cream or lightly whipped heavy cream to serve

Preserve to serve

Preheat the oven to 425°F. Lightly flour a large baking sheet. Sift the flour, baking soda, and salt into a large bowl, then stir in the sugar.

Sprinkle the butter pieces over the flour mixture, and rub in the butter until the mixture resembles medium crumbs. Blend in the currants or raisins, and make a well in the center.

Beat the egg with ¾ cup of the buttermilk in a small bowl, and pour into the well. Stir the flour mixture into the liquid with a fork until it is combined. Do not overmix. Form the dough into a rough ball, and place on a lightly floured surface: knead lightly 8 to 10 times until blended.

Roll or pat the dough into a ¾-inch-thick round. Use a floured, 2½-inch-wide, round cutter to cut out as many rounds as possible. Transfer to the baking sheet, arranging them about 1 inch apart. Press the trimmings together and shape into another ¾-inch-thick round, then cut out as many 2½-inch thick rounds as possible. Transfer these to the baking sheet.

Brush the tops of the scones with a little milk, and bake until risen and golden, about 15 minutes. Remove scones to a wire rack to cool slightly. Serve warm with fresh, whipped cream and raspberry or strawberry preserve.

> **TIP**
> *When cutting out the scones, cut straight down, do not twist the cutter, or the scones will rise unevenly.*

Cranberry-orange Biscuits

with cranberry-raspberry butter

These delicious, orange-flavored biscuits are filled with chewy, dried cranberries. If you like, use dried cherries instead, and serve with cherry compote (see page 425).

MAKES ABOUT 10 BISCUITS

3 cups all-purpose flour	¾ cup dried cranberries
1 Tbsp baking powder	2 eggs
½ tsp salt	½ to ⅔ cup heavy cream, plus extra for glazing
2 Tbsp sugar, plus extra for sprinkling	½ tsp vanilla extract
Grated zest of 1 orange	2 Tbsp milk
½ stick unsalted butter, cut into pieces	2 Tbsp firmly packed, light-brown sugar

Preheat the oven to 425°F. Lightly flour a large baking sheet. Sift the flour, baking powder, and salt into a large bowl; stir in the sugar and the grated orange zest.

Sprinkle the butter pieces over the flour mixture, and rub in the butter using a pastry blender or your fingertips, until the mixture resembles medium crumbs. Stir in the dried cranberries, and make a well in the center.

In a small bowl, beat the eggs and ½ cup of the cream until blended; beat in the vanilla extract and pour into the well. Using a fork, stir the flour mixture into the liquid just until it begins to combine; do not overmix. Form dough into a rough ball, and place on a lightly floured surface. Knead 6 to 8 times until blended. Pat the dough into a ¾-inch-thick round and cut out as many rounds as possible using a 2½-inch floured cutter. Transfer to the baking sheet, arranging them about 1 inch apart. Press the trimmings together and roll or pat to another ¾-inch-thick round, then cut out as many rounds as possible, and transfer to the baking sheet.

Brush the top of the scones with a little more cream or milk, and sprinkle with sugar. Bake until risen and golden, about 12 minutes. Remove to a wire rack to cool, about 3 to 4 minutes, then transfer biscuits on to the wire rack to cool until just warm. Serve with Cranberry-raspberry Butter.

Cranberry-raspberry Butter

MAKES ABOUT 1½ CUPS

1½ sticks unsalted butter, softened	1 Tbsp raspberry preserve
	1 Tbsp orange juice
1 Tbsp cranberry sauce	½ tsp ground cinnamon

Beat the butter until smooth and creamy in a small bowl. Beat in the cranberry sauce, raspberry preserve, orange juice, and ground cinnamon until well blended. Scrape into a serving bowl and refrigerate, covered, until ready to serve.

TIP

If the cranberries are very dry, plump them by covering with boiling water; stand for 5 minutes, then drain and pat dry with paper towels.

Goat Cheese and Sun-dried Tomato Biscuits

S erve these delicious biscuits instead of bread with a tossed salad or pasta dish with a difference.

MAKES 10 TO 12 BISCUITS

2 cups all-purpose flour	⅓ cup chopped, sun-dried tomatoes, packed in oil, drained
2 tsp baking powder	
¼ tsp baking soda	
¼ tsp salt	4 oz semi-soft goat cheese, crumbled or diced
Freshly ground black pepper	1 egg
1 to 2 scallions, finely chopped	½ to ⅔ cup buttermilk

Preheat the oven to 400°F. Lightly flour a large baking sheet. Sift the flour, baking powder, baking soda, and salt into a large bowl. Add a few grinds of black pepper, the scallions, sun-dried tomatoes, and goat cheese and stir well, being sure to coat the tomatoes and cheese, and make a well in the center.

In a small bowl beat the egg with ½ cup buttermilk and pour into the well. Using a fork, stir lightly until just combined, adding a little more buttermilk if necessary. Form into a rough ball and turn on to a lightly floured surface. Knead lightly 6 to 8 times until just smooth.

Roll or pat dough into a ¾-inch-thick circle about 10 inches in diameter. Transfer to a baking sheet and using a long-bladed, sharp, floured knife, score deeply into 10 or 12 wedges. Do not drag the knife through the dough or it will not rise evenly.

Dust lightly with a little flour and bake until risen and golden, 15 to 18 minutes. Remove to a wire rack to cool 2 to 3 minutes, then slide the scones on to the wire rack to cool until just warm. Serve warm with either salted or flavored butter.

Sesame Roquefort Crescents

These unusual biscuits are shaped like a croissant, and make a delicious alternative to sweeter choices.

MAKES 12 CRESCENTS

2¼ cups all-purpose flour	¾ cup buttermilk
2 tsp baking powder	2 Tbsp butter, melted
½ tsp salt	½ cup Roquefort or other strong blue cheese, crumbled
¼ tsp baking soda	
¼ tsp ground ginger	2 Tbsp freshly chopped parsley
½ cup shortening	
	Sesame seeds for sprinkling

Preheat the oven to 425°F. Lightly grease a large baking sheet. Sift the flour, baking powder, salt, baking soda, and ground ginger into a large bowl. Add the shortening and using a pastry blender or your fingertips, rub into the flour until the mixture resembles coarse crumbs, and make a well in the center.

Pour in the buttermilk, and stir lightly with a fork until just moistened. Form into a rough ball and place on a lightly floured surface. Gently knead 8 to 10 times until just smooth. Using a lightly floured rolling pin, roll into a ¼-inch-thick round, about 12 inches in diameter. Brush the dough with half the melted butter, and sprinkle with the crumbled cheese and chopped parsley. Using a sharp knife, cut into 12 wedges. Starting from each wide end, roll the dough toward the point.

Arrange the crescents, with their points tucked under, on the baking sheet (preferably nonstick), about 2 inches apart, pulling the ends toward the center to form a crescent shape. Sprinkle with the sesame seeds. Bake until puffed and golden, 15 to 20 minutes. Remove to a wire rack and cool for 2 to 3 minutes, then transfer crescents to the wire rack to cool until just warm.

Sweet-potato Pinwheels
with cinnamon, nuts, and raisins

These delicious biscuits are a cross between a coffee cake and a slightly sticky, sweet bun, and are great served with morning coffee. The nuts and raisins add a crunchy texture to the warm, spicy-flavored biscuits.

MAKES 10 TO 12 BISCUITS

1½ cups all-purpose flour	⅓ to ½ cup milk
2½ tsp baking powder	2 Tbsp butter, melted
½ tsp salt	**FILLING**
1 tsp ground cinnamon	¼ cup firmly packed brown sugar
¾ stick butter, cut into pieces	¼ cup chopped pecans or walnuts
1 to 2 Tbsp brown sugar	¼ cup chopped raisins
½ cup cooked or canned sweet potato, mashed	½ tsp cinnamon

Preheat the oven to 425°F. Lightly grease a large baking sheet. Sift the flour, baking powder, salt, and cinnamon into a large bowl. Sprinkle over the butter pieces, and rub in using a pastry blender until the mixture resembles coarse crumbs. Stir in the brown sugar and make a well in the center.

Put the sweet potato in a small bowl, and whisk in the milk until smooth. Pour into the well, stirring lightly until a soft dough forms. Form into a rough ball.

Place on a lightly floured surface and knead lightly 8 to 10 times. Using a lightly floured rolling pin, roll the dough to a ¼-inch-thick rectangle about 10 to 12 inches wide, and brush with the melted butter. Combine the filling ingredients in a small bowl, and sprinkle over the dough. Starting at one long end, roll the dough, jelly-roll style. Cut into 1 inch slices and arrange cut-side down on the baking sheet, about ½ inch apart.

Bake until puffed and golden, about 12 minutes. Remove to a wire rack to cool slightly, then transfer pinwheels to the wire rack to cool. Serve warm.

TIP

Scones and biscuits should never be over-mixed or over-kneaded, as they will be dense and tough-textured. Also, cut as many shapes as possible from the first rolling of the dough; extra flour and rerolling may cause drier, tougher results.

Baking for Christmas

This is the season when even the most reluctant cook takes to the kitchen. Here is a range of traditional Christmas specialties. There is the Yule Log from France, Mince Pies from Britain, Stollen from Germany, Lemańce from Poland, and Panettone from Italy. These wonderful treats should not just be lavished upon the family—make up a batch and present them as gifts.

Yule Log

Aclassic cake from France, where it is called *Buche de Noël*, which will help you celebrate Christmas in style.

SERVES 8–12

4 eggs, separated	1½ sticks unsalted butter
½ cup sugar	3 oz semi-sweet chocolate, melted
1 cup all-purpose flour	1 to 2 tsp dark rum
BUTTER CREAM	**DECORATION**
⅓ cup sugar	**Meringue Mushrooms**
6 Tbsp water	**Marzipan holly leaves and berries**
4 egg yolks	

Preheat oven to 450°F. Grease and line a 9 x 13 inch jelly roll pan.

Put egg yolks and sugar into a mixing bowl and whisk until the mixture falls in a thick trail.

Whisk the egg whites until stiff. Fold the egg whites and flour alternately into the egg yolk mixture. Pour into the pan and bake in the oven for about 10 minutes until golden brown.

Put a sheet of waxed paper on top of a dampened dish towel and sprinkle with superfine sugar. Turn the sponge out on to the sugared paper.

Peel off the lining paper and quickly trim the edges of the sponge. Make a shallow groove across one short side of the cake 1 inch from the edge. Fold the sponge over at the groove. Using the towel to support the cake, roll up the sponge with the paper inside. Cover with the damp cloth until cold.

To make the butter frosting, put the sugar and water into a small pan. Dissolve the sugar and then bring to a boil and boil to the "thread" stage (225°F).

Whisk the egg yolks in a bowl until thick and creamy. Slowly pour the hot syrup on the egg yolks in a steady stream, making sure you beat constantly until the mixture is light and fluffy.

Beat the butter until soft. Add the egg mixture a little at a time until the mixture is firm and shiny. Stir in the chocolate and rum.

Carefully unroll the sponge and remove the waxed paper. Spread a little butter frosting over the sponge and roll up again.

Put the cake on to a serving dish. Spoon the remaining butter frosting into a decorating bag fitted with a star tip. Pipe lines lengthwise down the cake. Add an occasional swirl to represent a "knot" on a log. Decorate with Meringue Mushrooms together with marzipan holly leaves and berries.

Christmas Pear and Nut Bread

This bread bears some resemblance to a Christmas cake, but a yeast batter is used as the basis. Bake 3 to 4 weeks before Christmas, wrap in foil, and store in a cool place.

MAKES 2 SMALL LOAVES

2½ cups dried pears

1 cup dried prunes

1 cup dried figs, chopped small

1 cup dried or fresh dates, without stones

½ cup candied orange and lemon peel, chopped

¾ cup raisins

¾ cup golden raisins

1 Tbsp pine kernels

⅔ cup hazelnuts, toasted and chopped coarsely

⅔ cup walnuts, chopped coarsely

1 tsp lemon zest

2 tsp orange zest

2 Tbsp Kirsch or rum

BREAD DOUGH

¾ cake (¾ oz) compressed yeast or 1½ packages dried active yeast

2¼ cups all-purpose flour

5 Tbsp superfine sugar

Pinch salt

1½ tsp cinnamon

Large pinch cloves

½ tsp star aniseed or allspice

2 inch vanilla bean, split

GLAZE

2 Tbsp granulated sugar

1 Tbsp cornstarch

2 Tbsp Kirsch or rum

Carefully wash the pears and prunes. Place them in a pan and just cover with water. Leave to soften for 2 to 3 hours. Then, bring to a boil and simmer gently for about 20 minutes. Drain the fruits but reserve the juice and leave to cool. Chop up the figs.

Place the figs, dates, orange and lemon peel, raisins, golden raisins, pine nuts, hazelnuts, walnuts, and the lemon and orange zests in a large bowl. Toss well together to mix and pour on the Kirsch. Chop up the cooled fruit roughly. Add to the fruit and nut mixture.

Combine ¼ cup of the reserved fruit syrup, warmed to blood head, yeast, ½ cup flour and 1 tsp sugar taken from the main quantity. Cover and set aside to rise and double in bulk.

Meanwhile, sift the remaining flour with the salt and spices in a large bowl. Make a well in the center, pour in the yeast batter and draw in a little of the flour. Scoop in the seeds of the split vanilla bean and sugar. Combine well together and moisten with about ½ cup of the fruit syrup. Knead the dough very thoroughly until it becomes less sticky and starts to roll off the sides of the bowl. When it is very elastic and large air-bubbles have started to form, gather into a large ball and place on the floured surface.

Pull the dough out and gradually knead in the fruit and nut mixture until all has been used. Roll into a large ball and lay in the large flour-dusted bowl. Dredge with a little more flour and cover with a clean dish towel. Set aside in a cool place to rise overnight.

Preheat oven to 350°F. Next day, break off pieces of dough and form into hand-sized 1½ to 2 inch rolls, or make two larger loaves 6 x 4 inch loaf pans, according to your choice. Lay small rolls, well apart, on greased baking sheets. Leave to rest and rise a little for 15 to 20 minutes, then bake until golden and well risen, about 1 hour.

Make the Kirsch glaze for the warm loaves. Heat 1 cup fruit syrup with 2 tablespoonfuls granulated sugar, bring to a boil. Stir in 1 tablespoon cornstarch and cook until thickened. Remove from the heat and stir in 2 tablespoonfuls kirsch. Brush on the warm loaves, press in a few almond halves for decoration, and leave to cool. Serve cut in thin slices with coffee or tea or even a glass of red wine. It also tastes good spread with butter.

Czechoslovakian Christmas Bread

This is a braided loaf, seasoned with ginger and nutmeg and full of fruit and nuts. It takes some work to knead in the fruit and to make the elegant braids. The loaf is baked in the oven. This recipe will happily fit both the 1-pound and 1½-pound pans.

BREAD MACHINE RECIPE—MAKES 1 SMALL LOAF

⅔ cup milk	1 Tbsp yeast
1 egg	¼ cup slivered blanched almonds
½ stick butter	
¼ cup sugar	¼ cup golden raisins
1 tsp salt	1 Tbsp candied orange peel
¼ tsp ground ginger	1 egg yolk beaten with 1 Tbsp water
¼ tsp ground nutmeg	
1 tsp grated lemon zest	2 Tbsp sliced almonds
3 cups bread flour	Confectioners' sugar

Put milk, egg, butter, sugar, salt, spices, lemon peel, flour, and yeast in bread pan in order suggested by your bread machine instructions. Set for white or sweet bread, dough stage. Press Start. You may add the almonds when the machine signals time to add fruit, but don't add the raisins and candied orange peel because the additional sugar in an already sweet bread could interfere with the yeast's rising action.

Oil a baking sheet at least 14 inches long. When the dough is ready, remove and punch down. Knead in the fruit and nuts. Cut the dough into four equal parts. Take three and roll each to form a rope about 18 inches long. Braid the ropes, pinch ends together, and place on the baking sheet.

Cut the remaining piece into four equal parts. Again, take three and roll each between your hands to form a thin rope about 18 inches long. Braid the ropes and center the braid on top of the fat braid. Run wetted fingers along the underside of the thin braid, then lightly press it onto the fat braid. Pinch the ends together and press them under the ends of the fat braid.

Cut the remaining piece into two equal parts. Roll each into a skinny rope about 16 inches long. Twist the two ropes together. Center the twist on the thin braid. Wet your fingers and run them lightly on the underside of the twist, then lightly press onto the thin braid. Pinch the ends together and turn them under. Use four or five toothpicks to skewer the braids in place. Otherwise, the top braids may slip off as the dough rises. Cover bread loosely, put in a warm place, and let rise until dough has almost doubled, about an hour.

Preheat the oven to 375°F. Lightly brush with the egg wash, then sprinkle the sliced almonds over the top and press a few into the sides. Bake until brown and a skewer inserted in a thick part comes out clean. Sprinkle with confectioners' sugar while warm.

Mince Pies

British Christmas wouldn't be Christmas without these little pies. They are served at drinks parties, with hot spiced wine after Christmas concerts, and as a dessert with brandy butter or cream.

MAKES ABOUT 18 PIES

12 oz Rich Pie Crust (see page 13)	I Tbsp milk
I egg	I lb mincemeat
	Confectioners' sugar

Begin by making the pastry and refrigerating it for half an hour. Roll out half of the pastry on a well floured surface with a floured rolling pin. Using a 3 inch circular cookie cutter, cut out 18 rounds, put the spare ones back in the refrigerator if you only have one muffin pan. Repeat the rolling process using the other half of the pastry and a 2 inch cookie cutter.

Preheat oven to 400°F. Beat the egg and milk together and set aside. Grease the muffin pan and fill with the 3 inch pastry rounds. Using a heaped teaspoon of minced meat, fill the pies. Brush the edges of the pies with a little of the egg and milk so to seal the pies and place the smaller rounds of pastry on the top pushing down lightly around the edges. Brush over the top of each pie with the egg mixture and prick with a fork.

Place the pies in the oven and bake for 20 to 25 minutes or until golden brown. Cool on a wire tray and dust with confectioners' sugar. Serve warm with cream or brandy butter.

Cinnamon Stars

Another Christmas specialty, decorative and delicious at the same time.

MAKES 30 COOKIES

2 egg whites	2¼ cups unblanched almonds, coarsely ground
I cup plus 2 Tbsp superfine sugar	I Tbsp ground cinnamon
	I½ Tbsp Kirsch

Beat the egg whites until stiff, then mix in the sugar and beat for about 10 minutes by machine (20 minutes by hand) until the mixture is very thick, white, and highly glossed. Reserve about 6 tablespoonfuls of the mixture. Mix the almonds, spice, and Kirsch into the rest of the meringue.

Gather into a ball, cover and chill for 30 minutes. Roll the paste out on a sugared board to ⅜ inch thick, and cut out star shapes with a cookie cutter. Preheat the oven to 400°F.

Transfer the cookies to a lightly buttered, baking parchment-lined baking sheet and smooth some of the reserved meringue on top of each. Bake for 15 minutes. Cool on a wire rack. These cookies keep for several weeks stored in an airtight container.

Cinnamon stars are often used as Christmas tree decorations. Use a toothpick or skewer to pierce a hole in the top of each cookie before baking.

◀ *Mince Pies*

Stollen

Full of fruit, peel, and nuts, this yeast bread freezes well so can be made a month before Christmas. Stollen makes an excellent gift so bake extra.

MAKES 2 LARGE OR 4 SMALL STOLLEN

2 cakes (2 oz) compressed yeast or 4 Tbsp active-dry yeast, 1 tsp sugar and 3 Tbsp warm water	1½ to 2 cups raisins
	¾ cup currants
Generous cup half and half	¾ cup chopped, candied orange zest
3¼ cups all-purpose flour	¾ cup mixed candied citrus peel, chopped
2½ sticks butter or margarine	½ cup almonds, blanched and chopped
6 Tbsp sugar	Melted butter or margarine, for glazing
½ tsp salt	
1 tsp grated lemon zest	⅔ cup confectioners' sugar mixed with 1 Tbsp vanilla sugar for decoration
1 tsp ground cardamom	
Pinch ground nutmeg	

Grease one or two baking sheets, depending on size. Crumble the compressed yeast in the mixing bowl and dissolve it in a few tablespoonfuls of the cream. (Dissolve dried yeast with the teaspoon of sugar in the warm water. Set aside for 10 minutes until frothy.)

Warm the rest of the cream and pour it on to the yeast. Stir in the flour, a little at a time and work the dough until it is smooth. Sprinkle a little flour on top, cover with oiled plastic and leave the dough to rise until it has doubled in size, about 1¼ hours.

Beat together the fat and sugar until fluffy and add the salt, lemon zest, cardamom, and nutmeg. Work the mixture into the yeast dough and add the dried fruit and almonds. Extra flour may be beaten in if necessary, the dough should be fairly stiff. Allow to rise once again, for 30 to 40 minutes, covered with oiled plastic.

Knead the dough and divide it into 2 or 4 parts. Shape them into round balls, flatten them a little and then fold them in the middle to make half-moons. Place the shaped dough on to the baking sheets, cover with oiled plastic and leave to rise for about 40 minutes. Preheat oven to 400°F and bake for 20 to 30 minutes until browned and cooked when tested with a skewer. Brush the Stollen with melted butter as soon as they are baked.

Allow them to cool slightly on the baking sheet(s). Dip the tops of the Stollen into the confectioners' sugar so that they are completely covered. The bread surface is then sealed by the butter-and-sugar coatings and the Stollen keeps well.

Swedish Christmas Bread

This is a dark, dense rye bread made with stout or ale, flavored with orange peel and molasses, and studded with bits of candied orange peel. It is best eaten simply with butter.

BREAD MACHINE RECIPE—MAKES 1 LB LOAF

¾ cup dark stout or ale	1½ cups rye flour
1 Tbsp vegetable oil	1 Tbsp grated orange peel
3 Tbsp molasses	2 tsp yeast
½ tsp salt	2 Tbsp candied orange peel
¾ cup bread flour	

Put all ingredients except candied orange peel in a bread pan in the order suggested by your bread machine instructions. Set for whole wheat bread, medium crust. Add candied orange peel after the first kneading, or when the beeper indicates time to add fruit.

Pulla

Pulla is a Finnish sweet bread seasoned with cardamom, a spice widely used in Scandinavian cooking. It is an everyday bread in Finland, often dressed up with raisins and candied orange peel for holiday celebrations.

BREAD MACHINE RECIPE—MAKES 1 LB LOAF

1 egg	**GLAZE**
½ cup milk	1 egg white beaten with 2 tsp water
2 Tbsp butter	
3 Tbsp sugar	2 Tbsp sliced or slivered almonds
½ tsp salt	
1 tsp ground cardamom	1 to 2 Tbsp sugar
2 cups bread flour	
2 tsp yeast	

Put all dough ingredients in bread machine pan. Set for white or sweet bread, dough stage. Press Start.

When dough is ready, take out and punch down. Cut into three equal pieces. Let it rest 5 minutes. Butter a baking sheet. Roll each piece into a rope, about 16 inches. Braid the ropes, tucking ends under. Cover dough and put in a warm place to rise until doubled.

Brush dough with egg-water wash. Sprinkle with almonds and then with sugar. Bake bread in preheated 375°F oven until golden, about 35 minutes.

Kolache

Kolaches are individual Czechoslovakian pastries with fruit or cheese fillings, often eaten at Easter or Christmas. Below are recipes for two fillings, or you can use your favorite recipe for other fruit, nut, or poppyseed fillings. For special occasions, serve a variety of fillings.

BREAD MACHINE RECIPE—MAKES 16

1 egg

½ cup milk

½ stick butter

¼ cup sugar

½ tsp salt

2 cups bread flour

1½ tsp yeast

Confectioners' sugar

APRICOT FILLING
(Makes enough for 16 kolaches)

½ cup chopped dried apricots

⅓ cup sugar

2 Tbsp apricot brandy, orange liqueur, or orange juice

CHEESE FILLING
(Makes enough for 24 kolaches)

3 oz cream cheese, softened

⅔ cup ricotta cheese, watery liquids poured off

1 egg yolk

3 Tbsp sugar

½ tsp fresh lemon juice

Put all the ingredients in a bread pan in the order suggested by your bread machine instructions. Set for white bread, dough stage. Press Start.

Lightly oil two baking sheets.

When the dough is ready, remove from the bread machine and punch down. Cut into 16 equal pieces. Roll each piece into a ball and flatten slightly. Place balls about 1 inch apart in baking pan. Cover loosely and set in a warm place to rise until doubled, about 45 minutes.

Preheat oven to 375°F. Gently use one finger to make an indentation in the top of each kolache, taking care not to deflate the roll. Gently widen the hole with your finger. Put about 1 tablespoonful of filling (see below) in each kolache. Bake until kolaches are golden brown, 15 to 20 minutes. Sprinkle with confectioners' sugar while still warm.

VARIATIONS

Apricot Filling
Put apricots in a small saucepan. Cover with water. Bring to a boil, then reduce heat to very low. Simmer until water evaporates, watching closely and stirring frequently so apricots do not scorch. Just as the last bit of water evaporates, add sugar and liqueur and heat just until sugar dissolves, about 1 minute. Let it cool slightly, then purée in a blender or food processor.

Cheese Filling
Beat all the ingredients together until smooth.

Cranberry Sandwich Stars

These beautiful sandwich cookies are big
enough to be a dessert.

MAKES ABOUT 20

2¼ cups all-purpose flour	**FILLING**
1½ tsp baking powder	1 cup fresh or frozen (defrosted) cranberries
½ tsp ground cinnamon	
¼ tsp salt	3 Tbsp sugar
1½ sticks unsalted butter, softened	¾ cup raspberry preserves
	1 Tbsp lemon juice
½ cup sugar	Confectioners' sugar for dusting
¼ cup packed light brown sugar	
1 egg, lightly beaten	
2 tsp vanilla extract	
Grated zest of 1 lemon	

 Into a medium bowl, sift together flour, baking powder, cinnamon and salt; set aside.

In a large bowl with an electric mixer, beat butter until creamy, 30 seconds. Add sugars and beat until light and fluffy, 1 to 2 minutes. Beat in egg, vanilla extract, and lemon zest. Stir in flour mixture until a soft dough forms.

Scrape the dough onto piece of plastic wrap or waxed paper. Using the wrap or paper as a guide, shape the dough into a flat disk, and refrigerate until firm enough to roll, 1 to 2 hours.

Lightly grease 2 large non-stick baking sheets. On a lightly floured surface, using a floured rolling pin, roll out one-third of the dough ⅛ inch thick. (Keep the remaining dough refrigerated.) Using a 3½-inch star-shaped cutter, cut out an even number of cookies. Using a 1-inch or 1½-inch star-shaped cutter, cut out the center of half the cookies. Arrange the cookies on baking sheets ½ inch apart. Refrigerate 15 minutes. Preheat oven to 350°F.

Bake until the cookies are just set and edges are golden, 8 to 10 minutes. Remove the baking sheets to wire racks to cool slightly. Then transfer the cookies to the wire racks to cool completely.

In a food processor fitted with a metal blade, process cranberries, sugar, preserve and lemon juice. Scrape into a medium saucepan, and, over medium heat, cook until mixture is reduced to about 1 cup, 8 to 10 minutes, stirring often. Set aside to cool, stirring occasionally.

Spread about 1 teaspoon cranberry mixture on each whole cookie star to within ½ inch of the edge. Arrange the cut-out cookie stars on a wire rack. Dust liberally with confectioners' sugar; then carefully place over whole stars, gently pressing together. Allow cookies to set 1 hour at room temperature.

TIP

To dust again with confectioners' sugar before serving, cover the filled centers with small rounds of waxed paper, and then dust with confectioners' sugar.

Christmas Cut-out Cookies

These cookies can be cut out in any shapes you can find: trees, angels, reindeer, bells, or stars.

ABOUT 6 DOZEN
(DEPENDING ON SIZE OF CUTTERS)

2 cups all-purpose flour	1 Tbsp vanilla extract
2 tsp baking powder	½ tsp lemon extract
½ tsp salt	
1 stick unsalted butter, softened	**FROSTING**
1 cup superfine sugar	3 cups confectioners' sugar
1 large egg	2 to 3 Tbsp milk
Grated zest of 1 lemon	1 Tbsp lemon juice
1 Tbsp lemon juice	Red and green food coloring (optional)

Into a medium bowl, sift together flour, baking powder and salt. In a large bowl with an electric mixer, beat the butter until creamy, 30 seconds. Add the sugar and continue beating until light and fluffy, 1 to 2 minutes. Beat in egg, lemon zest and juice, and vanilla and lemon extracts until well-blended. Stir in flour mixture until blended.

Form the dough into a ball, and divide into 3 pieces. Flatten each piece to a disk shape, and wrap each tightly in plastic wrap. Refrigerate for several hours or overnight until dough is firm enough to handle.

Preheat oven to 350°F. On a lightly floured surface, using a floured rolling pin, roll out one dough disk ⅛-inch thick. Keep the remaining dough disks refrigerated. Using floured cookie cutters, cut out as many shapes as possible, and, if necessary using a palette knife, transfer shapes to 2 large ungreased baking sheets 1 inch apart.

Bake until the cookies are just colored around the edges, 8 to 10 minutes. Remove baking sheets to the wire racks to cool slightly. Then, remove cookies to the wire racks to cool completely. Repeat with remaining dough.

Into a medium bowl, sift confectioners' sugar. Stir in 2 tablespoons milk and lemon juice, adding a little more milk if the icing is too thick. Spoon about ⅓ of frosting into a small bowl and another ⅓ into another small bowl. Add a few drops of red coloring to one bowl and green to the other, mixing until you have the desired shapes.

Spoon the three colors into three separate paper cones. Pipe designs and decorations onto each cookie. Allow to set for about 2 hours, then store in airtight containers with waxed paper between the layers.

Three Kings Bread

Three Kings Bread, or *Rosca de los Reyes*, is eaten in Mexico and Puerto Rico on Twelfth Night, January 6, the day the three kings brought Jesus gifts. A tiny ceramic doll, coin, or lima bean may be hidden in the bread. The person who finds it throws a party on Candle Mass, February 2.

BREAD MACHINE RECIPE—MAKES 1 LB LOAF

1 egg	2 tsp yeast
½ cup water	3 Tbsp chopped walnuts
2 Tbsp powdered milk	2 Tbsp raisins
½ stick butter	3 Tbsp candied cherries
3 Tbsp sugar	
2 tsp grated orange zest	GLAZE
1 tsp salt	3½ oz confectioners' sugar
2 cups bread flour	1 Tbsp milk or cream
	¼ tsp vanilla

Put all dough ingredients except fruit and nuts in bread pan in order suggested by your bread machine instructions. Set for white or sweet bread, dough stage. Press Start. Add fruit and nuts at beeper or after first kneading.

When dough is ready, remove from pan and punch down. Let it rest 5 minutes. Butter an 18-inch baking sheet. Roll the bread into a rope. Bring ends of the rope together to form a ring, and place bread on baking sheet. Insert a ceramic doll, bean, or foil-wrapped coin into the dough from the underside. Cover dough and put in a warm place to rise until doubled, 45 minutes to 1 hour.

Bake bread in preheated 400°F oven until golden, about 25 minutes.

Make glaze by combining sugar, milk, and vanilla. The glaze should be thin enough to drizzle it, but not runny. Adjust milk if necessary. When bread has cooled slightly but is still warm, drizzle the glaze over the ring.

Panettone

This is an Italian Christmas bread distinguished by its tall, domed shape.

BREAD MACHINE RECIPE—MAKES I LB LOAF

¼ cup milk	½ tsp anise seed
2 eggs	2 cups bread flour
3 Tbsp butter	2 tsp yeast
3 Tbsp sugar	3 Tbsp pine nuts
½ tsp salt	2 Tbsp golden raisins
I tsp grated lemon zest	¼ cup chopped candied fruit
I tsp vanilla	I Tbsp flour

Put all the ingredients except pine nuts, raisins, fruit, and the last tablespoonful of flour in bread pan in order suggested by your bread machine instructions. Set for white bread, dough stage. Press Start.

The high sugar content interferes with the rising action of the yeast, so it is kneaded after the first rising. Remove the dough and punch down. Toss candied fruit with I tablespoonful flour, then gently knead the fruit, raisins, and pine nuts into the dough. Put the dough in a buttered pan and turn so all sides are greased. Panettone is traditionally baked in a tall, cylindrical pan. Use a I pound coffee can or a 5-cup soufflé dish. Set it in a warm place, cover loosely, and let rise until doubled in volume.

Bake in preheated 350°F oven until golden and skewer inserted comes out clean, 30 minutes.

Lamańce

This is a traditional Polish sweet dish for serving at the Christmas eve feast. Lamańce means broken, reflecting the fact that some of the cookies are broken in the dip or that they should not be quite so perfect in shape.

MAKES 64

I½ cups all-purpose flour	DIP
¼ stick butter	⅔ cup poppy seeds, ground
Scant ½ cup confectioners' sugar	¼ cup ground almonds
	2 Tbsp honey
I egg yolk	I¼ cups sour cream
3 Tbsp sour cream	

Grease several baking sheets. Sift the flour into a bowl and blend in the butter. Stir in the sugar, egg yolk, and sour cream to make a soft dough. Cut the dough in half and wrap in plastic wrap. Chill for about 15 minutes, or until firm enough to roll out.

Preheat the oven to 350°F. Roll out half the dough to an oblong measuring 8 x 16 inches, then cut this into four 4 inch squares. Cut the squares in half diagonally to make triangles. Repeat with the second piece of dough. Place the cookies on the baking sheets. Bake for about 8 to 12 minutes, until golden. Cool on wire racks.

For the dip, mix the ingredients together, then lightly crush about four of the biscuits into it. Mix well, then offer the biscuits to dip into the creamy mixture.

◀ *Panettone*

GLOSSARY

Bake blind To bake an unfilled pastry case. To prevent the sides falling in and the base bubbling, non-stick paper and beans are used in order to weigh down the pastry during cooking.

Beat To mix food together with a wooden spoon or electric mixer in order to incorporate air into the resulting mixture.

Binding Adding eggs, cream, or melted fat into dry ingredients to hold ingredients together.

Beating

Blanch Parboiling usually refers to vegetables which are cooked for a short time in boiling water.

Boiling Cooking in liquid at 212°F.

Caramelize To cook sugar until melted and brown either by dissolving and boiling or by broiling.

Crimping Making a decorative edging to pie crusts.

Curdle When fresh milk separates into solids and liquids caused by overheating or adding acid. Also when beaten mixtures separate when adding eggs too quickly or when they are too cold.

Dredging

Dariole Small straight-sided round mold used for small cakes and desserts.

Dice Cut into small cubes.

Dredge Sprinkle food with sugar or flour.

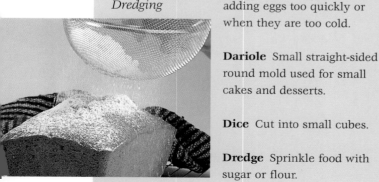

Dropping consistency The consistency of a mixture, neither stiff nor runny, when it will slowly fall from a spoon when shaken.

Dust see Dredge.

Fold To mix ingredients using a gentle figure-of-eight motion and a metal spoon. Usually applies to mixtures which have previously been beaten to incorporate air.

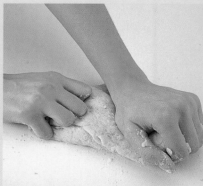
Folding

Frost To coat with frosting or confectioners' sugar.

Gluten Proteins found in wheat which form part of the chemical process when making risen breads.

Infuse To steep or heat gently in order to extract flavor usually from a spice such as a vanilla bean or a blade of mace.

Knead To stretch and fold mixtures to ensure even mixing of ingredients. Refers to yeast-based mixtures in particular.

Leavening see Rising.

Meringue Whisked egg whites and sugar beaten until stiff. Used to top pies or cooked in small mounds in a low oven until crisp.

Pass To press through a sieve.

Kneading

Praline Almonds and sugar cooked together to form a hard candy, sometimes crushed to garnish cakes or powdered and used as a flavoring.

Punch back To punch risen dough to expel air.

Purée To pass ingredients such as fruit through a sieve to form a liquid or thick paste.

Relax or rest Usually refers to pastry which needs to be set aside to allow the gluten, which has been stretched during rolling process, to contract. This reduces risk of shrinking during cooking. May also refer to batters that need to relax to allow starch cells to expand in the liquid, thus producing a lighter effect when cooked.

Ribbon To whisk ingredients until the mixture thickens sufficiently in order to leave a ribbon-like trail when the whisk is dragged through the mixture.

Rise To set aside mixture to allow rising agents to expand the dough to twice its original size.

Rising agents The active ingredient used to make mixtures rise either during the cooking process or before cooking. These include yeast, whisked egg white, and baking powder.

Roulade Thick, flat cake spread with cream or frosting and rolled.

Scald To sterilize cheesecloth or cooking utensils in boiling water or to heat milk until just boiling.

Scalding point The moment just before boiling when the liquid is bubbling around the edges of the pan but not bubbling in the center.

Sift To pass flour or confectioners' sugar through a sieve to remove lumps.

Spring-form pan Baking pan with hinged sides to facilitate the easy removal of your cakes.

Stirring Mixing with circular movements.

Tube pan Ring-shaped baking pan used for cakes.

Whipping Beating eggs or cream until frothy or stiff using a whisk.

Zest The colored part of citrus fruit skin. Used grated or thinly pared for flavoring.

Sifting

Whipping

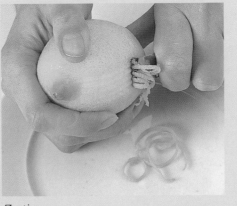

Zesting

INDEX